THE ANCIENT YEW

THE ANCIENT YEW

A History of *Taxus baccata*

Robert Bevan-Jones

WIND*gather*
PRESS

The Ancient Yew

A History of *Taxus baccata*

First published by: Windgather Press, 29 Bishop Road, Bollington, Macclesfield, Cheshire SK10 5NX, UK, 2002. This edition first published by Windgather Press, 2004.

Distributed by: Central Books, 99 Wallis Road, London E9 5LN

British Library Cataloguing-in-Publication Data
A catalogue record for this book is available from the British Library

ISBN 0-9545575-3-0

Typeset and originated by Carnegie Publishing Ltd, Chatsworth Road, Lancaster
Printed and bound by The Alden Press, Oxford

Contents

This book is dedicated to Lindsey

List of Illustrations

Figures

Plates (between pages 82 and 83)

Foreword

by Professor David Bellamy, OBE,
Fellow of the Linnaean Society and
President of The Conservation Foundation.

Having been interested in yews since I first saw one of these veterans shading the lych gate of our local church, I am delighted to write a foreword to this book.

The Ancient Yew presents a fascinating history of the yew tree. The detailed research describes the roles of the yew in botany, archaeology and history. Robert Bevan-Jones carefully illustrates the significance that the yew has had for peoples living in Britain over many thousands of years.

Each chapter provides an important contribution towards the study of this unique tree. This book merits attention from anyone who is interested in British trees and the complex ways they can contribute to the better under-standing of the British landscape, cultural heritage and archaeology.

Yews in our churchyards today are physically no different from those yews seen and used by Neolithic, Iron Age and Saxon populations. In many ways, this book brings the history of the yew to life and provides numerous referenced examples of situations where the yew has proven to be an indispensable tree for British populations. It is a book to come back to again and again.

15 May 2002

Preface

The yew is generally acknowledged as the British tree capable of longest life. Ancient examples often exceed a thousand years of age. These old sentinels are often found in churchyards, where they provide an evergreen impression of immortality. Large yews provide a sense of unchanging grandeur, silently witnessing centuries of parish services: baptisms, weddings and funerals. The yew is a distinctive tree that has, for thousands of years, been very much a part of British culture.

Today, almost every parish in Britain still has either a churchyard yew, a yew growing outside a cottage, or yews grown as formal yew hedging in the grounds of the local hall or park. It is unusual to live in Britain without passing a local yew at some time. The yew came to my attention when growing up in Rodington, Shropshire, where I often sat in the branches of the yew growing by the lych gate of the church, sheltering on hot summer days when playing Blockey 1-2-3, with friends. I often climbed the trees of the parish and was amazed by the dryness of the evergreen yew. It allowed good climbing on solid branches, free from rot, sheltered from wind, rain and sun.

British trees have played a significant role throughout my life. My father established Shrewsbury Timber Ltd in 1974. Before him, after the end of World War Two, my grandfather ran Llangadog Sawmills for over thirty years. Today, Border Hardwood Ltd at Wem in Shropshire continues this family tradition. At Shrewsbury Timber, while sticking planks of English timber for air-drying, I sold ash to coracle makers, and oak to joiners and cabinet makers. I also sold boards of yew. Yew was prized by cabinet-makers for its fine grain and colours. Craftsmen bought yew for making small tables and chairs and yew burrs were prized for turning plates and bowls. I noticed then that the red, orange and white boards of yew wood were narrower than that of most other British timber in stock. I pondered why this was. The grain also seemed tighter in most boards than those of other trees, suggesting that, perhaps, yew was a slow growing tree. The seeds of my interest in the longevity and history of this unusual British tree were planted.

The yew has been a significant feature of the British landscape since long before the last Ice Age. The yew will probably still be a significant landscape tree when the next Ice Age arrives. The archaeology of yew wood presents a fascinating picture of an indispensable tree, used as a weapon, a vessel, a linchpin, even as a god. There is evidence that early societies in Britain needed, feared and revered the qualities of this long-lived native evergreen tree over thousands of years. In Britain today, many people continue to find the yew uniquely useful. For example, Paclitaxel, a drug derived from compounds first found in the yew, is now frequently used for treating patients with cancer.

Botanists of the past have been inspired to investigate the ages of ancient yews. People have been examining the ages of living yews for over three centuries and are still analysing them today. A detailed consideration of the history of dating living yews is discussed in this text. I remark on the distribution of the oldest yews, suggesting more plausible reasons for their planting than have hitherto been suggested by most writers. I imply that perhaps the oldest specimens are not as mysterious as was long thought. I suggest that there is some evidence that many surviving ancient yews may have had roles in the churchyards of early saints and their descendants, in areas of England and Wales.

Estimates of the age of old yews can, I suggest, be used by archaeologists and local historians when observing the older specimens in the field, to use them as an indicator of early settlement, to help 'date' early churchyards or older hedgerows. In Wales there are instances of old yews in fields that mark pre-reformation lost chapels and well sites, where no other evidence remains above ground.

This book presents an exploration of the history of the yew in the landscape and cultural heritage of Britain, which I hope will encourage readers to take more notice of this ancient presence, yet enduring in our midst: to consider the yew as a botanical legacy within our ancient landscape. Echoing the words of Dr O. Rackham, 'I hope that conservation-minded readers may be helped to identify features which are worth preserving or restoring ... If they do their work properly they will have the satisfaction of ensuring that the achievements of our past civilisation have not been allowed to perish unrecorded.'[1]

Robert Bevan-Jones, January 2002

Acknowledgements

Many thanks are due to all who have helped make many researches at all possible; the staff of the inter-library loan system network, Stourbridge and Dudley Central Libraries and Wordsley Community Library, West Midlands, including C. Bogart, J. Guest and P. Turner; J. and S. Atkins of Summerfield Books, Cumbria; D. Curry, Keeper of Natural History at St Albans Museum; Gail Foreman, Keeper of Archaeology at Kingston Upon Hull Museum; Brecknock Museum and curator David Moore; Carmarthen Museum; and curator Wiltshire County Council Archaeologist, H. Cave-Penney; Hampshire County Archaeologist, David Hopkins; Archaeologist Professor Bryony Coles, of the Archaeology Department at the University of Exeter; Dr P. Sims-Williams, University of Wales, Department of Welsh; Dr M. Newton, writer on Celtic cultural history; medieval landscape specialists Dr M. Newman, The National Trust and Dr G. Coppack, English Heritage; Archaeobotanist Professor James H. Dickson of the University of Glasgow; botanists Dr D. Larson of the University of Guelph, Canada; T. R. Hindson, founder of the Companions of the Yew organisation; Professor David Bellamy, David Shreeve and Libby Symon of the Conservation Foundation; Paul Tabbush and Peter Crow at The Forestry Commission Research Centre; Alice Holt; Professor Mel Jones of Sheffield Hallam University; tree historians John Andrew, Allen Meredith, Andrew Morton, Tim Hills and Andy McGeeney. Many thanks to various Park Rangers and Forest Wardens for local advice and assistance, such as Angus Wainwright, G. Manning and James McCarthy. Additional help or advice was supplied by the Community Development Agency for Hertfordshire, Mr and Mrs D. L. Bevan-Jones, K. Nevitt and the Arachnoiditis Trust, J. Yates, G. Sage, M. Powney, J. Dams, Y. Shiarlis, M. Newman, J. Franklin, R. Purslow and R. Pederick. The archaeologists, historians and other authorities listed above, have all given varying degrees of advice or criticism wherever time has allowed, for which I am grateful. Any remaining errors or other inaccuracies are, of course, entirely my responsibility.

A note on measurements

Since the historical measurements of yew trees given in this book use the imperial system, feet (ft) and inches (in) have been used throughout this book. If, however, measurements have been made using the metric system – as in contemporary scientific studies – these are given in brackets after the imperial figures.

"Learning's root is bitter, but the fruit it bears is sweet."
Letters of Saint Jerome (347 AD–420 AD)

CHAPTER ONE

Botanical Features of the Yew

The physical characteristics of the yew are relevant to those examining yews growing in local churchyards, formal gardens, cliffs and hedgerows. They are also relevant to students of yew wood in the archaeological record, as they recur wherever yews grow, or have grown, in the British landscape. The yew has heavy orange-pink-red wood, occasionally mixed with purple, inside the outer white sapwood. The yew is unusual amongst British trees, being 'dioecious', having male and female features on separate trees. From the age of about ten years, the yews tend to become male or female for life, except for the rare monoeceous specimens, such as at West Felton, Shropshire and at Buckland in Dover, Kent.[1] These are very rare and tend to be wholly one gender, with only a branch showing characteristics of the other gender. Generally, only the female has berries.

The yew is often very slow growing and they are probably the longest living trees in Europe. There are several reasons why some yews may outlive other British trees. The main limitations to the longevity of any tree are environmental.[2] These factors may include the effects of storms causing damaged wood and fungal infection. In the damp British climate moisture can assist the decay of a tree, especially if already damaged. The yew is the only British tree of full forest stature that is dry under its canopy in both summer and winter. The evergreen canopy of the yew reduces infection and decay through rot. When a trunk is damaged the evergreen canopy grows new branches to protect torn areas from light, water and infections.

The dense, poisonous wood of the yew contains many diterpenoid alkaloids. These compounds discourage many parasites that beset other old trees. The yew has only two common parasites, when oaks may have two hundred or more.[3] The yew gall wasp, or midge, is the common yew parasite. In laying its eggs, it damages the terminal buds of branches. This wasp rarely plagues a yew to death, but it can be persistent. Infected buds flare up, having the appearance of small artichokes, hence the common name 'artichoke' galls. A similar insect creates oak apples on oaks.

The other key yew parasite is a relatively harmless fungus. The yellow bracket fungus called the *Polyporus sulphureus*,[4] is the only fungus commonly found on the yew. This exploits damaged areas of trunk, but rarely produces enough fungal growth to harm the tree. It is the only fungus that is common on the yew.

1

Botanical Classifications

The yew is an evergreen Gymnosperm of the order *Taxales*, family *Taxacae* and genus *Taxus*. Botanists disagree on the taxonomy, the exact classification of the genus *Taxus*, and allot six to ten species across the northern temperate zones of Asia, Asia Minor, India, Europe, North Africa and America. These species, including *Taxus baccata*, are all thought to come from one ancestor, *Paleotaxus redivida*, which grew on the landmass before it separated into continents. An example of this was preserved on a Triassic Age fossil laid down 200,000,000 years ago.[5] A later fossil of yew was found, of *Taxus jurassica*, 140,000,000 years ago. *Taxus jurassica* had the key characteristics of *Taxus baccata*, common or European yew, *Taxus cuspidata*, Japanese yew, *Taxus brevifolia*, Pacific or Florida yew and *Taxus canadensis*, the Canadian yew. *Taxus jurassica* evolved into *Taxus grandis*, and less than a million years ago, this species was almost indistinguishable from the European yew, *Taxus baccata*, just as today *Taxus baccata*, *Taxus cuspidata* and *Taxus brevifolia* are almost indistinguishable.[6] It has been suggested that the present day yews can all hybridise with each other and that they all have near identical chemical constituents and are near identical trees.

The yews of Irish history before *circa* 1780 were all common or 'English' yews, *Taxus baccata*, not 'Irish' yews, as suggested by Robert Graves.[7] The form called the 'Irish' yew, classified as *Taxus baccata fastigiata*, which has upright branch growth, was discovered growing on a hillside in Ireland in *circa* 1778. Cuttings grown from this tree are found today in many churchyards. The original parent Irish yew still survives at Florence Court, County Fermanagh, in Northern Ireland. There was no male tree, so all Irish yews have been berried females, cuttings from the one parent. The seeds revert to normal *Taxus baccata* form. The Irish yews are as poisonous as other types of yew. Many other forms and cultivars of *Taxus baccata* exist such as *Taxus baccata aureovariegata*, a golden-leafed yew. *Taxus baccata fructoluteo*, a yew with yellow arils (or berries) was a form first noticed growing on an estate in Glasnevin, Ireland in 1817.

The Etymology of *Taxus* and Yew

The origin of the botanical description of the yew genus as *Taxus* is somewhat obscure. In Italy the yew had often been known as *Tasso* and *Taxus*, as used in the botanical nomenclature devised by Swedish botanist Linnaeus (b. 1707– d. 1778). In Spain the yew is usually called *Tejo*. Pliny says that *Toxicum*, poison, was so named from this tree, although *toxon*, a bow is another, equally plausible derivation.[8]

In Britain yews have been called 'yew' for at least fifteen hundred years. This is frequently demonstrated in place-name, manuscript and personal name evidence. Examples of Anglo-Saxon spellings of yew, like *eow, iw, eoh*,[9] are recorded in Anglo-Saxon charters and manuscripts, some dating to the seventh century. (These are discussed in more detail, in chapter 6). In later medieval literature, Chaucer spells it alternately as *eu* and *ew*, while Spenser refers to *iun, yugh, yeugh, yewe, yowe, you, ewgh, ugh, u* and *ewe*.[10]

In Wales the yew has been known as *yw, ywen*, or occasionally *yreu-yw* or *yweu*.[11] According to W. J. Watson *ivo* is the early form of the Old Irish *eo*, a yew tree. *Eu* and *io* were recorded in use in 667.[12] Yew has various Celtic forms, 'Ealry Celtic, *eburos*, Old Irish, *ibar*, Scots Gaelic, *iubhar*, yew.' Another Gaelic equivalent is *ibor*, or *iubhar*,[13] pronounced as 'ure'.

The yew, like the oak, is a British tree likely to have retained a name recognisable to regional European populations since at least the Iron Age period. This suggestion is also reflected in the historical records of European words for yew. In France *l'if* signifies yew, in northern France, *ivis* is Breton for yew. In Germany it has been known variously as *Eibe, Ibenbaum* and *Ifenbaum*.[14]

Some yew place-name evidence

Place-name evidence contributes something to understanding the historic role of the yew in the British landscape. The parts of Britain where the historic distribution of large old yews has been recorded, seems to closely match the patterns of existing yew place-name distribution. Equally, no yew place-names are found in regions where large old yews have never been historically recorded, such as Suffolk, Norfolk and Cornwall. However most yew place-name parishes in Britain do not contain old yews today,[15] even though the place-names survive.

Any mature yews surviving in yew place-name parishes ought to be preserved, due to their rarity and potential significance. Sadly, such survivals are almost unknown. There is a Yew Tree Hill, in Netherton, West Midlands, recorded pre-1820, that seems to have no old yews today. There is also a North Yew Tree Heath in Hampshire, which has several types of prehistoric barrow within it, with disturbed summits, but no yews.[16] Yew Tree Batch near Yapsul Spring on the Long Mynd in Shropshire has no yews there today.[17]

Yews are often preserved in place-names, though such names are difficult to date empirically. We are mostly reliant on surviving records to reach as far back as we can go. Cumbria has Ivegill, first recorded in 1361, meaning 'deep narrow valley of the river Ive', an old Scandinavian name meaning yew stream.[18] Kent has Iwade, first recorded in 1179, the 'ford where yew-trees grow.' East Sussex has Iden, 'woodland pastures where yew-trees grow' in 1806, and Ifield, 'Open land where yew-trees grow' also in the Domesday Book. In south-west Yorkshire, Ewden, first recorded in 1290, signifies 'yew tree valley'.[19]

Hampshire, Surrey and Sussex have an early place-name, Ewhurst. According to Margaret Gelling, *hyrst* is cognate with Welsh *prys* meaning brushwood.[20] Ewhurst means 'yew tree wooded hill.' John Aubrey in 1719 recorded that Ewhurst, Surrey, was so named from 'the vast quantities of yew-trees that formerly abounded here'.[21] Iwode in Hampshire refers to an unusually large yew wood, possibly a forest, which may have been present in pre-Saxon times.[22]

These Anglo-Saxon names are thought to stem from old English *ig*, or *iw*, signifying yew. However, the Scottish place-name Udale, in Cromarty, first recorded in 1578, is thought to be a contemporary Norse derivation, *y-dalr*, 'yew dale'.[23]

Many yew place-names originate in Pre-Roman dialects. Somerset has Evercreech, Celtic *crug*, meaning hill with an uncertain first element, possibly Old English *eofor* 'wild boar', or a 'Celtic word meaning yew-tree'.[24] The extreme age of these names makes ambiguity of meaning a frequent hazard of interpretation. *The Oxford Book of Place-names*, 1991, explains that the name of the town of York in the Roman era, *Eborakon*, meaning 'yew tree estate', was recorded in *circa* 150 AD, also then known as *Eboracum*.[25] This yew name is thus the origin of Yorkshire and New York. The oldest yews in York town seem to have been removed many centuries ago.[26]

Many types of place-names have possible pre-Roman 'yew' place-name roots. It is well-known that many river names have Iron Age or Romano-British origins, whose meanings are often related to spirits of the water. In Dorset, there is a yew place-name, Iwerne, recorded in 877 as *Ywern*, that now features in Iwerne Courtney.[27] The Iwerne river name is a Celtic river name, possibly meaning 'yew river' or 'referring to a goddess'.[28] Boyd Dawkins noted that Iwerne originated as a Romano-British settlement called Ibernio,[29] another, earlier probable yew name. Yeoford, in Devon, is interpreted as 'possibly yew stream plus ford'. Nymet Rowland and Tracey, in Devon, has an earliest reference in 974, is interpreted as 'Celtic *Nimet* "holy place", probably also an old name for the river Yeo.'[30] Uley in Gloucestershire was known in 1086 as *Euuelege*, a 'clearing in a yew-wood'.[31] In 1312, a document records two further spellings *Yweleye* and *Ywel*, suggesting continuity from before 1086 to after 1312, up to modern day Uley. Recent excavations found Iron Age, Roman and Anglo-Saxon phases at Uley,[32] surrounded by rootholes of a contemporary religious grove, though the species was not identifiable.

There is some evidence for the yew in early place-names of Scotland although only a few ancient yews remain in Scotland today. A yew river name was recorded in Scotland by W. J. Watson; the river Ewe, Gaelic *iu*, from Irish *eo*, was a Gaelic usage of yew.[33] A cemetery in Inverness was known from some Gaelic sources as 'the Mound of the Yew-wood'.[34] It has been suggested that the clan Fraser Of Lovat's yew-badge was connected with Tomnahurich, 'the knoll of the yew-wood', near Inverness. There is a 'great Fraser yew on *Beinn a Bhacaidh* in Stratherrick, from which, alternatively, it may have been derived'.[35] 'Tomnahurich from at least 1500 was the gathering place of the clan, where courts and horse-races were held, which would associate place-name and clan.'[36]

The Fraser yew emblem seems to predate the accepted origin of the clan badge system, that was formalised in the early years of the nineteenth century. This clan emblem, allied with gatherings, seems to carry some echoes of early Irish native practices involving yews and other trees. Professor MacNeill suggested that a number of names met with in Gaelic literature, such as

Mac Cairthin, 'son of rowan-tree', Mac Dara, 'son of oak', Mac Ibair, 'son of yew' were the names of trees they held sacred, as Mac Cuill worshipped the hazel from which he took his name.[37] This shows family links with native trees in Ireland that mirror the later Scottish clan name links with plants and trees.

Place-names may refer to any feature of the landscape. 'Church of the yew' is found in both Scottish and Irish place-name traditions. In Ireland *Cell iubhair*, 'yew church', is found at least six times and *Cill-eo* and *Killeochaille* carry the same meaning in several places in Ireland, including, Derry, Sligo, Waterford, Kilkenny and Galway. Killanure, Killenure and Killinure all have the same root.[38] There are many other yew place-names in Ireland such as Mayo and Newry that rely on yew etymology for their meaning.

In England and Wales there are many 'Yew Tree Farm' names of uncertain antiquity, though this is certainly a very old tradition. Yew Tree Farm at Leigh in Lancashire, Yew Tree Farm, South Staffordshire, Yew Tree Farm in Highclere in Hampshire and Yew Tree Farm, West Wick, Weston-Super-Mare, North Somerset are randomly selected examples. At Scammonden, near Wakefield, a farm was recorded on the 1905 Ordnance Survey map, simply as Yews, and was called Ewse in 1616.[39] Several farms have had very large yews recorded on their sites, but are not called 'Yew Tree Farm'. Temple Farm in Wilts is such a site.[40] Some of these old yews relate to early churches now gone from the farm sites. One of the oldest yews at a Yew Tree Farm is to be found on the roadside at Yew Tree Farm in Discoed, Powys, perhaps marking an early church now gone. A complete analysis of Yew Tree Cottages and Farms could provide an entire volume.

Yews have been associated with sheltering cottages and farms, in many counties of Britain from the sixteenth century onwards. This is not surprising given the unique sheltering facilities offered by the canopy of the yew. It offers protection from wind and rain to 'table' tombs, churches, preaching crosses, wells, cottages and churchyard sheds. If not sheltering the entrance, Yew Tree cottages often have yews near their well, drain or privy, places that benefit from the dryness that yew canopies provide. Often, like the name of the cottage, the yew at a cottage may be three centuries or more in age.

Many public houses are also called 'The Yew Tree'. Some are not very old, such as the Gwent pub of that name with an 'Irish' yew on the sign.[41] A 'Yew Tree Hotel' existed in Wall Heath in the West Midlands, prior to June 1856.[42] An 'Old Yew Tree' pub existed in the Halifax area prior to 1822.[43] 'The Yew Tree Inn', in Kidderminster, Worcestershire, adopted an old yew, of just under five metres girth. This female yew was probably adopted from a now disappeared church that had certainly owned the land. A 'Yew Tree Pub' was recorded in Boxley parish in Kent, before 1840.[44] This parish also has a Yew Tree Farm. A Yew Tree Inn in Hampshire had ceased trading by 1870, where a Yew Tree Farm exists there today.[45] As an estimate, there could be 50 Yew Tree pubs, 100 Yew Tree Farms and at least 200 Yew Tree Cottages in Britain today.

Many of these names may have been prompted by yews seeded from yews elsewhere in the parish, frequently from an early church site. The yews of Yew Tree Farms most often indicate a church on the farm at some time. Often these original trees are removed due to their toxicity to cattle. Perhaps surprisingly for such a poisonous tree, the yew seems to have been popular as a marker for places, rivers, towns, cottages and farms, since the beginning of written records.

British yew distribution

Archaeobotanical records show that yews have been growing in many parts of the British Isles for at least 8,000 years. At Craven in Yorkshire yew was already colonising the limestone cliffs by 8000 BC.[46] Neolithic remains of yews and other trees have been excavated and radiocarbon dated from an island near Langstone Harbour in Hampshire.[47] Radiocarbon dates show that yews were growing there in *circa* 3000 BC. Neolithic and Iron Age yew charcoal has been excavated at Maiden Castle in Dorset. Neolithic yew charcoal has also been found at Whitehawk Camp in Brighton, Sussex. Bronze Age charcoal has been excavated at Holdenhurst in Hampshire.[48] These examples suggest local availability of living yews near these sites. A thorough consideration of yew distribution in British prehistory has been produced by Sir H. Godwin.[49] R. Switsur has dated yew trunks found in the Cambridgeshire fens, at 2000–1000 BC,[50] yet no large living yews have ever been recorded in Cambridgeshire in modern times. Yews in the Cambridgeshire fens, Yorkshire carrs and Irish peat bogs suggest that the yew had a wide distribution in Neolithic and Bronze Age Britain. However, J. H. Dickson of Glasgow University notes that no yew stumps have been found in Scottish peat.

Today, the yew may be still found in most parts of Britain. Parts of England, such as Shropshire, Cheshire, Hampshire, Sussex, Surrey, Kent, Gloucestershire, Yorkshire, Dorset, Devon and Somerset, have many old yews. Conversely, there are places that seem very barren, with very few or no ancient specimens today. Large yews of 16ft (5m) girth are rare or unknown in Cornwall, Essex, Suffolk, Norfolk, Bedfordshire, Cambridgeshire and Lincolnshire. These eastern counties are bereft of any yews of more than 400 years age, nor do they appear to have any historically recorded large yews. Oddly, nearby Kent has a collection of old yews to rival those in Hampshire or Powys. Old yews are almost unknown today in urban areas. Considerations of space were probably a factor when towns grew, increasing pressure on old trees, wells and other features.

Rural Ireland has few large yews today, yet the Irish sources show strong historic traditions of famous yews. The Irish sections of this book discuss the cultural role of yews in Irish society in more detail. The oldest surviving yews in Ireland today are usually found near large country houses. Equally, Scottish castle yews seem older than almost all churchyard specimens found in Scotland today.

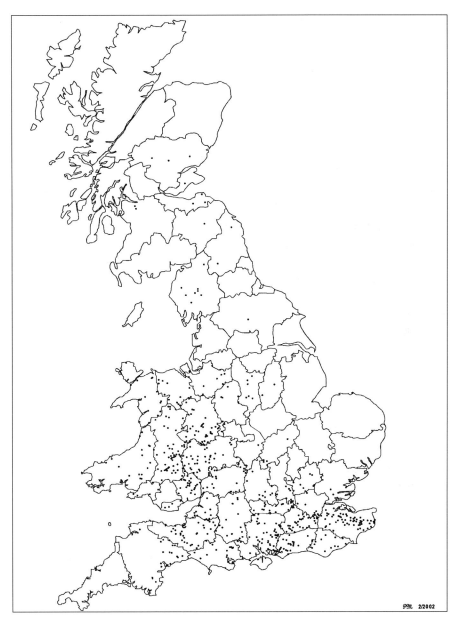

FIGURE I.
The distribution of
the oldest yews in
Britain, of 16ft (5m) +
girth.
ANDY MCGEENEY

The distribution of native cliff and hill stands of yew in Britain, probably the oldest surviving patches of 'wild' growth, is broadly similar to the distribution of older churchyard yews, especially in England. In Ireland however, the established cliff and crag yews are now more commonly found than old specimens in churchyards. Native stands of yews, up to 1,200 feet above sea level, have been frequently found on mountains in Ireland,[51] in most parts, including the north and western side.[52]

The evidence of native yews on limestone cliffs in 8000 BC in parts of Britain, coupled with man's inability to access these cliff sites, suggests it is possible that yews have been present on some cliffs for 10,000 years. The border regions between Wales and England display such a tradition of cliff yews, such as at Tintern, on limestone cliffs there. Limestone is the preferred rock but yews may root almost anywhere. Old specimens have been recorded on sandstone cliffs in parts of Worcestershire and on chalk on the south coast of England.

Celebrated wild yews can today be found on limestone in Dovedale, Derbyshire. Several caves in Derbyshire that have yielded Palaeolithic and Mesolithic occupation, have yew names. One called 'Yew Tree Cave', was excavated near Mansfield in 1937–1938. Another, 'Yew Tree Shelter', was excavated near Bolsover in 1866.[53] Yews there may not be planted but may be significant to the history of the sites, perhaps as vestigial native cliff yew growth of great antiquity with a link to the place-name.

In Shropshire, yews were recorded in the nineteenth century in woods around Eudon Burnell (a yew tree place-name) on the north side of the Wrekin, in woods along the Shatterford basaltic ridge between Bridgenorth and Kidderminster, at Limekiln woods near Wellington, sparingly in Wyre Forest, on Haughmond Hill, Lyth Hill and Blodwell Rocks. The seventeenth-century historian John Aubrey reported wild yews at Winterslow in his *Natural History of Wiltshire* (*circa* 1660).

Prior to 1789 Camden recorded 'the hills, whose summits produce forests of yew', at Whitedown in Surrey.[54] He also noted yew in hedges about Blidworth and Mooregreen in Nottinghamshire, although old specimens are scarce in that county today. In 1874 botanist Edwin Lees recorded native yews:

> scattered through the Wyre Forest, on Wichbury, Ankendine and Abberley hills in Worcestershire. In Berrow parish, near the southern end of the Malvern chain of hills, on the sides of the Ridgeway at the western base of the Herefordshire beacon, in a rocky wood at Cradley in Herefordshire, at Symonds Yat close to the forest of Dean, a fine assemblage of yews on the Wind Cliff, not far from Chepstow, Monmouthshire.

He also records wild patches in Somerset and at Combe Martin in Devon.[55] As the records clearly show, the yew has for centuries been noticed by botanists as a remarkable feature of the British landscape.

Toxicity of leaves, roots and bark

The yew is a poisonous tree. The diterpenoid alkaloids contained in the leaves, bark, roots and wood of the yew can be fatal to humans. These alkaloids have not all been identified, and they can vary slightly in composition as they evolve regionally. These variable compounds are mostly a combination of taxine alkaloids and volatile oils. Volatile oils are irritants that cause abdominal pain and vomiting. Ingestion of the taxine alkaloids causes heart stress and ultimately heart failure.[56] Ironically, it is the toxic taxine compounds (collected and processed from large quantities of yew clippings) which have proven useful to doctors treating patients experiencing many kinds of cancer. These pioneering products, including Taxol and Paclitaxel, are now synthesised by chemists. They have helped in some cases, to arrest the advanced stages of some cancers.[57]

Fatal poisoning by yew leaves in modern times is generally very rare. The only fatalities recorded in recent history are associated with the intentional ingestion of the sap or leaf by adults.[58] The British Medical Journal 1884 recorded the story of a young woman patient in the Cheshire County Asylum, who ate an unknown quantity of yew leaves, and was then 'immediately seized by an attack of faintness, followed by convulsions resembling epilepsy, and died within the hour'.[59] These are usually suicide attempts, although the use of yew as a stimulant for abortion has also sadly been tried in several countries. Another doctor recorded 'a lunatic dying in fourteen hours from chewing the leaves, another fatal case occurred in Shrewsbury Asylum'.[60] Mancunian Dr Percival recorded, before 1838, that a woman accidentally killed her three children when administering teaspoons of dried yew leaves, as a herbal remedy for worms.[61] Any ingestion of foliage should result in swift attendance at the hospital for activated charcoal or other treatment. Quick action is necessary to minimise damage.

Horses tied to yews have often died from browsing on yew leaves.[62] Most owners know that the yew is not a serious hazard in the field, if properly cut back, keeping stock from access to the foliage. The cut foliage must be picked up. It is thought that chemical enzyme changes occur when the leaves are cut and dried, increasing the toxicity perhaps 300 per cent. Pheasants have been recorded as being killed by ingestion of yew foliage.[63] If they had been bred in captivity, and then died shortly after release, they could not have developed a natural tolerance. By contrast, roe deer, fallow deer, grey squirrel, rabbit and hare, have all been recorded eating twigs and leaves as part of normal diet, with no ill effect.[64]

The hardy sheep in the Borrowdale region of Cumbria enjoyed plenty of bark from 'The Fraternal Four',[65] until a sturdy fence was recently erected. However, some sheep in Wales have been killed by ingesting yew foliage. Toxicity is therefore variable, and partly dependent on tolerance. Yew leaves have more often been fatal to stock, especially horses and cattle. However, cattle-feeding practices in Hanover and Hesse regions of Germany (pre-1838) supplemented cattle feed with yew leaves, gradually towards the winter, to build up a tolerance.[66] Total absence of exposure to yew foliage might accentuate the effect of yew on an animal.[67]

In 1994 the old female yew fragment on the parish boundary of Swindon and Enville in Staffordshire, at the top of Camp Bank, poisoned four cows that two days later died. Although protected by a wooden screen, unclipped foliage of the Camp Bank yew reached the animals and caused great expense to the farmer who still allowed the old tree to remain.[68] Old yews, such as those on field boundaries, rarely drop enough leaves to poison stock.

Their ability to shelter animals, including game, all year round may contribute to yews being allowed to remain as functional features. Several deer have been seen sheltering under a young yew of *circa* 100 years age at

FIGURE 2
The hollow Camp
Bank yew, in South
Staffordshire.
The foliage of this
tree has been fatal to
stock. The cavity is
shown facing the road.
ROBERT BEVAN-JONES

Ashridge Park, near Tring in Hertfordshire in 1998. Hampshire archaeologist
J. P. Freeman-Williams noted the large yews on the banks of John of Gaunt's
deer park at King's Sombourne, as good shelter for the deer. He measured
the largest in 1912 at 15ft 9inches in girth at 3ft from ground. This and other
yews there he considered as 'probably originals' planted when the deer park

was defined in the thirteenth century: 'this shows, of course, what is well known, that the yew is not poisonous to deer under ordinary conditions'.[69] R. Williamson, author and Park Warden of Kingley Vale, in Sussex, for many years, recorded deer often browsing back the young yews entirely.[70] For deer, unlike cattle, the yew provides good shelter *and* browsing material.

The berry, toxicity and variation

Male yew branches show yellow tips in February, preparing to disperse yellow pollen in March and April. From miniature soft cones, clouds of yellow dust are sent on the breeze, perhaps pollinating a female miles away. This results in the formation of berries containing seeds. The red yew 'berry' is actually called an aril. Thousands appear on female yews during September and November (Plate 1).

The black-brown seed is covered with a red surround. These red arils contain carotenoids, including Rhodoxanthin, one of the most intensely coloured carotenoids.[71] Rhodoxanthin is a natural red dye, synthesised many years ago for industrial use.[72] This dye can be obtained in quantity from one single female yew: enough dye for many garments from only one tree, yet this dye seems to have had no historic usage. (H. L. Edlin in *Man and Plants* shows a strong brown wool dye from yew wood chips, but not berries).[73] Once planted, the seed from the berry can take eighteen months to germinate, making growing yews from seed difficult.

The red coat of the berry may be eaten safely *if the seed is discarded.* The seed is toxic, though not as toxic as the leaves. It is chewing that would release the toxins in the seed, making them more harmful. In small numbers, even when chewed, these seeds should only 'increase heart beat, disorientate and confuse'.[74] Mild effects of nausea and vomiting have been recorded 'in a few cases'.[75] A huge quantity may obviously be more serious. The National Poisons Information Service (London) have not had a fatality reported from yew *berries* since their records began in 1963. Several chewed seeds would not kill.

Eating the seeds is not at all recommended, though unlikely to cause fatality. In 1950, Dr Kathleen Harding used to frequently eat and chew berries with seeds near Kingley Vale, to show the absence of toxicity.[76] This is not advised generally, as regional variation in toxicity may apply. R. Williamson, who for many years was warden of the Kingley Vale yew forest, recorded badgers and foxes in Sussex and Hampshire, eating hundreds of yew berries, at a single sitting, as valued autumn fare. Over eight species of birds have been recorded eating yew berry arils, including song thrushes and mistle thrushes at Kingley Vale.[77] Fieldfare, redwing, song thrush, blackbird, mistlethrush, robin and pheasant have been recorded as enjoying arils.[78] Owls occupying yews, as at Kingley Vale in Sussex and Camp Bank, near Ashwood in Staffordshire, may value yew berries indirectly as their food, since field and yellow-necked mice eat fallen yew seeds.

Medical treatment after ingestion of yew

Any person ingesting *any part of the yew*, except the red coat surrounding the dark seed of the berry, ought to attend an accident and emergency department. There is no antidote, but palliative measures are available to reduce morbidity. A common treatment available to patients who arrive at a casualty unit within two hours of ingestion, is activated charcoal and stomach washout. Other options may be available *depending on time elapsed since ingestion.*[79] There is no known antidote for Taxines, though most reported cases of yew poisoning do not result in serious health damage due to prompt treatment.

CHAPTER TWO

How Old are British Yews?

The estimation of the ages of yews has been a contentious subject for many decades, even centuries. Estimations of the ages of trees frequently rely on the size of the tree trunk. When trees increase in age, they lay down annual growth rings, leading to an increase in 'girth', the circumference the trunk. This is measured in metres today, though historical records adhere to feet and inches. Measurements of growth of trunk over known time periods gives an indication of the density of the growth rings laid down every year. One of the first botanists to recognise the growth rates of yew using ring-counting techniques and girth was Alphonse de Candolle, keeper of the botanical garden of Geneva, which he founded in 1818.

De Candolle travelled the world looking for ancient trees of many species, counting exposed rings and measuring the girths of trees. He considered the yew as being capable of very slow growth and accordingly suggested that the oldest living tree in Europe was likely to be a yew. He argued that for a typical yew, 144 annual rings were equivalent to an average of one foot of trunk diameter growth, an approximate annual ring growth of one annual ring per 1mm of radius of trunk. He assessed many yews in Britain and provided ages for many British yews, finding some of 1,500 years old, and some more than 2,000 years old. Most of these trees survive today. Though the findings of Alphonse de Candolle have been 'contended since his day',[1] his pioneering ring counting technique is still popular with many modern botanists.

The English naturalist Edward Jesse, 'after measuring trees at intervals, agreed closely with the Swiss botanist'.[2] Another Victorian, J. E. Bowman, favoured great ages for great yews, but argued that Alphonse de Candolle, made the 'young trees too old and the old tree too young'. John Lowe later contested the J. E. Bowman data, saying his trephine only reached the outer rings, and was therefore of 'no utility whatever'.[3]

Another Victorian botanist, Edwin Lees, having written his still unsurpassed *Botany of the Malvern Hills*,[4] gave ages for many yews, including ages of 800 years and 1,000 years for yews formerly recorded on and near Wychbury Hill. He considered the old shattered yew at Bromsgrove old church, probably now gone, to be older still. These Victorian botanists each provided assessments of the ages of yews that surpass 1,000 years.

John Lowe, author of *Yew Trees Of Great Britain and Ireland* (1897) was critical of the high estimates of age made by his peers. However, archaeologist W. Johnson (1912) [5] analysed several yews studied by Lowe (the Hurstbourne Tarrent and Basildon (Berks) yews) and found their growth was less than Lowe had suggested in his book. This encourages caution in the evaluation of dating evidence presented by Lowe.

The celebrated botanist Sir R. Christison, and his son Dr D. Christison observed 'that an increase of one foot for every 75 years would be more than an average increase'. This estimate falls between that of Lowe and Alphonse de Candolle. In brief, De Candolle estimated 144 years per one foot (30cm) increase in diameter, the Christisons, 75 years per one foot, Dr Lowe 60–70 years per one foot. The estimates of most modern researchers also provide estimates easily in excess of 1,000 years for the oldest yews.

Dating research, 1900–1975

Since 1900 many writers and botanists have assessed the ages of large yews. While producing no data on the ages of yews, W. Dallimore (1908) stated that 'numerous specimens exist whose ages are known to exceed one thousand years, whilst it is believed that the age of some almost double that number'.[6] This position has been held, before and since, by erudite men and it may be understood that this is today the received wisdom. Archaeologist W. Johnson argued in *Byways of British Archaeology* (1912), that the truth of the ages of old yews must lie somewhere between John Lowe and Alphonse de Candolle.[7] Though this is a vague concession, it basically accepts the view that yews live more than 1,000 years.

After World War Two, several authors retreated from this view. *The Churchyard Yew and Immortality*, by Rev. Vaughan Cornish was published in 1946. Cornish also wrote *Scenery of Sidmouth* and *Historic Thorn Trees of the British Isles*. Cornish was aware of Lowe and De Candolle, though he shied from assessing the ages of yews in detail like these researchers, and cautiously suggested 750–1,000 years as plausible ages for the oldest specimens.

H. A. Hyde, formerly a keeper of the Department of Botany at the Museum of Wales in Cardiff and author of *Welsh Timber Trees* (1931) is quoted in Cornish (1946) as saying, 'There is no evidence that Yew trees approach the age of two thousand years.'[8] Hyde wrote that 'the ages of yews have often been exaggerated: what appears to be one huge trunk sometimes consists of several vertical shoots which have fused'. Hyde's comments concerning fused trunks are not supported by evidence.

The appearance of fused trunks does occur from one yew seed, in multi-trunk specimens yet this has not been shown to affect significantly estimates of age relating to girth, as shown in avenue studies. Fused trunks represent the product of one seed, being formed of one sex, not made of fused multiple trees. A recent paper[9] by Dr D. Larson (1994) suggests that the *appearance* of fusion is possibly explained by the analysis of similar species such as *Thuja*, where radially sectored hydraulic pathways in the xylem (wood), as shown by the use of dyes, creates the appearance of fusion. This experiment also suggests a plausible scientific explanation for the physical development of re-growth stumps and fragment specimens of yew, as discussed later. Neither Hyde nor Cornish produced scientific data to support their views on the ages (or fusion) of yews.

The celebrated botanical expert H. L. Edlin suggested in 1958, that yews could grow 10–70 annual rings in one inch of trunk radius.[10] This indicates very high and low age estimates, at different times and places. E. W. Swanton published *The Yew Trees of England,* in 1958[11] and estimated around 1,000 years age for 10m girth yews, based on the general experience of yews, not specific data as such. Tree experts continued to appraise famous yews, especially in churchyards, in the 1960s and 1970s.

Local experts like Joshua Jones-Davies writing for Brecknock Museum News and A. J. Yarham in *This England* magazine 1975, wrote pieces on yews wondering at their ages but not producing scientific data, but acknowledging the recorded histories, produced by Loudon, De Candolle and Lowe. These students of yews between 1900 and 1975 produced little tangible data-centred research and often ignored the work of the Victorian botanists. This was to change dramatically as several botanists approached the subject from different perspectives after 1980, when once again the estimated ages of yews rose above 1,000 years.

Research, 1980–2002

The quality of research has greatly improved over the last twenty years and interesting data has been collected from new sources. When researching his book, *The Trees of Shropshire*, A. Morton had a small piece of rotten wood from inside the hollow trunk of the yew at Loughton churchyard radiocarbon dated. The Cambridge University facility gave a calibrated or normal dating of 550 years old for the piece, plus or minus fifty years.[12]

From where the sample was taken, as shown in the diagram, it seems that this tree was here long before 1435, the approximate date of the sample. The hollowness of the tree suggests this is unlikely to be the oldest piece of the tree, by several centuries. At least four centuries are fairly argued by A. Morton.[13] But this is not to deny the tree possibly being much older still, as the tree is twisted and the trunk leans to the south. This would place the tree as on site before the first recorded chapel in 1291. There was an unhewn lintel stone recorded at this church, that may have predated the rest of the building.[14] The age of the yew may imply an earlier, perhaps early medieval church at Loughton.

There has only been one other radiocarbon date of wood from a living yew in England. The celebrated Ankerwyke yew on the Thames was sampled and tested by Cambridge Radiocarbon dating Laboratory, using the Quantulus Scintillation spectrometer, dated a piece of the yew to only 190+/– 40 years before present: *circa* 1760 AD. This test sample was taken by A. Meredith from

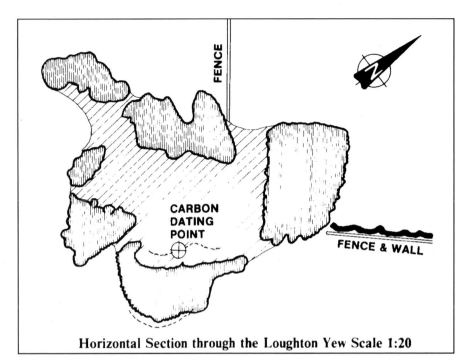

FENCE

CARBON DATING POINT

FENCE & WALL

Horizontal Section through the Loughton Yew Scale 1:20

inside the hollow yew. It is not accepted as a realistic reflection of the tree's age and more tests on both the wood from inside both the Loughton and Ankerwyke trees could prove interesting. In isolation these two results are not statistically significant, but suggest to me that if another ten or fifteen samples were taken from inside other old yews, then the two data results we already have would be unlikely to remain the upper and lower boundaries for the ages of samples tested.

American author H. Hartzell Jr, wrote *The Yew Tree, A Thousand Whispers* in 1991. He visited many churchyards and other famous yews, providing a gazetteer of them. He researched by correspondence historical favourites of De Candolle, Loudon, Lowe and Cornish. He managed to locate many trees. He concluded that 'It seems reasonable to me to consider a yew tree twenty feet in girth to be approximately fourteen hundred years old', adding 'yew trees of thirty feet and larger, by my estimate would be 2,200 years old.' Hartzell considered 35 rings to the radial inch as a likely 'typical' rate for the yew, suggesting that the David Bellamy scheme was using about 45 rings to the radial inch.[15] More cautiously, Oliver Rackham noted in 1994 that a yew could comfortably live to 1,120 years age, though he suggests no upper age limit.[16]

The 1990s saw David Bellamy and The Conservation Foundation assist the researches of Allen Meredith whose work is documented in *The Sacred Yew*.[17] This book brought many historic measures of yews together, revisiting many of the trees known to De Candolle, Loudon, Lowe and others. It provided a fresh start for modern British yew research as over 95 per cent of the old yews etched, measured and discussed by all of the eighteenth and nineteenth century botanists still survive to be assessed today. Allen Meredith's accumulation of historic measures and known plantings does suggest great ages for the largest yews. His lists of yews in *The Sacred Yew* (1994) is yet to be bettered.[18] His dating techniques are based on experience, instinct and large amounts of circumstantial evidence from these old trees. His list of known plantings and historic measurements constitute an impressive collection. His estimates have been to some extent, though not entirely, supported by several of the botanical papers detailed herein.

David Bellamy realised that the great ages of yews were plausible and began a campaign of awareness in order to preserve existing yews and encourage more research. However, the hollowing process continues to disallow totally empirical dates for many old yews. It must also be noticed that the Yew Tree Campaign age certificates were intended to provide estimates of the ages of each churchyard specimen, not empirical results. The Conservation Foundation Campaign brought more attention to yews and their ages, helping to preserve the oldest specimens from neglect, decline and removal.

Other figures in British botany became directly involved with yew trees in the 1990s. Eminent dendrologist Alan Mitchell worked for the Forestry Commission for thirty years. He personally created the template for the National Tree Register from his own collection of thousands of tree measures dating back to the early 1960s. Mitchell re-appraised his own estimates of yews and stated that he considered the largest yew at Ulcombe churchyard in Kent to be around 3,000 years old. He also considered that the age of the Tisbury yew 'must be considered in thousands.'[19] Alan Mitchell had experience of old trees of all kinds over many years and his recognition of the probable extreme antiquity of some old yews helped raise awareness nationally.

Forestry researcher Paul Tabbush[20] has examined yew growth rates at a number of different kinds of sites. Working with John White, he produced a paper on the Kingley Vale yews, published in the *Quarterly Journal of Forestry*.[21] He has described several features of tree growth in different circumstances. 'Open grown trees, not subjected to crown limitation, can show a strong correlation between crown diameter and stem diameter',[22] at least during a period of vigorous growth. Thus, as the crown expands unhindered by neighbouring trees, so stem girth expands in a regular way. At some stage, crown expansion will be limited by other factors, and girth increment will decline. These considerations led White (1994)[23] to offer a method of predicting the age of ancient, open-grown trees, and these ideas were later related to large yews growing in a woodland at Kingley Vale, Hampshire (Tabbush and White, 1996), producing high estimates of age, exceeding 2,000 years in some cases.[24]

In 1998 Paul Tabbush delivered to a meeting of Royal Agricultural Society Of England and The Royal Forestry Society, a paper on 'Veteran Trees: Habitat, Hazard or Heritage?' He recognised that 'the oldest tree in Britain is likely to be a yew, but there is considerable difficulty in assessing the age of old yews, which are invariably hollow', citing Dickson 1994.[25] He sensibly suggested that this problem prevents the coring of old yews, with borers being of no practical use. 'Since it is not acceptable to cause damage to these venerable specimens, ring-widths cannot be estimated from cores taken with a Pressler Borer. On the other hand, fragments of rotting wood, taken from the inner surface of the hollow tree, offer clear evidence of ring width from which estimates of girth increment in old age can be made.'[26]

The main result of the P. Tabbush paper suggests that a 'typical churchyard yew of 7m [23ft] girth, would be aged about 1,580 years'.[27] He significantly concludes that 'clearly, estimation of age from girth measurements in large yews is not an exact science, and the calculation must be modified for individual trees to take into account as much information as is available about history and growth rate'.[28]

P. Tabbush produced a graph showing some yew growth rates to accompany his churchyard yew research. 'Taking only those records where the girth was measured and the same recorded height (from ground) recorded on successive occasions, radial increment and mean ring width between successive measurements was calculated.' Tabbush concluded that 'The growth of individual yew trees is evidently quite variable, but the age of churchyard yews appears to be estimated fairly closely using equation 1 of Tabbush and White (1996),[29] or by using the fitted line in figure 1.

$$\text{Tree Age} = \frac{\text{Girth}^2}{310}$$

Where girth is expressed in centimetres. This offers an acceptable approximation and can easily be memorised.'[30]

This data from P. Tabbush presents an independent botanical analysis of churchyard yews in England and provides a scientific system for estimating the ages of yews.

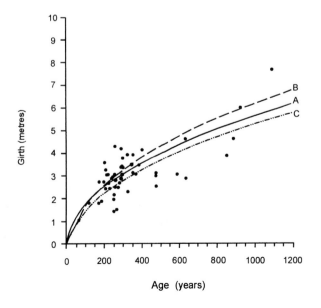

FIGURE 4
A graph plotting girth against age for trees of recorded age, drawn from the listing in Chetan and Brueton (1994). Curve A is fitted by least squares; curve B assumes a core of 40 rings of 3mm width and applies equation 1. Curve C assumes a core of 55 rings of 3mm.

P. M. TABBUSH

TABLE 1: Radial increment and ring width between successive historical measures of churchyard yews.

Tree	Date	Girth (mm)	Radius	Radial Ring increment (mm)	Average Width (mm)
1) SELBORNE (HAMPSHIRE)	1778	7010	1116		
	1823	7214	1148	32	0.72
	1859	7315	1164	16	0.45
	1877	7468	1189	24	1.35
	1897	7620	1213	24	1.21
	1912	7747	1233	20	1.35
	1947	7798	1241	8	0.23
	1981	7874	1253	12	0.36
	1996	8100	1289	36	2.40
2) CROWHURST (SURREY)	1650	9144	1455		
	1874	9373	1492	36	0.16
	1984	9601	1528	36	0.33
3) CROWHURST (SUSSEX)	1680	8230	1310		
	1835	8407	1338	28	0.18
	1879	8013	1290	−49	−1.10
	1894	8153	1298	8	0.54
	1982	8534	1358	61	0.69
4) DARLEY DALE (DERBYSHIRE)	1792	9754	1552		
	1836	9652	1536	−16	−0.37
	1888	9830	1564	28	0.54
	1933	10058	1601	0.36	0.81
5) ALDWORTH (BERKSHIRE)	1644	8230	1310		
	1972	8534	1358	49	0.15
6) CHURCH PREEN (SHROPSHIRE)	1889	6629	1055		
	1983	7036	1120	65	0.69
7) MUCH MARCLE (HEREFORDSHIRE)	1882	8687	1383		
	1989	8839	1407	24	0.23
8) PRIOR'S DEAN (HAMPSHIRE)	1850	7163	1140		
	1996	7700	1225	85	0.59

Source: P. Tabbush.

Toby Hindson, horticulturalist and founder of the 'Companions of the Yew' enthusiast network, recently produced some draft studies of entire ring-counted yew stumps he had examined, between 1996 and 2000. One study selected 40 recent woodland stumps at Alice Holt, on the Surrey-Hampshire border, aged from 0–350 years age, the majority of the sample being 0–210 years old. Only intact, fully readable, non-hollow, stumps were used. Using statistical analysis, he determined a slowing of growth in the woodland yews as the yews aged. The largest ring counted yew was determined to be 335 years old, girth at base at 3m 33cms.[31]

Hindson has developed several growth curves, yet feels that the principle of growth is more complicated than 'large yews grow slowly, small yews grow quickly'. His research implies that some 16ft (5m) + yews can have periods of fast growth, but usually return to slow growth for perhaps centuries. Appendix 3 from his Allen Mitchell Memorial presentation of 4 November 2000, shows a digest of measured yews in Hampshire and their growth over time, with measurements at a known height from the ground. 22 yews had a combined measured history of 2,000 years. This data suggests a growth in girth of *circa* 50 cms per century, for yews over 16ft (5m) in girth.[32]

Hindson has explored the ages of Hampshire yews for many years and his study is of similar merit to that of Tabbush, but relies more on ring-counted local stumps of known ages to support early growth rates. Both researchers imply that some 10m girth yews may be 2,000 years old and that 23ft (7m+) girth yews may often be 1500 years old. These totally independent botanical researches have yielded similar results that may have archaeological implications for the sites they refer to. It is important to realise that the estimations of age of yews given by all botanists emphasise the role of the site conditions of each tree: soil type, exposure, rainfall, etc.

At Hampton Court Palace 14 yews with a known felling date of July 1993 were assessed in 1999 for their dendrochronological potential by A. K. Moir. This dating system, comparing intact known rings distributions through time, is mostly applied to oak today to 'date' beams. He found good correlation between ring patterns of other species, such as oak, and the visible ring patterns of the yews of Hampton Court. At Hampton Court a corer had to be removed by tractor, such was the density of the wood.

The trees cored at Hampton Court were *circa* 10ft (3m) in girth and were found to be around three centuries old.[33] Most of the sampled 14 trees were 7–10ft (2–3m) in girth. He tentatively suggests that a 2½ft (75cm) increase in girth, equates to approximately 100 years growth in a yew, during the first centuries of growth, although growth is variable; the Hampton Court yews may not be typical in this respect, as London is warmer than many other sites across Britain. He found growth rate was linked to seasons, 'positively correlated with rainfall but ... inversely related to late summer temperature'.[34] A. K. Moir replicates a 303 year yew chronology, formed from Hampton Court Palace. This prompted him to suggest that yew may become the third most significant tree for dendrochonological analysis in Britain.[35]

In 1999 archaeologist Martin Bridge took core samples, counting annual growth rings of the Aberglasney yew tunnel. He dated it at most, at 250 years; J. Lowe, in 1897 described the Aberglasney tunnel as 'Jacobean'.[36] Most of the yews in the Aberglasney tunnel are below 3m (10ft) girth, with dense rings. This age estimate from Lowe and Bridge, would make the Aberglasney tunnel a deliberate garden feature, dating it to an era known for its fondness for yew hedging and topiary. Researchers such as Bridge and Moir have focussed their studies on younger yews that are not hollow, and have not assessed older specimens in the 4.75–11m (16–36ft) girth bracket, presumably due to the absence of countable rings.

Other studies produced since 1994 have actively contributed to the understanding of the ages of yews in England. Growth rate data published recently in *Nature*, concerned the ages of some cliff yews in Britain and Germany that were core sampled by D. Larson. Coring of yews is not recommended by many of those who have tried it, including Larson; two 'Haglof' corers were broken taking data for his study due to the dense nature of the yew wood. He found that cambium mortality, the death of parts of the living tree, was a key feature of these exposed trees. Larson took samples from dead wood within yews on cliffs. He took direct ring counts, from a corer, on a cliff yew from North Wales, not a huge specimen, which yielded in excess of 500 intact annual rings, for less than half the radius of the whole trunk, signalling an age in excess of a thousand years. This is in no way an absolute top marker for the age of cliff yews, only a high count. He found the width of rings for these exposed trees as consistently narrow.[37]

Larson has cored yews on cliffs in Germany, Wales, Yorkshire and Derbyshire. He considers that the trees he assessed are the oldest undisturbed forests in Europe. In his view the cliff trees of America and Europe represent unique ancient forests. The cliff woods he cored in Britain and France provide consistently dense ring patterns for this last millennium. Whether cliff and churchyard could produce similar age-growth rates is uncertain; Larson's research however suggests that the great ages of some churchyard specimens may not be overestimated.

Cliff yews can be quite small and ancient. Larson cited a yew at Whitbarrow Scar in Cumbria. From a dead portion on a living multi-stemmed yew tree, he counted 210 annual rings, in 2cms (¾inch) from pith to cambium, an average ring distribution of less than one annual ring per 0.1mm.[38] A. Mitchell recorded in 1985, a similar example of cliff yew growth. A yew from Britain's northernmost stand of yew, on a cliff near Strontian, Argyll, was blown down from the cliff; a section of 14cm (4¾inch) radius showed 310 rings.[39]

This extreme kind of data suggests that the Bonsai pursuit of 'Yamadori', as advocated by *Bonsai* magazine,[40] is a highly dubious activity. Yamadori encourages taking established trees from the semi-wild and wild. As long as the permission is granted by the landowner, the collector may transplant a tree from cliff or hedgerow in its entirety. The landowner, or collector, is unlikely to be aware of the potential age and landscape significance of these trees; most Bonsai enthusiasts enjoy the discipline without recourse to such questionable measures. The negative impact of rock climbers on cliff vegetation is another area of environmental impact on these stunted specimens. Since the yews of Britain, on cliffs or in churchyards, may not yet be dated absolutely, it would be unwise to assume that removing established yews will not deplete botanical heritage.

Assessing older yews in the field

A *rough guideline* indication of girth for specimens in 'average' churchyard circumstances is: 1m (3ft) girth 80–100 years, 3m (10ft) girth 250–350, 4m (13ft) girth, 350–500, 5m (16ft) 600–750 years. Below this size a yew is not normally visibly hollow, but often, as the tree reaches three metres girth and above, it will be growing internal roots that swell as the tree grows. Some yews do not have these. They settle in the decaying centre of the tree, using the rotting wood as soil or potting compost. Once rooted inside the trunk, they grow down, growing trunk-like structures inside the old trunk.

6m (20ft) girth yews often indicate an age of 700–1,000 years. 7–10m (23–33ft) must be considered in a wider band, 1,200–2,000 years, partly as decay and collapse and re-growth can blur the measure at this stage. These are *guidelines only*. All researchers in this field appreciate that the site conditions in churchyards are likely to vary over time, affecting growth patterns. Local nutrient supply, rainfall and humidity can be highly variable, affecting annual ring density.

Several factors can complicate the assessment of any large yew. The exposure of an aged yew to storm and lightning for several centuries can result in the tree splitting in two, creating a fragment specimen. This can allow a proportion of any percentage, from 15 per cent to 95 per cent of the tree to die. This usually only happens once in a yew's life, often producing hollowing, but the effects are visible for centuries. There are many sites where this has occurred and this phenomenon can result in dating difficulties, as girth is affected. Almost all yews where this has occured are already over twenty feet in girth.

Such loss is usually very substantial and would certainly be noticeable in data and in the appearance of the trunk. Reduced historic measures are almost unknown, except after such an event. Examples are the Aldworth churchyard yew, Berkshire and the Lorton yew in Cumbria, where a 27ft (8m) girth yew was reduced to 13ft (4m) in girth overnight, a chair being made for the mayor of Cockermouth from the wind-felled wood.[41] As discussed in chapter 4, the male yew at Strata Florida Abbey in Ceredigion, Wales (Plate 2), is a fragment of a very large yew. The tear is very likely to have been sustained before George Borrows visited to the site in *circa* 1854, when it was still entire, though split and literally half-dead.[42]

Deciduous trees often suffer fatally when fragmented; rot, decay and death may follow swiftly. The evergreen canopy of the yew and the alkaloids in almost every part, discourage rot spreading and a yew with even 95 per cent of the trunk dead and removed, can still recover completely, leaving only a jagged scar as proof of the experience. The epicormic shoots of foliage on the trunk turn to branches, often sheltering the site of the tear, while renewal occurs in other parts of the tree. At Shenleybury and Little Munden in Herts, there are churchyard specimens where this has occurred. Becoming a fragment has not yet been proved to affect the life span of a yew. In some cases, loss of parts of the trunk, leaving a hollow, can allow fairly swift re-growth, as light is increased on parts previously shaded, until maximum canopy is restored. When made hollow, the yew loses some live roots, affecting growth rate once the canopy has re-grown, post-fragmentation.

Sometimes both parts of the damaged tree survive. The Parted yew at Kyre Park, in Worcestershire, like the celebrated yew at Fortingall, in Perthshire, Scotland, has been two halves for over a century. Chapter 6 includes a photograph from 1889 showing the Kyre Park yew long split, as the supporting posts are not new. The other photo from 1999 shows little structural change in the Kyre yew over this period even though it has been exposed and split in two for over a century, all it has done is sink slightly. The survival of both halves is rare. I would suggest this is the also the case at Fortingall in Perthshire, Scotland. Interestingly, in Germany the Balderschwang Eibe (yew) in Germany is also formed of two 'gnarled trunks', dividing the opinion of German dendrologists, some of whom believe it is one tree, others who believe it is two.[43] It is almost certainly a split tree.

Another complicating factor for those assessing yews is that yews that have been cut down, can re-sprout and grow a renewing trunk or series of trunks. This ability adds to their reputation of impressive age, and the yew's symbolic connection with eternal life. When felled, the yew can often, though not always, re-sprout new growth, even after the majority, or all, the branches and trunk are removed. Without this facility for recovery, many of the ancient yews in Britain would not be here today. Sometimes the entire original trunk is felled and the stump regenerates, and a circle of small yews can occur. Re-growth stumps, such as at Thorley in Herts, at the other end of the site from the yew listed in *The Sacred Yew* gazetteer,[44] are deceptive and need an expert eye to determine the history of the tree.

In these instances a tree possibly in excess of 1,000 years can appear as a line, or semicircle of younger looking *circa* 7ft (2m) girth yews. These shoots from the old, often buried, stump can soon appear like several young trees. A specialist can determine the antiquity by looking at the bark on each stem, and the distribution of the small boles. An explanation for this pattern of growth is suggested in a paper by Larson on xylem pathways in Thuja trees, which have a similar structure.[45] This unusual circumstance of re-growth is physically different from one single trunk withering through antiquity, as at Farringdon in Hampshire, to become separate ruined stems.

These young looking re-growth circles may actually be 1,000 years old. The truth might be found by excavating around the trees to find the old base. An example of this type may exist near the old Enville Common, in Staffordshire, inside a pine plantation, called 'The Million'. A re-growth circle of yews may have grown back from a buried stump since the yew was felled to make way for the plantation. Re-growth clumps may mark the church of an abandoned settlement, in modern pine plantations, and may be worth investigating by local historians and archaeologists. The Forestry Commission is currently encouraging the mapping of archaeological sites within their plantations and yews within them may be an under-utilised resource.

FIGURE 5
A regrowth circle
from an old stump at
Thorley churchyard,
Hertfordshire.
G. SAGE

Hollowing

The majority of ancient yews, like most ancient oaks, are hollow. Hollowing in general is caused by a common fungus that affects many species called brown cubical rot.[46] The dense yew wood is slightly resinous and decays slowly. The evergreen canopy reduces the level of water falling on the trunk, probably reducing the rate of rot. The growing cambium (the fresh growth of living wood) moves over dead portions of the tree, sometimes closing an open hollow. The cambium of the yew seems undeterred by the process of hollowing. It flows and can continue movement for metres, around a dead branch, replacing dead wood with new life, so that the hollowing rarely significantly affects longevity or strength. Most hollow yews can remain hollow and healthy for centuries.

Hollowing invites a multitude of uses. The yew at Leeds in Kent, still alive as a hollow ruin, was lived in 'by some gypsies' prior to October 1833.[47] The hollow Boarhunt yew in Hampshire was also recorded as having been a 'home to a family for a whole winter'.[48] 'Of Talbot's Yew in Tankersley Park, it is said, that a man on horseback, could turn around inside its hollow trunk, and similar stories are told of other yew trees.'[49] At la Haye du Routot in Normandy, a chapel fills the hollow trunk, of one of a pair of enormous yews, while the other contains a statue of the Virgin Mary. Hollow yews are popular with birds. Owls occupy the hollow female yew at the top of Camp Bank on the Swindon-Enville parish boundary in Staffordshire. Owls often rest in

24

hollow yews at Kingley Vale. A feral cat was described frequenting the insides of hollow yews there also.[50]

Hollowing is usually a natural process. At Crowhurst in Surrey however, the yew was artificially hollowed out in 1820,[51] having all internal growth removed for leisurely human access, and at the same time the base of the yew was partially excavated.[52] The artificial hollowing may account for its frailty today (Figure 6).

Branch removal or the loss of a portion of trunk usually initiates the hollowing process. This occurs mostly in the hedgerow or churchyard, where space and access becomes problematic. In most cases the hollow entrance of the yew will face the road or pathway where branches have obscured access. In this way the loss of a branch three hundred years ago can remain a feature of a hollow yew. Factors such as burials cutting into roots may also promote hollowing in some cases. A once hollow trunk may close over time, much reducing the hole and therefore the projected width of a lost branch or portion of trunk.

Internal roots often occur within a yew, where roots are sent down inside the old rotting trunk. This transition of growth to root may effect the girth growth rate by slowing it. The internal roots of the yew can return a hollow yew to solidity again, reducing the need to increase girth. Fergus Kinmonth measured the famous yew at Betws Newydd in Wales at 31ft girth at 1.5m from ground. He also measured the internal trunk in 1998 as 7ft 6inches in girth at 3ft from ground.[53] This same yew was described as having a girth of 30ft 6in and 'a fine young tree growing within its decayed bole', in 1876.[54] The internal trunk visible today was there in 1876 (Plate 3). The same yew was etched at this time and has shown little change since then.[55] This internal root still grows inside the veteran shell of today, sprouting foliage and renewing the canopy. This tree is further documented by Allen Meredith.[56]

Yews when hollowing often split, allowing the 'soil' (actually rotting heartwood) to pour out. This can expose the internal roots. The internal root will remain, like a yew trunk within a trunk. Though burnt out recently, the Linton churchyard yew in Herefordshire, has a fine example of this. It is not known if these internal trunks can reach 16ft (5m) or 33ft (10m) in circumference. These are actually roots, with no pith, unlike a branch.[57] They grow down inside the trunk of the yew and help strengthen it from the inside, creating fresh growth. What triggers this process remains unclear, but the rotting wood inside the trunk or branches acts as a kind of soil; the internal roots use it to reach the ground and embed themselves. This has happened with many very old yews, making old growth difficult to discern from new, especially when the old shell disintegrates. Hollow yews can have several internal roots that can be as large as 13ft (4m) in girth and which end up as primary growth, very gradually replacing or coalescing with the older outer trunk of 23–33ft (7–10m) girth. This facility can allow the yew to live beyond the life span of its old trunk, leaving just internal growth. This point emphasises the importance of retaining internal growth for the long-term

health of hollow yews. Internal roots may have contributed to the appearance of trunk fusion.

These internal tree-like stems are usually internal roots, but occasionally a yew can seed inside other trees. A yew was recorded and depicted at Ribbesford churchyard, in Worcs, growing inside a hollow oak of 17ft (5m) girth. At the foot of Himley Hill in Worcestershire is an atypical, contorted yew that had seeded inside a hollow elm perhaps 150 years ago, with roots descended into the old elm bole. Today the elm is a dead stump, the yew having emerged from within as victor.

These features of older yew growth, often visible in the physiology of the trunks, need recognition in the field. They offer clues to the physical history of the tree, and are useful to researchers. A tree that can live more than a thousand years can have many phases of growth during that time. A landscape historian needs to recognise these traits in order to assess better the historic vegetation of the site he visits. Though exact empirical dating is still some way off, these features in old trees, coupled with an understanding of recorded growth rates, offer useful clues to a tree's age.

FIGURE 6 (*opposite*)
The Crowhurst yew, Surrey, artificially hollowed out around 1820.

ANDY MCGEENEY

FIGURE 7
A hollow yew at Farringdon, Hampshire.

T. R. HINDSON

FIGURE 8
Clun yew in
Shropshire: a
veteran tree.
ROBERT BEVAN-JONES

The largest yews cannot therefore yet be measured in terms of age with absolute conviction. A large body of information has evolved giving a broad picture of likely growth patterns. Though accidents like lightning and fire, pollarding and branch breakage can distort girth, the data gathered on younger yews allows estimates of age to be made of older yews. For the extremely large, decayed specimens, numbering perhaps thirty in Britain, that cannot easily be compared to the rest of the living yews, the known growth rate curves tend be fearful of their projected ages. Though 1,500 years seems a fair estimate, some support much older estimates. The 23–30ft (7–9m) girth yews, begin to leave the secure dating behind, not growing for centuries, they become more hollow and delicate, yet still very much a living tree. A yew such as at Farringdon, Crowhurst, Much Marcle or Clun can seem more like a small cave built of time itself.

Llangernyw in Clwyd; Tandridge in Surrey; Fortingall in Tayside; Clun in Shropshire; Betws Newydd and Mamhilad churchyards in Gwent; Farringdon, Hayling South and Long Sutton in Hampshire; Linton in Herefordshire all these trees deserve attention as genuine pre-tenth century relics. Yews of 23–33ft (7–10m) girth are exceptionally ancient and too much contact ought to be discouraged. Walking inside with groups of people could be detrimental in the long term, although I do consider the use of iron railings to be questionable. Most ancient yews can be entered if hollow, but for these trees it is perhaps asking too much of them. Only a handful of yews this age survive world-wide, most of them in British churchyards. There are usually younger specimens at these sites that are probably in excess of a thousand years old themselves, hollow but more sturdy. These can handle more contact.

Conclusions

The researches discussed in this chapter all add information that can contribute to the better understanding of the ages of yews found in the British landscape today. However, the hollow state of the vast majority of the oldest specimens leaves a significant degree of ambiguity in assessing their ages empirically. Historic measures are found to be useful indicators of age, but in the later stages of growth (i.e. between 16–33ft (5–10m) in girth) fragmentation of the bole, and the loss of portions of trunk and branches affect estimations of nearly all extant specimens. Hollow yews have, almost in every case, lost an uncertain portion of trunk, precluding scientific analysis of girth-based data involving the measurements of the oldest yews.

The hollowness of the largest trees indicates that, at some point, generally prior to the earliest measurement, the tree was once bigger. Age estimates linked to girth and ring counts, may be lower than the true age, as the missing portions of trunk may not be included in the data. The dating evidence based on ring counts and girth is, therefore, most accurate when the trunks are complete, prior to the later stages of disintegration. Hollowing due to branch and partial trunk loss clearly destabilises girth-based data.

The growth curves of researchers like P. Tabbush, A. Meredith and T. Hindson are most likely to be at their most accurate in the early and middle stages of yew growth, up to 16–20ft (5–6m) girth. This is the size when most rings may also be counted to the centre of stumps, providing very good evidence for yew growth rates, up to a certain size. This suggests that many of the largest yews above 26ft (8m) in girth are all likely to exceed a thousand years growth. Modern dating evidence suggests, and perhaps even proves, that yews of 32ft (10m) in girth are of pre-twelfth century origin. Furthermore, the accumulated dating evidence on younger trees suggests these yews may actually be at least 1300 years old.

The known planting data, of solid young yews up to four hundred years old, shows good evidence that all 16ft (5m) girth specimens are likely to exceed 500 years of age. This, coupled with the circumstantial evidence of the historic measured girths of hollow yews, seems to very strongly imply, even with the problems of latter stage decay, that the longevity of many yews in Britain reaches easily above 1,300 years of age. Precise proof of the exact age of each churchyard yew, is, however, still some way off. It is possible, that all churchyard yews of 25ft (8m) + girth, could in theory be *less* than 2,000 years old. The hollow trees which have all lost portions of trunk may be younger (or older) than current research suggests.

So why were yews planted in the first place? Within the time frame set out by the limitations of the dating evidence, the Anglo-Saxon church marker would appear to be a possibility. This theory is not borne out by the archaeology of known Anglo-Saxon churches, most of which do not have large yews recorded. Moreover, charter examples are always pre-existing trees in the landscape, not planted by the Anglo-Saxons as part of an organised scheme.

However, when we look at the early saints who flourished in the sixth and seventh centuries, there are many yews of 33ft (10m) in girth, of least 1,300 years of age, in the churchyards of their foundation in Wales. They seem identical in age and decay to specimens found in English churchyards, trees which have in the past been assessed at 2,000 years plus. I would argue that such specimens may be explained as 1,500 year-old remnant markers of early saint cells, which once existed on later Norman sites. Nothing more than lost post holes and the yews remain.

The difficulty of dating hollow trees like that at Discoed, in a seventh-century Welsh churchyard, allows the possibility that it may well be *circa* 1,400 years old (like the saint of the church), or as much as being 2–5,000 years old, as suggested by some researchers. Hollowing and resultant partial trunk loss brings the girth growth rate of the older trees into question, probably increasing the chances of girth growth variability. This reduces the probable accuracy of estimations of age based solely on girth. There remains a possibility that all the 26–33ft (8–10m) girth yews in British churchyards in England and Wales could be *circa* 1,500–1,600 years old remnants of Saxon era saint cells on site, of which we have little other evidence. This is the only explanation that to my mind satisfies the apparently anachronistic trees in churchyards today. If true, then the 26–33ft (8–10m) yews in English churchyards will suggest a more widespread historic early saint and post-Roman 'Dark Age' Christian presence across Britain. The absence of old yews in Norfolk and Essex may be consistent with this idea, being the most easterly counties, furthest from the homelands of native early saints.

Following this hypothesis, it may be no coincidence that yews at Clun in Shropshire, Linton in Herefordshire and Discoed or Llanfaredd are almost identical in size. Since Clun is near the Welsh border, there is a serious historic possibility of a Celtic saint presence. Peterchurch in Herefordshire, I would argue, may have a similar history.

This perspective, based on the strengths and limitations of the known dating evidence, could allow the oldest yews a role in suggesting the likely sites of lost early Christian cells. The cells or hermitages of early saints were tiny and in Wales, some were just 10ft by 13ft (3m by 4m) in size: barely enough stones to build a wall for a field, or more often just made of wood. Because their cells were so small, their archaeological evidence may often be hard to find, more than a thousand years later, at church sites where building and rebuilding have usually occurred. Thousands of burials also amount to thousands of unrecorded excavations, and may have removed post hole evidence.

We also know that many early saints are entirely unknown to us, except for one manuscript or mention in a place-name. Our knowledge of each individual early saint is often extremely sketchy, reduced often to a funerary slab, or a lone surviving church dedication. The history of this era of British church is incomplete, the original Celtic dedications having often been substituted for more English dedications. Many early saints died without any record at all. Even centuries later, the English-Welsh boundary was still marked at Worcester, suggesting a likely historic spread of cells through the west of England. The oldest 'mysterious' churchyard yews of England could be remnants of such a lost tradition: their physical ruin still hiding their exact ages, located in very complex archaeological contexts.

The early pre-Norman saints reached Brittany and Normandy. Large yews survive in Normandy, such as at La Haye Du Routot (on the same chalk as Hampshire); they are nearly identical, in size and age, to the pair at Discoed in Wales. West of La Haye-Pesnil there is a 9.3m girth yew. At Estry, Normandy, there is a specimen of 11.5m girth, suggesting as long a tradition as is possible for a yew in one churchyard. The early saints seem the likely culprits for these plantings, though the traces of their churches are elusive.

There is a 35ft (10.7m) girth yew at the church of St Ursin de la Manche in Normandy. This yew was measured by M. Lechevalier at 1m from ground, at 26ft (8.7m) in girth in 1802. St Ursin was a pre-tenth century saint, and this yew may genuinely be linked to a pre-tenth century foundation. These trees in Normandy have shown a growth rate of 1m per century, as measured by Victorian botanist Henri Gadeau de Kerville,[58] and then a century later by the Dutch expert Jeroen Pater.[59] The apparent swift growth may be explained by these trees all having become hollow, prior to the first measure, i.e. having lost parts of measurable trunk and root; they are renewing their canopy, to perhaps slow down again once maximum coverage is reached. In any event, one has to try to factor into the measures the missing, therefore unmeasured portions of trunk, that often represent lost metres of circumference.

These yews have invariably lost portions of trunk, prior to the historic measures taking place, suggesting that Normandy also had yews planted at early religious settlements, with yews dating from before the tenth century. This would make any later Norman church yew plantings, part of an existing communal tradition on both sides of the Channel.

I would argue that the powerful Anglo-Saxon church may have taken over some sites of early saint cells, which may have already been abandoned. The Anglo-Saxons were keen to establish their own cultural heritage and could have easily adopted the former site of an early saint's cells, often furnished with its convenient well and yew, thus providing British and French church-yards today with apparently anachronistic ancient yews. These ancient trees are indistinguishable in terms of age and size, from the ancient yews in early Welsh churchyards.

There is no evidence from Anglo-Saxon records of yews being planted at Anglo-Saxon churchyards, yet the converse is true of early Celtic saints. The laws of the Christian king Hywel Dda show that in 950 AD there was a very severe fine for felling yews 'associated with the saints'. These yews are most likely the yews of the early Welsh saints; even centuries later, i.e. in 950, their yews were still revered, and preserved by force of law, more powerfully than by a modern British 'Tree Preservation Order'. This law suggests that the yews of early Welsh saint cells in England may also have been preserved. Where later Norman churches grew the yews remained, which may be understandable given their historic Christian lineage. Settlement in 'Dark Age' Britain is still a subject of lively debate amongst archaeologists. Yet many existing yews may represent planting from this period. If this hypothesis is correct, then the mystery surrounding the oldest yews in England may not be quite so opaque and may assist the assessment of some church sites by landscape historians seeking contributory evidence for otherwise unrecorded pre-Norman activity in their parish.

The increasing attention of researchers in coming years, should help us hone our understanding of the significance and origins of these trees. Dendrochronological analysis will develop a clearer picture of historic growth patterns. In the future archaeologists may excavate more dead stumps of size in our churchyards and radiocarbon dated portions of these may offer us useful data.

'How old are British yews?' remains a question that cannot yet be answered empirically, but the researches discussed herein suggest our knowledge is significantly increasing. The evidence from many quarters emphasises the reality that these trees frequently exceed a thousand years growth. The yew may fairly claim to be the longest living British tree.

CHAPTER THREE

The Churchyard Yew

All of the oldest churchyard yews in Britain indicate a deliberate planting at some time to provide shelter and symbolism for the site, sites whose trees often preceded the Norman foundations of many churches. The exact origins of these earliest churchyard yews have long been shrouded in mystery. Part of the problem in assessing the context of old trees has been that most old churchyards have experienced several eras of occupation. Roman, Saxon, Norman and Victorian occupation stages are commonly represented. Because of these successive occupations, features such as wells or yews, difficult features to date empirically in themselves, can be difficult to place in context within one distinct phase of occupation.

The copious number of burials in churchyards also amount to multiple unrecorded excavations. The mixed, non-soil spoil of this activity often ends up under the yew. These factors can complicate assessments of context for features in churchyards, whether they are yews, wells or unhewn stones. However, botanical dating evidence of an old yew may indicate earlier settlement on the site than that suggested by present buildings or by other visible architectural remains.

Many old yews have been measured and observed for centuries and their histories are at least partly known. The examples shown below are famous yews in some cases with documented histories of at least 200 years, admired and measured by many botanists. The ancient yews detailed below show clearly that the idea of another yew being mistaken for the one historical example is very unlikely indeed. This evidence from individual trees strongly suggests that many British yews easily exceed a thousand years of age.

The Church Preen yew, Shropshire

At Church Preen in Shropshire is a famous churchyard specimen that domi-nates the site (Plate 4). The church is of a very narrow design, tucked away, below the yew. A. De Candolle visited this yew in 1831 and considered it about 1400 years old. John Lowe in 1897 considered it 750–1,000 years old.[1] The Church Preen yew is strange as the trunk is worn at the base in the photo, this clearly shows an arc of fragments of old trunk, disappearing at near ground level, that will, in years to come, not be visible for botanists to include in future measures. This could explain odd basal measures of 40ft 5in (12.33m) at base in 1889 and 36ft (11m) at base in 1833 while remaining almost the same girth at 3ft (1m) from ground during the same period. These measures may have varied how much to include of the rotting part of the base (which is far less than 40ft (12m) today) having effectively shrunk on this side, facing the path. The Church Preen yew was likely to have been 40ft (12m) in girth at one time, or larger still, making easily the largest ever recorded girth in

FIGURE 9
The Church Preen
yew, Shropshire.
ROBERT BEVAN-JONES

Shropshire, although the Clun and Norbury yews may fairly claim a similar age.

Another, much younger, entire yew, also in Church Preen, is in a private garden. This was 19ft 3in at four feet from ground in 1897. In 1983, it was over 6m, at 20ft.[2]

The Darley Dale yew, Derbyshire

FIGURE 10
The Darley Dale yew,
Derbyshire, as shown
in J. C. Loudon's
*Arboretum et
Fruticetum
Britannicum* (1838).

This tree is an unmistakable specimen growing near St Helen's church. The Darley Dale yew has been a noted landmark in the parish for at least four centuries.[3] It was estimated at only 700 years age in 1900, by Mr C. S. Greaves, in the Derbyshire Archaeological Journal, although he had heard it dated at 2,500 years old by J. E. Bowman.[4] Estimates made by C. S. Greaves were mostly based on three local churchyard yews, grown over the graves of churchwardens, even though the age of one was in doubt. He also reported several other plantings, which had grown more slowly and which he did not use in his assessment of the Darley yew.[5] The Darley yew is a very healthy female tree of 33ft girth at 3ft from the ground. The mean of several measures detailed in Loudon gave an age of 1356 years in 1838 according to De Candolle techniques.[6]

FIGURE 11
The Darley Dale yew
today, a protected
prisoner
MICK SHARP

This tree at Darley has been measured frequently:

1792: 28ft girth at base (Dr Burgh)

1792: 32ft girth at four feet from ground (Dr Burgh)

1838: 27ft in girth at base (Loudon [7])

1888: 27ft in girth at base (Paget Bowman)

1836: 31ft 8in girth at four feet from ground (John E. Bowman)

1876: 31ft 8in girth at four feet from ground (Dr Cox)

1909: 32ft 3in girth four ft from ground (W. Dallimore)

1933: 27ft at base (A. W. Smith)

1933: 33ft at four feet from ground (A. W. Smith)

Some of this data is from *The Sacred Yew*.[8] The Darley yew today is protected by railings and surrounded by tombs that make photographing the tree difficult. It remains one of the healthiest of the largest trees and shows few signs of decay, suggesting it must be tolerant of its current circumstances and may continue to be indefinitely.

The Fortingall yew, Perthshire

The Fortingall churchyard yew (Plate 5) survives today at the entrance to Glen Lyon in Perthshire. This place-name is understood today as 'church of the

FIGURE 12
The Fortingall yew,
Perthshire, as depicted
by J. G. Strutt in his
Sylva Britannica (1822).

The Great Yew at Fortingal.

fort', from Gaelic *Fartairchill,* in old records Forterkill. The fort stands on a commanding bluff near the church and is known as the 'White Fort', traditionally the residence of the legendary figure *Fionn mac Cumhaill.'* [9] The yew stands in the churchyard of the ancient church. This extraordinary tree has had many estimates and measurements. Any large yew of 23ft+ (7m+) in girth is almost unknown in Scotland, so to find Britain's largest surviving measured specimen, at Fortingall is, therefore, very odd. This is certainly one of the oldest yews ever recorded in Britain and is considered by many experts to be 2,000–3,000 years old. It may, however, represent a remnant of an early saint cell, of the sixth century, making the tree around 1,500 years old. Evidence of early saint activity has been recorded here, including a probable eighth century font.

The yew has been split in two since before 1769, when the Honourable Daines Barrington measured its girth at 52ft.[10] It today looks much as he

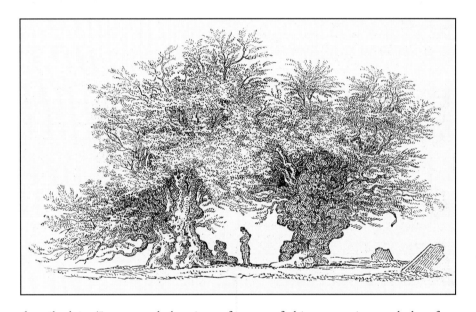

FIGURE 13
The Fortingall yew as shown in Loudon (1838).

described it. 'I measured the circumference of this yew twice, and therefore cannot be mistaken, when I inform you it amounted to fifty-two feet. Nothing scarcely remains but the outward bark, which has been separated by the centre of the tree's decaying in the last twenty years. What still appears, however is thirty-four feet in circumference.' He added, 'this, therefore is, perhaps, the largest tree we have any account of; as the great chestnut at Tortworth, in Gloucestershire, was only fifty-one feet when measured very accurately forty years ago by Greening, the father of the present gardener of that name.' [11]

Like the Tortworth chestnut, the Fortingall yew conceals its exact age behind a façade of ancient fragments, displaying by turn grandeur and decay. De Candolle's determination, of the tree in 1831, partly based on data collected in 1770, was between 2,500 and 2,600 years old.[12]

Dr Neill visited the Fortingall yew in July, 1833 and considered it around

2,000 years old then. He noted 'considerable spoilations' committed on the tree since 1769, noting 'masses of the trunk itself carried off by the country people, with the view of making *quechs*, or drinking cups and other relics, which visitors were in the habit of purchasing'.[13] Sir R. Christison, a celebrated Scottish botanist who measured trees at their narrowest part, estimated this tree to be 3,000 years old, based on several visible ring counts, and deemed it in 1879, 'the most venerable specimen of living European vegetation'.[14] Much later, with less expertise, C. T. Ramage based his estimate of 1,400 years on a growth rate of a single yew in Montgomeryshire.[15]

The Kyre Park 'Parted' yew in Worcestershire, like the Fortingall yew, has also been in two halves for more than a century. These rifts probably occurred through storm or lightning damage and had either tree lost a portion of trunk during a storm, they would now be fragments, leaving little clue to their original sizes. It is unusual for both halves to survive. Evidence from Benington in Hertfordshire and from the failed resurrection of the Selborne yew also suggests that leaving fallen yews in situ, wherever possible, may be the best approach to encourage survival after trauma.

De Candolle was a good scientist. Most modern dating evidence from contemporary researchers to some extent supports his estimates of growth, in that A. Mitchell, A. Meredith and others agreed that the Fortingall yew could exceed two thousand years growth. The yew may equally be a veteran remnant of a post-Roman early Christian hermitage on the site. This would make the yew at least 1,400 years old. (Plate 5)

The Forestry Commission looked at care and maintenance for this tree in 2000. The management programme included trimming a nearby tree that had been competing for light with the old yew.[16] I would even argue quite strongly for a trial period of ivy removal and moving the walls away from the tree; indeed for any measure to increase light access. This may trigger fresh growth, though a trial such as this could take two or three years to show benefits. Certainly, with two trunks still growing, potentially there is plenty of life left for this yew, perhaps the oldest tree in Europe.

Buckland in Dover yew, Kent

At Buckland in Dover, Kent, in the churchyard, there is a great monoecious yew. It was recorded as a 'hollow butt', in 1946,[17] due to it being struck by lightening around 1770.[18] The pre-1838 print shows traces of internal roots ripped during the fall, before it was moved, in February 1880, 62ft to the west, to allow the extension of the nave. This process required a long trench, huge planks, rollers and windlasses.[19] The whole tree, root and earth moved measured 6ft 5inches by 11ft 8inches, by 3ft 6½inches deep.

In 1987 it was battered by the Great Storm, and yet the tree still continued to thrive. Other large yews have been successfully moved. At Amberley church in Sussex, 'by the door of the church is a magnificent yew which was moved 200 years ago and is no worse for the change. It must have been 300 years

FIGURE 14
The fragmented yew
at Buckland in Dover,
Kent, as shown in
Loudon, 1838.

FIGURE 15
The Buckland in
Dover yew in the
process of being
moved in the 1880s.

old when it was moved from the vicarage garden, and it is an almost miraculous thing that it should have survived such an adventure'.[20]

The Selborne yew, Hampshire

The Selborne yew was documented by the celebrated Rev. Gilbert White in his *Natural History and Antiquities of Selborne* in 1789.[21] The yew was 23ft in girth in 1778, at five feet from the ground, ten years before White measured the tree finding the same girth. William Cobbett measured it at three feet from ground, finding 23ft 8inches, in 1823. A. Meredith measured at the same height from ground and found 25ft 10 inches.[22]

Britain's most famous authority on silviculture, the late A. Mitchell, also contributed an estimate of 1,400 years, based on the growth rate recorded since Gilbert White measured the tree.[23] Meredith contributed an age estimate of around 1,400 years. Since then, Hampshire horticulturalist and tree ring researcher, Toby Hindson has estimated 1,150–1,200 years, from available ring counts, and also by reconstructing the core, from ring count studies of

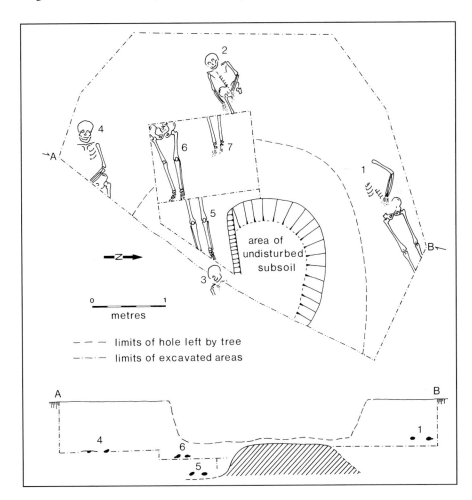

FIGURE 16
The Selborne yew root hole excavation plan.

HAMPSHIRE FIELD CLUB
AND ARCHAEOLOGICAL
SOCIETY

41

several hundred Hampshire yew stumps of 0–300 years age.[24] The Selborne yew was not the oldest yew in Hampshire, as Gilbert White knew, himself having been very familiar with the church at Farringdon, where the yew is much older, yet it was certainly an impressive ancient yew.

When the Selborne yew was blown down in the storms of January 1990 an 'opportunity to learn' was presented to botanists and archaeologists alike. This large in situ dead stump presented an interesting archaeological experiment that sadly has yet to be repeated. Hampshire archaeologists D. Allen and S. Anderson took the opportunity to excavate the hole the stump left. Their dig had bad weather which often drowned the site, and was made more difficult as the tree remained partially in situ, in the hope that it would revive.

The dig took into account the distance that the earliest burial had eaten into the undisturbed subsoil beneath the tree. No burial passed entirely under the yew to give a baseline for dating. However, the archaeology, based on the deepest burial being dated at 1200–1400 by pottery in the grave fill, suggested that, 'an age of a thousand years or more therefore seems possible for the great yew'.[25] The tree was *circa* 9ft (3m) in girth at the time of the earliest burial. Attempts to resurrect the Selborne tree following the fall failed, hampered by poor weather. The stump remains today as a decaying habitat. Other pieces of the yew now form a memorial altar.

FIGURE 17
The Selborne yew
circa 1940.

FIGURE 18
The Selborne yew
crater in 1990.
HAMPSHIRE FIELD CLUB
AND ARCHAEOLOGICAL
SOCIETY

An age of a thousand years or more for the Selborne yew seems a balanced conclusion. This does not resolve many questions concerning the origins of the Selborne yew but it adds to the picture. It also tells us that any yew stumps of this size or antiquity, *circa* 16ft+ (5m+) or more, could prove very profitable for archaeologists to excavate, as other yews could be far more ancient. If this yew were a stone, deliberately placed a thousand years ago there would be far more interest from archaeologists. Old stumps that are of the size of the Selborne yew exist in some Hampshire churchyards, such as Privett and Soberton. They are totally dead and ideal for excavation or coring analysis.

FIGURE 19
Portions of the
Selborne yew live on
as a war memorial
altar.

43

Reasons for planting churchyard yews

The role of yew inside the churchyards of Britain seems to stem from the early saints who began their cells in the sixth century AD. These earliest Christian missionaries seem to have used the yew as a symbol of immortality. Many of their trees yet survive, especially in Welsh churchyards. However, many rumours and beliefs concerning the origin of planting of churchyard yews persist today. The idea of yews being planted where stock (cattle) could not reach them has no historical evidence to support it. Although timber for bows is not really a realistic planting motive for old churchyard specimens it is said that Charles VII of France (1422–1461) ordered the yew planted in all of the churchyards of Normandy for crossbows.[26] John Lowe, author of *Yew-trees of Great Britain and Ireland* uses many such references to English yews being planted for bows that have not been found by researchers today. His post as physician to the Prince of Wales some time before 1898 may have entitled him to access a Royal repository or library that no longer exists. Certainly most yew for medieval bows was imported from Spain. The historic origins of planting yews in the churchyard, has nothing to do with bows.

Several existing early accounts suggest a combination of motives for planting the yew. R. Turner in his *Botonologia* of 1644 suggested that 'if the Yew be set in a place subject to poysonous vapours, the very branches will draw and imbibe them, hence it is conceived that the judicious in former times planted it in churchyards on the west side … being fuller of putrefaction and gross oleaginous vapours exhaled out of the graves by the setting sun.'[27] This theory has not been proven scientifically, but the shade of the yew, keeping ground below it dry and clear of undergrowth and also sterilising the soil with decaying falling needles may contribute something to the health and safety of burial grounds. This belief may neatly explain the later widespread popularity of yews planted outside Victorian privies.

As a spiritual symbol, the yew has always retained a strong presence. In 1656, the Rev J. Collinson, when writing of the churchyard of Ashill in Somerset, wrote, 'Our forefathers were particularly careful in preserving churchyard Yews which by reason of their perpetual verdure were emblematical', 'of the immortality of the soul'.[28]

Donald Gregory noted that Edward I in 1307 decreed that groups of yews should be planted in all churchyards in the land to 'provide protection to the fabric of the church from high winds and gales'.[29] In the Book of Llandaff, a twelfth-century document, sanctuary is stated to be available to those 'who sought it between the yew and the church door'.[30]

This idea of sanctuary or shelter is also implied in the thousands of records of those buried under yews in England and Wales. On 12 January 1875, diarist-curate Frank Kilvert mentioned a gypsy girl, aged 12, called Limpedy Buckland, who was buried in 1809, under the 'great yew', in the SE corner of Langley Burrell churchyard in Wiltshire, after she had died in the 'tents of her people'.[31] The will of Thomas Aldy, dated 19 December, 1520, stated that he wished to be buried 'under the yew tree, beside my father',[32] in the local churchyard of Ash village in Kent. These examples perhaps couple the ideas of sheltering the dead and symbolising immortality of the soul.

Apart from burial, the yew has long been incorporated into other church rituals. In 1858 one writer wrote of the long established role of the yew as a palm substitute in Ireland. 'One of the great ceremonies of the Roman Catholic Church is the blessing and distribution of "palms" on Palm Sunday, the last Sunday in Lent. In Ireland the branches of the yew are always used for this purpose, and sprigs of yew are worn in their caps and hats by the peasantry for the whole of Passion Week up to Easter Sunday. On entering a peasant's cottage or the "room" of a dweller in towns, branches of "blessed palm", i.e. yew will be seen placed by the crucifix or at the head of the bed, where they will remain until replaced by fresh ones on the next Palm Sunday.' [33]

Although not commonly brought into churches, the yew has played some roles in church ceremonies, such as a tradition recorded in 1854, at Leigh church in Worcestershire. 'The custom of dressing the church with flowers, green boughs, or holly and ivy, prevails at Leigh, Worcestershire, at the three great festivals of the Church, on Good Friday too, the church is dressed with yew, which gives place to the flowers on Easter Day.' [34] In the village of Berkely near Frome in Somerset it was recorded in 1850, that the church was decorated 'on Easter Sunday with yew, evidently as a symbol of the resurrection'.[35]

The origins of churchyard yews

R. M. Tittensor suggests that most very large yews occur in churchyards are of probable pre-Norman Saxon origin.[36] Some yews in churchyards are likely to have been plantings of the Norman era. Many of the 16–23ft (5–7m) girth yews are such trees. As we have seen, it is not possible at this time to identify the ages of each and every tree. Church records rarely relate back this far and even traditions of Norman plantings are unknown. Yews do not seem to have left much record on the folk memory of the parishes or more importantly in their documents.

Britain's Norman yews were certainly in part the continuation of an older tradition on both sides of the channel. Perhaps specific records would not have been necessary. As the yew has certainly been present continuously in churchyards since long before the seventh century, it seems strange that no carving in wood or stone, or any decorative depiction of a yew, or its foliage, exists in any church in the whole of Britain, from much before 1870 AD. This is very hard to understand given the role it has played in villages in most counties. Nor do misericords, wooden church carvings that often depict oak leaves, offer evidence for pre-1900 representations of yew.

Several records of early documents support the role of the yew at religious sites from the seventh century onwards. J. G. Strutt, a very talented engraver of identifiable famous trees, cited an original charter that refers to the building of a church at Perone (or Peronne) in Picardy in 684. In this charter was a remarkable clause, giving instructions for the preservation of a particular yew tree. The writer adds that the same tree was in existence in 1799.[37] This tree must have been large in 684, like the 'yew on the barrow' mentioned in a Anglo-Saxon charter of 625. These yews, now probably gone, at least suggest the role of the yew in funerary traditions long before 625, as they were preserved and noted as established significant features in the seventh century.

Another piece of charter evidence is the oft-cited 1152 reference to the Eastham yew in Cheshire. The manor of Eastham was handed to the abbots and monks of St Werburgh, by Earl Randall of Chester. The villagers apparently entreated the new owner 'to have a care of ye olde yew', obviously at least four centuries old at that time.[38] This famous yew today is certainly extremely ancient. The clerical novelist Charles Kingsley, who also founded the Natural History Society of Chester, often admired this tree. In 1975, E. R. Yarham estimated it to be around 1,500–2,000 years old.[39]

Because of the time scale involved some suggest a replanting may have occurred, to explain the 'apparent' great ages of huge yews. This is very unlikely in most instances. Any other replacement, with a younger yew would be distinctly apparent. Any great discrepancy of age would show considerably, since it takes at least five centuries for a yew to begin to look ancient. We know this from the hundred or so known plantings in churchyards in this country, from church records. Many of these have been collected by A. Meredith[40] yet many more must exist that are unknown to researchers. Almost a hundred trees planted since 1500, recorded in the church records, suggest that yews do not generally reach 16ft girth until at least five hundred years of age.

A typical example of the quality of the post-1500 evidence comes from Derbyshire. 'In the copy of the register of Carsington, it is stated that a yew was planted in that churchyard in 1638,[41] in 1877 it was measured at ten feet in girth at four feet from the ground.'[42] In November 1775 in Woodbury churchyard in Devonshire, 'a yew or palm tree was planted, as appears by the register'.[43] These are trees that are difficult to lose in the records. Any 'replacement tree' would show as a much smaller specimen.

F. Moss records two little known plantings in a Cheshire churchyard, in his Chronicle of Cheadle, published 1970: '1686, planted then in the east side of the churchyard near the road by John Ryle of High Greave a younge yewe tree.' He also recorded another known planting in the same ground. '1857 the rector planted a yew at the NW entrance.' These clear records show that yews in fact have probably the longest and most complete record of measured growth of any British tree.

Where pairs of large yews occurred in the same churchyard it is possible that attention might switch from one to the other, if one died. One would most likely have been the same age as the other, if mature enough to make a serious attempt at seeming old enough to be the same tree, say of 23ft girth, a size that takes at least eight centuries to realise.

In many counties pairs of large yews exist in churchyards. There are similar records of 30ft pairs of yews in some churchyards in Normandy. At sites like

La Haye De Routot, pairs survive of yews that must be over a thousand years age. The pairs of yews at La Haye De Routot, 32ft (9.66m) and 36ft (11m) girths, suggest identical traditions to Hampshire, Kent and Shropshire. There are at least ten examples of 'paired girth' yews in Kent churchyards alone, all these trees being over 20ft (6m) in girth, suggesting paired plantings.

The origins of yews sometimes remain obscure. Large hollow yews offer little solid dating evidence. Unless historic measures are retrieved, an excavation report done of the root hole at time of the death of the tree, photographs taken, ring counts taken etc it is hard to speculate about them. Some old yews are remembered using that flawed device, 'folk memory', the stuff of pseudo-history and factoids i.e. 'A dead yew, under-propped, and chained together so as to preserve the upright position, stands in the grounds of Kersal Cell, Lancashire. This cell was founded about the middle of the twelfth century, and Mr Arthur Mayall, has suggested that the seed was brought back from the holy land at the end of the second crusade.' [44] Another yew with an unlikely myth is the old yew that was formerly at Duffield church, in Derby, Derbyshire. Tradition spoke of it being planted in commemoration of the battle of Crecy, in 1346.[45]

Vanished churchyard yews can easily leave a site with little evidence remaining above ground concerning the age of the tree and its associated link with early settlement. A church at Hampstead Marshall in Kent once had recorded a yew of 47ft in girth, one of the largest ever recorded in England. At Hardham church of St Botolph in Sussex was a yew of 21ft girth (in 1835) that 27 people could fit into.[46] The ancient yew at Lullingstone in Kent has been replaced by a cedar.[47] At Hagley parish church in Worcestershire, Edwin Lees recorded 'a massive yew', that had 'renewed itself by deposition of alburnum from above'. These internal roots and the size of the tree suggested it was 'at least seven centuries old', according to Lees in 1882.[48] According to parish minutes this 'shapeless' yew was 'cut down and burnt' in 1971 as part of a churchyard levelling exercise.[49] Other local problems can make finding old yews difficult. The yew at Upton-cum-Chalvey, Bucks, was 'an ancient yew, near the lych gate, of great girth and with spreading branches', pre 1946.[50] The place today is called Slough, so the tree may have partially been 'lost' due to the change of name.[51] The ancient yew that once stood on a mound outside the grounds of St Patrick's church at Patterdale in Cumbria, as photographed in John Lowe's *Yew Trees of Great Britain and Ireland*, implies a marker of a possible lost early saint cell. Patterdale is named after a Patrick, which adds something to the explanation for the parish having had unusually old yews.

Many yews are much older than their current churches. At Claverley in Shropshire the giant 26ft+ (8m+) yew by the road is far too large and decayed to have had a post-Norman origin. An excavation of the church interior did reveal human burials, lying north to south, buried with a small animal. A small urn was also found. The church was found to have been built on a large unhewn stone and concrete platform, nearly the length of the nave, seven feet thick at one end, in the form of a buttress.[52] This, of course, does not automatically date the yew though encourages, with the estimated age of the yew, ideas about pre-Norman occupation on the site, possibly by an early saint, who adopted an abandoned Roman site.

The relevance of Roman artefacts in churchyards to yews is frequently dubious. At Uppington in Shropshire, the Roman altar is much defaced and is thought by local archaeologists to have been robbed from a local Roman site, simply for building materials. The much better preserved altar at Gresford, in Clwyd, does not link to the yew, even if it may have been used locally by the Romans. Roman coffins and other items are often taken to the churchyard by superstitious farmers, such as the Roman coffin at Corhampton, Hants. These are sparse examples and the most venerable yews in these churchyards suggest to me a link with a pre-tenth century cell, now lost, with trees of early christian missionaries. It is likely that the yews themselves will one day be dated by dendrochronologists, and their exact chronology will be produced without argument. The current dating (and historic geographical evidence) points to Anglo-Saxon era saint cells rather than anything necessarily earlier than this. Many cumulative examples, especially from Welsh churchyards, suggest this is the case.

Churchyard yews of Wales

Wales probably has the largest collection of ancient yews in the world. It has a wealth of unique churchyard sites including a number of sites with several ancient yews, yews of more than 23ft (7m) in circumference of trunk. Strangely, there are few or no patches of ancient yew woods recorded in Wales, except on cliffs. However, there are many amazing Welsh churchyard specimens of probable early saint origin, of the sixth–seventh centuries AD.

Probably the earliest written record relating to the yew in Britain occurs in a Romano-British, funerary inscription found at Llandysilio, Pembrokeshire: '*Evolenggi fili Litogeni hic iacit*'. *Evolenggi* is noted by J. MacNeill as certainly a yew-based personal name.[53] This name is of Irish origin and later became the personal name *Eolang*. This traditional personal name shows a historic association with the yew that was not linked to funerary ritual but to a living tradition, possibly with royal associations, that has coincidentally been preserved in a Welsh churchyard. Certainly though, it is an apt place for a person with a yew name to rest.

In Wales, as in England, the role of the yew as shelter for the dead lives on. A phrase often heard in Wales, as noted by J. Jones-Davies of Brecknock Museum in 1970, was that rich and poor alike referred to their demise as '*gorwedd dan yr Ywen*', 'sleeping under the yew'.[54] Another old Welsh saying runs, '*Is yr Ywen ddu ganghennog dwmpath gwyrddlas cwyd dy ben*', 'Under the green-leaved branching Yew a grassy mound is soon raised'.[55]

Welsh yews have also been long admired for their beauty as landscape features. The Victorian diarist and curate Kilvert noticed many aspects of the countryside, during his times in rural parishes in England and Wales. Kilvert often described yews he saw. He wrote of 'Cae Noyadd, in its black yews', in the vicinity of Clyro in 1870. In 1874, he described Llanvareth church, on the Wye river, as 'half-hidden by its great yew'. On 30 August, 1870, he describes Capel-y-ffin, 'church of the boundaries', South of Hay on Wye, as 'squatting like a stout grey owl among its seven black yews' (Plate 6).[56]

The largest yew at Capel-y-ffin today is a huge fragment, with a missing portion facing the path, bordering a track to the river fifty yards away. It has lost perhaps half its trunk. Many of the oldest yews in Britain are fragmentary, their remaining portions not representing their original sizes. The oldest yews at Capel-y-ffin may have originated as shelter for a pre-tenth century cell.

Numerous early saint sites in Wales have yews of 30ft (9–10m) girth associated with them. It is more than likely that most of these trees are literally, 'yews of the saints', in the region of 1,400 years old. At St Afan's church, at Llanafan Fawr, a yew of 39ft girth thrives today. It was once a larger tree, as remnants of old trunk stumps testify. It is near the tomb of St Afan, who was martyred in the seventh century.[57] This circumstance bears some similarity to the huge yew at Llanerfyl, where the immense tree had a similar seventh-century funerary stone under it, before it was moved into the church. These examples may suggest a real relationship between the early saints and their yews.

The yew at Llangernyw is almost certainly one of the ten oldest yews in Britain. A possible derivation of Llangernyw in Clwyd, is put forward by Canon Doble. 'It seems possible that Cerniu might be derived from the name of the Cornovii who inhabited the Welsh border in Roman times, that the name might have been carried to Cornwall ...'[58] However, D. Gregory notes a couple of early Welsh saint tomb markers at this site, from before the ninth century. Saint Digain of the church dedication fits this picture of a genuine early saint yew. This evidence, like many other early saint sites, points mostly to a yew of *circa* 1,500 years age. This provides, in my opinion, a tangible, living link to an ancient Christian presence on the site in the post-Roman period.

At Llansantffraid-in-Elwell, Powys, at the St Bridget churchyard, there is a pair of giant, broken yews that also support this argument. St Brides Super Ely in South Glamorgan has an 26ft+ (8m+) girth yew that has been estimated as 1,600 years old.[59] At Llansantffraed in Gwent, there are indications of significant ancient re-growth clumps and large stumps, which may confirm another link with this early saint.

At Rhulen St David's church, Powys, it is said that 'a formidable yew tree curtailed the extension of the chancel (in the fourteenth century). Even so, the east wall was pushed right up against the tree to enlarge the sanctuary as much as possible.'[60] This observation implies some early yew presence at this site, perhaps reaching back towards the time of the early saints. John Andrew records the probable removal of a large 'medieval' yew at Oystermouth, Gower, just south of the medieval church porch in an illustration of *circa* 1790, gone perhaps due to the turning of the old church into the north aisle of a larger new one in 1860.[61] A similar case occurred at Mathern in Gwent.[62]

If these ancient trees or stumps have to be removed today, they ought to be excavated. 23ft+ (7m+) dead stumps, of at least eight centuries age, await investigation in England at Privett and Soberton, both in Hampshire, Ashford Carbonnell, in Shropshire, Portbury, near Bristol, and elsewhere. Their excavation, could assist us to further understand the origins of such plantings, without significant ecological damage.

Wales has a unique tradition of yew circles occurring in circular churchyards of great antiquity. As essayist J. Harte concedes, 'these trees were evidently planted at a time before the circular *llan* had been replaced by the rectangular churchyard, although the date of this change is open to question, and in some cases may be no earlier than the thirteenth century'.[63] Some of the yews within these circles are thought to be 1,500 years or more, by criteria currently used to assess their ages.[64] The Overton on Dee yew circle is a celebrated 'Wonder of Wales' near the Shropshire border. This fine site does not contain the oldest yew circle in Wales, although it is a fine example and is currently the most famous yew circle in Britain.

Circles of large yews, with up to 40 trunks of 16ft+ girth in a round churchyard, is a truly Welsh phenomenon, not recorded anywhere else in Britain, except perhaps as remnants at Ashford Carbonnell in nearby Shropshire. The Ashford Carbonnel yews may perhaps, originally have been such a circle, including the giant ivy covered stump inside the wall bordering the field, and the hollow yew outside the churchyard, perhaps offering faint evidence of an early saint occupying the site.

There are perhaps 25 examples of yew circles, intact or fragmentary, to be found today in isolated sites around Wales. At Penpont in Brecon is a circular churchyard with a circle of young yews that is known to have replaced an older circle. How the old circle was removed is not recorded.[65] One key element of old yew circles is that where there are many of these trees in the circle, usually a pair of yews will be at least several centuries older than the rest. For example, if the circle has 15 yews, 13 may be 20ft in girth (or under) and two will be more than 26ft in girth. This combination indicates two spheres of deliberate planting, separated by several centuries, the latest sphere of planting, perhaps *circa* 900–1100, the earlier planting between 600–800. The oldest yews on these sites are most likely directly associated with the era of early saints.

D. Gregory notes a significant yew circle at Halkyn. 'Further east, in Clwyd, south-east of Holywell is Halkyn (Helygain). Near and under a circle of large and therefore ancient yew trees' … 'a grass-covered table-land, where the former church once stood; beyond this platform and the yews in the lower-lying south side of the churchyard may be found by the patient seeker a spring of water, bubbling up from the well, which supplied an earlier age with water'. 'After Christian sanctification the well provided for many years the water for the font of the first church to be dedicated to St Mary on that site.'[66] Springs are known to be favourite landscape features of early settlements, in Wales they are most commonly associated with early saints. With the ancient yews, the well may indicate a lost early saint cell.

Cefnllys near the river Ithon, has 'an impressive circle of yew trees, which mark the boundaries of the churchyard'.[67] Llanspyddid, Powys, above the River Usk, is a circle that includes specimens of over 26ft (8m) girth. Llanspyddid has a round churchyard, its outline marked by ten large yews. Nash-Williams dated an early saint stone in this churchyard to the sixth century.[68] The churchyard of Nantmel has a semi-circle of yews on the south and south-east sides.[69] Llanelly in Brecon has a church that had '13 ancient Yews', pre 1946.[70] Other yew circle sites include Llanycil and Llanddwywe, Gwynedd, south of Llanbedr.

At Llanfeugan, Powys, 12 very large yews mark the raised circular boundary, where specimens include 33ft+ (10m+) yews, in the north-east of the churchyard, where there was once a cockpit.[71] There were 13 yews here for most of the nineteenth century. Fergus Kinmonth measured the male yew to the north of the site at 37ft 3inches in girth.[72] This clearly predates the 1272 church and must be associated with an earlier sphere of influence, perhaps an early saint. Similarly, at Llanfihangel-nant-melan, St Michael's churchyard in Powys there is another ancient circle, including specimens of *circa* 33ft (10m) girth, suggesting an early saint presence.

At Cwm-Du church, near Llanbedr Ystrad Yw, is a circle of 'more than twenty yews', marking a very large round churchyard. Here early Christian sixth-century memorial stones, in Latin and Ogham, commemorate the death of Catacus, son of Tegernacus.[73] Nantmel church, five miles from Rhaeadr, has a semi-circle of yews on the south and south-east sides. The church is associated with St Cynllo, a sixth-century Welsh saint. The largest of the yews in these churchyards, when over 26ft (8m) in girth are usually indicators of a pre-tenth century planting.

The examples discussed here demonstrate the significance of the early saints, in the history of the ancient yews that survive in the churchyards of Wales. My research also implies that many churches (even some in England) have yews probably linked with their era, rather than the later Norman dedications, that their churches are currently named after. In my opinion, the 30 largest or oldest yews in English and Welsh churchyards, are likely to be of similar age.

Conclusions: churchyard yews today

Several hundred yews, of more than 800 years age still survive in British churchyards. Many older specimens in Wales (and England) are forgotten today, swamped with ivy or rubbish. Many have disappeared through pressure for churchyard space, for burials or buildings. The legendary 33ft (10m+) yew at Llanthewy Vach, with huge internal growth, was present until 1946,[74] yet was felled or burnt, in the 1970s.[75] It was 36ft (11m) girth and was hollow enough to contain several people. The painter Thomas Henry Thomas painted this yew in *circa* 1900. His watercolour pictures of this and several other yews, resided in the 1970s as a set, at the National Museum of Wales, in Cardiff.[76] This was likely an original early saint era tree.

A number of ancient yews are still used for storing planks, paint and other materials. At Llangernyw in Clwyd, one of the oldest yews in Wales or England, an oil tank stood inside the tree, until the possible age of the specimen was appreciated. A 20ft+ (6m+) yew in Sidbury churchyard, in Shropshire, formerly housed timber panels discarded from church usage. In an ever-busier world, these trees will need more monitoring and care. The encroaching legions of sheds, piles of rubble and polythene are taking their toll on some venerable churchyard specimens.

Yews outside churchyards are not necessarily much safer. At Craigends in Kilbarchan parish (a parish name linked to early saint activity) lives the second oldest yew in Scotland. Now seriously encroached by a recent housing development, it has suffered greatly in recent years and its long-term survival may be threatened by these recent changes to its locality.

The fondness for old yews displayed by the Victorians resulted in a spate of railings; these have caused a lot of problems since the trees they surround have grown. Branches collide with the iron, growing round them, or, become impaled on the railing spikes. The South Hayling churchyard yew, Hampshire, has this problem. The railings, provided to protect the tree by a parishioner now buried next to the yew, hamper it today.[77] To resolve many railing problems would be expensive and difficult. Often there are chains, now overlain by the cambium, which were formerly placed there to help prop the tree up. The expense of sorting these problems out may be beyond the purses of some parishes, which have many other deserving concerns. It is also often a difficult situation to treat without risking harming the tree.

In past years I have encouraged criticism of piling stones around the bases of yews. However, stones seem better than railings and the old yews with long established stone supports seem in better condition generally than those without. This may be because the stones dissuade burials too close to the trunks, or because the weight of stones helps secure the trunk from storms and other basal damage, including fire.

Fire is a very common problem; Peterchurch, Herefordshire, Tettenhall, West Midlands, and Thorley, Hertfordshire, have all been particularly unlucky, almost losing their fine trees. According to Ken Mills, the largest of the yews at Borrowdale, Cumbria has recently been badly burnt-out, by visitors staying in the area.[78] Several medieval churchyard yews in Wales were recorded by J. Andrew as having being killed by burning of uncertain origin.[79] According to Toby Hindson, hollow yews in different areas of England have been burnt out to try to kill the trees, such as at Cobham churchyard in Surrey. Equally, much burning on yews is probably caused by lightning.

A yew in Kenley in Shropshire was burnt out, removing portions of trunk. Fragments of dead burnt trunk are wrapped in ivy and this may be hastening its demise. The current girth, when the dead, burnt fragment falls, will soon be a fraction of a once enormous tree. From what is left this fact will not soon be apparent to the visitor.

The churchyard yew is restricted in many ways, as pressure for space has demanded limits for the yews, often concealing their natural tendency to cover ground with shade. Severing branches causes hollowing in most cases, usually on the side facing a pathway. In recent times, the preservation of the yew has been highlighted by successful projects, like the Millennium yew campaign planting scheme, organised by The Conservation Foundation. In November 1996 key Conservation Foundation members David Bellamy, David Shreeve and Libby Symon organised a collection of cuttings, initially from 20 yews from England and Wales thought to be in excess of 2,000 years age.

The main collection of cuttings was supervised by botanist and tree expert Fergus Kinmonth. He was helped by climber Bertrand Maurer to reach the best samples. These cuttings were then prepared by Martin Day at his Bedfordshire nursery. By 2000 the yews had reached 7,000 participating parishes. These 'Millennium Yews' have been ceremoniously planted by Bishops, vicars, celebrities and members of the Royal family. These trees, of ancient stock, carry ecological and spiritual significance for each community. The importance of recording the origin of each tree will become clearer as each year passes. The millennium yews celebrate the ancestry of the English yew planting tradition and also represented the celebration of the third Christian millennium. These yews provide a significant collection of known plantings that will doubtless form part of botanical surveys of yews in centuries to come.

The past history of the churchyard yew is still imperfectly understood, yet we have gleaned much information from the various records of our peers and forbears that help illuminate some aspects of yews. Further excavations of dead yew stumps by adventurous archaeologists will bring us even closer to predicting the ages of our yews and their historic contexts. The radiocarbon dating of more yews and renewed interest in the use of yew in dendrochronology will take us much further towards knowing the history of the yew in greater detail. Campaigns like the Yews for the Millennium Campaign will help keep the ages of all yews in the minds of those who see the small millennial yews growing as they pass through parishes across Britain. They contribute to a continuous British tradition of at least 1,400 years practice, of planting evergreen yews at places of burial and worship: trees symbolic of immortality of the soul, that shelter buildings and people, in all seasons.

CHAPTER FOUR

Yews at Abbey Sites

The vast majority of known abbey yews today are under 13ft (4m) girth, indicating a planting later than 1100. Most of these are later still, post-dating the Reformation. Of perhaps 500 abbey sites in Britain today, only three or four have yews thought to be growing before 1100. Yews at Ankerwyke Priory, in Berkshire, Strata Florida, Ceredigion, and Fountains Abbeys, Yorkshire, are certain examples. At Strata Florida, I suggest that there is evidence for an early Welsh saint cell having been responsible for the extraordinary yews there. The extreme rarity of old yews at abbey sites suggests that, except at these few sites mentioned above, they were generally not planted there in the thirteenth or fourteenth centuries. No evidence suggests any other abbeys in Britain had ever grown old yews. If they had, one source or another would mention them – whether the sixteenth-century traveller Leland, or George Borrow, or William Cobbett, or engravers such as J. G. Strutt. Yews of great age on abbey lands are many times rarer than 'normal churchyard' specimens.

Younger yew plantings are well represented at many abbey sites. The yew walk at Buckland Abbey in Yelverton, Devon is likely to be a post-reformation garden feature.[1] The many yews at Lilleshall Abbey in Shropshire are similarly *circa* 10ft (3m) girth and are likely to have been planted after the reformation, perhaps around 1750. The largest yew at Lilleshall Abbey, of a different coloured wood and leaf to all the others and growing among the buildings is *circa* 13ft (4m) girth. It is probably pre-Reformation, but post-foundation, a yew that the monks probably knew. Some other yews at Lilleshall may not be seen as the property is divided in terms of access. There have been recent yews planted at some abbey sites. At Hailes Abbey in Gloucestershire, an ornamental golden yew, a cultivar, was planted to mark the site of the high altar, but this has now gone.[2]

Yews that monks may have known are not common. The Bolton Abbey yew once stood at the centre of the cloister. Although venerable, its age may never be known. The Muckross Abbey yew is a cloister yew and is considered a fifteenth-century foundation tree. In 1776, Arthur Young recorded its trunk diameter as two feet (up to 12ft from ground) which implies a girth of *circa* 6ft 4inches girth. By 1860 it was 10ft in girth, up to 10ft from the ground. In 1994 it was 12ft in girth.[3] One more possible example is that of Dryburgh Abbey, where a yew near the abbey church is today less than 16ft (5m) in girth. This is supposed to be a foundation yew of the abbey, which dates from 1136. This abbey also has a known planting of (1789) noted by a memorial stone. J. C. Loudon (1838) and Lowe (1897) mention these trees.

At Jumièges Abbey in Normandy, France,[4] the yew is certainly post-Reformation. The yew at Abbey Dore in Herefordshire is certainly not earlier than 1200 and may be later than 1500. All of the specimens listed above are probably some of the most famous abbey yews, and none are hollow or exceed 16ft (5m) girth. This places these trees easily in the post-1100, or post-1536 bracket.

An unusual arrangement of yews exists at Llanthony Abbey in Wales. A large yew growing above cellars at the ruins, perhaps a sheltering yew planted to keep the cellar dry, is certainly several centuries old. A very strange yew grows against the wall of the old St David's church at the same site, perhaps as a forgotten grave marker. Neither yews are hollow or have 16ft+ (5m+) trunks, making dating difficult, although the age of these trees is at least several centuries. The Llanthony yews remain enigmatic.

William Stukely recorded his visits to Barnwell Abbey, Cambridgeshire in the first decade of the eighteenth century. He 'frequently took a walk to sigh over the Ruins of Barnwell Abby, and made a Draught of it, and us'd to cut pieces of the Ew trees there into Tobacco stoppers, lamenting the destruction of so noble monuments of the Piety and Magnificence of our Ancestors.'[5] Although the well at Barnwell is acknowledged to have been part of pre-Christian, well-centred activity by some authorities,[6] the yews are not famous or necessarily very old.

Waverley Abbey, Surrey, has a famous yew that causes historians of trees many problems, a contested specimen, depending on how it is measured. By one reckoning it is *circa* 20ft (6m), possibly suggesting pre-foundation, as it seems clearly a larger girth than all but two abbey yew sites in Britain. Yet it grows on a wall of the abbey, therefore it must post-date the abbey foundation, and possibly the Reformation. I would argue that its girth, made up of writhing roots over rocks, is not a natural trunk, suggesting historic damage to the tree. It cannot be compared easily to most other yews. Yews can survive great upheaval when smashed and then not disturbed, as at Kyre Park and Powick churchyard, both in Worcestershire and Benington, Hertfordshire. The yew may have been damaged during the Reformation and walls tumbled, regrowing through the rubble, prior to the tidying operation needed when the site was taken into the care of the state.

A pre-Reformation status seems appropriate, based on the age and condition of the tree. An excavation of the stump when dead, might empirically determine the relationship between the wood and the surrounding stone. There is too much of both at the moment, which I think could obscure a result in the short term. Coring such a specimen may not resolve the debate, as the contorted trunk is unlikely to present enough continuous ring data. This is a probable pre-Reformation yew in my opinion, though debate about the origins and age of this tree will continue amongst botanists. The Waverley yew is one of the five oldest yews at abbey sites in Britain. However, a few yews at abbey sites in England and Wales strongly indicate earlier settlements there prior to the arrival of the Norman era monastic communities.

The Ankerwyke Priory yew, Berkshire

The Ankerwyke yew, in Berkshire, is certainly a very rare pre-Priory yew, of a kind worthy of consideration as an indicator of pre-Priory settlement on the site (Figures 20 and 21). John Lowe wrote in 1897, that 'The National Trust Society, which has done such splendid work in preserving monuments of antiquity, would do well to cast a protective glance over these veterans',[7] referring to such trees as the Ankerwyke yew. About a century later, the organisation purchased the site where the legendary Ankerwyke yew grows today. The late Bill Bowen of Bath University had intervened in the mid 1990s at Ankerwyke to prevent tree surgery happening to the tree. This effort

FIGURE 20
A detail from Strutt's 1822 portrait of the Ankerwyke yew.

Yew Tree at Ankerwyke.

56

and those of A. Meredith brought the yew to public attention. It is certainly very ancient and stands close to the Thames surrounded by ditches. It cannot possibly be less than 1400 years age. Exactly how much older it is, cannot yet be scientifically determined. Archaeological investigation of the ditches may provide some sense of context for the tree.

Measured at over 30ft in 1806, in 1989 it was over 29ft in girth. J. Lowe, measuring in 1894, found 30ft 9inches at three foot from ground. He recorded the base 'a good deal broken away', as at Church Preen. The Ankerwyke yew had lost parts of its trunk, yet it still exceeded 30ft in girth in 1822. Excepting two sites, this tree is still twice as large as any other abbey site yew in Britain. It may have been incorporated into a local Anglo-Saxon boundary marking scheme as a mature tree.

Matthew of Westminster (1215) records that Runnymede was the field of council where the Anglo-Saxons met to consult on the welfare of state. There is no direct evidence that this tree, at Ankerwyke, was used by the Anglo-Saxons as a meeting place. The origination of the tree could easily have been as a marker for a sixth-century saint cell that could have been deserted by the time of the arrival of the nuns.

The Ankerwyke tree certainly predates the nunnery on the site. I have not seen any direct evidence that the Magna Carta signing occurred under the Ankerwyke yew. This idea was, however, already current before 1800 as a poem suggesting the link was published by 1822.[8] It is certain that this tree

FIGURE 21
The Ankerwyke yew today: a tree still recognisable from Strutt's 1822 portrait.
ANDY MCGEENEY

was full-grown at the time of the signing. The Ankerwyke yew also seems an ideal location for a Court of the Hundred tree. Situated within the ditches and water features on the banks of the Thames it may have had a significant role in history. The engraver J. G. Strutt in 1822 made several measures of it, noting 27ft 8inches girth at 3ft from ground, and at 8ft from ground 32ft 5 inches in girth.[9] The huge severed branches on either side of the trunk, discernible in the etching, are visible today on the trunk of this tree, as healed stumps.

There is a large fallen limb that lies below the yew today, that has not been cored and ring-counted. It may contain upwards of five hundred rings. A radiocarbon dated piece of the Ankerwyke tree produced a date of *circa* 150 years age.[10] Unfortunately, this is not representative of this hollow tree's actual age and may reflect re-growth from when the tree lost a portion of trunk.

This is only one of two known radiocarbon dates ever undertaken on living yews in Britain. The Ankerwyke yew sample may have been contaminated prior to testing. Another sample or two may provide more data. Many other hollow yews need to be tested in this way to assist in determining how useful the technique can be in assessing the ages of hollow yews. No funding has been found for researchers to test more specimens, including testing another piece of the Ankerwyke yew. This would need to be done to put together a representative collection of data; to even give us an idea of the range of ages we are likely to find, one from *circa* 1850 and one from *circa* 1450 is not enough. Two more tests would need to be done on the Ankerwyke yew to gain a chance of an indication of its age, although other yews may well date better. Based on modern growth ring analysis and girth-based research, the age of the Ankerwyke yew cannot be less than 1,400 years old.

Fountains Abbey yews, Yorkshire

At Fountains Abbey, there is a historic group of yews, once known as 'The Seven Sisters', whose original trees certainly predated the arrival of the Cistercian monks who founded the abbey in 1135 (Plate 7, Figure 22). These trees have been famous for four hundred years. During this time, various measures and estimates of their age have been made.

The remnants sit on an earthwork called Kitchen Bank, south of the abbey, with younger yews forming a line on it. Though a postcard of *circa* 1900 claims to depict the 'last of the Fountains Abbey yews', W. Dallimore in 1908 described these trees as 'the Famous Fountains Abbey Yews of the present day'.[11] Two of the original sisters were reported as still present in 1994. One of these had fallen but was healthy and therefore, unlikely to have a limited life as a result of the fall.[12]

J. C. Loudon, writing in 1838, cites a manuscript that implies they were there before the Cistercians arrived. 'The history of Fountains Abbey is minutely related by Burton, from the narrative of Hugh, a monk of Kirkstall, which is said to be now preserved in the library of the Royal Society:

FIGURE 22
One of the Fountains
Abbey 'Seven Sisters'
from Loudon's 1838
illustration.

At Christmas, the archbishop, being at Ripon, assigned to the monks some land in the patrimony of St Peter, about three miles to the west of that place, for the erecting of a monastery. This spot of ground had never been inhabited, unless by wild beasts; being overgrown with wood and brambles, lying between two steep hills and rocks, covered with wood on all sides, more proper a retreat for wild beasts than the human species. This was called Skeldale; that is, the vale of the Skell, from a rivulet of that name flowing through it from the west to the eastward part. The prior of St Mary's at York, was chosen abbot by the monks, being the first of this monastery of Fountains, with whom they withdrew into this uncouth desert, without any house to shelter them in that winter season, or provisions to subsist on, but entirely depending on Divine Providence. There stood a large elm tree in the midst of the vale, on the lower branches of which they put some thatch and straw; and under that they lay, ate and preyed; the bishop, for a time, supplying them with bread and the rivulet with drink. Part of the day some spent in making wattles, to erect a little oratory; whilst others cleared some ground to make a little garden. But it is supposed they soon changed the shelter of that elm for that of seven yew trees, growing on the declivity of the hill on the south side of the abbey, all standing at this present time (1658) except the largest, which was blown down about the middle of the last century, They are of extraordinary size: the trunk of one of them is 26ft 6in in circumference at 3ft from the ground; and they stand so near to each other as to form a cover almost equal to a thatched roof. Under these trees, we are told by tradition, the monks resided till they had built the monastery.' [13]

This tempting text offers clues to the age and history of these trees, yet we must be wary of the evidence it provides. I could not find a mention of yews in the earliest account of 1207; the first oratory there was built under an elm. This 1207 manuscript is referred to as a rare authentic contemporary account by historian J. Patrick Greene. Postholes of this original oratory were excavated, within the main abbey building, by Glyn Coppack, though the elm root hole was not found within the limits of the dig. [14]

The earliest manuscript of 1207, mentions only the elm, not yew, though an 1658 text cited by Loudon, recorded that the monks, having left the elm, settled under the yews. These yews are some considerable distance from where we know the oratory (and possibly the elm) to have certainly been. The historic yews at Fountains, are certainly pre-Cistercian trees and it is

Yew Trees at Fountains Abbey

FIGURE 23
An engraving of the Fountains yews, drawn in 1822 and printed in Strutt's *Sylva Brittanica* of 1830.

interesting that J. C. Loudon finds records dating back to 1658 which associate them with the abbey, even if the earliest manuscripts do not contain yew references.

De Candolle, based on visible ring counts, gave *circa* 1,280 years for the age of the oldest yew there in *circa* 1815.[15] By 1822, the remaining six yews had been neglected and Strutt noticed axe-marks and limb removal. It is a shame that four have been lost since 1820, having been looked after carefully since 1132 when they were probably already many centuries old. A group of yews such as these do not ever flourish together so closely, in a natural situation, as the shade generally prevents them surviving together.

Botanically speaking, it is impossible for these yews to be younger than the abbey. To become a group like this, either they were re-growth trunks of one tree, or they represent the disintegrated remains of one enormous bole, making it possibly one of the oldest pieces of vegetation in Britain. The 'Seven Sisters' may have been one disintegrated female. Interestingly, venerable single oaks, split through age have also been known as 'The Seven Sisters', denoting one shattered tree. The engraving by Strutt, a fastidious draughtsman, suggests that it is possible that this clump of yews at Fountains, could have been one tree, like the circle of limes described by Oliver Rackham as being 6,000 years old.[16]

However, a fragmented single sixth-century planting might offer a similar looking situation. With one Fountains Abbey yew measured at 30ft girth and another at over 26ft girth, *circa* 1822, this interpretation could make the Fountains group, historically at least, as large as the Fortingall yew. The most likely possibility is that the Fountains yews represent fragments of an early saint marker yew, like that at Fortingall church and possibly at Strata Florida Abbey. A careful excavation around the area of surviving trunks may unearth some more data concerning context. The Fountains yews are certainly a pre-Norman piece of vegetation that may themselves indicate pre-Cistercian early Christian settlement near Fountains Abbey. A site suited to the monks of one era is likely to have appealed to the monks of another.

It is interesting to note that a large portion of a tenth-century Anglo-Saxon ornamental stone cross was discovered in a study of the stonework collected from the ruins by J. Laing.[17] It is thought unlikely to have travelled far since its original use and may offer a clue as the significance of the yews, being the only other above ground pre-Cistercian features yet found on the site. However, unlike at Strata Florida, extensive antiquarian activity at Fountains, decorating the ruins with romantic stonework in the eighteenth century, may be responsible for this find; it that has no known context. It is not possible to state whether the cross was of the Roman or Celtic church, though the Celtic monastery at Ripon suggests that the yews (and cross) may represent the lost location of an outlying daughter cell. Kitchen Bank, where the yews occur, has not yet been excavated. The age of the yews and the Anglo-Saxon era cross, together offer indicators of pre-Cistercian settlement on the site, perhaps within the vicinity of today's remnant yews.

The yews of Strata Florida Abbey, Ceridigion

The Strata Florida yews (Plate 2) seem to have considerable archaeological relevance. The origins of the oldest yews at Strata reach into antiquity beyond the site's era as an abbey. Their extreme age and historic records suggests that, as at Fountains Abbey, they are likely to be the remnants of an early Celtic saint settlement. The excellent spring that fed the abbey main building at Strata Florida may like the yews, have been a feature of a cell of an early Welsh saint. The yews at Strata Florida are valuable for several reasons. One of the surviving yews at Strata Florida has the poet Dafydd ap Gwilym buried under it. Which of the two Strata Florida yews he most probably rests under is, however, a moot point.

Strata Florida Abbey lies in the angle between the Glasffrwd brook and the river Teifi, in the same way as Fountains Abbey has the river Skell nearby, Rievaulx Abbey has the Ure and Ankerwyke Priory has the Thames. Access to water was a dominating factor in choosing most church sites, Saxon or Norman. The river Teifi was a living boundary for regional kingdoms of early Welsh princes and kings long before the abbey was built at Strata Florida. The founder of the abbey, Rhys ap Gruffyd, used his rivers carefully. 'Rhys ap Gruffydd accompanied the Archbishop as far as the river Dovey, which was the boundary of his dominions and of the diocese of St David's.'[18]

The founder of Strata Florida often frequented early saint sites near rivers. In 1184 Rhys ap Gruffydd 'in the presence of many of our army in the Church of St Bridget at Rhayader', confirmed his previous donations and set forth in considerable detail the boundaries of the large estates he granted to Strata Florida Abbey. This parish church of Llansanffraid Cwmteuddwr, dedicated to the sixth century St Bridget, is situated on the west bank of the River Wye in modern day Powys. S. W. Williams stated that, 'the church of St Bridget stands in an extensive graveyard, and there is ample space of level ground around the church for the assembly of a large number of people. This is not the case with the church of St Clement; the space there is and always must have been, very confined.'[19] This large graveyard compares well with that of Strata Florida, a site that was also used for important assemblies. When in 1238 'Llywelyn Fawr summoned his assembly of Welsh Chieftains at Ystrad Fflur'[20] this would have almost certainly taken place under the yews of the abbey, in the spacious cemetery.

When Leland visited Strata Florida in the middle of the sixteenth century he recorded the principal features of the abbey including many large yews. These are the only yews he mentioned in all his travels. They must have been spectacular:

> The chirch of Strateflere is larg, side ilid and crosse ilid. By is a large coloyster. The fratry and infirmitori be now mere ruines. The coemiteri wherin the cunteri about doth buri is veri large, meailey waullid with stone. In it be xxxix great hue trees. The base court or camp afore the abbey is veri fair and large.[21]

These 39 yews, described as great in *circa* 1539 were all of significant size and of at least several centuries antiquity. These are the only yews that Leland found worthy of comment in all his travels. This description suggests that the yews were a very remarkable feature of the abbey site that would have been a feature of the background to daily monastic life at Strata Florida.

Two yews that remain today at Strata must be counted amongst Leland's 39. One of these measured 22ft in girth in 1874.[22] Another ruined yew was etched in 1874 that is now gone. This is discussed in detail later. The ages of the old yews at Strata support a pre-Cistercian, probably sixth century origin. When in 1741 the engravers Samuel and Nathaniel Buck depicted the Strata Florida site for the Stedman family, their etching shows no trees identifiable for species type. This family had had control of the site since 1567. As no yews were depicted in the 1741 etching, though several were still present, it may be suggested that the Stedman family were not interested in yews, that probably 36 of the 39 had already been removed by 1741. The natural erosion of numbers of yews between 1537 and 1741, from 39 to three is very unlikely. I would argue that three yews were preserved, partly because of their age and links to the Welsh poet Daffyd ap Gwilym.

By 1848, the accumulated turf over the ruins made examination of the ground difficult, although some excavation was completed. The *Archaeologia Cambrensis* 1848 (p. 127) reports that the yews at Strata were, 'so reduced in number as to seem like the last of a once flourishing and noble race, mourning in their own decay over the magnificence of the past, and the desolation of the present.' This appearance was probably symptomatic of the storms that had battered those left, after the majority of yews were removed.

The report by S. Williams of 1889 itemises Cistercian finds and a couple of finds from later occupations. No flints, postholes, or any pre-Cistercian items were recorded at all. The area his excavation covered is not clear in the report although he built, 'retaining walls of the rough rubble stone taken out of the ruins to fence in the site, and also to form a revetment wall for the deposit of the enormous mass of soil and debris, amounting to about 3500 cubic yards, which had to be excavated, but which could not be removed outside the limit of the churchyard.'[23] This activity was not supported by a diagram in the report. In his site he refers to the site being initially 'encumbered with trees',[24] but this would probably have been of young trees, seeded from the locality. The two yews on site today, could not have been disturbed by this movement of soil.

The Dafydd ap Gwilym yews

The yews of Strata Florida are most famous for their association with Dafydd ap Gwilym. Dafydd ap Gwilym is the most famous name in the history of medieval Welsh poetry. The court poetry of his day was strictly governed by rules of rhyme and intonation, making the process of making poetry very complex and ritualised. Poems attributed to Dafydd generally concern the heart, poems to women, set mostly in leafy bowers and greenwood cathedrals.

FIGURE 24
The Strata Florida
female yew.
ROBERT BEVAN-JONES

Dafydd was probably born in 1320. His burial at Strata Florida is widely accepted as fact. Several medieval poems record this fact, many of them recording his burial under 'the' yew. Strangely he himself mentions yew only in passing, in a poem where he speaks of an ironic silver-backed yew bow, that breaks, demonstrating that pretty things are not always as functional as they are beautiful.[25]

It is possible that versions of the Welsh legends known today as the *Mabinogion* were kept at Strata Florida, as it was a very important library and manuscript centre. Based on a margin note in the *Book Of Basingwerk*, 'we have here the record of the Cistercian Abbey of Conway by a colony of monks from Strata Florida'.[26] This literary link may have in turn fostered the welcome of poets to the site. Gutyn Owain, 'one of the most distinguished poets of the fifteenth century' and equally celebrated as a herald and historian made this his principle residence.[27] This may suggest that the memory of Dafydd ap Gwilym's burial site, marked by a yew, was remembered and recorded by those poets at Strata Florida in the fifteenth century, admiring their greatest poet and his immortal poetry.

On Saturday, 7 July 1951, Mr Gapper's memorial stone to Dafydd ap Gwilym was 'erected at' Strata Florida, at the large female yew. The President of the Honourable Society of the Cymmrodorion, the celebrated Keeper of Manuscripts at the British Museum, Sir Idris Bell, unveiled it. The ceremony

FIGURE 25
The Strata Florida female yew, next to the parish church of St Mary.
R. PURSLOW

celebrated the burial of the Master poet, Dafydd ap Gwilym, under a yew at Strata Florida. This has not been disputed since 1879. In 1879, D. Long Price in an article in *Archaeologica Cambrensis*, questioned the statement about Dafydd ap Gwilym being buried at Strata Florida' and claimed him for Talley Abbey.[28] This was unsuccessful and since that time most, possibly all, are agreed that the evidence seems clear, Dafydd was buried at Strata Florida. Professor Rachel Bromwich[29] and many other scholars have stated that this is more than likely. I would agree but I will also suggest the Dafydd yew was not the yew that the Honourable Society assembled around in 1951.

An elegy from a poet contemporary with Dafydd, Gruffydd Gryg,[30] describes the location of the burial vividly. Professor T. H. Parry-Williams, delivered an address to the society in 1951, and read a translation:

> At Ystrad Fflur, beside the hall,
> There grows a yew against the wall.
> God bless this yew for whom 'tis bliss
> To be the house where Dafydd is;
> For now the yew has gleaned a fame
> From his beauty and his youthful name.

King David said, before you grew,
That you would be the poet's yew,
And consecrated for his home
Your leaves, when he to dust should come;
Death's fort against the wind and snow,
Like the trees which Dafydd used to know,
Your roots and boughs have grown to be
A family vault where men can lie.

It was not my wish your roots should have
A narrow and silent grave,
There a brave man lies, the bee-hive where
The angels of the world consorted were.
Before the voice and that great heart,
Which Dyddgu loved, were laid apart,
Their bond had made her thrall, the yew,
Put on his foliage anew.

But let your tripod roots and boughs
Repay your lord his fitting dues,
And guard his tomb in gentleness:
And let his aunts your branches bless.
Yew tree grant this boon I crave
Step not from the head of Dafydd's grave.

The straying goats you need not fear
Will waste your branches, browsing here;
No love shall break you, nor fire consume,
No carpenter cut you, nor shall come
The cobbler with his knife to peel
And from your body the garment steal.

No churl nor firewood gatherer
Will cut your weighty boughs from fear
That they will suffer on their backs
Who dare to lay you to the axe.
For roof your leafs; good your place;
God keeps your wonders from disgrace.[31]

(Translation by David Bell)

Many shorter, later poems are recorded that reiterate the point that this poet was buried under 'the yew' at Strata Florida, confirming a continuous tradition of his resting place as a famous medieval grave site. According to Joshua Jones-Davies, the scholars in 1951, 'declared, once and for all, "that Dafydd's grave is under *the* tree at Strata Florida".'[32]

The fame of the tree had somewhat waned by the time the Honourable society arrived in 1951. I would not claim that Dafydd's grave is not under *a* yew at Strata. There are *two* surviving ancient yews of similar age at Strata Florida, of the 39 that Leland saw. This would possibly have not been apparent to the scholars, as they would have looked at the site and seen one big yew, big enough to look 1,000 years old. It is probably in excess of 1,400 years old. No wonder they chose this yew, it is a fine ancient berried female. What they probably did not do was to look carefully at the other yew, over by the north wall. This fragment is much smaller, less than half the girth, but perhaps a tenth of the bulk. From the large yew it looks like a shrub. Underneath the foliage however is evidence it was once an enormous yew, of equal age to the other.

Dafydd could have been buried under either, or any of the original 39 yews, as seen by Leland, *circa* 1539, though there is evidence to suggest that he was buried under a yew that remains today, the 'small' male yew not the 'large' female one. It is very likely that these two yews, were saved from felling, probably when the manor house was built on the site, and probably because of Dafydd ap Gwilym associations. The burial sites of poets in Wales are not easily forgotten, as George Borrow discovered.

There are direct clues in the poem to the exact location of his grave. The actual yew marking Dafydd's grave in the contemporary poem, is described as 'gleaning a fame', so it was well known exactly which yew it was, when

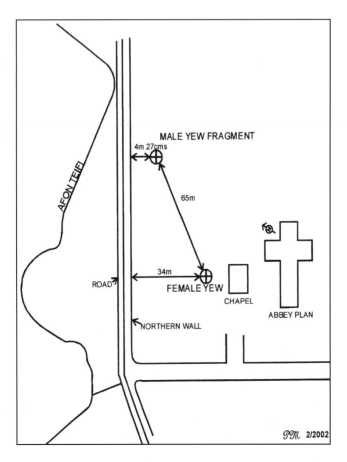

FIGURE 26
The location of the
Strata Florida Abbey
yews in relation to the
abbey plan.
L. YATES

39 yews were there. The poem also suggests that the yew was famous as the marker, of a much frequented grave of a celebrated master poet. These directions in the G. Gryg elegy are deliberate; he wants Dafydd's 'aunts to bless the branches', of the yew that guards Dafydd's grave. There are several directions he gives. Using Leland's guide to the Abbey, 'wallid with stone', the current wall around the site is probably the one Dafydd knew, at least in plan.

In the poem the yew 'grows against the wall'. This does not apply to the 'large' female yew today accepted as the Dafydd yew. The 'small' male fragment, when intact, would have literally grown against the northern wall of the cemetery. The torn surface of this fragmented yew faces the wall concerned. When Allen Meredith visited the site in 1986 he also noted that the yew in the northern corner of the cemetery was a small fragment of a much larger yew. This was also noted as an ancient fragment of an older yew by Arthur Chater, former Keeper of Botany at the National Museum of Wales. This is not the only evidence.

In the elegy, the tree of Dafydd is described by someone who is familiar with yews. The scholars eyeing the large yew in 1951 were not botanists. Their belief in Dafydd being buried at Strata was based on scholarship, but they were not to realise that the little fragment, when intact, would have fitted the criteria and was also alive before Dafydd's day. Nor did they know that the fragment male was intact but split, when George Borrow visited and accepted it as the Dafydd yew in 1854, not the female.

The yew is an unusual British tree in being of two separate sexes. The male tree emits pollen, the female has berries. The 'large', traditionally accepted Dafydd yew is female, and has berries. This is a key feature of female yews, and the bright red berries would be ideal for a poet to describe. There are no berries mentioned in the poem. This suggests that it could not have been a berried female. No medieval Welsh poet would ignore berries within such a descriptive poem.

Another source suggests that historically the small male yew was originally bigger and was known as the Dafydd yew: George Borrow.

George Borrow and the Dafydd yew

Novelist George Borrow wrote *Wild Wales* as an account of his journey through Wales in 1854. Not published until 1862, it was undertaken for one purpose alone, to visit the graves of Welsh poets he admired. He was well educated, could speak many languages and excelled at Welsh, unusually for an Englishman. Borrow spent four years learning the medieval Welsh of Dafydd ap Gwilym. Few Welshmen he met in Wales in 1854 could understand it, because the stylised Welsh language of the medieval poets was so removed from modern Welsh.

He visited the graves of many Welsh poets in *Wild Wales*, talking to locals in Welsh, who often led him to desolate locations. We know that his descriptions of yews in Wales are accurate, because large yews are there today, where he described them to be. At Mallwyd, there is a huge yew he mentions, when visiting a poet's grave there. The same situation happened at Llancilin. A very large yew is there also. Such was his zeal, he even travelled to Anglesey to visit a little known poet he admired.

Borrow visited Strata Florida to visit the grave of Dafydd ap Gwilym, possibly the poet he most admired. Borrow recorded that the poet was by

FIGURE 27
The male yew visited by George Borrow in 1854.
ROBERT BEVAN-JONES

legend married 'under the greenwood tree',[33] 'their hands joined under it by Madawg Benfras, a poet and friend of Dafydd'.[34] Borrow states that the joining of hands by bards was probably a relic of 'druidism'. He adds that unions of this kind were, 'long practised in Wales and were rarely set aside'.[35]

Borrow even records that at Strata Florida he asked locals for information, to ensure he found the right yew. He knew the verses written by Gryg describing the Dafydd yew, so he knew when he had found the correct tree, by following the directions given in the poem. This was over a hundred years before Mr Gapper erected his stone and the Honourable society of the Cymmerodorion met at Strata in 1951 to assemble around the female yew.

Borrow spoke to a local before entering the churchyard, who spoke something about worshipping sticks and stones. Having sat on a mound, surveying the scene inside the old cemetery Borrow said to himself, 'I would give something, said I, to know whereabouts in this neighbourhood ap Gwilym lies. That, however is a secret no one can reveal to me.' Here he possibly infers that the location is given in the poem of Gryg he has in his head. He then describes what I refer to as the 'small' male tree, as he viewed it then, lamenting, as a strike of lightning had laid low half the tree.

'At length I came to a yew-tree which stood *by the northern wall* [my italics] which is at a slight distance from the Teivi. It was one of two trees, both of the same species, which stood in the churchyard, and *appeared to be the oldest of the two*.' (my italics). This is the 'small' male yew, as it is the only Strata yew, of those that remained of the original 39, which is both near northern wall and at a slight distance from the Teivi.

'Who knows says I, but this is the tree that was planted over ap Gwilym's

FIGURE 28
The Strata Florida male yew, pictured with the author.
L. YATES

70

grave, and to which G. Gryg wrote an ode?' I would argue it was a favourite of Dafydd's in his life at Strata Florida; it is far too old to have a fourteenth century origin. Borrow was a keen researcher of the sites of Welsh poet graves, not a botanist. Gryg did not state the yew was planted.

Borrow continues, 'I looked at it attentively and thought there was just a possibility that this was the identical tree. If it was however, the benison of Gruffydd Gryg had not had the effect which he intended, for either lightning or the force of wind had splitten off a considerable part of the head and trunk, so that though one part of it looked strong and blooming, the other was white and spectral. Nevertheless, relying on the possibility of its being the sacred tree, I behaved just as I should have done had I been certain of the fact; taking off my hat I kissed its root, repeating lines from Gruffyd Gryg ...'[36]

Borrow certainly viewed the yew the poem clearly refers to, the now small male, by the northern wall. He was lucky to have documented the tree at the time it was becoming a small fragment. This is the male tree there today, a tree still bearing the scars of being torn by storms. Dafydd ap Gwilym, may yet lie below it, as visited by Borrow, not under the larger Dafydd ap Gwilym yew. These two trees once had the same size trunk. Since the male became fragmented, some modern burials have taken place under it, perhaps disturbing the sleep of the most famous bard of Wales. An exploratory excavation by archaeologists under the trees may lay this possibility to rest.

An ancient Strata Florida yew now gone
Only three old yews were ever recorded at Strata of the 39 Leland saw in *circa* 1536. This third, older, more decayed yew survived until at least 1874 and was carefully drawn in a print.[37] This was never associated with Dafydd ap Gwilym, it is not near a wall, and so does not fit the description of the existing male yew fragment visited by Borrow as Dafydd's yew. The other prints of yews in the same 1874 article are directly comparable to those trees that exist today; including Llanfoist, near Abergavenny, the Tettenhall male in Staffordshire and the Staunton yew in Worcestershire. The picture of this large old yew that was at Strata is therefore very likely to be physically accurate.

This amazing yew was described in 1874 by Edwin Lees, author of *Botany of the Malvern Hills*. 'When I visited the locality, only three battered yews remained, and the largest of these was divided into two parts, leaving a passage through it, this was 22ft in girth, and another was in six fragments at the base thus indicating great antiquity.'[38] This is a crucial piece of observation. This yew he measured as having 22ft girth, missing portions of trunk, in 1874, would have then been easily in excess of 1,200 years old; it is the yew Borrow saw as Dafydd's, the now small male fragment, where I suggest Dafydd is most likely buried.

The 1874 print shows another kind of old yew, more decayed than flourishing, as fits the description by E. Lees of the other yew he saw. This decay through antiquity, leading to separate fragments at the base, as shown in the print, is very rare. This yew suggests the existence of yews at Strata Florida

before the arrival of the Cistercian monks. There are only two yews in the whole of Wales that today fit the depiction of the Strata yew now gone. Discoed, Powys and Llangernyw in Clwyd. These trees are often thought to be 3,000 years old,[39] though based on geographic evidence and the flaws in existing dating techniques, I would argue that an early Welsh saint origin is most plausible.

Although most of the 36 older yews were removed between 1539 and 1848, this old yew may have been swept away during the 1899 dig, having disappeared after 1874. This yew was far too old, like the remaining two yews, to have been planted in the eleventh or twelfth century. As a group they suggest a planting pattern seen in many sixth-century Welsh saint sites. These sites often have no surviving trace of their founding church, except their huge yews, a pre-Norman slab and perhaps a well, like those found at Strata Florida.

Indications of early settlement at Strata Florida
In the charters of Rhys ap Gruffydd and Henry II almost all boundaries of the properties belonging to Strata Florida Abbey seem to have been rivers and springs.[40] The Arth is mentioned in this context, '. . . from Abermeylir upwards, along the Arth as far as the Foss which runs from the spring of

FIGURE 30
The chambered
feature at Strata
Florida, in the monks'
choir by the high
altar. Established at
the earliest era of
building at the site, it
was fed by the
medicinal spring
Dyffryn Tawel.
ROBERT BEVAN-JONES

Bleydud Orvanaun ...'[41] Strata Florida, by the river Teifi, had a spring that was probably used prior to the establishment of the abbey. It is simply called 'Dyffryn Tawel',[42] which may be translated as 'spring of the valley'. Today it is just off the abbey site on farmland. It has never been excavated and may have been a feature frequented by man prior to the foundation of the abbey, possibly by early Welsh saints. Certainly it would have been known to Rhys ap Gruffyd.

F. Jones, mentions records of the spring Dyffryn Tawel, 'valley spring', at Strata Florida. It fed the feature in the centre of the main abbey building. Considering Dyffryn Tawel, he stated that 'Near Strata Florida there are wells whose waters contain mineral properties, and were much used by people at the beginning of this century.'[43] The secular name 'Dyffryn Tawel' is unusual for a monastic spring, with no saintly association. This perhaps suggests a prior local usage, prior to the Abbey being built. This 'excellent'[44] spring flowed from a two feet by three feet, stone sewer, rising from a rock near the lime-kiln by means of a lead pipe, four inches in diameter, three-eighths to half an inch thick.[45] The feature it fed is not quite straight in the building; it is slightly off-centre, even on the plan. This is referred to as a *mandatum*, an abbot's footbath, or drain, by D. Robinson in the current Cadw guide to Strata Florida.[46]

Examples of these features in Britain are almost unknown.[47] The back cover of the 1998 edition of F. Jones' book has a photograph of an ancient holy well in Anglesey, at Rhoscolyn, St Gwenfaen's Well. St Gwenfaen was a sixth century saint, many of whom were directly associated with wells. It is a similar stone lined basin, with rough-hewn small slabs, two sides straight, two sides stepped, exactly like the Strata Florida example. These features are often difficult to date, but the similarity is striking.

Not only were many Welsh kings and princes buried at Strata Florida, but they were also often brought to Strata Florida, when wounded or otherwise diseased, to subsequently die, or recover. 'In reading the records of the deaths and burials at Strata Florida, one cannot but be struck with the fact that in so many instances it is recorded that the individual mentioned died *at* Strata Florida; and it would appear as if in those days it was not uncommon for a person stricken with sickness to repair to the abbey … when any person of rank and importance died there, the conventual scribe duly entered the fact in the monastic chronicle.'[48]

The prominent position of this chambered feature, in the monks choir, fed by the medicinal spring, suggests that it could have been a well. This may have been popular with medieval pilgrims, perhaps seeking cures while the monks tended their wounds and provided hospitality. This feature may have been a key component in the reputation the monks cultivate for healing at Strata Florida, which may also have encouraged the site's later literary and poetic reputation. Dafydd ap Gwilym himself certainly admired many wells and often went on pilgrimages to them. He went on pilgrimage to a holy well in Anglesey, to the martyred female saint Dwynwen's well, by which she was murdered on Llanddwyn island, just off the main island. She is the patron saint of lovers in Wales, and knowing this seems to make Dafydd's pilgrimage

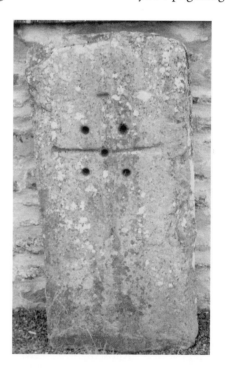

FIGURE 31
The pre-Cistercian slab at Strata Florida, comparing an etching from *Archaeologia Cambrensis* of 1850 with a recent photograph.
ROBERT BEVAN-JONES

74

even more understandable.[49] It seems possible that this feature was a well at Strata Florida, fed from the ancient spring, near already old yews that served as shelter for those visiting or resting near the spring, before the arrival of the Cistercian monks.

There are other pointers to an early cell at Strata Florida. There is a fine incised slab that was found in 1848 to have been covering a 'skeleton of considerable size', in the cemetery, with no apparent grave goods. This may have been the grave of an early Welsh saint.

Most authorities describe this slab as of pre-Norman and pre-Cistercian design. V. E. Nash-Williams in 1950 described it as seventh to ninth century in date.[50] This slab, found covering a grave, would not have been brought from afar, given the enormous quantities of fine stone that were available on site.

This pre-Cistercian slab, as at Fountains Abbey, could help explain many of the very old pre-Cistercian yews here, as at other similar early Welsh ancient yew sites, often co-located with slabs of this period.[51] The Strata Florida site, in my opinion, was based on the deserted site an early saint cell, with its many yews and excellent spring, far from the 'concourse of men', but already known to an earlier era of Christianity. The yews that survive at Strata Florida are archaeologically significant. Not only does one yew mark the grave of a great Welsh master poet but also these trees may help indicate the site of a lost cell of an early Welsh saint.

Cadw are the principal custodians of Strata Florida abbey buildings, yet the yews are in the care of the local parish church that shares the site, the small church of St Mary. In 1998 I suggested, in an unpublished paper, that the wall around the female yew in 1951 could damage it. I now admit this may not be the case. The wall will stunt the trunk growth, yet the trunk is equally protected by it. The Norbury yew wall is still there from pre-1790,[52] as is the pre-1790 wall around the Llanfoist yew,[53] near Abergavenny and the Peterchurch yew in Herefordshire has its wall. All these are 26ft+ (8m+) girth yews with more intact trunks than most unprotected 26ft+ (8m+) girth specimens. Although imperfect, a cement-free wall would certainly be better than railings.

I would suggest preventing further burials under the immediate vicinity of the 'small' male. Burials have already affected the area where I believe George Borrow probably visited the grave of Dafydd ap Gwilym. The remaining yews at Strata Florida are susceptible to loss as they display serious damage since 1850, having previously grown for centuries protected by other yews. Perhaps 37 yews could be grown from seeds gathered from the on-site old female to continue what may be a dying line.

If either of these old yews perishes then the possibility of original Strata stock, from male and female, would also disappear. Young yews could provide windbreaks and shelter for the surviving older yews and persons visiting the church or abbey. They would also echo the splendour of the 39 seen by Leland that every medieval monk and poet in Ceredigion knew well. The added yews with a (restored) well could attract many more visitors to a lovely historic site.

CHAPTER FIVE

Yews at Wells and Springs

The yew is most commonly associated with the sites of British churches and cemeteries. Another historic role in the British landscape that the yew has played is as a marker for wells and springs. The yew is, by any measure, the largest growing native evergreen. This implies that the yew is uniquely suited amongst British trees as a marker and shelter for people visiting places, like churches and wells, during all seasons. The yew has been recorded as marking the locations of at least 25 well sites across the British Isles.

Many British trees have been associated with wells in all parts of Britain. A pamphlet dated August 1600 describes an English well in the village of Utkinton, Cheshire, as 'issuing fromn firme ground at the roote or foote of a shrubbie hull or hollin-tree,' a holly, 'the well or Cesterne being bordered with three or foure flagge stones.'[1] An individual holly may, unfortunately, not survive a few centuries, like a single rowan, elder or other single small tree, necessitating replacement. A single yew, in contrast, can last a thousand years. An old yew near a well may be the oldest above ground surviving evidence of human use of the well, especially if there is little early record of the well and no obvious masonry.

Trees have been associated with wells as long as the records of wells themselves. The early ecclesiastical councils forbade tree, well and stone worship in equal measure. At Arles (452), those 'who offer vows to trees, or wells, or stones, as they would altars', were denounced.[2] In 567 in Tours, one of the canons of St Cummin proscribed the worship of wells and trees.[3] Other similar dates and meetings indicate that the church long held a steady position on the subject. This position seemed to have mellowed somewhat by the twelfth century, when the bishop's permission was sought in the year 1102, before 'attributing sanctity to a fountain'.[4]

Wells in Britain have had many applications. The water from wells has been used for healing ailments and to supply water for brewing the ale for village fetes.[5] In England alone there have been over eighty wells whose water has been used for baptism at some time.[6] Most village wells are usually found in the churchyard, at fort sites, or are found at the side of roads forming the boundary of parishes. These locations were where local people and pilgrims would visit, often on days associated with the local saint. This diversity of well types, locations and uses, represents the repeated value of the well or spring for different eras of British populations. Some religious wells, such as that at St Augustine's Well, the eponymous Sandwell of Sandwell Priory in the West Midlands, were probably used by Bronze Age settlers.[7] Similar sites are often forgotten today, their locations sometimes marked only by trees.

Hawthorn, hazel, oak, ash and yew have all had a long and widespread association with well sites in Britain. F. Jones lists ancient hawthorns and old oaks overhanging wells in Wales,[8] as in northern France and Ireland. Trees have been associated with all kinds of wells for many centuries. In Wales alone F. Jones recorded over thirty wells associated with trees of various kinds, and commented that there were probably 'many more'.[9] The number of significant trees at wells recorded in Ireland is several hundred, at least.[10] Many well trees survived the Irish shortages of timber in the eighteenth and nineteenth centuries, because of their holy status.[11] There are many ancient tree traditions at well sites in Wales and Ireland that are yet to be investigated or recorded. Trees or dead stumps at wells should be recorded for species and size, or photographed, as part of any well survey or excavation. The consistent role of trees at well sites in Britain allows the landscape archaeologist to benefit from studying the long history of tree and well traditions, as recognising significant old trees may help locate lost or silted wells in the field.

Existing yews today feature at well sites in many counties across Britain, especially at wells associated with early Welsh saints. Yews within ten yards of a well are clearly deliberate plantings, maintained for good reasons by the local people, often many centuries ago. Interestingly, some yews at early Welsh saint wells are often of similar size to those yews in early Welsh saint churchyards. It is possible to suggest that some early Welsh saints used yews as markers, not only for their church sites but also as markers for their wells, and possibly as markers of ecclesiastical ownership of the well.

Like the wells themselves, many trees at wells were dedicated to the local saint. A common type of story is told of a well with an oak tree, inscribed with a cross, recorded in 1260: 'Fons Suani, Swein's Well, on the boundary of the parish of Winmarleigh (Lancashire)'. At St Juthware's well (Dorset) the oak there is the tree of the saint and the tree features in a typical folklore tale of martyrdom by beheading. St Juthware's oak was 'just by the well, which was also held in great veneration', in 1727.[12]

In the established Welsh laws recorded in the time of Hywel Dda, *circa* 950,[13] the value of a yew dedicated to a saint was a pound, but otherwise only 15 pence. A 'holy yew', was called *ywen sant*. The other less valuable kind was called a 'yew of the woods', *ywen coet*.[14] Other sources describe these as *Taxus Sancti*, 'a saint's Yew', and the less valuable *Taxus Silvestris*, a 'woodland yew'.[15] The fine for removing the holy yew was the equivalent to 60 sheep, which amounted to three flocks at that time. (The oak, for comparison, was valued at six score pence). The more valuable holy yew is called a 'consecrated yew', in some other sources.[16]

The Welsh historian Rachel Bromwich noted a link between yews and wells in Wales.[17] The laws of Hywel Dda are usually thought to be the latest version of previously existing rules, which may have existed since the sixth century.

The holy yews of Hywel Dda may have been valued in 950 because of their association with the early Welsh saints, whose wells are often today surmounted by large yews. Old yews are common enough features overhanging wells, often away from churches, that the trees may provide an estimate for dating evidence of the earliest visitors to the well, especially in cases where modern Victorian and post-Victorian masonry obscures any other above ground evidence of age. At sites with aged yews near the well, the age of the yew ought to be considered as an indicator of antiquity of the well site, in the absence of other above ground evidence.

Yews at wells associated with early Welsh saints

Jones listed many yews planted in obvious relationships with the wells of Wales, such as Ffynnon Bueno in Holywell Parish, Flintshire, now Clwyd. F. Jones said it had a yew growing above it. He describes the well being 'beneath a tree in a meadow near Castle Hill in Holywell Urban parish'.[18] The yew that grew at Ffynnon Bueno, at Aelhaiarn Clwyd no longer exists. 'Ffynnon Bueno, Cappel AylHayarn in ye borders of Lh. Elidan (Denb)' (now Clwyd) was recorded at the turn of the century as being 'ruinous since time out of mind. There's only an yew tree there at present'. The yew serves equally to shelter and to mark places that parishioners and pilgrims visit. At this well, cattle were sprinkled with a yew bough that had been dipped in water.[19] Jones only found six Bueno wells in a list of *circa* 200 well saints in Wales, several of these having large yews nearby. Another Bueno well had been mentioned in Leland's *Collectanea*, II, 684, under the title 'Superstitious practices prevailing in Wales in 1589 AD', recording 'offering heifers to St Bueno, at Clynocgvaur'. This healing well was near a cromlech.[20] This suggests a possibility that Bueno chose some well sites that were probably pre-existing.

The spring Ffynnon Bedr, south of Conwy in Gwynedd, has a *circa* 23ft (7m) girth female yew yet surviving today (Plate 8). It has lost parts of trunk facing the photographer. The yew has quartz stones at its roots where the spring flowed. It is listed in *The Sacred Yew*, and estimated as being 1,400 years old.[21] This seems to concur with data from several other pieces of recent research published in 1997–2000, as outlined earlier in this book. I would suggest that this tree may have been put there by Christians in the 'age of the saints', offering a 1,400-year-old marker of human usage. The yew today is ailing from an unknown disease, possibly poisoned or affected by local changes in water level, that have also dried the well.[22] F. Jones recorded this yew and well, 'about a quarter mile S of Llanbedrycennin: it is overshadowed by a Yew: it was once covered by a building 10 feet by 6 feet: up to about 1844 children were bathed there and afterwards taken to a little chapel outside the cottage garden, St Bedr (Peter) was a dedication popularised in Wales in the twelfth century by Norman rulers, who frequently replaced early Celtic saint dedications, with his name'.[23]

Pre-existence of the yews before the arrival of the saints might perhaps be argued. Certainly 'it has been noted that the Church decreed that pagan sites were to be converted to Christian solemnities, and this missionaries did by rededicating the well, megalith and the tree, and by erecting chapels or churches near them'.[24] However, the link with early Welsh saints and very large yews is certainly a consistent thread.

The place-name of Ystrad Yw, known today as Llanbedr Ystrad Yw, has a yew and a well story attached to it. J. Rhys, in his 1880 text *Celtic Folklore*[25] relates the romantic story of the place named after a yew at the source of a river. Initially J. Rhys approaches the Ystrad Yw site from its mention in the *Mabinogion* tale of Kulhwch and Olwen. It is the earliest source for the mythological Welsh hero Arthur, a magical story dated to at least the tenth century by K. H. Jackson.[26] In the mythological tale, a human king is transformed into the magical boar called Twrch Trwyth. This boar is similar to the magical pig of Irish traditional tales called Formael. The other swine died across Wales and 'Lwydawc' a boar offspring, 'having made his way to Ystrad Yw, and, after inflicting slaughter on several of his assailants, he is himself killed there'.[27]

Llanbedr perpetuates the name of Ystrad Yw, although it is situated near the junction of the Greater and Lesser Grwyne and not in the Strath of the Yew, which Ystrad Yw means. So one can only treat Llanbedr Ystrad Yw as meaning that particular Llanbedr or St Peter's church which belongs to the district comprehensively called Ystrad Yw.

This place-name may be based on yew. There is a note on the meaning of Ystrad Yw by J. Rhys:

> A river may in Welsh be briefly called after anybody or anything. Thus in North Cardiganshire there is a stream called the Einon, that is to say, 'Einon's River'. Here yw is in English 'yew' but Ystrad Yw and Lygad Yw have to be rendered the strath of the Yw burn and the eye of the Yew burn respectively.[28]

The place-name has a long history.

> Now if one glances at the Red book list of cantreds and Cymwds, dating in the latter part of the fourteenth century, one will find Ystrad Yw and Cruc Howell existing as separate Cwmwyds. So we have to look for the former in the direction of the parish of Cwm Du; and on going back to the Taxatio of Pope Nicholas IV dating about 1291, we find that practically we have to identify with Cwm Du a name Stratden', p. 237, which one is probably to treat as Strat d'Eue (also 1234), or some similar spelling. Most of the parishes of the district are mentioned by the names they still bear. Interestingly, John Leland recorded in 1536–39 AD, that 'Tretour and Creghouel stand in Estrodewe hundrede.'[29]

He then discusses the 'the spring emanating under the but of the yew-tree'.[30]

From Cwm Du a tributary of the Usk called the Rhiangoll comes down and receives at Tretower the waters of a smaller stream called the Yw. The land on both sides of that Yw burn forms the Ystrad or strath of which we are in quest. The chief source of this water is called Lygad Yw, and gives its name to a house of some pretensions bearing an inscription showing that it was built in the middle of the seventeenth century by a member of the Gunter family well known in the history of the county. Near the house stands a yew tree on the boundary line of the garden, and close to its trunk, but at a lower level is a spring of bubbling water: this is Lygad Yw, 'The eye of the Yw'. For Lygad is a succinct expression for source of the Yw burn and the stream retains the name Yw to its fall into the Rhiangoll; but besides the spring of Lygad Yw it has several other similar sources in the fields near the house.[31]

The current status of the yew is unknown. This somewhat fanciful story from Rhys implies an established tradition in 1880. However reliable the story is, the fact it links yews, wells and St Peter, in a Welsh context, is of interest.

Another ancient well site in Wales has old yews that probably act as settlement markers. At Ffynnon Fair (St Mary's Well), Caernarvonshire, now Gwynedd, 'In a field called Cae Ffynnon in Llanfairfechan: once a potent well, it has been filled up since around 1874: the site is in a plantation by the remains of some Yews: its water was used for baptism at the church: children were baptised in the well, and articles that were believed to have been bewitched were bathed in it: bent pins were offered.'[32] This would make an excellent location for excavation or restoration of the site, perhaps to preserve the yews and contents of the well. The tradition of offering bent pins may be traced in Iron Age and Romano-British temple wells where miniature silver spears, some deliberately bent, have been found at several locations. Miniature votive iron spears were found at the Uley shrines in Gloucestershire.[33] This Llanfairfechan site demonstrates the landscape archaeology potential of large yews locating potentially significant, otherwise lost sites. A site like this ought to be placed on the National Monuments Register. The remnant yews described here may possibly be, if huge and decayed, remnants of an early Welsh saint yew, as described in the Hywel Dda laws. If so, this should make them an integral part of the ancient site. If felled, the stumps will still be in situ and measurable, as removal of yew stumps is rarely undertaken. Total decay of large yew stumps takes at least a century.

Near the river Wye, St Eluned's Well at Slwch Tump in Breconshire similarly had a yew that may have been a sixth-century planting. The hollow dead stump remained in 1998, where it grew directly out of the depression where the well issues. The yew may have been felled before the Rev. S. Baring-Gould wrote, 'the well is there, but choked with mud and stones'.[34] Any recovery of quantities of yew seeds from this site would establish a female gender for the yew. Jones explains some of the history of St Eluned's well. 'St. Lludd, also called Alud and Almedha, was a daughter of Brychan, and was martyred by a stone near a mound. This mound is at Pencefngaer, above one mile E of

Brecon, and near Slwch farmhouse. To the N of the mound the sanctuary of the saint once stood. One tale states that her pursuer was a Pagan Saxon chief, that she hid at this mound, but was discovered and beheaded. She was buried at Usk. Jones calls it Penginger Well, and compares the name Penginger with the Cornish Treginegar, derived from Tre + Old Welsh Cynidyr, from Old Celtic Cuno-setros 'bold-chief'.[35] There is evidence of a Saxon coin having being called a Pinnginn. The beheading by a chieftain is similar to the legend at Ffynnon Wenfrewi, the well of St Winefride at Holywell. Another tale, involving a well and a severed head is an account from Ffynnon Ddigiwg, near Clynnog associated with St Bueno.[36] The yew here was probably felled more than fifty years ago, probably to help restore the area as usable for farming. The church here stood until 1698. The whole hilltop, around the well, was the scene of 'great crowds of ordinary folk', celebrating the virgin saints' day, which fell on August first, Lammas Day. These crowds could have benefited from the sheltering yew over the well, if it was a sixth century planting, like some other huge yews above other wells dedicated to sixth century saints. Giraldus Cambrensis recorded this festival having occurred prior to 1188 at this site, where people ran around the site, singing songs, leaping in a frenzy, miming ploughing, cobbling, tending oxen and ladies spinning, while singing traditional songs, before entering the church.[37]

Another Welsh holy well recorded with a yew that grew over it is Capel, in Llanfihangel Rhos y corn, 12 miles from Gwernogle: 'a yew grew over it and there was the tradition of a chapel'.[38] 'Elias, in Llansanffraid Deuddwr (Deythur) Montgomeryshire, near the Shropshire-Wales border, was 'visited by people who suffered weak eyes: a large Yew grew over it, but the well was silted up.' This would be another example of the archaeological potential of locating and preserving old yews, as the yew may yet survive, still marking this lost well. 'Sugared water was drunk there.'[39]

The yews at Welsh sixth-century well sites may also have deterred people watering animals at the wells of the early saints. Shelter for those visiting the wells for healing may have helped preserve the yews. Whether a sterilising effect from the needles falling into the wells exists, is unproven but it could help explain the healing reputation of many wells overshadowed by large yews. The toxins in the needles are not released by immersion in cold water.

Jones wrote of 'Ff. Gwenlais, Carmarthenshire (Dyfed): In Llanfihangel Aberbythych parish. Gwenlais springs at Capel Gwenlais. There is no chapel today.'[40] This well is the source of the river Gwenlais. Local researcher Jan Fry has worked hard campaigning protect this yew, located next to the rare mainland ephemeral turlough pool. Quarrying the site and the yew being felled have been attempted in recent years.[41] The naming of this well is obscure but may pertain to an otherwise forgotten early saint. The age of the yew may fit the early Welsh saint scheme, yet due to attempts at recent felling and storms, the yew has lost most of its branches and possibly portions of trunk.

This is certainly a historic tree. According to Fenton it was already a large specimen in 1804, a tree that clearly marked the well by 'growing over it'. He added:

> The tradition is of this spring, as that of Holywell, that a virgin was murdered, and that on the spot a spring gushed out. The spring has two eyes, they say, of a very different nature ... They shew a cavity, about the size of a grave, near the well, on very dry ground, of which it is said that, fill it as often as you please to the surface ... it will always sink to the same depth, that is about a foot or fifteen inches from the surface.[42]

The yew can assist researchers seeking wells in the field. Oxwich church well is near the sea on the south coast of the Gower peninsula. D. Gregory found the yew there a useful tool in locating the well:

> The underlying reason for visiting the churchyard for the visit was to try and find the well in the churchyard, which in former times had been essential to those who lived there. After much vain searching a damp patch of ground was observed, that widened and eventually led to a

FIGURE 32
The yew at Ffynnon Gwenlais.
MICK SHARP

PLATE 1. Yew berry and foliage.

PHOTOGRAPH: A. MCGEENEY

PLATE 2. The Strata Florida male yew, with the female yew and the parish church of St Mary in the background.

PHOTOGRAPH: RICHARD PURSLOW

PLATE 3. Betws Newydd yew in Wales: an old trunk with internal root growth reviving the fortunes of the tree canopy.

PHOTOGRAPH: A. MCGEENEY

PLATE 4. The Church Preen yew, Shropshire. The most decayed portion of trunk faces the camera and path. The trunk is shown with new metal banding, as the original had begun to constrict the tree.

PHOTOGRAPH: ROBERT BEVAN-JONES

PLATE 5. The legendary Fortingall yew. At least fourteen centuries old, these ruins perhaps represent the oldest living piece of vegetation in Britain. The other main trunk of the tree is visible to the rear left of the picture.

PHOTOGRAPH: A. MCGEENEY

PLATE 6. The Capel-y-ffin fragment yew, one of several forming a remnant of a yew circle.
PHOTOGRAPH: ROBERT BEVAN-JONES

PLATE 7. Fountains Abbey, with two of the 'Seven Sisters' in the foreground.
PHOTOGRAPH: A. MCGEENEY

PLATE 8.
The Ffynnon Bedr yew, Gwynedd,
marking the site of a holy well.
PHOTOGRAPH: A. MCGEENEY

PLATE 9.
The Hope Bagot yew, Shropshire,
located above a holy well.
PHOTOGRAPH: ROBERT BEVAN-JONES

PLATE 10. The Largest yew on an Iron Age earthwork, at the entrance to Merdon Castle hillfort.
PHOTOGRAPH: T. R. HINDSON

PLATE 11. Yews (and holly) at Newlands Corner, Merrow Down, Surrey. The shade of the living branches and fallen needles both discourage undergrowth, even in summer.
PHOTOGRAPH: ROBERT BEVAN-JONES

PLATE 12. Yews at Newlands Corner, Surrey. Burnt out and dead for more than 25 years, this represents at least 500 years growth. This stump could take a century to degrade fully.

PHOTOGRAPH: ROBERT BEVAN-JONES

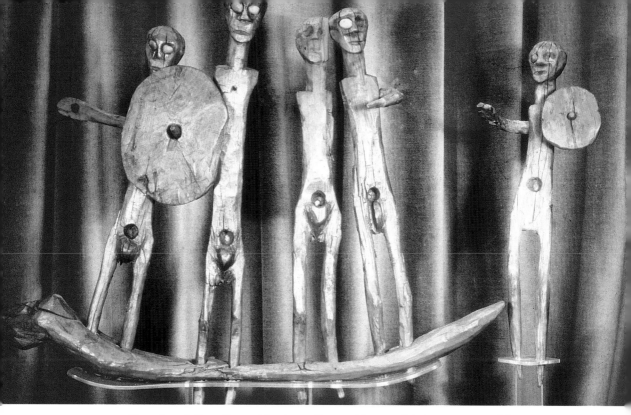

PLATE 13. The enigmatic Roos Carr prehistoric yew figures with some of their equipment and fragmentary transport.
PHOTOGRAPH: HULL AND EAST RIDING MUSEUM, KINGSTON UPON HULL MUSEUMS AND ART GALLERY

PLATE 14. Detail of the Roos Carr figures showing quartz eyes and other fine workmanship.
PHOTOGRAPH: HULL AND EAST RIDING MUSEUM, KINGSTON UPON HULL MUSEUMS AND ART GALLERY

sloping bank, above which a yew was bowing. Here, quite overgrown with ivy, was the well, which would have remained hidden from view but for a wet patch which was unexpected after so dry a summer as 1989 enjoyed. [43]

Without the yew, this well could easily have become lost.

In south Wales, an old yew was recorded as a feature of a well in the seventeenth century. Richard Symonds, who was at St Fagans with King Charles in 1645, wrote, 'In the orchard of this howse under an old ewe tree, is a spring or well within the rock called St Faggin's Well: many resort from all parts to drink it for the falling sickness (epilepsy) which cures them at all season. Many come a yeare after they have drank of (it) and relate there health ever since.' [44] This yew was clearly several centuries old in 1645, emphasising the longevity of the tradition.

Yews at wells in England

English wells with yews do exist although the majority of the oldest examples are near the Welsh borders. Some English sites with ancient yews at churches may be borderline comparisons, as the yew can be more than 33ft (10m) from the well, but if the yew is 33ft (10m) in girth, then the well and yew, even if 150 yards (50m) from each other, may pre-date the existing church building. This circumstance, however, is rare. Churchyard yews and water sources may be the oldest visible above ground evidence of settlement at a heavily restored church site.

Yews can be ambiguously associated with wells. At Gawton's well, in Cheshire, the yews may not be significantly old, and there is no early record to support the age of the yew. According to Ron Hornsby, at Burton upon Stather churchyard in the Humberside region, a well was filled in a few years ago, that was near a 'large ancient yew tree standing on its own', that is close to the north-east corner of the chancel. This churchyard has other yews, but this one is very close to the site of the former well. [45]

There is a 'Yew Tree Well' in Tissington with a male yew very near it. Shelter must have been a motive here as the canopy envelops the well space. This male yew does not appear that old, perhaps 150 years old. It is not a healthy specimen. There are records that state that the 'Yew Tree Well', was formerly known as Goodwin's Well, making the relatively young age of the tree match the known place-name history.

As with a yew growing over the Ladywell at Wombourne, West Midlands, the yew was probably planted to help shelter Georgian pilgrims. The tradition of well dressing at Tissington is established and is better documented than most. In 1823, the wells of Tissington were decked with 'Scripture and other religious sentiments, that are placed among the greens and other flowers about these wells, together with the service solemnised at the Church, shew the grandeur and sublimity of a Christian worship.' [46] The tradition of placing

FIGURE 33
A well dressing at Yew
Tree Well in
Tissington, the
photograph was taken
in 1960.
COLOURMASTER SERIES

evergreens (as well as flowers) by wells in Derbyshire is shown by the pre-1871 example of the Whit Tuesday dressing of the well at St Alkmund's.[47]

An evergreen yew and an ancient well are found together at some old church sites. In the churchyard of Hope Bagot near Ludlow in Shropshire, beyond

FIGURE 34
The shallow well
chamber, still filled
with water, under the
yew at Hope Bagot.
ROBERT BEVAN-JONES

an apple orchard hung with mistletoe, a giant roadside yew stands at the top of a high bank, beneath which runs an ancient well (Plate 9). The church is fittingly dedicated to St John the Baptist. Hidden below the yew a stone-lined chamber, where the churchyard well flows under the yew canopy. It is easily possible that the yew and well here both exceed a thousand years of age.

A Victorian well chamber also exists across the road, erected in 1879. The *circa* 23ft (*circa* 7m+) girth female yew is certainly pre-Norman in terms of date and size, perhaps indicating a lost early Welsh saint site. The ancient well and ancient yew are clearly associated. The yew canopy is enormous and represents the average cover provided by a yew when it is not heavily cut back as most are in other churchyards. The Hope Bagot yew could shelter several hundred visitors, keeping them dry when visiting the well. According to a current parish leaflet, this well, like many others, is associated with healing eye complaints.[48]

Another Shropshire well with a deliberate yew is documented in detail. In 1777 John Dovaston, at West Felton in Shropshire, having sunk a well with his own hands, was unhappy with the wooden boards that were inadequate in preventing the sand from collapsing into the well. So, 'he planted near to the well a yew tree', 'rightly judging that the fibrous and matting tendency of the yew roots would hold up the soil'.[49] He purchased the young yew 'of a cobbler for sixpence',[50] This tree still exists. It was 5ft 11inch in girth at five feet from ground, in July 1836.[51] In 1985, it was 12ft 11inch in circumference, no height given.[52] It happened to be a unique variety, its pendulous habit becoming *Taxus baccata Dovastonii*, the West Felton yew. As a huge coincidence, it is monoacious, having male branches and a female berried branch. It is a rare yew indeed; bearing both pollen and berries, a well yew and a known planting rolled into one. At Shrawley in Worcestershire, on the churchyard boundary, facing the road, is what appears to be a Victorian pump, with a similarly aged yew directly above it, echoing early traditions.

Often only fragments of records show evidence of yews at wells in England. In 1893, Jacobs' Well near Hensting in Hampshire was recorded as being 'surrounded with yew-trees'.[53] An ancient spring/source of a river in Surrey, marked by yews was recorded by the historian and antiquarian John Aubury in *circa* 1670. He states 'A little below, in a Grove of Ew-Trees, within the manour of Westhall, in the Parish of Warlingham, as I have frequently heard, rises a spring, upon the approach of some remarkable Alteration in Church or State, which runs in a direct Course between Lille Hills to a place called Foxley Hatch, and there disappears ...'[54] This is a dubious entry that has difficult to research further.

Funtington church in Sussex had a large old yew recorded as being 21ft girth in 1946. It has a village pump at the base of the tree.[55] The shelter of the yew from its excellent canopy seems to have played a part in its popularity. This yew must be in excess of 900 years old and is probably older still. Some accounts link the place-name Funtington to fountain. If so, this must be it.

Norfolk, like Suffolk, Essex and Cornwall, have had no apparent records of any yew over 16ft girth being recorded in their churchyards. In 1946, Vaughan Cornish published a comment that, 'Grigor, writing a hundred years ago, said there were no Yews in Norfolk churchyards, but in the grounds of Walsingham Priory, there is a sturdy Yew close beside the wishing well.' [56] The wells at this site were visited by Henry VIII and the well tradition is traced to a vision of the Virgin Mary in 1061, followed by later reverence of her image at the wells, where the apparition appeared. [57]

An elusive record of a yew at a well in England is the small yew stump found 11ft 9inches under the earth, in the vicinity of The Chalice Well, near Glastonbury Tor. This was discovered during excavations. Only measuring 10inches (25cms) girth, it was carbon dated *circa* 300 AD by Professor R. D. Preston. It was also buried under a landslide at some time. This yew may or may not have been a deliberate feature. An avenue of mature yews of ambiguous age exists today near the site.

Yews at wells in Scotland and Ireland

Yews at wells in Scotland and Ireland are rare. The clan yew of the Frasers of Lovat in Scotland, is almost 16ft (5m) in girth. It is on the course of a spring, without much soil, facing a lake. It is male, an unusual gender for a well yew. It seems old. It is developing new trunks from extended roots. It has possibly been growing there since *circa* 1500. Axe marks suggest this tree has been threatened in the recent past; apparently it was a gathering site for the clan in troubled times. [58]

A much older Scottish yew of possible Pictish origin, stood at the *Tobar an Iuthaiir*, 'Yew Tree Well' in Easter Ross, Scotland. This yew was certainly cut down before 1904. Professor W. Watson [59] provides the only record of this old yew at a well. It was situated 'at the western side of *Cnoc coille na tobarach*, "Well wood hill", which is the Gaelic name of the so-called Fairyhill or Danish fort, at Easter Rarichie. Hard by this well once stood a tree whose branches bent over the water, and while the tree stood, the well cured "white swelling." The tree was cut and the well struck. The following rhyme in connection with this tale demonstrates a deep concern for the well tree:

> *Tobar na h-iu, Tobar na h-iu,*
> *'s ann duit bu chumha bhi uasal*
> *tha leabaidh deis ann an iuthairnn*
> *do'n fhear a ghearr a' chraobh mu d' chluasan.*

> Well of the yew, Well of the yew!
> To thee it is that honour is due;
> A bed in hell is prepared for him
> Who cut the tree about thine ears. [60]

Of 210 holy wells with trees assessed by A. Lucas across limited parts of Ireland, 103 were marked by whitethorn, 75 by ashes, seven by oak, six by willow, five by elder, four by holly, three by rowan, two by elm, but only one was a yew well. This well had a typical story; staff of the saint (not named in the text) sprouted to become the tree of the well myth associated with it – Yew Tree Well, Kilklienagh, County Laois.[61] Only Munster and Leinster were covered by Lucas. Other counties may hold a similar quantity of material. As in Wales, several more yew tree wells with historical yews may emerge with further research. A holy well was recorded in the townland of Kiltierney in the parish of Magheraculmoney, in the district of Fermanagh:

> On a S facing slope within the ecclesiastical enclosure, all that remains of this holy well is an oval well hole defined on the N side by 6 visible courses of masonry. The wall has been dug into the slope with the N side higher than the S, only two courses are visible defining the latter side. The well hole is 2m N-S by 1.5m. E-W. It is 0.8m deep at present. Starrat writing in 1720 gave an account of the well devotions that took place there three times a year and mentioned a large yew-tree growing there.[62]

The 'Irish' yew, *Taxus baccata fastigiata* is a recent form of yew. Like the West Felton yew from Shropshire, it too originated from one sapling later in the eighteenth century, so any yew recorded in Ireland before *circa* 1770 must be a 'Common' or 'English' yew, *Taxus baccata.*

Another yew well located in Ireland is *Tobar an Iubhair*, Roughgrove, County Cork. It had a legend attached to it that a local man, while felling the tree above the well for firewood, saw an illusion that his house was on fire, while chopping. He returned home and the mirage vanished, so he went back to the tree. This happened twice and the third time, he ignored it and finished the job of felling. When he reached home, it was burnt to the ground. This bears some similarity to the story of the Easter Ross yew tree well *Tobar an Iuthaiir*, in Scotland. A note relating to Irish well-tree tradition recorded by Lucas, 'It is a curious fact that up until very recently and, in some cases, even yet, trees and bushes growing on the sites of these ancient dwelling places were treated with the utmost respect. To cut or mutilate them was considered extremely unlucky.'

These sites, collated from topographical records of all British nations, show that the tradition of planting yews at wells and springs has been significantly widespread and popular for many centuries. Generally, trees have not been observed or recorded by the National Monuments Register, The National Trust or English Heritage as integral parts of ancient well sites. Recognising and recording aged yews, remnants of ancient hawthorn and other trees, could help us better understand the obscure yet recurrent roles played by specific native trees in the well cults of England, Wales, Scotland and Ireland. Well restorations can also ignore the significance of such trees and sweep away much important vegetation, without record, or replacement, when 'restoring' a site. Sadly, a tree at or near a well is rarely mentioned by species in most texts produced on wells.

Some of the yews over wells are hollow and seem decayed, yet are physically strong and healthy. Hollowness and decay, of course, does not indicate a finite future for this tree. This appearance of decay may lead to unnecessary removal by over-zealous restorers of well sites. Agricultural use of land has also probably contributed to the removal of many yews at wells, due to the poisonous yew foliage being a small risk to valuable stock. Almost all yews hanging over holy wells in Wales or England have been berry-bearing females. The male yew has no red fruit. This obviously suggests a deliberate planting scheme.

Unlike British deciduous trees, the yew provides excellent shelter and dry kindling all year round for visitors to the well or churchyard. They also keep an area of ground dry all year, a very useful attribute near watery well sites. Though the yew foliage is extremely toxic, these compounds are not considered soluble in cold water. It is interesting to note that where such old yews sheltering wells have been removed, as at Slwch Tump near the river Wye in Brecon, Wales, the well becomes very muddy, which the evergreen yew, when present, will prevent. These features, along with its striking deep green colour in winter, may have led to the yew being preferred as a well tree.

The yew as a well marker seems widespread and recurrent, especially at well sites associated with early Welsh or Irish saints. Tabbush suggests that a 'typical churchyard yew of 7m [23ft] girth would be aged about 1,580 years'.[63] Yews of around a thousand years of age or six metres girth have been found at several holy well sites. These examples of yew and wells are by no means exhaustive and many are as yet unrecorded; there are 'many others', according to F. Jones.[64]

The longevity of the yew suggests it is clearly possible some yews at wells may survive from the 'age of the saints', in England as well as Wales. Few of these wells have been located, mapped or valued. Tracing and recording surviving significant specimens of yew in the landscape can offer rewards to local historians.

The exact roles of native trees at well sites in Britain are still quite obscure and it is only by scrupulous research and meticulous recording of vegetation by enthusiasts and archaeologists that this picture may become clearer. Oak, ash, yew and hawthorn seem to have been the most frequently preferred well tree. This chapter emphasises the place of the yew in this category.

CHAPTER SIX

Old Yews in the Wider Historic Landscape

Some of the oldest yews in the landscape today were certainly growing before the Norman Conquest. Yews growing in the Anglo-Saxon period in Britain are known from various sources. These include yews of early saints, those mentioned in charters and possibly those trees known as 'hundred court' trees.

W. G. Hoskins[1] recorded the history of Hundred Lane in Suffolk, with a massive earthwork, from the Roman era, that became an Anglo-Saxon boundary, Hundred Lane, dividing the hundreds of Bosmere and Hartismere. Most hedgerows that contain hollow old yews are similarly as complex in composition as Hoskins' example. Equally, it is difficult for landscape historians to even describe fields as 'Anglo-Saxon', as there is little evidence of a specific 'Anglo-Saxon' style of boundary division.[2] In most places they worked with native British populations, settling existing managed lands.[3] Therefore, assessing the context of a living tree in such an evolving landscape is difficult, especially as dating techniques for the older yews only provide estimates of age.

Although there are problems for those assessing trees of early medieval origin in the hedgerow, there are yews that we certainly know were landmarks in the Anglo-Saxon landscape; those boundary marking yews mentioned in the charters. It is likely that our understanding of vegetational Saxon boundary markers is limited, due to the loss of many records. Vegetational boundary markers are rare in surviving Sussex charters and only 17 per cent of 1,885 boundary markers in Hampshire Saxon charters studied were vegetational, with only three being yews.[4] This suggests that yews were not planted as boundary markers, but were included as such, if they were already present. One of the Hampshire Saxon charter boundary markers was marked 'old yew', suggesting that an existing tree was incorporated into the emergent Anglo-Saxon hundredal boundary marking system.

In the known extant charters yew ranks thirteenth in frequency of tree species mentioned. Although the incomplete nature of the surviving evidence prevents too much analysis, if the tree was used commonly for this purpose this ranking would probably be higher. Some of the yews listed in the charters mentioned below may be traceable today as existing trees.[5]

A charter mentions a yew at Barnhorne (attached to a perambulation of

Bexhill) in Sussex. The place-name occurs on a boundary, as '*Iwedise*' – '*iw*,' 'yew' + '*edisc*', a term of unknown meaning related to cultivation. (Charter reference Birch, *Cartularium Saxonicum* f. 208, dated 772.) At Hannington, Hampshire, we find '*ywyrstac stigel*', Yewhurst stile or gate. Yewhurst is probably the name of a wood. (Charter reference Kemble f. 739, dated as 1023.)

At Martyr Worthy in Hampshire a place was called '*Iwigap*', interpreted as 'Yew eyot', an island in the river Itchen. (Charter reference BCS, f. 740, dated 939.) Also in Hampshire, at Havant, '*ywwara haga*' appears in two places. It may mean either 'yewen hedge' or 'hedge of the group called *Ywword*'. (Charter reference BCS, f. 707, dated as 935; another version is in Kemble f. 624, dated 980.) Another yew feature was recorded at Michelmersh, three and a half miles north of Romsey, Hampshire. Place-name or feature mentioned is '*iww cumbe*', Yewcombe. Feature '*ealde iw*', old yew. (Charter reference Kemble, f. 652, dated 985.) This description as elderly suggests the yew was an established feature in 958.

Another example occurs at Stoke Bishop, north-west of Bristol, place-name or feature '*eow cumb*', Yewcombe. (Charter reference BCS, f. 551, dated as 883.) At Tidenham, Gloucestershire, the yew place-name or features is '*Iwe's heafden*' Yewshead – 'head' in a geographical sense, also '*iwdene*' Yewdean, yew valley. (Charter reference BCS, f. 927, dated to 956.) In 1904, James G. Wood noted that 'Iwes Haefda', or 'Yew's Head', of the Edwy Charter of Tidenham, was situated on the 'high point above but rather to the left of the Tunnel',[6] near Tintern Station, facing south. 'It can be seen all the way round to, and from, the Abbey.' This feature is the probably the location of the charter yew feature. Yews there today could be the same yews as those seen in the tenth century. The cliff yew studies by D. Larson covered in chapter two suggest this is easily possible.

At Upton on Severn, Gloucestershire, the yew place-name is on a boundary, as '*Eow rhyc*', 'yew ridge'. (Charter dated to 962.) A house called 'Yew Tree' stands today near where Della Hooke suggests this feature was located.[7]

At '*Manaur Troumur*', near the Wye, in Monmouthshire there is '*cumuleu iriuenn*', 'yew barrow' that claims to be of date 625.[8] Barrows have often been recorded as having large old yews on them. Examples include Taplow Court, Buckinghamshire, Wormelow Tump, Herefordshire and Duck's Nest Barrow in Hampshire. A significant yew was once recorded at 'Ty Illtud', Llanhamlach, in Gower. It is a Neolithic chambered tomb, named after an early Welsh saint: 'Illtud's House' where local assemblies traditionally took place.[9]

Pre-existing barrows, rivers, wells and trees were incorporated into the landmarks that marked out ownership in the landscape of early medieval Britain. The charter yews were, therefore, probably there already. W. G. Hoskins wrote that, 'Everything in the landscape is older than we think', and that, 'we are not just dealing with a series of isolated sites, but rather with overlapping and often interrelated prehistoric, Roman and Saxon landscapes underlying the present surface.'[10] Though not common, these references give a picture of the distribution and significance of yew in the landscape of Anglo-Saxon era Britain.

R. M. Tittensor noted many Sussex place-names containing a yew element of Saxon or Jutish origin. Ifield, Iford, Iridge Place, Ewhurst, Iden, Ewhurst Manor, Iwood, Ebernoe, Eridge, Ifold House, Ibrook Wood, Ewhurst Place and Ifield Wood, all in Sussex, all contain pre-Norman Conquest place-name evidence.[11] This suggests a widespread topographical relevance for yew in Anglo-Saxon England.

Tittensor also noted that 15 of the 16 yew wood sites studied at random by her in the Hampshire-Sussex region fall on one or several parish boundaries. She suggests that these woods originated with yews that may represent Saxon boundary markers or their descendants, including one site near Bow Hill, at West Dean, that occurs on a now defunct East Marden parish boundary.[12]

Other examples cited by her include: Earthham boundary clumps, on the Eartham-Slindon boundary; 'many' at Slindon on the Madehurst-Arundel boundary; 'many' also at Robin Wood, Rowlands Castle (Idsworth), Compton boundary; At Kingley Vale on the Funtington, Mid Lavant boundary. Droxford, Wield, Midhurst, Haslemere and Duncton are other examples.[13] She explains that this pattern suggests evidence of Anglo-Saxon era boundary yews that are not preserved in any charters. Only the yews at Fairmile Bottom, of Kingley Vale, are recorded by Tittensor as being a charter example.

Large specimens occur in other counties on parish boundaries, such as the fragment yew on the Swindon-Enville parish boundary at the top of Camp bank in South Staffordshire (Figure 2). In an adjacent parish to Kyre Park in Worcestershire (where a 'court of the hundred' yew occurs on the historic county boundary) there is another significant ancient marker yew. On the Bromyard to Ledbury road, is a 'gospel yew', in a hedge, on the junction between the parishes of Bosbury, Castlefroome and Canonfroome. A Victorian writer George Piper noted it was of 'great antiquity'.[14] This description suggests that it may be old enough to be a pre-Norman boundary marker.

The yew was a common feature of the landscape when the Saxons arrived. Dedicated yews of churches of early saints would have already been present. In 950, Hywel Dda, a Christian king of all Wales, endorsed a huge fine of sixty sheep on those who cut down yews 'dedicated to saints', encouraging their preservation.[15] The early Celtic saints were known to have yew trees directly associated with them, yet the famous, later Anglo-Saxon churches in England have had few or no large yews recorded. This may suggest that where large yews thought to be of 1500 years age or more occur in English churchyards today, they may possibly indicate lost churches of early Welsh or Irish saints, rather than later lost Anglo-Saxon churches.

The limited surviving evidence of sixth- and seventh-century Celtic church cells in England may be explained by the idea that the Saxon churches that came after them, were equipped with better organisation, bigger, more permanent buildings and more power: an imported culture that may not have cared much for the 'holy, humble ill-organised',[16] small cells that they gradually displaced. 'Native' Celtic cells could have become isolated, or even perceived as subversive, their little cells easily forgotten in later Anglo-Saxon England, where new churches dominated the landscape.

This perspective could explain the near total absence of ancient churchyard yews recorded in East Anglia, furthest from the homelands of the early Celtic church, yet densely populated in the Anglo-Saxon period. The distribution of yews recorded as meeting-places of the hundred courts also do not occur in East Anglia. The distribution of known Anglo-Saxon charter yews also matches this pattern, as does the yew-linked place-name evidence. This adds more circumstantial evidence to the argument concerning the propagation of yews by early saints in England and Wales.

Court of the hundred yews

There are many British trees that were recorded as meeting points for the courts of the hundreds.[17] These hundreds were land parcels of probably a hundred hides of land, which often used pre-existing features and boundaries. Most hundredal usage of boundaries date from the early tenth century, documented for the first time in a manuscript of King Edgar, 957–975,[18] though regional organisation probably occurred along similar lines, prior to this date. The hundredal court could issue punishments, make outlaws of offenders and probably controlled the hundredal execution site, usually located on the boundary of the hundred.[19] After the County Court Act of 1867 was passed, the hundred system became totally extinct, having been in decline for many decades. The hundred trees were known in many English counties throughout much of this era, as meeting places for the hundredal courts.

Old oaks and yews, both over eight centuries old, have been recorded as having marked the locations of hundredal courts in England. The origins of the typical court of the hundred tree is indirectly speculated on by Charles Phythian-Adams. 'It is tempting to speculate whether at least those Hundredal place-names ending in *treow* (and often prefixed by a personal name) may indicate an association between the pre-hundredal administrative meeting place and … an ancient sanctuary.'[20] The ruinous yew at Heavitree (Devon) was a hundred court tree. It was chosen in 2002 by the Tree Council as one of the 50 UK trees of the Golden Jubilee. By assessing their girths it becomes clear that the examples of yews with a recorded reputation as having been 'hundred court yews' all happen to be trees of great antiquity. Had any later replanting occurred (for example) after 1600, they would all be less than half the size they are today, 10 to 12ft (3–4m) in girth, instead of 20 to 30ft (6–9m). All of the yews with a hundred court meet-place tradition, are of a size indicating an age of more than 800 years.

Some hundred court yews are as large as yews may grow. Oliver Rackham has suggested that many of the largest churchyard yews may be, at earliest, of Anglo-Saxon origin,[21] though this is a vague concession. The early Welsh saints of the sixth and seventh centuries could have easily provided sixth-century plantings on some sites that were later adopted by later churches, especially in Herefordshire and Gloucestershire. The enormous specimens, found in conjunction with early Welsh saint sites, as detailed in the relevant chapters, suggest that 1,500 years of age is frequently reached by the largest churchyard specimens. These sixth- and seventh-century saint planting would technically have to be Anglo-Saxon era plantings.

The yews associated in texts as meeting places of the hundredal court system, like the boundary yews listed in Anglo-Saxon charters, may have been pre-existing when large enough to be used as boundaries or meeting points. This may be especially true of those court yews in regions where once existed many early Welsh saint churches, such as in Herefordshire and Gloucestershire.

As a nationally occurring tree, the spreading yew, protected by law in many areas of Britain in 950, at the time of the emergent hundredal system, would have made ideal meeting places for the hundredal courts, providing shelter for those waiting for justice, on sacred ground. Most villagers in most counties in Britain could have easily understood where these places were: the rath, barrow or churchyard of the parish, under the yew.

Though this pattern cannot be dated exactly, I would argue, as with early Welsh saint yews at circular churchyards, that there is enough evidence of aged yews at unusual locations of regional significance for some pattern to have been responsible for their occurrence, such as plantings as markers for the cells of Anglo-Saxon era saints. The trees with hundred court reputations are all very old yews, though when the associations with the courts began, is difficult to trace in an absolute fashion. I discuss such records that I have been able to find. There must be many more that have been lost without trace and others that reside unnoticed in archives across Britain.

The old yew on Wormlow Tump Herefordshire
A 'decayed' yew stood on this mound until 1855.[22] It was an ancient meeting place for one of the Herefordshire hundreds. It forms the meeting point of three parishes and six roads.[23] It is implied that by the mid-tenth and eleventh centuries, meeting-places of assemblies were moved from neutral sites to sites at estate centres.[24] This Wormelow yew, like the St Weonards tump old yew, stood until 1855. These trees certainly indicate deliberate plantings and it seems strange that so many old yews on burial mounds, like the huge Taplow yew, were removed around 1855. The Wormelow tump is certainly a Saxon moot site, believed to be on a prehistoric funerary mound, with a plausible record of an yew, of more than five centuries age, pre-1855. It could have been a thousand years plus or more at that time, when it was described then as the most significant tree on the mound. The old yew here suggests a probable pre-Norman church site on the mound, or in the immediate area.

A court of the hundred yew at Totteridge, Greater London
The Totteridge yew is known to have been the meeting place for the Court Hundred of Cashio, in Hertfordshire.[25] This tree is well recorded, and appears

FIGURE 35
The Totteridge yew,
Greater London: the
meeting place of the
court of Cashio
Hundred.

ROBERT BEVAN-JONES

not to have grown in girth in over three hundred years. How long this had been the case before measurements began in 1677, can only be conjecture, but the latest estimate dates it to early in the Anglo-Saxon period. It is also said to be on a fort site, though the fort is not visible above ground; some forts are hard to discern, especially in built up areas. The simple St Andrews church building is almost all Victorian, the yew clearly being the oldest above ground feature.

According to E. W. Swanton in *The Yew Trees of England* (1958). The antiquary Gough recorded this tree, in a letter to the Rev. M. Tyson. 'Sir John Cullem met with a yew tree in Totteridge churchyard: its trunk everywhere of nearly the same girth., 3ft above the ground is 26ft in circumference, I measured it myself in 1777, one hundred years after, it was precisely the same size …' Dr S. Lysons, in his *Environs of London* (vol. iv, p. 43) says that in 1796 it measured 26ft in girth at three feet from the ground. Eighty years later, J. E. Cussons, County Historian, found it to be 26ft also. Allen Meredith measured the yew in 1983 and it was 26ft.[26] It was 26ft girth in 1999.

However, it has obviously lost a large branch and a slice of trunk at some point, on the side facing the photograph (Figure 35). This may have allowed a growth and loss between historic measures. This is an example of a probable pre-existing yew, used as a convenient meeting place for the court of the hundred. This kind of yew can be useful to the archaeologist, being an indicator of early settlement, in absence of other evidence above ground. This was also probably a boundary marker; the yew now belongs to Barnet, Greater London, as the regional boundary has recently changed.

A court of the hundred yew at Langsett, South Yorkshire

G. L. Gomme states that, 'In the beginning of the last century there was at Langsett, in Yorkshire, an old yew-tree in Alderman's-Head grounds, near the river, under which the court for the manor of Penisale had been held from time immemorial. Around this tree the market and fair were said by tradition to have been held, on a green plot in which it stood, and there is a tradition that there was once a town called Panisale around this tree. (Hunter's *South Yorkshire*, ii, 359.) The name Alderman's-Head, which belongs to a house and farm near this place, seems to take us back to the time when the alderman was simply the oldest man of the community, for there is no trace of this locality ever having belonged to the municipal alderman.'[27] Perhaps this refers to the late Saxon Ealdorman, who was a powerful figure in charge of the reeve who conducted the judicial hundred courts. This court yew has not been located recently and is probably gone. It has been said that gypsies may have occupied its trunk and at around this time the yew was burnt.[28]

A court of the hundred yew at Churchill in Worcestershire

The yew at the St James the Great churchyard in Churchill, Worcestershire is a probable hundred court tree. The yew at Churchill was described by one local historian: 'It is probable that these commissioners met at the "great tree in Churchill", which was one of the places where the King's Leet (or Court), for Lower Halfshire Hundred was held.'[29] G. L. Gomme mentions that 'suit and service are done at the Court Leet held under a tree at Churchill, as recorded in T. Nash's *Collections for History of Worcestershire*, 1781 (vol. i, p. 57).'[30] The church is on low ground near a rounded hillock Margaret Gelling considers the root of the place-name Churchill, not 'church on the hill'.[31] The brook by the yew at Churchill (in Halfshires) is called the Churchill or Wannerton brook, an ancient boundary that in 866 was known as 'River Wenferth'. It is a tributary to the Stour river of the Midlands. This ancient tree by such an ancient boundary would have been ideal for a hundred court meeting.

Inside the tree many internal roots have welded together; some are several feet in girth. A quarter of the tree is dead, being overlain with new growth. It was measured in 1998 as 5.67m (18ft 7 inches) at 1m from ground. 5.27m (17ft 4 inches) at ground level. This is not an intact bole, a large branch and portion of trunk is missing clearly indicating a larger girth at one time, probably 23ft+ (7m+) judging by the scale of the tear in the trunk and cavity. Like the Lorton yew in Cumbria and the Sandhurst yew, in Berkshire, this is certainly a fragment of a larger tree. This would not only have been a large tree in Nash's day, but is large enough to have been a tree known to people in the late Anglo-Saxon period.

The large diameter of the internal stems may suggest more time exposure to light, rather than less. The tree at this quiet church in Churchill is healthy and is appears structurally safe, having shaken off much weight. The old shell

FIGURE 36
The yew at Churchill
in Worcestershire: a
probable meeting
place for the
hundredal court.
ROBERT BEVAN-JONES

is fading as the internal stems now have branches and take the weight of the tree. Internal stems appear to now be yews within a yew. One day only these will remain. One fairly old box tree is within 16ft (5m) of this tree. Other yews in the vicinity, one on the hillock in a private garden across the road, may indicate associated plantings.

A court of the hundred yew at Kyre Park, Worcestershire

The beautiful lakes and gardens at Kyre Park (pronounced *Keer*, from Old Welsh *Cyr*) in Worcestershire were landscaped in the 'Capability' Brown manner, though the actual name of the designer at Kyre remains a mystery. There are young yews of *circa* 10ft (3m) girth around the lakes that date from the era of Georgian design. The Georgian landscape designers usually improved an existing landscape, already populated with veteran trees and other features, and this happened at Kyre.

Repton himself stated that 'the man of science and of taste … will … discover beauties in a tree which the others would condemn for its decay … sometimes he will find an aged thorn or maple at the foot of a venerable oak … these he will respect … not only for their antiquity … but knowing (also) that that the importance of the oak is comparatively increased by the neighbouring situation of these subordinates …'[32]

The Hundred Court Yew and its partner yew at Kyre were ancient yews that certainly saw the era of Georgian designers like Humphry Repton come and go. It also seems that the paths around the grounds at Kyre were designed to take in these trees as significant features of the estate, the Georgian designers perhaps sympathising with Repton on the merits of historical ecology.

In the shrubbery, there is a yew called The Parted Yew, that has much decayed in its probable 1,500 year history, having split in two, like the Fortingall yew, long before 1895. Its partner tree, identical in size and age, was a court leet yew, once measured at *circa* 33ft (10m) girth, now suspected lost.[33] This closely planted pair of similar age were both on the banks of the Kyre brook. The remaining Parted Yew would no doubt have also provided shelter for visitors during the hundred court era. It must have been established at that time, coming into the elite category for size even when compared to the largest churchyard specimens. They were doubtless connected historically as contemporary plantings, in the same location.

Kyre Park has its origins as a medieval park. 'The grant from Edward I, in 1275, to John Wyard to enclose and plant the park at Caer Wyard, still exists but neither of the yews are in the park or enclosure.'[34] In 19 July 1895, Lady Baldwyn-Childe, the then resident of Kyre Park, wrote to John Lowe. 'Outside the Wood-patch grove stands a yew-tree 30 ft at ground level, 26 feet at 5 feet, sound and growing; top not broken; with plenty of young growth. Forty or fifty years ago this tree was hollow, and an old man remembers 12 persons standing inside it, but this is now filled.' 'It stands by the river Kyre, which divides the counties of Worcestershire and Herefordshire, and the courts of the Leets were formally held by the owners of Kyre under its shade.' This suggests that both yews are at least pre-1275, although this probably marks less than half their actual age, in light of likely ages for yews of 33ft (10m) girth, suggesting planting in association within an earlier boundary marking system, both planted by the river Kyre, an old county boundary. It is unlikely that a yew would have a court leet reputation without having previously been an existing church marker, making it a perfect choice for such a purpose.

The two famous yews at Kyre Park may indicate early settlement here, possibly the cell of an early pre-Norman saint, later adopted by the Saxon hundredal system as a convenient meeting place on a significant boundary, probably not far where the Parted yew is today. Perhaps the yews originated

FIGURE 37
The Kyre Park 'parted yew' in 1889.
A. BERTIE-ROBERTS

FIGURE 38
The Kyre Park yew in 1998, little changed since 1889.
ROBERT BEVAN-JONES

as the markers of an early saint cell, eclipsed by later settlement patterns which found the building of the church nearer the road more convenient for a new community. This may also have suited the owners of the park.

These oldest yews at Kyre Park definitely predate the planting of the park in 1275, and to have two 30ft girth yews, on a county boundary, one with a court leet reputation, suggests possibly some very early occupation, planting a twin pair, for boundary or meeting purposes. It is in ways such as these that old yews can offer some faint indications of early settlement. A small example of the antiquity of the surviving tree may be seen in an 1889 photo, post-collapse, and a photo from 1998, that shows little structural change since that time, suggesting that the tree may yet survive many more centuries in two halves (Figures 37 and 38).

Other significant yews in the landscape

There are also other similarly sized yews found on or near significant prehistoric earthworks. These may represent, for example, the remnant marker of a lost early saint cell or later church on the site, lost when the settlement pattern changed. Few of these sites have been excavated and many of the yews have gone. Most of these earthworks occur on farmland and yews are, understandably, often discarded by farmers cautious of protecting their livestock. Yews on mounds and earthworks may have survived as the cows may not have been able to use those sites for grazing. Records describing yews on earthworks may provide clues of meeting places and churches that are otherwise lost.

St Weonards Tump yew, Hereford and Worcester

The west and south of Herefordshire was a stronghold of churches of the early Welsh saints in the sixth and seventh centuries. St Weonard was Sant Guainerth, a saint found in the place-name Llanwenarth, near Abergavenny. The flat-topped castle mound near the church of St Weonards, Herefordshire, has been claimed, 'on the testimony of the spade', as having been a prehistoric grave-hill.[35] Mr Thomas Wright, who opened this mound in 1855, declared that 'Beyond a doubt', it had been used for 'sepulchural purposes'. 'The summit of the present mound is a circular platform about 76 feet in diameter … a rough oval … A cutting was made through it. Two interments were found, one a central one … the whole of the ashes of the funeral pile were placed at this spot … when the small mounds roofed with stones had been raised over the deposit of ashes, a circular embankment was next formed round the whole. It may be mentioned that a 'decayed yew, of considerable age, together with other trees, adorned the hillock'.[36]

A yew does not tend to appear decayed much before reaching 20ft (6m) girth, an age of more than seven centuries, probably more. This tree would have provided excellent shelter and kindling for five centuries, and have been capable of covering in excess of one hundred people. Wright also stated that it was 'until recently the scene of village fetes, especially chosen for Morris dancing'.[37] These facts suggest, when coupled with details of the other decayed yews on burial mounds, a deliberate planting, perhaps marking the site of an early saint cell. There is evidence that early Celtic saints were knowledgeable about land ownership and ancient monuments. One manuscript records that a king of Gwent called Idon, on a mountainside near the river Trothy, having heard Saint Teilo pray and talk there, ceded to him, 'the land surrounding the cumulus on which he stood'.[38] As we have seen, a law of Hywel Dda of 950 protected yews 'dedicated to saints' in Wales, with a severe fine. These separate facts, coupled with the probable ages of some yews on prehistoric mounds, allows speculation about the significance of old yews in such locations.

Large yew on the summit of an Anglo-Saxon mound at Taplow Court, Buckinghamshire

This yew was planted on top of the summit of an Anglo-Saxon burial mound in Taplow churchyard in Buckinghamshire. The burial mound or 'low' was of 'an early seventh-century Saxon prince who may have been the eponymous Taeppa'.[39] The place-name type is consistent with others that were used by Anglo-Saxons as markers for meeting places. These names including 'low' are often to be found at the centre of hundreds and are often part of the hundred name. Thus Taplow, though built for a burial, may have become a focus for meetings which sheltered under the yew. Within 50 yards of the mound there is evidence of prehistoric occupation and burial, providing an explanation for the location of the church next to the mound.

The ancient yew grew 15ft up on the mound, which was 80ft in diameter, and 240ft in circumference. The mound yielded a hoard of gold and silver only surpassed by the Sutton Hoo burial goods. The burial also included several large wooden buckets, some banded by iron, some by bronze.[40] This common Anglo-Saxon funerary practice at least suggests a local availability of yew, as yew is the usual material for Anglo-Saxon funerary buckets. The yew was measured at 21ft in circumference of trunk in 1882. The tree fell during the excavation, taking the shoring with it, the fall of earth injuring a local archaeologist, Mr Rutland.[41] The fact that the excavators tried to preserve the tree suggests some local respect for it as a curiosity.

'The church itself is no longer visible, though its ruins remained on the spot until 1853. On clearing away the masonry, it was seen that the foundations of the building passed through an ancient ditch. The church had been erected at the Eastern end of an enclosure, the centre of which was dominated by the barrow. The whole occupied high ground, known locally as Bury Fields. From time to time fragments of pottery – British, Roman, and Saxon – together with well-worked flint flakes, had been collected on, or near the surface of the village graveyard.'[42] Parch marks mapped in 1995 suggest an Anglo-Saxon church existed on the site, not far from the barrow. The examination of these marks by archaeologists suggested contemporary populations here in the seventh century were pagan *and* Christian, using the same site at the same time.[43] The Taplow yew may have been a late Anglo-Saxon era planting, santifying the older mound.

The old yew at Cranborne Chase

The celebrated archaeologist General Pitt-Rivers stumbled across another significant yew on a prehistoric site of importance in Dorset. 'Gen, A. Pitt-Rivers, in describing a British barrow which he opened on Winklebury Hill, seems to supply an instance. He states that he found no relics within the mound, and this absence was probably due to a dead yew, locally called a 'scrag', which he removed. Gen. Pitt-Rivers call the yew an 'insertion', but was the tree 'inserted' alive or dead? A dead yew would scarcely work much havoc. He continues – and the addition is noteworthy – 'I afterwards learnt that the people of the neighbourhood attached some interest to it, and it has since been replaced by Sir Thomas Grove.'[44] The yew was 'dead', yet the local reaction may suggest it was alive and hollow. He may have presumed it useless as timber and dying. Either way, it was likely to have been a venerable specimen, possibly linked to early settlement as boundary markers.

The yew on the top of Duck's Nest Tump, Rockbourne, Hampshire

On the summit of Duck's Nest Tump in Hampshire, as noted by County Archaeologist J. P. Williams-Freeman in 1915, there is an enormous yew. It has not yet been officially dated or assessed by tree researchers. The yew here, is difficult to date, beyond stating that these yews are of such size that the most likely origin is at least early medieval. Dating them is a difficult problem, due to splitting, hollowing and the loss of trunk(s).

The enormous specimen at Ashbrittle churchyard, in Somerset is said by several authors to be on a prehistoric Neolithic barrow.[45] Other earthworks in Hampshire involve yews of at least several centuries antiquity. Situated close to the River Wey, 200 yards south of Bramshott Court, is a mound 46ft (14m) in diameter, five and a half feet (1.7m) high with no ditch, that is 'known locally as "Druids mound" and is surmounted by old yew trees'.[46] These are probably Georgian garden design features, as at Weston Park, Staffordshire, around Pendrills Cave. Danebury hillfort still has some large yews, which were referred to by Freeman-Williams as 'old yews on banks at Danebury'.[47] Also in Hampshire, in the New Forest, at Denny Lodge, by the River Beaulieu, is Yew Tree Heath, with six bowl barrows and a bell barrow. One barrow, 85ft (26m) diameter by eight feet (2.5m) high is mutilated by a giant central crater.[48] Large craters are often the places where large trees have been removed, by early antiquaries or looters who opened the barrows. The site may bear comparison to barrows found at Yew Down in Oxfordshire.[49]

These examples together suggest that yews on interesting archaeological features may have been deliberately planted. These records represent a fraction of the extant evidence as many trees will have been removed without record and many will be recorded in county volumes not accessed by this writer.

The implications are that the majority of these very old yews represent the markers of lost churches, some of which were Anglo-Saxon (or Welsh) saint in origin. As we cannot yet empirically measure their exact ages, we must preserve these trees carefully, for future generations to assess their contexts, using as yet undeveloped techniques.

The Wall Hill yews in Worcestershire

A pair of very large yews were reported on a large earthwork near Kyre Park and Thornbury, by botanist Edwin Lees of Worcester on a field trip with the Worcestershire Naturalists' Club. He considered the pair of yews on the earthwork of Wall Hill as ancient. He had seen many large yews in his botanical career, including those at Himley Park, Kyre Park, on Wychbury Hill, in Hagley churchyard and at Bromsgrove church, which was probably the oldest yew in Worcestershire.[50] He was present on Tuesday, the 8 June 1880, when Worcestershire naturalists assembled at the Wall Hill. Mr H. H. Lines, described the earthwork.

> It is 1,220 feet long, by 650 in breadth, within the ramparts. There are two original gates of remarkable width, one on the SE corner 60 feet wide between its two crests, the other on the NW 50 feet between the crests. In addition there are four other openings which seem to be of subsequent formation. On the western side are two yew trees growing on the line of the rampart, which has been diverted from its proper line in order to leave them outside the camp area, as though they grew where they stand before the camp was made.[51]

Though fancifully described this is obviously an Iron Age site. The pair of yews described that day may, like many old yews in the landscape, have marked a site of an early church. We know from churches that survive across Britain today, that the old fort sites were popular church sites. These yews on forts may indicate the presence of such a failed cell or hermitage, that may only have left the yew (and postholes) as evidence.

The Merdon Castle yews at Hursley, Hampshire

The hundred court at Merdon Castle was still set up within the earthworks of the Iron Age hillfort during the nineteenth century. The Iron Age fort at Merdon was constructed in *circa* 500–100 BC. It has not been fully excavated. The Normans later altered the earthworks significantly, perhaps sinking the well inside the fort.

A source from 1808 records that the yews at Merdon were noted as being 'of great age', at the fort site.[52] The yews on the Norman earthwork may bear some comparison to those on the Norman mound recorded at Astley, Hampshire.[53] The yews growing at Merdon were considered by Hampshire archaeologist J. P. Williams-Freeman, in 1915, as being of probable Norman origin on the inner earthwork and probable Iron Age yews on the outer.[54] J. Freeman-Williams measured the yews growing on the Norman earthwork as 15ft 9inches girth, the same measure he made of a yew at John of Gaunt's deerpark, coming to the conclusion both were probably Norman in origin.[55]

The oldest yew on the British earthwork at Merdon (Plate 10) stands by the original entrance of the fort. It is growing on bare chalk, a soil that usually suggests slow growth rates. This tree was described in 1915, as being 'the biggest yew, on the right-hand side as we come in, stands on the British bank and may date from before 1138. It is difficult to measure, as it grows on such a steep slope, but below the spring of the main limbs, four feet up from the lower roots, it is no less than 22ft 9inches in circumference.'[56] From his own data he also extrapolates an age of 1,050 years for this yew.[57] This same yew was measured by Toby Hindson as 24ft 6in in girth, in July 1997, at an unknown height from the ground, 'including some unavoidable ephytic growth'. Based on ring counts derived locally, he suggested an age of *circa* 1,750 years old.[58] A. Meredith gave an estimate of around 2,000 years.[59]

The vagaries of yew dating, understood from a conservative position, allow me to suggest the possibility of 1,500 years age. It could be therefore that it represents a post-Roman early saint church planting. 'The name Mer*dun* together with its earlier importance as the centre of a Saxon Hundred and the chief manor of the district would suggest that the Saxons found it a Celtic stronghold when they conquered the country.'[60] These recordings suggest it was a powerful Anglo-Saxon stronghold, before it became the site of a Norman castle, or Bishop's Palace, perhaps requiring an Anglo-Saxon era church. The *Anglo-Saxon Chronicle* records how Cynewulf, King of the West Saxons, was caught in a bower with his mistress in the fort of 'Merdon', and murdered by Cyneheard. In 871 King Alfred and Ethelred are said to have fought the Danes at Merdon and lost. There remained some buildings in the fort until the end of the eighteenth century, when, 'excepting a room or two, necessarily reserved for the purposes of the Manorial Court', they were removed.[61] Like Knowlton Henge, Merdon Castle was an ancient community site when it was used by the Saxons as a hundredal court centre. The huge yews at these sites are of archaeological importance, signifying pre-Norman Christian settlement and assembly.

The Knowlton Henge yews, Dorset

At Knowlton, 'the pre-Roman earthworks contained no building material to entice the churchmen within their boundaries ... Here a ruined church built by Norman labour, though not necessarily representing the first church on the spot, stands within a round British earthwork. The Knowlton earthwork is one of a group, and close by is a cluster of ancient, storm-beaten yews.'[62] Several of these yews survive today.

A partial investigation of the site was recently conducted by J. Gale and S. Burrow of Bournemouth University, who surveyed the site, in conjunction with English Heritage in 1994–1996 using limited digging and geophysics. This revealed ploughed away ditches and suggested a very complex site. The prehistoric site has a series of complex earthworks, some of which are

FIGURE 39
Knowlton Henge in
Dorset from the air.
The yews, of at least
pre-Norman date, can
be seen on an
earthwork marking a
defunct boundary of
unknown date.

FIGURE 40
One of the
pre-Norman boundary
yews at Knowlton
Henge.
ANDY MCGEENEY

Anglo-Saxon. The site almost certainly contained a court of the hundred, as the local hundred was known as the Knowlton hundred. The topographical surveys by J. Gale implied the existence of an Anglo-Saxon church, of which nothing remains to today, though this remains unproven.

One earthwork has several large 23ft+ (7m+) girth yews on it, in a line, touching the base of the Bronze Age feature upon which the church sits. This line of yews runs along a remnant of a disused hedge boundary and two of the oldest yews border the edge of the mound. I suggest this was a pre-Norman boundary hedge bank. It ran further than it does today, perhaps suggesting a longer row of yews in former times. Some of these yews of 23ft+ (7m+) in girth, are probably original Anglo-Saxon era boundary markers.

There is also an arc or semicircle of old yew remnants at the Southern Henge, some way from the Church Henge. As the churchyard enclosure itself is so small, I would perhaps argue that this semicircle of yews, on a prominent local feature, may represent vestigial growth of a possible meeting place yew. This location would have allowed more people to assemble, than in the churchyard itself. The Southern Henge has two roads meet on it, with one running through and an adjacent trackway meeting the road at the southern tip of the henge, whereas all the other prehistoric features have only one road by each feature, including Church Henge. As at other sites where similar aged yews planted apparently in lines no longer make useful sense (such as Middleton Scriven in Shropshire and Tettenhall in the West Midlands), these yews may be plantings of a pre-tenth century church boundary marking system.

The Wychbury Hillfort yews, West Midlands

Near Himley in the West Midlands lies the Iron Age Wychbury Hill hillfort. Like many hillforts it has a well by its earthworks. There are many yews, mostly on the southern outer ramparts, nearest the well. A. Meredith recorded many are dead stumps. The destruction of many of the yews has left fragments of great yews that, coupled with the recorded yew on the high ground of nearby Round Hill, suggest a possible early church site somewhere by the hillfort.

The Victorian botanist Edwin Lees observed old yews as a specialist interest. He reported several features of the Wychbury hillfort yews and visited the site several times. The 'dense umbrage' of the 'grand old yews', 'covered the vallum', in 1870 and 1882, as it still does today. In 1870 there was noted a larger yew than the others.[63] It was measured at 30ft (9m) in girth much larger than those there today. In 2002, T. Hindson assessed a yew stump near the summit. The tree had been recently burnt, requiring felling. The rings were intact to the pith. There were 385 annual rings. The girth was approx 16ft (5m) at 1m from ground.

Nearby, south of the fort, a natural hillock called Round Hill, was known to have had an enormous yew on its summit, preserved in photographs held by the Wychbury Archaeological Society. This huge yew was present until *circa* 1936 and may have been a deliberate shelter or boundary feature. The site of the stump on the summit was partly excavated by Herefordshire County Archaeology Service, as part of a proposed road building scheme. Finds recovered from the features were of nineteenth- or twentieth-century date.[64] No significant archaeology was unearthed, it being considered a natural hillock. The assessment of whether it was a hundred or similar assembly tree is not affected by whether it is on a natural or man made hillock, as Saxon meeting-places were held on both types of mound.[65] This result from the excavation below a yew, unlike the Taplow Court dig, matches the Pitt-Rivers result when he opened an empty barrow on Cranborne Chase, mentioned earlier in this chapter.

The old yew at the entrance to Old Oswestry hillfort

At the western entrance to the Old Oswestry hillfort in Shropshire a large mature yew was recorded in 1999 by P. Martin: 'there is one mature tree which must be of some age. This is a yew by the western entrance.'[66] This must almost certainly be a deliberate planting. All other old trees, including many oaks, on this fort site were harvested in several phases, as discussed by Martin. He says it was 'probably spared because of a superstition about felling yews or because yews are very hard and so difficult to fell'. The yew is probably the hardest British tree to fell, or to remove entire. In the same parish, St Oswald's Well was marked by a yew in 1813. (Cambrian Register). Also, in 1780 human remains were excavated near the well. The significantly old yew on this site, like other yews planted at entrances to hillfort earthworks, was probably a church or well marker.

Conclusions

Other records of ancient yews signifying settlement at deserted sites exist. At Walterstone Iron Age Camp in Herefordshire, in 1812 the location of a lost chapel, dedicated to the obscure St Ailsworth, was reported as 'nestling by the NE entrance' of the camp. The writer added 'a venerable yew tree yet remains'.[67] In the western ditch of 'The Knapp' earthwork in Herefordshire in 1933 was recorded by the Woolhope Club, 'an ancient yew in the western ditch of the Knapp earthwork'[68] Not all of these trees are certainly associated with early church or cemetery sites, but their locations and ages, on land often farmed for centuries, suggests a likely deliberate planting. Similarly old yews at Capler Camp in Herefordshire suggest an early church now lost. During any excavation of sites with a history of yews such as these, the yews ought to contribute to the description of the site *prior* to excavation. The survival of such poisonous trees, in many agricultural locations where stock may be affected, suggests a deliberate preservation of the trees as a traditional practice. A huge 'wild' yew was recorded on the top of Conygree Hill near Bromsberrow in Gloucestershire, by the Malvern Naturalists Club.[69] This is another enormous yew that probably has a significant planting history, as a remnant church marker.

Other yews of pre-Norman size that still exist suggest the sites of lost pre-Norman churches. Another pair of yews probably demonstrating the site of an old church now gone was described in the Woolhope Club transactions of 1933. On the way down the hill from 'Arthur's Stone' (a Neolithic burial chamber) towards Dorstone, the field club passed between two yew trees, 'nine yards apart', at the top of one of the meadows. 'One of these trees being of unusual size, measuring seven feet across' from there the stream was traced to another yew tree at the bottom of this meadow where the stream came into sight crossing the lane and going under the road.'[70] These yews, with a well called the Hind Well, in this meadow, suggest a probable pre-Norman lost church site located within fifty yards of the largest yew; the whole meadow, with the yew by the road, may mark the lost ecclesiastical enclosure. In an agricultural context, the retention of the most poisonous British tree must be viewed as significant, as at Wall Hill Camp, Worcestershire and in the field opposite the modern church at Middleton Scriven in Shropshire, as documented by Andrew Morton. All these trees are likely vestigial early church markers, of easily more than 1,000 years antiquity.

The yew at South Hayling churchyard, Hants, is probably one of the ten oldest in Britain. Its girth is 33ft+ (10m+), placing it in the oldest category of yews in Britain, plausibly aged in excess of 1,400 years. The current church, near the old yew, is not the original parish church. It was on Church Rocks in Hayling Bay, a mile from the mainland. The old church fell into the sea in 1066, after severe storms eroded the cliff. This begs a question: as the South Hayling yew is at a Norman churchyard and the yew is most probably older, where did it come from? Was it a Anglo-Saxon era yew, of a lost wooden church for which we have no record?

The 'new' church was built near a mysterious prehistoric earthwork, called Tournorbury or Tunorbury. The earthwork, which is a roundish camp of eight acres, with a bank three or four feet above the area, nine or ten feet above the ditch, almost surrounded by water. It is close to the sea down a lane from the church. It was noted in 1915 as being covered in wood, 'old yews being a conspicuous feature upon the banks'.[71] The earthwork yews may also be archaeologically significant and may corroborate the early yew presence in the area and together, the South Hayling yew and the fort yews may suggest a local pre-Norman yew symbolism, that may have used the South Hayling yew as a meeting place for open air assembly, which made it a desirable place to put a church, where people assembled, perhaps a Saxon court, or a deserted early saint cell.

It is clear from these examples that there may be some considerable benefits to be gained by the landscape historian by assessing the historic vegetation of historic sites. The botany of a place often bears direct relation to its history. Ancient yews at historic sites, perhaps above all other British trees, indicate a deliberate planting. Their unique toxicity to stock, suggests a decision taken historically not to remove them. Their unique status as church markers, may have helped in this regard. In many situations, the old yews at significant sites such as hillforts, would have been selected to remain again and again.

I would suggest that almost all these examples of yews over five centuries old, on funerary mounds and hillforts, represent plausible lost church markers and perhaps some meeting places. Being more poisonous to livestock than any other British tree, yews are unlikely to have been preserved by chance. The early churches of the Anglo-Saxon period, of the Celtic saints and later churches, are known to have used hillforts and prehistoric mounds, often situated near the earliest local roads, as convenient sites for founding churches. Many lost churches hidden in the landscape may be marked by such large yews as are described here. These yews may still survive or exist only in topographical-botanical records. Yews must be recognised as possible indicators of an era of early settlement not necessarily indicated by other known evidence. They were put there deliberately, and need to be preserved.

CHAPTER SEVEN

Yews in Woods, Hedges and Gardens

British woodland yews

The natural seeding of yews in most parts of the British Isles and the copious records of prehistoric yew, show that it is a native tree: an authentic, naturally occurring feature of most British woodland types. Yet yews are not very common in most British woods today. Where they may be found, it is usually in the counties where ancient churchyard yews are historically recorded and similarly, in the same regions where yew place-names most often occur. Their rarity in woods may be attributed to a number of causes. Yew trees are too slow growing to be generally planted as a timber crop. Equally, in woods where standard oaks or similar large British timber trees are grown, yews may be considered undesirable, especially if left to produce seedlings, as their evergreen canopies can compete with other trees or saplings. Yew being poisonous to cattle and horses may also contribute to their regulation by foresters and wardens.

Pockets of woodland dominated by yews have become significantly more rare since 1900. In 1980 R. M. Tittensor assessed many pieces of yew-dominated woodlands, of all ages, across Sussex and Hampshire.[1] Tittensor found that several of A. S. Watt's yew woods of the South Downs, studied in 1926, had completely disappeared. In 1927 the Forestry Commission acquired the Holt Down site, near Butser Hill and War Down, both near Petersfield, and planted them with timber trees. Tittensor found that 'consequently there are only remnants of the original yew'.[2]

The Deep Coombe yew site, wooded with yew since at least 1597 and studied by Tittensor, was leased to the Forestry Commission after the Second World War. They cleared the scrub and downland to plant it with beech and conifers. Three hectares of yew described by A. S. Watt remain within this plantation, who thought they would be 'likely to remain undisturbed for the next 100 years until the beech crop is harvested'. Stead Coombe was similarly noted in 1980 'as a remnant of its former extent, swallowed up in a forestry plantation'.[3] The Alice Holt Forestry Commission research station in Surrey (near the Hampshire border) had many 16–27ft (5–8m) girth yews in its woods until most were felled and sold in the 1860s, and the area replanted with oak and then conifers. Some ancient yews remain at Alice Holt today. They may be more than 1,000 years old, reminders of a much larger yew-dominated woodland that once stood there.

R. M. Tittensor noted that most of the younger yew woods studied by her were probably seeded by parish boundary marker yews. She posits that changes relating to rabbit warren farming and sheep grazing in the late eighteenth and nineteenth centuries allowed the old yew pockets to form small woods that had hitherto been grazed back. Like A. S. Watt, she noted that the thorn and juniper played a key 'seral' role in protecting the small yews from being browsed. Dead junipers and thorns were found under many of the yew woods of Sussex and Hampshire; their presence demonstrated the young ages of most of the yew growth. The near total decline of juniper may therefore signal a problem for future yew wood development.[4] This suggests that many young yew woods may represent an important ecological resource that may be difficult to replace easily.

In Ireland, the famous Killarney yew wood on the Muckross peninsula has many yews over several centuries old. Although none are of great girth this yew wood can be viewed cautiously as a remnant native yew site. The main yew wood is Reenadinna Wood in Killarney National Park. These yews occur on Carboniferous limestone outcrops, bordered by lakes and Muckross Bog, with Devonian Old Red Sandstone marking the western boundary. It is crossed by many walls of probable eighteenth-century date, suggesting the spread of the wood occurred after that time. Naturalised sika deer damaged and killed many yews at Muckross. The ring counts on twenty debarked yews did not exceed 200 years.[5]

Though some yews here have been kept free from deer for over thirty years, they still show no natural regeneration, as in many English yew woods. At Killarney the dense shade and deep moss-filled forest floor discourages yew spreading. The yews of this wood have unusual bryophytes – mosses and liverworts – that grow on the yews and on the ground. These plants occur rarely on yew, and perhaps only the yews growing on the wild, wet hillsides and cliffs of Cumbria have similar moss-laden trunks. These examples show the diversity of yew growth in the British landscape. The trees adjust to the conditions where they occur.

Yews occurring on cliffs across Britain, such as the historic stands at Tintern, near Chepstow and along Dovedale in Derbyshire, are plausible representatives of undisturbed yew growth in their locations since before the tenth century. As we have seen earlier in this book, seemingly small yews grown on cliffs may be of great age. Until non-invasive dating techniques of these trees improve, we should protect the finest examples for future generations to enjoy.

There are pockets of ambiguously old yew growth in parts of England, that merit preservation, such as those found at the Aston Rowant National Nature Reserve on Watlington Hill, in Oxfordshire, adjacent to both the M40 motorway and the Ridgeway prehistoric track. The yews there include remnants of old growth that may be historically important.

Similarly ambiguous are the old yews growing freely on the north side of the Wrekin hill in Shropshire, near the Ministry of Defence shooting range. Many of the Wrekin yews were recorded as venerable in the middle of the

FIGURE 41
Maturing yews at
Aston Rowant Nature
Reserve. If deer and
sheep do not prevent
fresh growth, the yews
will in time dominate
this hill.

ROBERT BEVAN-JONES

nineteenth century. Wyre Forest in Worcestershire has areas that contain many young yews, browsed into tell-tale parasol shapes by numerous deer. The yews are mostly between six and nine feet in girth, seemingly seeded naturally before 1900, in times when deer were known to have been less common. The Castle Eden Dene estate in the north east of England also has established pockets of younger yew woods. Though few trees are of great girth they are worthy of protection and management. These 'lesser' sites are habitats that encourage the settlement of red squirrels, many species of owls, mice and shrews, and represent valuable yew resources that cannot be replaced without at least three centuries of growth.

Excepting pockets of natural yew woodland on cliffs, there are only three or four woods left in Britain containing several ancient yews, with a girth of 16ft or more. These small groups of ancient yews in woodlands seem to have all survived in the south of England; at Kingley Vale in Sussex, near Chichester, Newlands Corner, near Merrow in Surrey and Druid's Grove, at Norbury Park, near Dorking, in Surrey. At a private estate at Odstock in Wiltshire there is also a dense yew wood of considerable age. The yews on these sites have been growing continuously for more than a thousand years.

Three of these sites in the south of England all retain a degree of public access and are discussed here. Many British woodland yew sites have very sensitive environments and one needs to be careful when visiting, seeking advice locally where possible. These sites are probably not suitable for very large groups. All these British woods have small portions of woodland that have several recorded 23ft+ (7m+) girth yews in close proximity. There are probably no other places in Britain, where the principal woodland trees, in small areas, are ancient yews.

Newlands Corner near Merrow, Surrey

Newlands Corner is owned by Surrey County Council. It is open to the public for much of the year. It is probably the most convenient place for anyone to access and enjoy areas of very old yew growth. As these yews are on flat ground they are the easier to access than other yew woods, which are more usually found on very steep slopes. Pockets of unusually old yews are grouped together in distinct areas.

In Tupper's Victorian tome, *Farley Grange*, the Newlands Corner yews get a romanticized reference: 'On Merroe Downs, in Surrey, are two distinct concentric groves of venerable yews a thousand years old with remnants of little avenues, possibly Druidic.'[6] It would be unwise to discount totally the possibility of yews being old enough for this kind of speculation, though any association with living yews and druids is distinctly unlikely and owes much to the Victorian imagination.

These ancient avenues at Merrow were also recorded in 1787. 'Having spent my days on chalky downs I had many opportunities to study various collections of yew trees ... Not many miles from Guildford, a great number of yew trees, of some former century, are growing on so rude a waste, that, had they not stood in straight lines, it would be difficult to persuade many that they were placed there by the hands of man.'[7]

Old tracks weave among the trees and an early settlement has seemingly left traces of tracks, ditches and small earthworks, though no archaeological excavations have taken place to my knowledge. I would argue that it is possible that the oldest yews at Newlands may have originated as remnants of early church cells from a deserted settlement and have thereafter allowed to seed naturally for many centuries. We know that no native forest is entirely natural and most areas of British woodland reflect man's historic usage of plants. Keepers of game such as deer frequently appreciate the yew for winter feeding, for foliage and also as shelter. This may be an important reason for the preservation of yews that had already seeded or been planted on lands that later became parks or similar estates.

One of the largest surviving yews at Newlands Corner borders the main road, en route to the car park. There are no circles (or avenues) discernible today. Toby Hindson estimates several specimens there as *circa* 800–900 years and a couple at 1,200–1,300 years old (Plate 11).

His assessments of ring counted stumps of known felling date across Hampshire, in churchyards and in woodlands, support his estimates.

There has been much destruction at Newlands Corner. Several hollow yews have been killed by being burnt out, possibly by lightning, though manmade fire is equally plausible (Plate 12). Young yews are relatively rare here and a healthy deer population probably discourages much renewal of yews.

The ebb and flow of the fortunes of many of the Newlands Corner yews may be seen in the twisted broken nature of their boles, making it difficult to measure them sensibly. Some of the ancient yews are ruined by storms, some are bloated by polling of lost branches. Holes in the trunks gape where branches have been removed, the saw marks still visible today. Most of these were burrs, taken, it is said, by shepherds for making nutcrackers. Oliver Rackham presented a study on Newlands Corner and suggested that wood-pastures existed here, where the yews grew in open downland.[8] He was puzzled as to why the old yews at Newlands Corner were pollarded. We may never know. Bow wood may perhaps have been obtained from pollarding these yews, or wood for making buckets, as both traditions show at least a thousand years of yew usage in England. The appearance of the Newlands yews may owe as much to natural loss of trunk through storm.

There are few or no young yews at Newlands Corner, between the relics. This is probably for two reasons. The oppressive shade of the yews discourages most plant growth, except when opportunist seeds have taken where the shade has been broken by storm or limb removal. Local deer may eat the small yews before they have time to mature, as at Wyre Forest in Worcestershire where yews 150–300 years old occur without sign of offspring, their canopies bitten by deer to above three feet from ground. Deer populations are known to have ballooned in many British woods since 1900, suggesting deer populations may be inhibiting much natural yew wood development. Initial studies recently undertaken by Hindson at Newlands Corner suggest deer populations are restricting the regeneration of yew in an absolute fashion.

'Druid's Grove' at Norbury Park, Surrey

The history of the place-name of 'Druids' Grove' does not seem to have been traceable much before *circa* 1850. This romantically named yew wood is on a steep slope consisting mostly of chalk. This presence of old yews on cliffs and steep slopes may partly be a result of steep sites having evaded agricultural use, longer than anywhere else, rather than as a necessary environment for yew growth.

This secluded yew wood has suffered greatly from storms in recent years. Many trunks are now prostrate but many sprout vertical shoots from their horizontal trunks. As at Newlands Corner, many large yews here seem to be in lines. Several living yews spread out over the entire site exceed 20ft in girth. Other yews here, as at Kingley Vale and Newlands Corner, may have once been over 20ft girth but have lost major portions of trunk. In 1897, John Lowe recorded yews at Norbury Park, some along a path called Druids Walk. He recorded a 'great many fine trees' [yews] measuring from 12ft to 22ft in girth. He measured trees below the house, near the railway station, near Keepers Lodge and near established paths. Many of these yews probably survive today, even though snow damage had affected the yews of his day and many later storms, such as the Great Storm of 1987 have ravaged them since.

Surrey County Council Park Rangers at Norbury Park are keen to preserve as many of these yews as possible, and are systematically working the woods around the oldest yews.[9] The 1991 storms resulted in the widespread death of large yews, although many prostrate yews by 1998 had risen again, sending fine trunks out vertically from wherever they had fallen. The regeneration process continues. The woods are on a steep slope and are not the easiest to access, and perhaps this has helped their survival. This wood has not been mapped for all the yews and is a still a very wild place.

The Kingley Vale yew forest, Sussex

The steep chalk downland at Kingley Vale Reserve is one of the main natural habitats of the British yew. Richard Williamson, in his book *The Great Yew Forest*, provides an affectionate portrait of his experiences looking after the yew forest for over fifteen years. The site is full of archaeological remains. Goosehill Camp and Bow Hill Camp, have Kingley Vale yews on them.[10] 'The group of yews at Kingley Vale stands in the neighbourhood of four barrows, and numerous excavations, probably prehistoric, dot the turfy slopes of the hillside.'[11] The yew wood on a private estate at Great Yews, at Odstock in Wiltshire is also near an Iron Age hillfort with prehistoric barrows nearby. As we shall see in chapter nine, yew was certainly highly prized in the Iron and Bronze Ages, though we cannot prove an association. However, I would argue that post-Roman populations, attracted by the earlier settlements, might equally have brought yews to such locations, as holy markers.

Almost all the yews at Kingley Vale are under two centuries old, and cover huge areas of ground, having been carefully managed since the Second World War. Only a few ancient trees survive at Kingley Vale, in a much diminished form, on the Chilgrove ridge, which became apart of the park in 1968. Lowe, in 1897, thought that some Kingley Vale yews were around 500 years old.[12] Richard Williamson feels this is a reasonable estimate of their age.[13] A survey of Kingley Vale was completed by Dr A. S. Watt in 1926 who considered the oldest there were at least 700 years old based on ring data he collected on other trees.[14] Mr Newbould in 1963 cored some young yews at Kingley Vale and found that some younger yews yielded 10–20 rings per radial inch, falling to 50 rings per radial inch for older yews, which allows an age of 500+ years for older specimens in the five feet diameter class. A. S. Thomas 'in the 1950s' counted the rings of a blown yew from the Kingley Vale grove and showed it to be 500–550 years old.[15]

Kingley Vale has changed dramatically since 1900. Richard Williamson noted that many venerable yews were grubbed out to expand the agricultural potential of the area. Many of the oldest yews at Kingley Vale were also deliberately blown up by the army on manoeuvres during the Second World War. Several soldiers were killed in the yew woods during these manoeuvres – Richard Williamson records the account in his book, having seen pre-war photographs of many large yews, he was amazed to find no evidence on site of these trees. According to a local witness 'that was our army ... they had to see how many mortar bombs they could use to knock the yews over ... they would go on all day and half the night if there was a moon.' Bullet marks can still be seen

today on some specimens that survived.[16] These upheavals make dating the
ruined trunks that remain at Kingley Vale very difficult.

The paper by P. Tabbush in *The Quarterly Journal of Forestry* on the ages
of yews in Kingley Vale in Sussex was a scientific assessment, and consequently
gave a necessarily wide range of ages for trees there. The oldest trees he found
at the site were growing on a flat terrace, not on a slope as with the younger
trees. He dated a ruinous yew at Kingley Vale as being 2,800 years+ to possibly
5,500 years+.[17] This 23ft+ (7m+) stump, topped by a large trunk, could be a
single tree, having been partly smashed by the military activity. This tree
grown in the chalk of the vale, must be at least 1,000 years old. The oldest
trees may yet be the stubborn remnants of a much larger ancient yew wood
established before the Norman Conquest. Because of the Second World War
devastation of the site, other fragments of ancient trunks may also survive in
parts of this huge woodland, appearing as small fragments, or clumps of
seemingly young trees. The young yew forest that surrounds the remnants
of old yew growth at Kingley Vale make up an extensive yew woodland that
supports rare wildlife. In former times its type may have been far more
commonly found in the British landscape.

The Borrowdale yews, Cumbria

As at Newlands Corner in Surrey, the famous yews of Borrowdale in Cumbria
may indicate another deserted religious site, rather than a vestige of 'native
forest'. These yews are sometimes referred to as a grove. At Borrowdale all
the yew trees are female. They have been famous as very old yews for at least
two hundred years. Marked on the old Ordnance Survey maps, not far from
Seathwaite Farm in Borrowdale, these yews were a favourite subject of
Wordsworth. In 1803 Wordsworth wrote of the Borrowdale yews,

> But worthier still of note
> Are those Fraternal Four of Borrowdale,
> Joined in one solemn and capricious grove
> Huge trunks! and each particular trunk a growth
> Of intertwisted fibres serpentine ...

The old yews of Cumbria together represent a nationally significant ancient
yew resource. Wordsworth planted eight yews at Grasmere church.[18] He also
wrote a poem entitled 'Lines left upon a seat inside a Yew Tree', set in the
same region. He wrote another poem to the Lorton yew. The chair made for
the mayor of Cockermouth from a fragment of the Lorton yew, may one day
be useful for dendrochronological analysis. The Lorton yew was carefully
depicted by Harry Goodwin in 1887. His picture shows it was a boundary
marker; a fence running from it, to the river, perhaps suggests a remnant of
an early ecclesiastical enclosure.

The Borrowdale group are certainly the oldest group of yews in the north
of England. Sited on the banks of the river Derwent they are unique. It is

very difficult to understand this site, without suggesting early human occupation, or native yew woods, here 1,500 years ago. These yews are far too old to be associated with the time that Borrowdale was the property of a thirteenth century Cistercian monastic grange.

W. J. Watson recorded Borrowdale as meaning dale of the fort. It is perhaps possible that these yews mark the site of an early ecclesiastical settlement, perhaps of an early saint. Early Welsh kingdoms once stretched across Cumbria and the churches of Celtic saints were common in the region. These trees are as old as many of the oldest yews found at early saint sites in Wales.

The Borrowdale trees are certainly over 1,300 years old. In December 1883 a great storm ravaged the Borrowdale yews. They have not yet recovered. Ken Mills noted in 1999 that a recent visitor had set a fire inside the largest hollow yew, damaging the tree.[19] The fame of some of Britain's yews may actually damage them, as much as protect them. This may serve as a warning for those visiting old yews in woods, as the impact of visitors must be kept to a minimum. Climbing on hollow yews ought to be discouraged. Respecting the environment of the trees is as important a part of the experience as viewing the trees themselves. The places detailed here are the only sites where one can find groups of yews of this age. There are no more known sites of this kind in Britain; these trees must be respected, since a replanting would take upwards of seven centuries to begin to reach the sizes they are today.

Hedgerow and boundary-marker yews

Yew is a rare but persistent hedgerow tree nationally, and has probably been retained for its sheltering habit. Many hedgerow yews provide temporary shelter for flocks, villagers and farmers. At Easthope in Shropshire, near Easthope National Trust car park, yews of 10–13ft (3–4m) girth grow along damp drovers tracks; they have provided shelter from wind and rain for sheep and herdsmen for several centuries. Hedgerow yews tend to be in England and Wales, where the distribution of old growth in churchyards and native cliff yews are more frequent. Mysteriously, although the yew tends to reach 33–36ft (10–11m) girth in churchyards, no recorded hedgerow yews of 26ft+ (8m+) in girth survive today. Small hedgerow yews in pairs can represent vestigial ruined cottage entrances.

There are several 16ft+ (5m+) yews in the hedgerows of byways around Claverley in Shropshire that may be boundary markers of more than 700 years age. The yew on the Enville-Swindon parish boundary in South Staffordshire is on a crossroads, on the summit of a hill, is probably a deliberate planting. A few miles away, there is a large roadside hollow specimen coming into Wolverley, Worcestershire on the A456. This parish adjoins Churchill in Worcestershire, which has a 'Court of the hundred' yew, mentioned by Nash in his *History of Worcestershire*. Enville parish church has several large specimens in nearby hedgerows; these are much larger than in the churchyard and could be late medieval boundary markers. Also in Enville on 'The Sheepwalks' are

FIGURE 42
One of the famous
Borrowdale yews.
ANDY MCGEENEY

FIGURE 43
A hollow yew in a
hedgerow at Claverley,
Shropshire.
ROBERT BEVAN-JONES

a line of similar sized yews marking the southern boundary of Prestwood, running within 50 yards parallel to the parish boundary. These were noted by Edwin Lees in the nineteenth century as ancient trees.

There are large hedgerow yews, of 20ft+ (6m+) girth, in Hampshire, Shropshire and Staffordshire, which may perhaps be Anglo-Saxon boundary marker remnants. Yews of *circa* 20ft (6m) girth follow the parish boundary of

Acton Burnell, Shropshire. Some old yews occur in fields, as at Knowlton in Dorset, where the old boundaries they marked are now redundant. Hampshire and Sussex have many similarly large parish boundary yews in their hedges. R. M. Tittensor recorded 15 examples of yew growth on parish boundaries in Sussex and Hampshire, suggesting they were remnants of Anglo-Saxon boundary marking. Some of these pockets straddle two or three parishes.[20]

It is difficult to know whether any single scheme is responsible for these trees, though the presence of a yew of great age in a hedgerow may provide evidence of human settlement along the route it is on, perhaps even a lost church. The dating of the yew may contribute something to the understanding of the age of the hedge or boundary it marks.

The now outmoded hedge-dating techniques of Dr Hooper, based on the number of tree and shrub species as an indicator of centuries becomes impossible to use in studying hedges containing large yews as the canopy of the yew usually excludes most species growing within 60ft (20m) either side of it. This may also be said for hedges where holly dominates. The age of

FIGURE 44
A postcard dating from around 1900 of the historic hedgerow yew at Rocky Lane in Perry Barr, West Midlands. Note the lost branches facing the road, a sign of management to facilitate passage past the tree. This tree must be at least one thousand years old, suggesting this lane and boundary are also of considerable antiquity.

yews in such a hedge may therefore provide the best dating evidence for the hedge or boundary, in the absence of other evidence.

Documentary evidence of a yew as a historic boundary marker is supplied by the perambulations of the manor of Sheffield. The 1574 perambulation of the estate boundary describes, 'one ewe tree standing upon my lordes land called Benettfield is thought to be a meere [boundary marker] betweene my lord of Ecclessall, and so upwards to a place called Stowperstocke. This evidence given and showed by one John Stone of Whitley-wood aforesaid, beeing of the age of sixty yeares and above; as hee hath heard his elders say the same.' [21] This is interesting, especially as the rare place-name Eccleshall involves *ecclesia* (originally latin), a loan word from primitive Welsh, 'believed to have been used by pagan Anglo-Saxons when referring to communities of British Christians'.[22]

Within the parish of Eccleshall in Sheffield today, a much decayed boundary yew still exists at Thrift Farm, on a significant boundary. It is thought to be the oldest tree in Sheffield [23] and may be a genuinely ecclesiatical planting, perhaps marking a daughter cell of the manor church. (Such status may have preserved such a poisonous tree on farm land). Very old yews are also recorded at Eccleshall in Staffordshire.

FIGURE 45
Topiary of the
Harlington yew,
Greater London.
originally drawn in
1729, it was reprinted
in Loudon in 1838.

120

Formal hedging avenues and topiary

The fashion for formal yew hedging seems to have grown in popularity throughout the seventeenth century. Evelyn, in 1644, probably erroneously, claims to have started the fashion himself, 'without vanitie', he claims to have brought the yew, 'into fashion'. He described yew hedging as unparalleled for 'beauty', and as a 'stiff defence', presumably as shelter from wind. When removing a yew hedge, therefore, a consideration of resultant exposure to wind must be undertaken. J. Lowe lists many hedges of known date as does H. Hartzell.[24] Lowe described yew hedging as affording 'excellent protection from the wind and sun'.[25]

There are many fine formal yew hedges and avenues in many parts of Britain that have known planting dates. Planted yew avenues and hedges occur in Wales, England, Ireland and Scotland. Whole books have been devoted to the

FIGURE 46
The Harlington yew drawn again by Loudon in 1838, having recovered.

subject of formal hedges alone. Most country houses and stately homes in the care of the National Trust or English Heritage have hedges whose lengths include trees two centuries old. The most commonly recommended feed for yew hedges is the preparation known as 'blood, fish and bone': not unlike the nutrients it enjoys in churchyards. Yews usually thrive as a formal hedge, but tend to grow narrower trunks when so closely planted; original plantings in formal garden designs may seem too small to be originals at first glance.

Yew avenues, like yew hedges, have been planted for at least several centuries. The Westbourne churchyard avenue in Sussex, formed of eight yews, is said to have been planted by the then Earl of Arundel in 1544.[26] The eight avenue trees have a mean girth of 11ft (3.33m). T. Hindson has studied the Monnington Walk yew avenue in Herefordshire and has produced a mean girth of 10ft 4in (3.08m) for this avenue of 43 widely spaced yews, planted 376 years ago. These results, when coupled with most of A. Meredith's list of known plantings, suggests a general slowing of yew growth for typical yews, at *circa* 10ft (3m) girth, indicating the onset of adulthood.

T. Baxter observed many formal hedges, especially those at Blickling Hall, near Norwich, Norfolk, where the East Hedge alone measures 290ft long and 15ft thick. They are certainly at least 250 years old. In each hedge 100 trees were planted out, three feet apart, of which approximately 75 remain as originals. 'One large yew measured six ft 5in, in circumference but in general, the circumference of the yews at two ft from ground was less that 2ft.'[27] Girth measurements are poor indicators of age when yews are densely grown so coring can be an ideal tool in dating yew hedges.

The fashion for topiary, the sculpting of yew into recognisable cones, pyramids, animals etc., also began to be popular in the late seventeenth century. The yew of Harlington churchyard (near Brentford, London) was depicted in 1729, having been newly carved with a globe and weathercock. It ceased to be clipped in 1780 or 1790, and still survives today.

These varied roles for yews, as hedges, sculptures and avenues seem to have attracted plantsmen for centuries and in almost all parts of Britain yews can be seen clipped to suit the designs of the owner. The gardens at Levens Hall (Cumbria) could be described as the finest yew-dominated scheme in England. The organic development of designs means that no two examples of topiary, as single trees or as hedges, are ever identical.

Lancelot 'Capability' Brown and yews

Landscape designers of the eighteenth century such as Humphrey Repton and 'Capability' Brown worked within a great tradition. In most cases they brought fresh ideas to existing sites which were already equipped with woodlands and other features already many centuries old. Their talents as designers lay in the sympathetic arrangement of new with old, planting where appropriate, while respecting existing features of great beauty or age, and enhancing their effect where possible by avenues, paths and other strategies utilising perspective.

Their new plantings, of single trees or clumps, were for specific visual effect, often tastefully complimenting the existing British trees of the parks they aspired to improve. Yews feature as significant trees in several of the garden landscapes known to have been influenced by Brown. When Oliver Rackham visited Hatfield forest in 1987 he saw 'three magnificent yews', on 'the dam of the western arm of the lake', which 'must date from 1757',[28] when Brown was adding trees to the medieval park. Rackham measured the largest, a female yew, at 14ft 7in in girth. This tree provides the largest girth measure of any yew of known age, ever found in Britain.

Rackham reports that 'it cannot be more than 230 years old and should always be remembered by anyone who supposes that big yews must always be of fabulous age'.[29] In May 1998, it measured 15ft girth at 3ft and 5ft from ground. Other yews near this portion of the lake are much smaller. In 1998 one measured 8ft (2.15m) and another nearly 9ft (2.70m) in girth all at 3ft from ground. One large dead yew stump hard by the lake had an intact basal measure of 12ft 8 in girth near ground level in May 1998. This yew may have been one of the three yews Rackham referred to as being plantings from 1757.

A comparison of the 1987 and 1998 measures of the largest yew is helpful. The growth rate ought to at least assist us estimate the age. 5in in 11 years, suggests an average probable age of 396 years, not 243 years. The trunk of this yew is prematurely hollow, though not through branch removal, with slightly splayed vertical trunks. It is atypical, whereas the size of the 12ft 8in solid stump, better matches the known growth of yews *circa* three centuries in age. However, it is not impossible that the Rackham tree was perhaps damaged when young, perhaps when transferred from a hedge when a hundred or so, to accelerate the maturity of the 'Capability' Brown design. The growth rate in the recent ten year period suggests a slower growth rate that would fit this pattern. Admittedly, more measuring time may provide a better picture.

In corroboration of my transplantation theory, it may be noticed that in 1897 John Lowe blamed Lancelot 'Capability' Brown for the removal of hundreds of metres of yew hedging when implementing his open style of landscaping.[30] He also comments that Brown often moved adult trees. Could Brown have selectively recycled removed yew hedge specimens for the better effect of his 'new' landscapes? This may imply the yews were semi-mature when planted. Lowe seems certain that Brown removed many yew hedges, wholesale, as part of the new trends in landscape design. This could explain the apparent size of the largest Hatfield specimen and its slow recent growth.

At Himley Hall, in Staffordshire, the grounds of which were also probably landscaped by Brown, there is a yew by the wishing pool, of a similar size to the Hatfield specimens, which is a historic landscape design planting. There are probably more examples to be found. At both Hatfield Forest lake and Himley Hall wishing pool, the yews are female, by water and are *circa* 13ft (4m) in girth. Both of these examples are atypical, odd yews, anatomically, when compared to the majority of yews of this age. The Himley yew has branches covered in burrs, while the Hatfield yew seems to have hollowed prematurely, without branch loss. It is even possible that Brown may have removed yew hedges and selected interesting looking specimens from the hedge, to selectively plant in his 'new' landscapes. These two sites seem to have yews incorporated in Brown's design, and further field researches may uncover more examples of prominently planted 10–13ft (3–4m) girth yews of his planting or re-planting.

Richard and Nina Muir, in *Hedgerows, their History and Wildlife* (1987), recorded a 'straggly hedge of yew' near Grafham, Cambridgeshire. Though seemingly part of a typical hedgerow, they record that Christopher Taylor, 1985, identified the yew hedge as forming part of a 'relict lost garden'. Such examples emphasise the importance of recognising yews and their landscape significance. Successful core sampling of such trees in yew hedges can identify their exact chronology in the formal garden design.

The yew deserves a unique mention in the history of formal gardens, as the archetypal hedging plant, clipped into walls, towers and all manner of topiary. As a landscape tree it was used artfully by designers of the eighteenth and nineteenth centuries, for singular effect, draped over water, or as an imposing avenue. This evidence survives today in the grounds of many halls and country houses, often providing the last visible vestiges of original schemes, and may be enjoyed for centuries to come.

CHAPTER EIGHT

The Yew in Folklore Traditions

The yew in British folklore tales is often invested with dark or magical associations. On a more practical level, many tales also report the durability of the wood and longevity of the tree. These facets of the yew are constant features of folklore tales from around Britain. Much material mentioning the yew is of purely Irish origin, allowing a discussion here of mainly Irish historical tales as a group. Features of Irish legend are often present in faint traces in Welsh tales and one may conclude that some of the tales have distant, but shared origins. Fewer pure 'native' texts have been preserved from Wales and mentions of trees of any kind, are rare. Sir John Rhys, author of *Celtic Folklore*,[1] noted in 1880 that he had difficulty in getting older Welsh people to discuss Welsh folklore. They believed that to speak of such things was immoral or simply silly. As with the permanent loss of most of the diaries of Kilvert, Wales has lost much of the folklore that once existed to amuse, inform and entertain. The extant Irish texts perhaps offer some clues as to how some of the early populations of the British Isles may have perceived their mountains, rivers and trees.

British tales that survive today, are often difficult to assess in an empirical way as the exact date of their origination can be obscure. There is, therefore, some ambiguity in the historical value of each passage of text that involves the yew. What usually survives is the date they were first preserved in print, rather than the date when they were written. This ambiguity of origin implies that we should not easily discard any material, since we cannot fully quantify its worth. As Canon G. H. Doble wrote, 'Legend is history, in the sense that the legends and traditions of a people are a part of its history.'[2] This reminds us that we must recognise some historical value in all British folklore texts that mention the yew, recorded in whatever form history has allowed.

Modern storytellers have contributed to the description of the yew in British folklore. Robert Graves in his vivid 'historical grammar of poetic myth', *The White Goddess*, created powerful images for the yew based on his own readings of many British myths and legends. 'The Night Mare is one of the cruellest aspects of the White Goddess. Her nests, when one comes across them in dreams, lodged in rock-clefts or the branches of enormous hollow yews, are built of carefully chosen twigs, lined with white horse-hair and the plumage of prophetic birds and littered with the jaw-bones and entrails of poets.'[3] This kind of dark, magical imagery pervades many British folklore tales that involve the yew, linked perhaps to the sombre evergreen shade of its canopy and the poisonous compounds it contains.

A Hertfordshire St George fights a dragon

Hertfordshire local historians such as W. B. Gerish in 1900, recorded the story of Piers Shonks, who was considered a 'St George'. In the legend Shonks slew a dragon whose cave was under the roots of a large hollow yew tree. 'The lair of the Brent Pelham dragon was a cave under the roots of a great and ancient Yew tree that once stood on the boundary of Great Pepsells and Little Pepsells fields. A terror to the neighbourhood, the dragon was said to be a favourite of the devil himself ...'[4]

Canon Wigram documented this yew in a tithe audit *circa* 1895–1900. He was a Hertfordshire scholar who archived ecclesiastical histories of St Albans during his long career. Canon Wigram at a tithe audit reported:

> ... there was a little stile over which you used to go from Great Pepsells into little Pepsells: it was in the hedge, inside a gurt Yew tree that you used to go through ... Now when this yew tree was cut down, it was Master Lawrence that cut it down (the grandfather I think of the Lawrence who now is at the Post Office), they do say sir that the men could not get that yew tree down. And at last they all went away to breakfast, and when they all came back that yew tree had fallen down of itself, and when they looked there was a gurt hole right underneath it, underneath the roots like a gurt cave.[5]

As the canon says, 'cavities are often found under at the roots of venerable trees but the connection of this one with the legend is decidedly interesting. I have since been informed that fragments of the tree were carried away as relics by the villagers; and Mr Skinner, of Cove Gate, Anstey village has some of the loppings in his garden.'[6] The fact that some of these loppings survive could be significant and ought to be located and preserved.

The tomb of Shonks lies at St Mary's church in Brent Pelham. Shonks cast an arrow as he lay dying to decide the site of his burial, fulfilling a prophecy that he would not be buried in or out of the church, and the arrow flew through a window and embedded in the wall of the church where he now lies. 'With regard to the place of burial being indicated by an arrow's flight, this incident is a common feature of the Robin Hood type legend.'[7]

These legends are interesting. The tree's root hole location could still be explored, perhaps with significant archaeological results; it may be an Anglo-Saxon era boundary tree, or may mark an early cemetery. It is interesting that it formed the route of a footpath, with the stile being set inside the hollow tree. It could even be replanted today from cuttings of the loppings from Cove Gate, Anstey. It would have been at least a thousand years old to reach the hollowness and size described at the time it was felled *circa* 1820. If a churchyard were discovered at this location then any excavation could help place the yew, now gone, in an archaeological context.

A Welsh folklore tale

Francis Kilvert, the 'curate of Clyro', recorded the yews of Llanshifr in association with a folk tale he had heard. On 13 March, 1872, Kilvert walked through the rain:

> Below lay the black and gloomy peat bog, the Rhos Goch', ... 'As I returned I paused at the stone stile above Llanshifr to look down upon the strange grey dark old house lying in the wet hollow among the springs, with its great dismal solitary yew and the remains of the moat in which the Scotch pedlar was buried.

From within the house he describes the 'bank rising steep in front of the window'.

In 1870 he had found 'the tall dark yew' of Llanshifr. The owner of the site, Mr Morgan, showed Kilvert where the body of a pedlar was found, the man having been murdered for his pack. The body was discovered when the moat was being cleaned.

> One of the twin yews was lately blown down and cut up into gate posts which will last twice as long as oak. The wood was so hard, Morgan said 'it turned many of the axes as if they were made of lead.' He also added, 'I wonder which of these yews Gore hid the penknife before his death which made him restless, as hidden iron is said to do, and caused his spirit to come back rummaging about the house and premises and frightening people out of their wits.[8]

Unfortunately, more than 22 volumes of Kilvert diaries were destroyed. Only three volumes were retained from burning. These missing volumes undoubtedly would have contributed greatly to our understanding of rural culture, including much folklore gleaned from old parishioners. The evidence we do have from him, relating to yew trees and other tree traditions suggests we have lost a lot.

A mermaid tamed by yew and a rowan pin in Marden, Herefordshire

> Marden church in former times stood close to the river, and by some mischance one of its bells had been allowed to fall into it. It was immediately seized by a mermaid who carried it to the bottom and held it fast, so that any number of horses could not move it. According to some, the people of Marden were told by a 'wiseman' how to recover it; others said that the bell itself gave instructions from the bottom of the river. At any rate, a team of white Freemartins [sterile female cows] was to be attached to the bell with yokes made of yew wood and bands

of 'wittern' [rowan] and it was to be drawn up in silence. The instructions were followed and the bell hoisted up on to the bank, with the mermaid asleep inside it. But in his excitement, one of the drivers called out:

'In spite of all the devils in hell,
Now we'll land Marden's great bell.'

This woke the mermaid, who darted back in to the water again, taking the bell and crying:

'If it had not been
For your wittern (rowan) bands
And your yew tree pin,
I'd have had your twelve free-martins in.'[9]

This Marden bell story exemplifies the strength and magic of the yew (and rowan). The parish of Marden is close to the modern Welsh border and this tale may contain residual Welsh-Irish influences from the time when most of Shropshire and Herefordshire was still Welsh. A 33ft (10m) girth yew was historically recorded at Marden churchyard, which also has a famous well. The role of the 'wiseman' in the Marden mermaid tale, may be paralleled with the role of the 'conjuror' in the following Welsh tale of 'Twm and Iago in the Forest of the Yew Tree', collected in 1880.[10]

Twm and Iago in *Ffridd yr Ywen*, 'The Forest of the Yew', in Powys, Wales

A tradition is current in Mathavarn, in the parish of Llanwrin and the Cantref of Cyfeillioc, concerning a certain wood called *Ffridd yr Ywen*, 'The Forest of the Yew', that it is so called on account of a magical yew tree which grows exactly in the middle of the forest. Under that tree there is a fairy circle called 'The Dancing Place of the Goblin'. There are several fairy circles in the Forest of the Yew, but the one under the yew in the middle has this legend connected with it.

> Many years ago, two farm-servants, whose names were Twm and Iago, went out one day to work in the Forest of the Yew. Early in the afternoon the country became covered with so dense a mist that the youths thought the sun was setting, and they prepared to go home; but when they came to the yew tree in the middle of the forest, suddenly they found light all around them. They now thought it too early to go home, and decided to lie down under the yew and have a nap.
> By-and-by Twm awoke, to find his companion gone. He was much surprised at this, but concluded Iago had gone to the village on an errand of which they had been speaking before they fell asleep. So Twm went home, and to all enquiries concerning Iago, he answered, 'Gone to the cobbler's in the village.' But Iago was still absent next morning, and now Twm was cross-questioned severely as to what had become of his fellow-servant. Then he confessed that they had fallen asleep under the

yew where the fairy circle was, and from that moment he had seen nothing more of Iago.

They searched the whole forest over, and the whole country round, for many days, and finally Twm went to a *gwr cyfarwydd* (or conjuror), a common trade in those days, says the legend. The conjuror gave him this advice: 'Go to the same place where you and the lad slept. Go there exactly a year after the boy was lost. Let it be on the same day of the year and at the same time of the day; but take care that you do not step inside the fairy ring. Stand on the border of the green circle you saw there, and the boy will come out with many of the goblins to dance. When you see him so near to you that you may take hold of him, snatch him out of the ring as quickly as you can.' These instructions were obeyed.

FIGURE 47
Twm and Iago in the
Forest of the Yew.
WIRT SYKES 1880

Iago appeared, dancing in the ring with the *Tylwyth Teg* (Welsh fairy folk) and was promptly plucked forth. 'Duw! Duw!' cried Twm, 'how wan and pale you look! And don't you feel hungry too?' 'No,' said the boy, 'and if I did, have I not here in my wallet the remains of my dinner that I had before I fell asleep?' But when he looked in his wallet, the food was not there. 'Well it must be time to go home', he said, with a sigh; for he did not know that a year had passed by. His look was like a skeleton, and as soon as he had tasted food, he mouldered away.[11]

The archaic address for this 'Forest of the Yew' is an authentic location, even if it may be a late addition to the tale. There is a village in Powys called Llanwrin, halfway between Machynlleth and Cemmaes. The *cantref* or cantred, as mentioned in the tale, means literally a 'hundred hamlets'. It was the administrative land unit in Wales and Ireland before the end of the twelfth century, when the commote was then introduced. It is now extinct, much like the English hundredal system. The court of the *cantref* was important locally for judicial matters. The Welsh prince of Powys Owen Cyfeilog granted a charter to Strata Marcella in 1170.[12] He was excommunicated by Gerald of Wales for not coming 'with his people', to meet the Archbishop upon his arrival at the commote of Cyfeiliog, that he had held since 1149.[13] This may be the same location as mentioned in the tale, though the tale may only be late Victorian romance.

This story of Twm and Iago could contain themes echoing those of the ancient Irish story, the 'Yew Tree of Mac Aingis'. The Irish tale involves a yew of the Irish fairy folk, people of the *'sidhe'*, an Irish word for magical dwellings, usually burial mounds.[14] In Wales, these same beings were called the *'Tylwyth Teg*, the fair folk, or family'.[15] These small peoples were not inherently evil and were most often helpful or merely mischievous. Tales of these small magical peoples, such as described in the Twm and Iago tale, were already established in Wales by 1190.[16]

The yew of Mac Aingis: an ancient Irish legend

This story is of great antiquity. Not only is it of interest as an early tale of a special yew tree: it is also considered to be the earliest recorded story from Ireland involving a harp. This same yew tree is also mentioned in another text as a Wonder Of Ireland; it is described in a poem ascribed to Cuan Ua Lothchain (d. 1024) which describes three famous yews of Ireland.[17]

This tale of a magical yew tree is recorded in several versions, many of them certainly originating over a thousand years ago. The tale is preserved in very old language in the *Book of Leinster*, a twelfth century compilation. The tale is thought to have been taken from the *Psalter of Cashel* written by Cormac Mac Cuileannain,[18] the king-bishop of Cashel (d. 908). Oilioll Oluim, mentioned in the text, was the ancestor of the great families of south and north Munster, was king of the province, died after a long reign, in 234 AD.[19]

The fairy harper mentioned in the text, Fer Hi, may be a personified deity. W. J. Watson states that Fer Hi, meaning 'Man of Yew', who was son of Eogabul, 'fork or cleft in a yew-tree', were probably yew deities. Eogabul was a king of the 'sid of Knockainy' where grass was burnt every Samhain, where his son, Fer Fi, 'Man of Yew', was to play his music.[20]

> At a certain time Eoghan, the son of Oiloll Oluim, and Lugaidh Mac Con, his stepbrother, set out to pay a visit to Art, the son of Conn, monarch of Erinn. Conn was their mother's brother, who was then on a visit in Connacht, for the purpose of receiving some bridle-steeds from him.
> Now, as they were passing over the river Maigh or Maigue, at Caher-ass, in the county of Limerick, they heard music in a yew tree over the cateract and saw a little man playing there. After that they returned back

to Oilioll with him, that is, with the little man whom they took out of the tree; because they were disputing about him as to who should have him, so that Oilioll might give judgement between them. He was a little man, with three strings in his *timpan*. 'What is your name?' said Oilioll.

'Fer-fi, the son of Eogabhal', he said.

'What has brought ye back?' said Oilioll.

'We are disputing about this man.'

'What sort of a man is he?' said Oilioll.

'A good timpanist', they said.

'Let his music be played for us', said Oilioll.

'It shall be done', said he. So he played for them the crying tune (*Goltraighe*), and he put them to crying and lamenting and tear-shedding, and he was requested to desist from it. And then he played the laughing tune (*Gen traighe*), till they laughed with mouths so wide open, that all but their lungs were visible. He then played the sleeping tun (*Suantraighe*) for them, until they were cast into a sleep (so deep, that it lasted) from that hour till the same hour the next day. He then went away from them to the place whence he was brought [i.e. back into the yew clump] leaving a bad feeling between them, such as he particularly wished should exist.

The bad feeling which the little timpanist left between the stepbrothers arose not so much in regard to himself, as about the ownership of the wonderful yew tree in which he was found, and which appeared to have sprung up spontaneously by necromantic art for their misfortune. [21]

Wood-Martin states that:

the little man was one of the Tuatha De Danann race from the neighbouring hill of Knockany (Cnoc Aine). The famous Tuatha De Danann lady, Aine, from whom the hill takes its name, had been some short time previously abused, and herself and her brother Eogabhal slain in a fit of anger, by king Oilioll Oluim, and was to have revenge for this deed that the little timpanist, Fer-fi, the son of Eogabhal, raised up the phantom yew tree at the falls of Caher-ass, in order to excite a dispute between the sons and stepson of Oilioll. In this he succeeded to the full. Oilioll awarded the yew tree to his own son Eoghan, and Mac Con charged him with partiality, and challenged him, with all his forces, to a battle, at a time to be fixed afterwards.' Huge battles ensued and six sons of Oilioll including Eoghan Mor and much of the forces of Munster were killed. So the little timpanist, Fer-fi, had ample revenge for the death of his father and his aunt.

A more modern translation of the tale has been produced by C. Matthews, who provides some other details. The yew is called a 'wonderful, poisonous, handsome tree', created at Ess Mage of the great clans. According to C. Matthews, Mac Con claimed the old wood and the green growth, all that he could see. Cian claimed it whole, from the seed, both the straight and crooked growth.

Eogan, claimed it entire, all that grew above the ground, and all that grew below. Each stalwart fellow claimed the whole tree for himself. The ensuing conflict is also named, as the Battle of Mag Mucrama.[22] On Tuesday the battle of 'Mag Mucrama of the red grasses' was fought, 'the heads of Ireland fell'. Art Mac Conn, High King of Ireland fell, as did the seven fine sons of Ailill. Wounded Lug Laga slew Art Mac Conn the Fair and Benne Britt of the Britons. Mac Con and Ferchess mac Comman and Sadb, daughter of Conn fell, 'from the venom of the beautiful yew'.[23]

This tree was revered and feared:

> It is no tree but an apparition of the *sidhe*, its nature is not of this world; not of wood is its trunk, but of an horrific gloom. The tree gave shelter from the cutting winds, enough for three hundred warriors; its seasoned wood would have been sufficient for a house, it was a protection against all dangers. It is mysteriously hidden by the people of the *sidhe* with artful skill. Only one in a hundred is unlucky enough to find it; then it is everlasting discovery of misfortune. From north and south fell warriors, from the venom of the russet-boughed yew; from east and west they fell – do not seek further to ask me why.[24]

The Scottish Glaistig yew

In a Scottish tale recorded from an oral tradition in *circa* 1891, a female fairy of a common type, called a *Glaistig*, was recorded as having lived in a yew. On the coast of Morvern, a mountain tract, called Garlios, stretching along seven miles, from the Sound of Mull to Kingairloch, was haunted by a *Glaistig*, fairy woman, who herded sheep and cattle. 'Tradition said she was small but strong, taking refuge at night in a particular yew tree (*craobh-iuthair*), which used to be pointed out, to protect herself from wild animals that prowled over the ground.' In this legend she out-rowed a local man rowing to Lismore in his coracle, whereupon she disappeared from his view, having much embarrassed him.[25]

Tales of hangings from a yew

A yew at Nevern in Ceridigion has a hanging myth, possibly a monk.[26] Crowhurst in Sussex had a reeve hanged from its famous yew in the time of Harold, who once owned the manor.[27] A reeve at that time had a significant judicial role, administering the hundred court. This may imply the yew was a court of the hundred yew, as justice and execution were often conducted in the same vicinity as the court.

In Scotland, recorded at Mains Farm, Kincardine, Perth, near the ruined Kincardine Castle, there is an ancient yew named 'Jeddart Justice'. The origin of the name is obscure but there appears to have been a lynch legend, 'hanging first, trial afterwards'.[28] In Scotland in 1550, a Jeddart staff was a military weapon with a four foot steel blade and a spike. Other castles in Scotland, like in the walled garden of Hunterston Castle have yews reputed to be over 600 years old.

The head of a virgin hung from a yew near Halifax, Yorkshire

There are several documented hangings from yews, including the legend of the naming of Halifax mentioned in Gough's *Camden*. The veracity of this etymology of Halifax may be queried, since it is folklore. The tale was old in 1789. A. Chetan and D. Brueton traced the Halifax yew story to Camden in 1586.[29]

> A certain priest, as they call him, had long been in love with a young woman without success, and finding her virtue proof against all his folicitations, his love suddenly changing to madness, the villain cut off her head, which, being afterwards hung upon a yew-tree, was reverenced and visited by the common people till it began to corrupt, every person pulling off some twigs of the tree. The tree, stripped of its branches, maintained its reputation for sanctity among the credulous, and the vulgar fancied the little veins spread between the bark and body of the tree were the maiden's identical hairs. A pilgrimage was established for the neighbourhood hither, and such a concourse came that the little village of Horton grew into a large town, and took the new name of Halifax, '*Hali-fex*', q.d. 'Holy hair', signifying hair among the English on the other side of the Trent.[30]

This etymology is not acceptable today other that as an antiquarian curiosity.

Trees of Trystan and Esyllt

This Welsh version of the Arthurian tale of Tristan and Iseult has clear affinities with the Irish tale of Diarmuid and Grainne. Many authorities have suggested a Pictish origin for a legend perfected in south-east Wales, in perhaps the tenth century.[31] A sixteenth-century Welsh manuscript exists wherein Trystan falls in love with Esyllt, wife of March ap Meirchion. March complains to Arthur and a series of musicians and the Hawk of May encourage Trystan to attend the court of the king. Trystan is thus brought to Arthur and promises to obey the king. Arthur arranges a compromise: he decides one of the rivals must have Esyllt during the leafless period, the other having her when the leaves are on the trees. March ap Meirchion is offered the choice. He chooses the leafless period because the nights are longer, and Essylt, overjoyed, sings a stanza saying that the holly, ivy and yew always have leaves, so March loses Esyllt forever.[32]

The yew in Anglo-Saxon documents

B. Griffiths has studied various Anglo-Saxon documents in great detail, and has translated several passages that mention yew. The diversity of text styles studied by him, results from the diverse early medieval cultures in these islands, an amalgam of influences of Roman, British, German, Danish and Norwegian. Though valued, the yew is not accorded exceptional respect in the texts. In a mid-tenth century Saxon charm against the 'Water-Elf Disease', thought to be measles, causing 'discolouration of nails and watery-eyed aversion to light', yew-berry is one of many British plants, like wormwood and comfrey, listed as ingredients.[33] A medicinal recipe including a yew berry must have been a powerful treatment.

The yew is appreciated in practical ways in most Saxon era manuscripts. An old English rune poem has a verse on the properties of yew wood:

> Yew is on the exterior an unsmooth tree,
> Tough, firm in the ground, a keeper of fire,
> with roots undertwined, a joy (to have) on the estate. [34]

'A keeper of fire', is also recorded in another document, presumably implying its suitability for kindling. Another text from the twelfth century, states that, 'Yew is the greenest of trees in winter: it is liable to crackle as it burns.' [35] None of these records refer to planting yews, only to making use of their qualities.

Riddle 55 from the Exeter Book, a late tenth-century text,[36] involves yew, with other woods, to make a 'wolfs-head tree', 'in a hall where warrior's drink'. A wolf's-head tree is explained as meaning possibly an outlaw gallows tree. This is one of the few unresolved Saxon riddles in the book. Some recent research suggests that the answer to the riddle is mead drinking vessel and barrel. A maple cup (or mazer) with a yew barrel, made with staves of 'hard yew'.[37] This description emphasises its durable nature.

The link with warriors mentioned in the riddle is further cemented by other Anglo-Saxon references. Though Anglo-Saxon yew bows are very scarce in European archaeology, a verse of an Anglian Old English rune poem in Old Norse does celebrate yew wood, relating to bows:

> A bow (yew) is for nobles and for every man,
> a joy and an honour; it is fine (to the view) on horseback
> firm in its place, an item of battle equipment. [38]

An Icelandic rune poem states, '*Yr* (yew) is bent bow, and (also means) brittle iron, and arrow's giant.' [39] The Saxon link between bow and yew is emphasised by the links between the early Scandinavian hunter deity Ull, his abode in the yew dales and his association with bows. This deity was familiar to the Swedes, Danes and Germans during the Saxon era of Britain. Udale, in Cromarty (first recorded in 1578) is thought to be a Norse derivation, '*y-dalr*', yew-dale.[40] The Scandinavian god Ull, who lived in a yew dale, was likely to have been worshiped by many Scandinavian settlers in early medieval Britain. Cumbria has Ivegill, 'deep narrow valley of the river Ive, an old Scandinavian name meaning yew stream.[41]

This evidence suggests that some Scandinavian and Germanic settlers in early medieval Britain would have had a sincere regard for yew: for its roles in carpentry, medicine and religion, though other timber types, like oak and ash were equally important. In the only mention of a living yew, in a Anglo-Saxon text the tree is described as 'firm in the ground', probably referring to the difficulty of cutting it down or its resistance to storm damage. The range of different uses of yew, from many different Anglo-Saxon sources, celebrate a useful tree, in a practical sense.

The yew in early Irish traditions

The yew features in many early Irish tales, including stories that had previously passed down through oral traditions. Irish tales were first transcribed by church scribes, who blended the traditional stories with their Christian values. Many Irish tales frequently involve kings, poets and even the fabled druids of early Ireland. Some of the earliest Irish stories involve magical characters that are partly based on native deities. The records of such traditions, ritual and belief from early Ireland are unlike those surviving today in France, England and Wales. The Roman, Anglo-Saxon and later settlements of France, Wales and England obscured and disturbed most vestiges of similar traditions.

The 'native' tales surviving from Wales are few. In Welsh tales one often has only an echo of many themes paralleled in greater detail in the Irish texts. Many pre-tenth century regional Welsh kingdoms were founded by Irish families,[42] so there may well have been shared storytelling traditions. Surviving Irish annals, records and tales are therefore uniquely important, as their influence may have been great on early British mainland populations. Irish influences had reached the Humberside region long before 200 BC.[43] The role of the yew in the later legends and histories of Ireland may be read for clues as to how the yew was perceived within contemporary early societies throughout the British Isles.

In many early Irish texts the yew, its berries and wood, are often associated with royalty, tradition and magic. The social hierarchy that is described was established by the time of the Roman invasion of mainland Britain and survived in Ireland into the fifth century AD. P. Mac Cana has argued that 'given the pivotal role of sacred kingship in early Irish society, it is hardly surprising that the mythology, and to some extent the ritual, of sovereignty bulks large in the extant literature, even if trimmed of some of their most uncivil features'.[44] The yew features in many early tales of Irish sovereignty. The celebrated Irish historian J. Carney considered that the most important evidence of survival of native traditions in Irish literature were the 'oral archives of the kingship of Tara'.[45] The kingship of Tara and Munster, as will be shown, was inextricably linked to the yew in several early accounts.

The Settling of the Manor of Tara
This tale is directly concerned with this famous royal palace site and it involves a yew of symbolic importance. The story is said to involve the High King,

Diarmuid mac Cerball, who reigned from 545 to 565. In this famous story, nobody is keen to apportion the land around Tara and the oldest, wisest man is sought to arbitrate the dispute. In front of the kings of East and West Meath, poets and druids, a wise man is found. He is named Fintan mac Bochra, a grandson of Noah, who has survived 'the deluge', by staying on a high place in Munster. This figure is the oldest and wisest man in Ireland. He recounts the history of Ireland, but then is asked how good his memory really is. The ancient figure of Fintan answers by telling them a story about a yew tree.

> I passed one day through a wood in West Munster: I brought home with me a red berry of the yew tree, which I planted in the vegetable-garden of my mansion, and it grew there until it was as tall as a man. I then took it out of the garden, and I planted it in the green lawn of my mansion; and it grew in the centre of that lawn until an hundred champions could fit under its foliage, and find shelter there from wind, and rain, and cold, and heat. I remained so, and my yew remained so, spending our time alike, until at last its leaves all fell off from decay. When afterwards I thought of turning it to some profit, I went to it and cut it from its stem, and I made from it seven vats, seven *keeves*, and seven *stans*, and seven *churns*, and seven *pitchers*, and seven *milans* (i.e. an *urna*), and seven *medars*, with hoops for all. I remained still with my yew-vessels, until their hoops all fell off from decay and old age. After this I re-made them, but could only get a *keeve* out of the vat, and a *stan* out of the *keeve*, and a mug out of the *stan*, and a *cilorn* (*pitcher*) out of the mug, and a *milan* (an *urna*) out of the *cilorn*, and a *medar* out of the *milan*; and so I leave it to Almighty God, that I do not know where their dust is now, after their dissolution with me from decay.[46]

E. O'Curry wrote that the ancient, ancestral figure Fintan is the 'cultivator and craftsman of the yew', and that 'the first household vessels in Ireland were made out of the timber of this tree'. He adds that, the account of Fintan arriving at Tara provides valuable archaeological evidence in, 'the list it contains of the different household utensils of the earlier ages'.[47]

In the same tale Fintan cites a story from the earliest times, to illustrate ways Tara was settled and divided in the past. He introduces a character called Trefuilngid Tre-eochair, 'a primal ancestral figure' who brings a branch, with three fruits, 'these are the fruits which were on it, nuts, apples and acorns in May-time'. He needs no food from the party of people, for 'the fragrance of this branch which is in my hand will serve me for food and drink as long as I live'. This branch in other sources involving St Finnian (who lived *circa* 550) is named as the 'Immortal food of the Gael'.

After copious descriptions of territories, the figure leaves Fintan, 'some of the berries from the branch that was in his hand, so that he planted them in whatever places he thought it likely that they would grow in Ireland. And these are the trees that grew up from those berries: The Ancient Tree Of Tortu and The Tree Of Ross (a yew), the tree of Mugna and the branching tree of Dathi, and the ancient tree of Uisnech.'[48] These trees are discussed further in detail as at least one, Eo Rossa, was a yew. Once the trees become ancient Fintan recites a long poem,

> I see clearly to-day
> In the early morn after uprising
> From Dun Tulcha in the west away
> over the top of the wood of Lebanon.

Another verse continues,

> Bile Tortan, Eo Rosa,
> one as lovely and bushy as the other.
> Mugna and Craebh Daithi to-day
> and Fintan surviving. [49]

He resolves the boundary matters by setting up stones, marking the five territories just as Trefuilngid Tre-eochair had set them. In one version, the story ends with Fintan borne away to Paradise, 'as Elijah and Enoch', to 'some secret divine place'.

Five legendary tribal trees of Ireland

Tree-centred traditions seem to have evolved gradually in Irish culture, with many types of trees being accorded great status by the tenth and eleventh centuries. Long before the arrival of St Patrick, there were well-known regional centres in each of the five provinces of Ireland, where recurrent tribal symbols, including tribal trees, were found. 'At Uisnech and Tara 'not only did the provinces and their kingships converge on these centres and fuse together, but there was an assemblage of symbols, as a hill, a stone, a palace, a seat, a tree, a well, a fire – and they were places of contact with the supernatural world.'[50]

The famous sacred trees of Ireland were often located at the inauguration sites of the early Irish regional kingdoms. 'Society in fifth and sixth century Ireland, Wales and Scotland, was of small independent tribal kingdoms, with a rural, hierarchical and familial character.'[51] According to P. Mac Cana, the trees at such centres were, a talisman and *crann bethadh*, a 'tree of life',[52] that embodied the security and integrity of the kingdom.

Watson notes that only trees of 'full forest stature' could be used for this role. According to Irish records only four tree types qualified for this. The yew, the ash, the oak and the elm.[53] Elm was considered generally unsuitable because of hollowing and branch loss. This seems strange, as the ash, yew and oak could also be said to suffer in this way. Many scholars have said that the yew was a tribal symbol in early Ireland.[54] C. Matthews states that 'the ancient trees of Ireland were focal points of tribal meeting and were thought to possess memory and to have the power of witness. Trees were central emblems of tribal continuity.'[55] Several of these important trees, such as the famous 'Yew of Ross', were described as yews.

The five sacred trees in the Settling of the Manor of Tara 'grew at the inauguration site of the king as a symbol of sacred wisdom and sovereignty. Fitting into certain schematic divisions of Ireland, trees like this marked the centre of the tribal territory, where it stood as an *axis mundi.*'[56] B. Raftery lists four known tribal centres that had trees as ceremonial features. He adds that these important features, leave little trace in the archaeological record and are of certain 'Pagan Celtic' character and that similar tribal tree practices are seen in early settlements in France.[57]

The sacred tree called the 'Yew of Ross' is particularly well documented. 'Eo Rossa which also grew in Leinster, stood at what is now Old Leighlin, County Carlow.' This tree was certainly a yew. The tree of Ross fell north-east as far as Druim Bairr.[58] The sites where Irish sacred trees were reported to fall is always far from the site of rooting. It is suggested that some regional symbolism was vested in this apparent anomaly. The 'Yew of Ross', was said 'to be the offspring of the tree that is in Paradise'. It 'brought lasting virtues to Erin, and filled its plains with its fruit; for as each berry of it fell to the ground and the next berry ripened, and the flood ripened it without destroying it.'[59]

The 'Yew of Ross', did not die of natural causes. The Life of St Laserian describes a group of clergy, desiring the wood of Eo Rossa. They 'dared not cut it outright, but took turns in fasting and praying ...' The most devout man's prayers, those of St Laserian, 'brought the tree down'. St Laserian is said to have given St Moling enough timber from Eo Rossa to roof his oratory,[60] founded near the modern settlement of St Mullin's in the county of Carlow.

O'Curry suggests that, in the seventh century, the 'Yew of Ross' was a 'great ancient yew tree',[61] which implies a locally significant role for the tree prior to the arrival of the early saints. The 'Yew of Ross' features in the twelfth century texts, *The Rennes Dindshensas* which records great natural features in Ireland and their naming. These texts were recorded in many different versions. The *Dindshensas* contain some residues of traditional Irish beliefs that may, in part, stretch back to Iron Age traditions. The description of the 'Yew of Ross' is a song of praise to a regional sacred tree, implies many things about the role of this particular tree in this Irish region.

Tree of Ross, a King's Wheel, a Prince's Right, a Wave's Noise, Best of Creatures, a Straight Firm Tree, a Firm Strong God, Door of Heaven, Strength of a Building, the Good of a Crew, a Word Pure Man, Full Great Bounty: The Trinity's Mighty One, a Measure's House, a Mother's Good, Mary's Son, a Fruitful Sea, Beauties Honour, a Mind's Lord, Diadem of Angels, Shout of the World, Banba's Renown, Might of Victory, Judgement of Origin, Judicial Doom, Faggot of Sages, Noblest of Trees, Glory of Leinster, Dearest of Bushes, a Bear's Defence, Vigour of Life, Spell of Knowledge, Tree of Ross. [62]

Many of the lines are open to interpretation. 'A King's Wheel', is said in some cases to be his breast-brooch. 'Renown of Banba' is 'Ireland's Renown'. The lines concerning faggot of sages, judicial doom, word pure man and judgement of origins may be associated with local roles of the Irish druids or filidh, later called poets. This famous 'Yew of Ross' was also recorded as half the answer of a riddle. In the ancient text called *Imtheacht na Tromdhaimhe*, Marbhan confounds Dael Duileadh, one of the professors of the great bardic institution by asking 'which are the two trees whose green tops do not fade til they become withered?' Dael could not answer and the answer was given as 'The two trees whose green tops do not fade are Eo Rosa and Fidh-Sidheang, namely Holly and Yew,'[63] naming two famous specimens including the yew of Ross.

Eo Mugna, another famous tribal tree, apparently stood in ancient Leinster, at a place now identified as Ballaghmoon, County Kildare. *Eo* 'most oftenest connotes the yew (but) it may also mean a tree in general'.[64] The oak is often associated with this tree. It fell south to what is now Garryhundon, County Carlow. This felling involved a group of poets. Eo Mugna was felled by poets because the king Aed Slaine, who was murdered in 600 AD,[65] refused them a request and thereby proved his own ineligibility to rule and they felled the tree to show their disgust at his actions. Like the saints these poets 'cast and chanted their incantations', the most powerful words felling the tree, according to one account, the words of Ninine, master-poet, did the task, perhaps empowered with the facility to cast spells.[66] This compares directly with the story of St Laserian and his prayers felling Eo Rossa.

The human factor, of poets, priests, invading Danes and local forces, all accounted for the destruction of famous trees in Ireland. The felling of special trees is described in the *Annals Of Tigernach* ascribed to the year 1151. 'A great raid by Ruadri Hua Conchobair and by the Sil Muredaig, into Munster; they burned the trees of Port Rig, the best that were in Ireland, and carried off many people and kine' (cattle). Port Rig is often translated as a 'king's residence'.[67] Under the year 982 the 'Annals of the Four Masters', record that the bile of Magh Adhair 'was cut after being dug from the earth with its roots', by Mealseachlainn of Meath.'[68] Magh Adhair, now Moyre, near Tulla, was the inauguration site of the people known as the Dal gCais.

The yew in the Cattle Raid of Cooley

Though Professor K. H. Jackson suggested that some early Irish myths, especially the 'Cattle Raid Of Cooley', might be perceived as being 'a window on the Iron Age',[69] this view is not generally accepted by historians today. Still, such tales and manuscripts are the earliest texts we have yet surviving in the British Isles and some texts have been compared to Iron Age archaeological material by some recent scholars, such as B. Raftery. When discussing his own archaeological excavations of the Iron Age roadway at Corlea, Raftery found that the methods and materials of wooden trackway construction, as preserved by both the peat bog and the manuscripts compared favourably.[70] The eighth century tale of the Cattle Raid, containing yew references twelve centuries old, may perhaps represent vestiges of material even older still.

The Cattle Raid of Cooley is set in the district south of Carlingford Lough in County Louth. The tale forms the centrepiece of Ulster's celebrated eighth-century cycle of tales. The cattle of this raid were imbued with mythological symbolism. In the first few pages of the tale, the king Conchobar, uncle of Cuchulainn, is described with his retinue at Emain Macha, a royal house known as the 'Red branch'. The king's house is vast, 'one hundred and fifty inner rooms … the houses and rooms were panelled with red yew'.[71] This description associates yew with ancient Irish royalty. In a poem-story ascribed to Flann Mainstretch (who died in 1056) in the mid-twelfth century *Book of Leinster*, yew also features as royal building material, at the foundation of a king's house. 'Frigriu of Fothart', 'noted above the field of exercise for his great force', built a house of 'red yew, bent after splitting, with pure unwrought mass of silver of gold of bronze'.[72] This palace was built in the stronghold of the O'Neill dynasty. As will be discussed further, the use of yew as ornamentation of the palaces of chieftains across Ireland is a persistent, seemingly Iron or Bronze Age tradition.

In the Cattle Raid of Cooley, the magical head-hunting warrior Cuchulainn, visits a prophetess called Scathach. 'After three days the girl told Cuchulainn, if he really wanted to learn heroic deeds, he must go to where Scathach was teaching her two sons Cuar and Cat, and give his salmon-leap up to the big Yew tree where she was resting, then put his sword between her breasts and make her promise three things: thoroughness in his training, a dowry for his marriage, and tidings of his future – for Scathach was also a prophetess.'[73] Cuchulainn met her on a mound, where she was reclining '*in* the great yew-tree', according to another version.[74] Cuchulainn is mentioned in another tale as trysting with a magical royal figure, the goddess Fand, 'in his own country by the yew-tree at the head of Baile's strand'. This being a place on earth where they could meet safely, her being a deity, the pearl of beauty and wife of Manannan, the Irish Sea-god.[75] These yews of Irish legend imply magical as well as royal associations.

The inauguration of the first king of Munster under a yew

The region of Munster has been described as 'the primeval world, the place of origins', and the west coast of Munster was the site of mythical invaders, like 'Banba and Fintan, mythical ancestral figures thought to have survived the flood by staying on a height in West Munster, called Tul Tuinde, according to Fir Bolg divisions of territory.[76] In west Munster, at the great regional centre Cashel, stood a ceremonial yew from the time of the first king.[77]

This capital of Munster, like Tara, had a stone, well, fire, seat, palace and a tree, in order to function as a tribal centre of legendary Irish history. 'Great centres had similar concentrations of symbols. For example, some of the principal features of Cashel, capital of Munster, may be gleaned from two tales. The first tells of the return of Conall Corc to Munster after a sojourn in Scotland. On that day, the swineherd of Aed, King of Muscraig, was tending his swine and at night told the king of a wonderful sight he had seen. He saw a Yew tree on a rock and in front of it an oratory with a flagstone before it and angels ascending from the flagstone and descending on it. The vision was interpreted by a druid: the place (Cashel), would be the residence of the kings of Munster forever, and the kings would be the descendants of the first man to kindle a fire under that Yew tree ...'[78]

Lucas noted that 'the stone is, of course, the Rock of Cashel in Tipperary, now crowned with a cluster of ecclesiastical ruins'.[79] An early reference comparing the king to a golden tree of Munster is from 'A stanza of a poem in praise of Aongus Mac Natfraoich, king of Munster (d. 489), quoted in the Annals, contains the line, 'Died the branch (*craobh*), the spreading tree of gold (*dosbhile noir*).'[80] Here, the tree is personified as the dead king himself.

Yews and Irish royalty

MacDermot, Lord of Moylurg, of County Roscommon, who died in 1458, was written about in a Scottish-Irish verse between 1430 and 1458, by Giolla CriostBruilingeach.[81] In the poem, he is compared with a stick of yew, as a 'manly very generous timber', whereas Maguire, the King of Fermanagh, was compared to a 'rotten alder brake'. The poem continues in a similar fashion, one 'a beautiful man of noble lineage', the other compared to 'an old, outlandish starveling cripple'. Yew and alder are compared at the outset and end of the long poem, both times the yew is a complimentary comparison, epitomising the qualities of a good king.

Kings and yews combine in a story recorded *circa* 1160, called 'The Dream of Oengus'. Oengus, is a divinity, son of deities Boand and the Dagdae. He is described as having a dream of a beautiful woman from the province of Connachta, called Caer Ibormeith, meaning 'yew berry'. Oengus encourages his family to help get hold of this woman. She turns out to be a daughter of the King Ethal Anbuail, the king of the Sidhe, people of the otherworld mounds. Head-hunting ensues, to a place called Cruachu, in a bid to get Ethal to give his shape-changing daughter Caer Ibormeith away.[82] Oengus and Caer Ibormeith met and were then transformed at Samhain, a seasonal Celtic festival of great importance. Caer Ibormeith, meaning 'yew berry'[83] is clearly a magical, otherworldly, royal woman and her name may be of no mean significance.

Yew berries were clearly highly prized in early Ireland. In the 10th century Irish poem 'The King and the Hermit', Marvan the brother of King Guare of Connaught, commends the yew berry highly as food.[84] Another early Irish source records 'Excellent fresh springs – a cup of water, splendid to drink – they gush forth abundantly; yew berries bird cherries ... Beer with herbs, a patch of strawberries, delicious abundance, haws, yew berries, kernels of nuts.'[85]

In the celebrated early tale 'Niall of the Nine Hostages' (who is said to have flourished between 379–405) the yew becomes an unexpected feature of his trial of kingship before he became accepted as king. This trial was set for several men. Fergus, during a trial, accidentally picked up a stick of yew without recognising it, when collecting a bundle of firewood. Fergus was punished for failing to recognise the value of the yew, a prized timber not for kindling. This mistake made him ineligible and he was pronounced sterile and therefore unsuitable for kingship, hence the proverb, 'a stick of yew in a bundle of kindling'.[86] No flaws would be allowed,[87] as the god-king 'Nuada of the silver hand' found out; he had to replace his arm to regain his eligibility.

In 1897 Lowe sceptically recorded a tradition concerning a king of Ireland who defeated the Vikings, and a yew. It seems an authentic early record, perhaps from Irish annals. 'Tradition is again at fault in the case of a tree at Yew Park, in Clontarf, County Dublin, where is a fine specimen, 12ft in girth, of which the owner, H. Brougham Leech, Esq., LL.D., writes, "It is surrounded by young shoots; it presents the appearance of a tree in the midst of a small plantation." Lowe noted that this dense shade prevented shoots occurring on the original trunk. 'The branches project horizontally, and touch the ground, and then, without taking root, strike upwards again. The circumference of the shade is 76 yards ... About forty years ago a portion, including part of the trunk, fell out owing to the weight of snow after a snowstorm.' 'Tradition would make it nearly 900 years old and says that Brian Boru, king of Ireland, died under it at the battle of Clontarf, in which he defeated the Danes on Good Friday, in the year 1014.'[88] This king is perhaps identified with the tree as a tribal symbol.[89] Brian Boru was the leader of the Dalgais, when they attacked the Vikings in Clontarf in 1014 and also had contributed to the decline of the *Eoganact* dynasty of Cashel.[90] It is interesting that another Irish tale cites Brian Boru offering a reprieve to a relation of his, king Mailmora, after finding him hiding in a yew, after a lost battle.

Lowe was sceptical of accepting a yew of 12ft having such a great age, without himself having viewed the condition of the tree. Yet his correspondent clearly states it lost a portion of trunk forty or fifty years ago. This implies the trunk was once larger, perhaps by a great amount. This could well be the Brian Boru yew of the tradition, and it may still survive today. The fragment specimen could easily be of this age and being a 12ft fragment need not affect its longevity. Fragment specimens can be less than half the size of the original tree and usually carry evidence of antiquity in the character of wood and hollow decay, that is never present in a more typical 10–13ft (3–4m) girth yew. Survival of famous Irish trees into the present day has been mostly prevented by extreme demands on timber stocks, for eighteenth- and nineteenth-century industrial purposes.

The yews of Suibne, the mad poet-king

According to Irish tradition, 'Suibne was King of Dal nAriade.'[91] This area is also known as Dal Riada, bordering on the sacred lake of Loch Neagh. It included parts of County Antrim and County Down. This territory includes many of the places that the poet-king hid, often inside trees. Some of these were yew trees. Suibne knew where these trees were in churchyards and woods around his Kingdom. He had one place that he most adored, Glenn Bolcain that had many fine yews.

His feral story is apparently sparked by an incident involving St Ronan, who cursing him, gives him the habits of a bird, though not the appearance of a bird. He is sentenced to live among the treetops, often with periods of human lucidity. In his tale, when battle joined noisily, Suibne sprang up in a fearful frenzy, settling in a yew far from the battlefield. Suibne soon flew to Glenn Bolcain. 'It was there madmen used to abide when their year of frenzy was over, for that valley is always a delight to madmen. Glenn Bolcain has four gaps to the wind and a lovely fragrant wood and clean-bordered wells and cool springs.' In this tale yews are found at this place and Suibne is associated with the yews. He remained for some time, then flew to a well, at Cluain Cille, on the border of Tir Conaill and Tir Boghaine. He went to the well for watercress and water. Then he went into the old tree of the church.'[92]

Suibne uttered a long poem about his plight. 'Suibne of Ros Earcain ... a crazy madman', ... 'I am the crazy one of Glenn Bolcain,' ... 'Frosty wind tearing me, already the snow has wounded me, the storm bearing me to death, from the branches of each tree.' He returned to Glenn Bolcain after seven years of wandering. 'Though I live from hill to hill on the mountain above the valley of yews, alas I was not left to lie with Congal Clain.'[93] Suibne came to Ros Ercain where he had a house and settled in a yew tree there. Loingsechan tries to capture him but he fails. Loingsechan explains that Suibne's parents have died, and his brother, daughter, 'is the needle of the heart', and son, 'the drop that brings a man to the ground'. Upon hearing this last misfortune, he fell from the yew tree. He heard a hunting call that signified an army, he heard a stag bellow and then he spoke of the trees of Ireland one by one 'praising oak, hazel, alder, blackthorn, sloe-trees, watercress, apple, quicken, briar', with verses for each.

Of the yew, he says, 'yew-tree, little yew-tree, you are conspicuous in churchyards', He continues with verses on ivy, holly, birch, aspen, then oak. 'My aversion in woods – I conceal it not from anyone – is the leafy stirk of an oak swaying evermore ... Glen Bolcain, my constant abode, twas a boon to me ... many a night have I attempted a stern race against the peak. "The old tree of Cell Lughaide wherein I sleep a sound sleep ...'

In Benn Boirche Suibne came to where Moling was. He sat at the fountain and ate watercress in front of Moling's student. Moling says, 'O mad one, that is eating early', and a long debate ensues. Moling says during the debate 'delightful is the leaf of this book, the psalter of holy Kevin'.

'More delightful is a leaf of my yew in happy Glen Bolcainn.' Suibne replies.

Suibne is speared by a swineherd of Moling, thinking he was having an affair with his wife. Suibne while dying confessed his faults and accepted the body of Christ.' [94] In this tale Suibne was associated with the yew, his sanctuary, a symbol fit for a legendary poet-king.

Poets, druids and the yew

'In the Lives of the Saints, Irish tales of poets and kings, even the druids and their magical arts figure conspicuously; as for instance in the *Tripartite Life of St Patrick* (a ninth-century text) and in the earlier memoir of the saint, by Muirchu, as well as in Adamnan's *Life of Columba*; and not less so in the historical tales.' [95]

In a variety of ways, trees, especially yews, are involved in these early tales of sovereignty, magic and heroism. The druids and poets were essential to the ritual of sovereignty in Ireland. Irish historian P. Mac Cana argues that 'oral literature and learning enjoyed high status long before the coming of writing' ... 'they were cultivated and controlled by an elitist and privileged class of semi-sacred savants and poets: the druids and, subsequently the filidh, who were closely associated with religion and ideology and had their close counterparts in Wales, and, earlier still, among the Celts of Britain and the Continent.[96] Both continental and Irish druids claimed superiority to kings, unless of course, they held both offices.[97] Later, kings would become bishop-kings in the same way. Regional kings needed their druids to officiate at the seasonal religious ceremonies that made their own kingships sacred.

An authority on the Irish literature of this period, Dr J. Pokorny, has explicitly stated that the Irish druids are never mentioned in connection with the oak. Their holy tree was the yew.[98] O'Curry also held this opinion.[99] Irish scholar P. W. Joyce lauds O'Curry as the 'first to describe in detail the Irish druids from native sources'.[100] J. A. MacCulloch stated that 'the Irish druids attributed special virtues to the hazel, rowan and yew, the wood of which was used in magical ceremonies described in Irish texts'.[101]

According to O'Curry, the Druid's 'wand of divination' was usually made of yew.[102] The druids of Ireland are usually recorded as having carried wands of yew and they were also noted as kindling druidic fires with yew fag-gots.[103] An Irish source, of around 1100, notes that 'Patriarch of long-lasting woods is the yew, sacred to feasts as is well known.' [104] This description of the yew as 'sacred to feasts', is spoken by an ancient king of the otherworld *sidhe*, Iubdan, king of the Lepra folk. Yew's sacred role at feasts may indicate the significant presence of yew at seasonal festivals that were widely celebrated in early Ireland, ceremonies that often involved sacred kingship. The story of the inauguration of the first king of Cashel in Munster was foretold by a druid in a vision. He foretold that the first to light a fire under a yew there, by a rock, would become the person to start the hereditary royal line in Cashel. Kings, magic and yews seem inextricably combined in many Irish myths and legends.

Yew *Ogam*

In most Irish tales the wood used for inscribing *Ogam* (a symbolic language written in carved notches) was the yew, although oak and alder were also used. Some scholars maintain that *Ogam* was used by continental druids, as a symbolic language, possibly as early as 500 BC, though its written form became widely known in the fourth century AD.[105] It is probably a tribute to the durability and general importance of yew wood in Irish courtly culture that it seems to have been valued for this special purpose.

In one Irish tale, a King of Tara called 'Conn of a Hundred Battles' (who ruled over Northern Ireland in the second century AD) was presented with yew *Ogam*, with prophetic content. In the story he was with his poets and druids when he first encountered the magic stone of Fal. They then become lost in fog, then they found a golden tree, cups of gold and a girl in a crystal chair, with a golden crown, amongst other items. A phantom explains that he is not a phantom, but the god Lugh. He recites his ancestry back to Erimon son of Mil of Spain, and tells the King, 'I have come to tell you the span of your sovereignty and that of every prince that will come of you in Tara for ever.' 'When he had named every prince from the time of Conn onwards, Cesarn wrote them down in *Ogam* on four staves of yew.'[106] There are other examples of yew staves bringing prophecy in early Irish tradition and W. J. Watson noted yew as mentioned in several *Ogam* inscriptions.[107]

Ogam plays a role in the tragic folklore tale of Baile and Aillinn. This tale is similar to The Ballad of Fair Margaret and Sweet William, a tale of tragic lovers wherein a briar grew out of his grave and is united with a rose grown from hers over the churchtop in a symbolic reunion of lovers. Baile and Aillinn 'died from the false tidings conveyed to them out of spite that each had been unfaithful to the other. A yew sprang out of Baile's grave and an apple out of the grave of Aillinn. These trees were afterwards cut down and made in to writing-tablets, in which stories of courtships and lovers were inscribed, in *Ogam* script by the poets of Leinster and Ulster. On one occasion these tablets were brought into the kings presence at the same time, and as he held them they sprang together and were bound together, 'as a woodbine to a green twig', so they that they could never again be separated. They were laid up in the king's treasure-house at Tara, but eventually perished in a fire which destroyed the palace.'[108]

Records of yews at Irish church sites

As in Wales, yews in Ireland have long been associated with churches of early Celtic saints. When Giraldus Cambrensis (Gerald of Wales) arrived in Ireland in 1184 he recorded some yews he saw there. 'Yews, with their bitter sap, are more frequently to be found in this country than in any other place I have visited; but you will see them principally in old cemeteries and sacred places, where they were planted in ancient times by the hands of holy men, to give them what ornament and beauty they could.' [109] Ancient yews in 1184 suggest an early, pre-tenth century, established tradition, as with the regional tribal plantings.

As we know, very few old yews survive in Ireland today. Myross church in County Cork, Ireland is said to still have very old yews. The yews at Tullyallen, 'beautiful hill', churchyard, and at Drogheda in County Louth may also be ancient. The churchyard is bordered by wells and a pump with 'huge stones in the churchyard, ruined churches and old yews'.[110] There are few sources available relating to large churchyard yews in Ireland today. It seems that few of the yews mentioned by Giraldus still survive.

The yew of Newcastle churchyard in Dublin is said to hold Ireland's oldest surviving yew, though there is only one 21ft (7m) girth specimen known in the whole of Ireland, at Glencormac in County Wicklow.[111] Unlike in England or Wales, where the reverse is true, in Ireland there are fewer living old yews than than dead ones in historic records. Many factors have conspired against the survival of the Irish trees, including fierce timber shortages. However, Ireland does have a fine historic archive that indicates great yews at churchyards were, historically at least, once a noteworthy feature of the landscape.

The Glendalough Yew in County Wicklow was:

an immense tree, and shaded from the sun and storm, not only the ruins of a small church under it, but the greater part of the churchyard. Samuel Hayes was informed, on undoubted authority, that on one hot summer's day, when this tree was in its full beauty, the agent for the bishop to whom the church belonged had all its principal limbs and branches cut off close by the trunk and sold. About forty years afterwards, when Samuel Hayes saw it [*circa* 1794] the trunk was decaying at the heart, and a holly was growing up through one of its fissures.[112]

Many forces have conspired against the survival of ancient Irish holy trees. In Leinster there was an account of a group of elms having replaced older yews. 'A writer of the last century, referring to a rock bearing the impressions of St Cuimin's hands and knees in Rutland townland, Kilcomin parish, County Offaly, states, 'There are three very remarkable elm trees called 'Cuimin's trees', still growing around and close to this rock. It is said they were planted many years ago by the owner of the property, in place of three yew trees of unknown age, but straight as an arrow, which had previously grown in the same spot, and which were supposed to have been planted by the saint himself. These last mentioned trees, however were, as was also said, cut down, as the result of a wager between the owner of the place and a neighbouring gentleman.'[113] It is interesting that the yew is often associated in Ireland with early Irish saints like Cuimin and Patrick, just as the oldest yews in Wales often occur in those churchyards and wells associated with early Welsh saints.

The yew has been embedded in the landscape of Ireland in many ways. An entry in the Irish annals under the year 1162 states, 'The monastery of the monks of Iubhar-Chinntrechtra was burned, with all its furniture and books, and also the yew which Patrick himself had planted … It will be observed that the name of the monastery incorporates the word "yew" (*Iubhar*) and it was doubtless named after the sacred yew itself. The place is of course, Newry, Co. Down, which even in its anglicised form contains the "yew" (*Iubhar*).' [114]

Another source, from 1015, cites Iubhar Arnun, that means 'Arnun's yew', associated by one scholar with Cell Iubhair, 'church of the yew', in Kilconnell barony, County Galway, now anglicised Killure. [115] Though the yews may have perished, they live on in their place-name legacy.

Although apparently very frequent the association of yew with churches was not unique; many churches at this time bore the names of different types of British tree that grew by them. An interesting note from Lucas supplies another early, established yew site. 'A tantalisingly brief notice from the year 1077 seems to bear witness to yet another sacred grove being attached to a monastic site: Gleann Uiseann, with its yews, was burned. Gleann Uiseann, now Killeshin, County Carlow, was the site of an early monastery.' Lucas lists other situations where such woods were places where early monks would deliberately position their oratories and suggests that for these yews at Gleann Uiseann to receive special attention in the annals, it must have been 'a sacred grove'. [116]

The *Chronicum Scotorum* records a story from Clonmacnoise in 1013. 'Great winds in the autumn, the like or equal of which have not been witnessed in these times, by which the great oak of Regles-Finghin [a name of a church on the site] at Cluain-muc-Nois, was prostrated.' A century later another great tree was brought down at Clonmacnoise, a yew of great size. 'In January 1149, lightening took effect on the yew tree of Ciaran, so that it was through the power of men it was extinguished; and it killed 113 sheep under the yew.' Here, as elsewhere, the tree is called after the founder saint whom later tradition represents as having planted it with his own hand. [117] It has been suggested by Macalister that Clonmacnoise (like Iona) was formerly a pagan sanctuary. [118] Though the oak and yew of the site may not be dated with any certainty, it is clear that they were likely to have been standing there before 800.

An eighth-century text by the Venerable Bede recorded that when 30 Anglo-Saxon monks fled the island of Britain, in the sixth century, Colman founded a monastery for them at Magh Eo, 'plain of the yew', a place-name that today gives the county of Mayo its name. [119] It is said that the tree formerly existed in the vicinity of the modern Mayo Abbey. This tree must have survived some considerable time before and after the arrival of Colman, suggesting that the yew was a valued feature of the Irish landscape from at least the sixth century onwards.

Several early Irish saints valued the yew. It is said that St Kieran was the first saint born in Ireland. In one early manuscript, a pupil of his, St Cellach, the son of a king, is torn apart by four creatures, resulting from a prophecy of Kieran, which said that if Cellach neglected his studies, he would die. One of the four creatures is a kite that lived in Cluain-eo's yew, in the parish of St Kieran. Cellach's church is also described as a 'beautiful yew-shaded church', in a manuscript dated to 1411, describing the sixth-century saint's cell. [120]

There is evidence of Columba praising the yew of the Black Church, in Manus O'Donnell's *Life of Colmcille* of 1532:

And in especial above in the yew tree in front of the Black Church, where Colmcille and his saints were wont to chant the hours, were there ten hundred angels keeping guard, as Colmcille, or Columba, hath said in these quatrains:

> This is the Yew of the Saints
> Where they used to come with me together.
> Ten hundred angels were there,
> Above our heads, side close to side.
> Dear to me is that yew tree,
> Would that I were set in its place there!
> On my left it was pleasant adornment,
> When I entered the Black Church.[121]

Yew was also often used inside Irish churches. O'Curry cites a poet who lived between 1220–1250, who describes the cathedral of Armagh founded by Saint Patrick:

> The church of Armagh, of the polished walls,
> Is not smaller than three churches;
> The foundation of the conspicuous church,
> Is one solid, indestructible rock.
>
> A capricious shrine of chiselled stone,
> With ample oaken shingles covered;
> Well hath its polished sides been warmed,
> With lime as white as the plumes of swans ...
>
> Upon the arches of this white-walled church,
> Are festooned clusters of rosy grapes,
> From ancient yew profusely carved;
> This place where books are read so freely.

O'Curry says he 'quoted these verses in order to show that down to the middle of the thirteenth century the cathedral of Armagh, though its walls were built with chiselled stone, was covered with oak shingles or boards in place of slates; and in the second place, that the arches at least, of that venerable historic edifice were festooned with clusters of the ripe vine-berry, carved from ancient yew, and apparently coloured to imitate the natural grapes, probably some part of a more ancient roof of the church itself. From this curious fact, for, as a fact I am satisfied to receive it, we may easily imagine in what way the yew was applied to the adornment of the ancient palace of the Royal Branch at Emania, the Great House in Rath Cruachain, and many others which may be met with in our ancient writings.'[122] It may be noted that the yew described by O'Curry as having been used inside Armagh Cathedral,

148

being of purple colour, may have lain for centuries in peat bogs; purpling is often very pronounced in carved bog yew items.

The peoples of Ireland have had a complex relationship with the yew tree over thousands of years and the surviving documents leave a fascinating impression of elements of that history. It has been used as a royal tribal symbol, as a religious symbol for early saints, and in the decoration of churches and royal houses, valued equally by kings and saints.

The oldest of woods

In many Irish sayings the yew is referred to as the 'oldest of woods, or 'of most ancient fame'. The royal associations with yew in many Irish texts may be partly based on the longevity of the yew, a quality with which their kings wanted their own dynasty identified. Longevity in creatures and trees is an admired attribute in many early cultures. Lists of ages of things, denoting the passage of time, working back to the beginning of the world, are a recurring cultural theme.

Many versions of the list below found in England and Ireland have the yew as the oldest living thing in the list. The Irish versions are probably the oldest surviving examples. This Irish version is from the *Book Of Lismore*:

> A year for the stake
> Three years for the field
> Three lifetimes of the field for a hound
> Three lifetimes of the hound for a horse
> Three lifetimes of the horse for a human being
> Three lifetimes of a human being, the stag
> Three lifetimes of the stag for the ousel
> Three lifetimes of the ousel for the eagle
> Three lifetimes of the eagle for the salmon
> Three lifetimes of the salmon for the yew
> Three lifetimes of the yew for the world from its beginning to its
> end.[123]

And from the Book of Ballymote:

> Three fields to a tree
> Three trees to a hound
> Three hounds to a horse
> Three horses to a human being *
> Three human beings to a deer
> Three deer to a chain
> Three chains to a salmon
> Three salmon to a yew
> Three yews to an age
> Ever living God.[124]

CHAPTER NINE

Yew: An Archaeological Perspective

The yew re-colonised Britain soon after the last Ice Age retreated, some 10,000 years ago. Trees with this kind of heritage are celebrated as 'native' British trees. These 'natives' are the only types of wood one can typically find in British archaeological contexts. The 'native' tree species, including oak, elm, ash, hawthorn and yew, have had a continuous impact throughout the history of human settlement in Britain. The yew tree is generally considered the only British tree to have retained its earliest known name, a name used by re-Roman populations. The word 'yew' was probably even understood by many Iron Age and Bronze Age populations of Britain, as demonstrated by surviving early Gaelic and Welsh forms.

The yew seems to have had a wide distribution across Britain during many prehistoric phases. Unfortunately, wood and other plant remains are usually rare survivals at prehistoric archaeological sites. Stone and metal more often survives and the record is known therefore to show a bias against wooden evidence due to its organic, transient nature. Even so, British yew-wood finds in prehistoric contexts are exceptional in terms of variety and quality. As archaeobotany flourishes, these finds are developing ever more attention.

Yew wood finds of the Palaeolithic period

There are yew wood artefacts found in Britain that date from long before the last Ice Age, from the Palaeolithic period. This stretches from *circa* 2.4 million years BC to *circa* 240,000 years BC. The yew lance tip found at Clacton, Essex, is still the earliest wooden tool yet found in the whole of Britain. It was discovered in 1911 and is known to be from the Middle Pleistocene Holsteinian warm stage. This dates the yew spear to *circa* 400,000 years BC. Palaeolithic expert Dr Hartmut Thieme has remarked on the extremely limited evidence for the organic component of Lower and Middle Palaeolithic technologies. Until recently, when several silver fir branch javelins from this era were discovered by him,[1] the yew lance tip found at Clacton was one of only two wooden tools *ever* found from this huge period of earth history.

The only other wooden artefact ever found from this early prehistoric period, was a lance from Lehringen, Lower Saxony, in Germany. It was excavated from the Late Pleistocene warm stage deposits, in 1948, and it too is made of yew wood.[2] It was found between the ribs of a now extinct tusked mastodon.

This is thought to have been deposited around 200,000 years BC. These extraordinary yew finds demonstrate the common usage of yew as a European spear material around a quarter of a million years ago, predating the much later Neolithic usage of yew across Europe, when yew was sought for making bows.

Yew bows

In 1994, a walker called Dan Jones found a yew bow in good condition in a peat bog, in Carrifran Glen, near Moffat in Dumfriesshire. The 'Carrifran bow' was dated to 'about 6,000 years'[3] age, *circa* 4000 BC. It is now exhibited at the National Museum in Edinburgh. Another Neolithic yew longbow in very good condition, was found close to underlying mineral layers, in a peat bog type situation, at Rotten Bottom, Games Hope Burn valley, Tweedsmuir Hills in Dumfries and Galloway, Scotland. It was dated by the Oxford Radiocarbon Accelerator Unit to 5040 +/− 100 B.P.[4] (B.P. denotes before present, always taken as 1950, the benchmark 'present' by which the radiocarbon dating system operates. The +/− refers to possible error margins.) This dating indicates a 'normal', or 'calibrated' date of *circa* 3000 BC for this Neolithic yew bow.

Continuity of prehistoric yew bow usage in Britain is suggested by the later yew bow found in Cambridge, also in peat deposits, in 1855, by General Pitt-Rivers. Now in the Pitt-Rivers museum in Oxford, this early Bronze Age find was dated at Cambridge University facilities at 3680+/−120 B.P.[5] This indicates a 'normal' date of *circa* 1700 BC. At Edington Burtle, Somerset Levels, a segment of yew bow was excavated, dated by Cambridge facilities at 3270+/−110 B.P.[6] This indicates a 'normal' date of *circa* 1200 BC. It was about 5ft (1.5m) long.

These bows from Neolithic and Bronze Age Britain were carved from split timbers from trunks of fairly mature yews. Unlike later yew bows, they did not use sapwood as a feature of the bows. The bows are carefully made in D-section, curving round the archer when drawing the bow, with the flat side facing away from the body. With a notch cut at the top, to secure the bowstring, the prehistoric bows were, like some yew bows in 1500,[7] sometimes covered in lattices of webbing, to perhaps strengthen the bow. A fine example was preserved from Meare Heath in Somerset, from the Somerset levels. (Radiocarbon date: 2690 BC +/-120 years (calibrated).) Its webbing is beautifully preserved. It was *circa* 6ft (2m) in length when whole.[8]

'Prehistoric yew bows have also often been found in Switzerland, Austria and Germany.[9] The 'Iceman' found preserved by a glacier near the Austro-Italian border in 1991, had preserved with him a fine unfinished yew bow. His possessions included a copper-headed axe, complete with an unusual yew wood 'knee-joint' shaft, utilising the natural joint where branch meets trunk.

It has been suggested that he was killed by an arrow, shot from a similar bow to the one he was carrying. The frozen situation allowed archaeologists to examine for the first time a man preserved with a bow and arrows that he had made himself in *circa* 3300 BC.[10] Typically for prehistoric yew bows, the bow-maker had removed the sapwood. Splinters from the bow wood were found to have 16 annual rings per centimetre (0.39in), showing very slow growth indeed.[11] Brenda Fowler suggests that this density of rings does not occur locally there today on cliffs or in valleys, suggesting the Iceman used and perhaps cultivated the dense growth deliberately, using obscure techniques.[12] I would suggest that the ring density would probably have occurred naturally enough, in very old pockets of yew woodland, taking many centuries to form, which rarely survive today. The dense shade produced, especially on rocky exposed sites, would often encourage such dense ring growth.

Such sites could have been periodically visited by local people for the bow wood they sought, using renewable coppicing techniques, taking suitable young growth from within the most shaded places in the wood. The yews at such locations must have been protected and cropped by people who saw the yew timber as a uniquely useful material for making the bow, an essential technology. The bow was an instrument at the centre of these early European societies. The sources of material for its manufacture must have been highly prized sites.

The usage of yew as a bow material, throughout the Neolithic period to the end of the Bronze Age, across Europe, seems not inconsistent with the perspective of Colin Renfrew, when considering the heritage of European ancestry:

> Many people believe that the first Celtic inhabitants of Britain and Ireland arrived in these areas somewhere around 2000 BC from a homeland elsewhere in Europe. Others would prefer a date fifteen hundred years later. I shall argue that there is no evidence whatever for that, and the Celtic languages may have much longer antecedents in the areas where they are now spoken. Such an argument has the effect of removing the hiatus between the British and Irish Neolithic periods – the time of the megalith builders and of the art of Irish passage graves – and the succeeding phases of prehistory. It means, if we accept it, that our origins – and in general this is claimed here for other parts of Europe too – go very much deeper. These lands have been our lands and the lands of our forefathers for very much longer than is widely thought.[13]

Strands of cultural continuity could apply to technology and ritual behaviour, involving native animals, trees and plants, developed from the Neolithic and Iron Age, continuing into Roman Britain and beyond.

However, no examples of bows from Iron Age and Roman Britain – a huge period of time spanning a thousand years – seem to have been found. Although probably used as a bow material by some Anglo-Saxons, from *circa* 400–900, evidence for this is also slight, though some mentions of yew bows do occur in Anglo-Saxon literature.[14] We know that even by 1188 the yew bow was unknown in Wales. Gerald of Wales commented, 'The bows they use are not made of horn, nor of sapwood, nor yet of yew. The Welsh carve their bows out of the dwarf elm trees in the forest. They are nothing much to look at, not even rubbed smooth, but left in a rough and unpolished state. Still, they are firm and strong. You could not shoot far with them; but they are powerful enough to inflict serious wounds in a close fight.' These short elm bows were ideal for forest skirmishes, such that forests were always considered the harbours of thieves and outlaws at that time.[15] Interestingly, in parts of Europe where yew was not used for Neolithic bows, elm was frequently preferred.

A brief consideration of later yew bows is appropriate, as they (perhaps) represent linear successors of the prehistoric examples. Continuity of usage may be masked by the perishable nature of wood in most archaeological circumstances. The prehistoric bows were 'self' bows, made of a single piece of yew, which differentiated them from most later 'longbows', which had a pronounced grip and horn fittings.

After the end of the Bronze Age, the first example of a known surviving British yew bow seems to come rather late. The yew crossbow from Berkhamsted Castle, of 'early thirteenth century date', is only 4ft (1.2m) long.[16] One characteristic of most yew bows of this period is that they seem roughly made, often half-finished in appearance. Until the raising of the *Mary Rose* Tudor ship, which contained many yew bows in a good state of preservation, we had more specimens of bows surviving from extreme antiquity, found in ice and peat, than we had been able to assess from the entire medieval period. The *Mary Rose* sank in 1545 and the yew longbows on it averaged nearly six feet (two metres) in length.[17]

The glorious era of celebrated yew usage, between 1200 and 1650, is documented copiously in various texts, like G. A. Hansard, *Book of Archery*, 1840 and other books by R. Hardy[18] and R. Wilkinson-Latham.[19] John Lowe[20] cites many charters and statutes pertaining to protecting and planting yews passed by various monarchs in Britain during this period. Researchers today have had difficulty in tracing proof of the charters, although in 1897, John Lowe was honorary physician to the Prince of Wales. This could have positioned him well for such researches.

One yew wood that is likely to have been planted and polled for late medieval bows is at Cherkley Court, near Leatherhead in Surrey, where in 1897 over 90 acres of yew remained.[21] In 1999 T. Hindson studied ring counts from dead stumps there, brought down in the storms of October 1987. He assessed the ages of some of the older yew stumps, at *circa* 600 years, indicating a probable bow plantation. Their boles give their story away, as their twisted swollen forms show that these trees were probably pollarded several hundred years ago. Many of these trees have been lost since Lowe's day.[22]

Most authorities on bows are in general agreement that much Spanish yew was imported for battle bows between 1300 and 1650, as English yew was found to often be brittle and knotty, even having had a lower value than the Spanish yew.[23] Although the tradition of English yew bows lives on today, the English yew bow had generally already fallen long into disuse by the time of the publication of Evelyn's *Sylva* in 1644.[24] It may be fair to say that the most culturally significant era for bows made of English yew occurred between 4000 BC and 1000 BC, a period when bows were an essential survival tool. Yew seems to have been almost exclusively used for bows for this entire period of British prehistory.

Bronze Age boats of oak, moss and yew

In 1938, 1940 and 1963, E. V. Wright excavated the 'Ferriby boats', all found in the Humberside region. They were buried in thick blue clay in the intertidal regions, on the northern foreshore of the river Humber. All in very good condition, all were made of oak, moss and yew. 'Ferriby One' was measured as being 43ft 6in long. These Ferriby boats were all caulked (sealed) with moss and were stitched with yew 'withies' (lashings). A sample of yew withy, from Boat One, was tested by Cambridge University at 3312 +/- 100 B.P.[25] Another yew withy from that boat was dated at 2980 +/- 55 B.P,.[26] and another, 3020 +/- 40 B.P.[27] This indicates a normal (or calibrated) dating of *circa* 1100 BC. Recent radiocarbon dating on one of the boat withies, after removal of preservative agents, suggests that they were built at an earlier time of around 2030 BC.

Several other examples of this yew withy, oak plank and moss-caulked boat type, from the same period, have been excavated. In 1992, a Bronze Age boat was excavated in Dover, Kent. The oak boards were found to have been stitched with yew withies, and were caulked with moss. This boat was 49ft (15m) long, similar in length to Ferriby One. The Dover boat had a scrap of Dorset shale found in it, suggesting it was possibly a sea-faring craft. It was in a good state of preservation, and was dated to *circa* 1300 BC.[28]

Another prehistoric boat found in Britain, from yet another part of the country, also involved yew withy lashings. This boat fragment, with oak board and yew withy, was found in a former bed of the river Neddern, a tributary of the Severn, near Caldicot Castle in Gwent. It was dated to *circa* 1500 BC.[29] This evidence all suggests a continuity of materials and design (moss caulking, yew lashings and oak planks) possibly for sea journeys, involving places as diverse as Dover, South Wales and Humberside, between 1600 BC and 1100 BC. As with the yew bows, this evidence suggests organised communication across these European prehistoric societies; they valued yew in precise roles, in order to sail and hunt, and to develop their culture.

Yew leaves and branches in a Bronze Age barrow

In February 1930 A. S. Newall excavated Barrow 85 in Amesbury, Wiltshire.[30] He recorded that the parish boundary of Boscombe and Amesbury, 'passed over the centre of the barrow'. This may, therefore, have been a Anglo-Saxon boundary feature.

Inside the round barrow, Newall found a grave, lined with yew wood and leaves.[31] The barrow was constructed of reddish soil layers, 'not caused by heat', alternated with white chalk. 'It is possible that the whole body had been laid in and covered by yew branches and mosses.'[32] According to Newall, this primary burial, in which carbonised yew wood remains were found, was probably of a local chieftain. The bones examined showed little dental wear, a large skull and an age of 50 or so years for the man. The burial also contained sections of red deer antler, with a knife. Wrapped in 'abundant' yew leaves and 'abundant' sphagnum moss was a flat-grooved bronze knife, with remnants of a sheath and handle.[33] The estimate of date for this burial, based on the bronze knife, was 1700–1300 BC.

These barrow finds provide very rare, perhaps unique, evidence of yew in a context of Bronze Age burial ritual in Britain. The presence of yew seems to have been an important feature, and even the colour of the wood seem relevant. The foliage of the yew turns bronze-red when dried. The bronze knife would have been red-gold in colour. The alternating layers of white chalk, with reddish soil, red yew and red deer antler, suggest a colour symbolism that occurs elsewhere in the traditions of Bronze and Iron Age Britain.[34]

Bronze Age yew figure from Ralaghan, Ireland

'The Ralaghan Figure' is a finely carved yew sculpture, standing about 45in (1135mm) high. The figure was recovered from turf-cutting in the parish of Shercock, County Cavan, Ireland. Grains of quartz-type granules were found in the 'pubic' hole. The Ralaghan figure once had a square plinth, now lost, that its pointed feet stood in. 'Probably associated with a shrine, there is no doubt of its religious application.'[35] It is dated to a normal (or calibrated range) of 1096–906 BC, *circa* 950 BC.[36] This figure has much in common with the Late Bronze Age yew figures called the 'Roos Carr Assemblage', found near Holderness, Humberside. This pair of sites with similar anthropomorphic yew figures and quartz elements, watery deposition and very similar carved 'pubic holes', could suggest a similarity in custom over at least a four-century period.

Five late Bronze Age figures from Roos Carr, Humberside

'The Roos Carr Assemblage', is a group of five Bronze Age yew figures standing 14–16 inches (350–400mm) high (Plate 13). They were found in 1836 in the parish of Roos Carr, by labourers working in a storm drain or tidal creek, an ephemeral tributary of the river Humber. They were found six feet below the ground, in a bed of blue clay. The Roos Carr figures, their transport and equipment, are all made of yew. They were recently correctly identified as being made of yew not pine by wetland archaeologist Allen Hall.[37] These very rare figures have been radiocarbon dated to a normal (or calibrated) age range of 606–509 BC, *circa* 550 BC.[38]

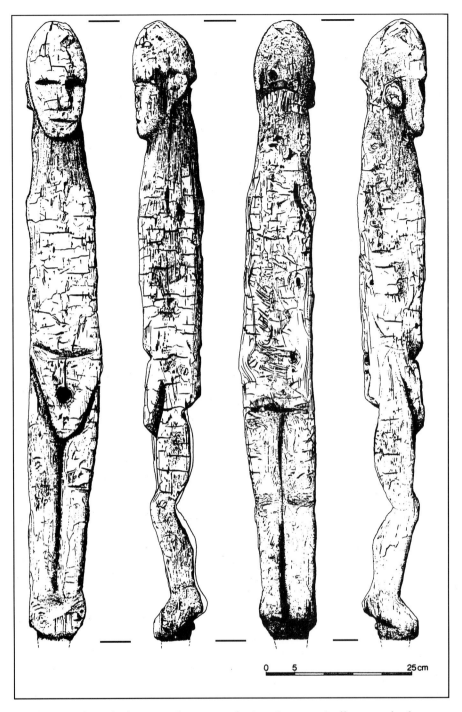

They are breathtaking in their complexity. Symmetrically carved, they are equipped with assorted items, transport and tools. The figures stare with quartz and limestone eyes. All other British prehistoric wooden figures (numbering less than ten in total) have been found without any kind of equipment. The yew figures from Roos Carr are of exceptionally fine workmanship, especially when compared to most other non-yew prehistoric wooden figures, such as the Somerset God-Dolly (ash) and the Lagore figure (oak).[39]

Bryony Coles has noted, like Thomas Sheppard in 1901,[40] that the Roos Carr figures seem to fall into a group of three and two, though a crew of four for the craft is still generally accepted.[41] Perhaps the original observation, soon after discovery, of suggesting a crew of originally eight figures may have been correct. The four figures were joined by the fifth in 1901. Undoubtedly genuine, once separated from the crew, it had spent many years in a local house where it was known as 'the ancient doll'.[42]

The Roos Carr collection has posed difficulties of interpretation since its discovery. These Roos Carr figures were found travelling in what is described as a yew wood, animal-headed 'boat'. There may have been other wooden items, perhaps a box and other pieces that were not preserved, as being too decayed to survive. Two round holed 'shields', of very different sizes, implying different uses, were recovered with the figures, with short curved yew sticks and a long-holed pole. The short yew sticks are thought to be arms, or penises for the 'pubic holes' of the figures.

Coles notes a reference to a missing 'box', in one paper, that could not be saved at the time of discovery. This box may represent the lost frame of a cart or chariot and other related pieces seem to fit this interpretation. The largest of the two round, holed 'shields' could represent a surviving chariot wheel, of a wheel type similar to prehistoric Irish wooden examples.[43] There is also a Hallstatt sixth-seventh century BC bronze animal-headed chariot that has horse heads, several passengers and four wheels. Of Celtic tribal origin, it dates from a similar time.[44]

The Roos Carr 'boat' is possibly horse-headed and its fragmented partial state allows an open-minded approach to its reconstruction. There is a reconstruction of an Iron Age chariot from Wales, showing a long timber leading to the horse that has a hole in it,[45] exactly like the one longer timber that survives from the Roos Carr assemblage. The stylised horse on the Roos Carr 'boat' suggests perhaps a vehicle pulled by a horse. There is no exact evidence to prove which pieces were lost, but the idea of another lost 'boat' is entertained as a possibility by Bryony Coles.[46] Certainly pieces are missing. Though the craft is widely accepted as a boat by the archaeological community, as many pieces were thought too decayed to keep this kind of speculation must not be dismissed out of hand. Whatever the exact nature of the transport, the incomplete pieces inevitably retain a degree of mystery.

Even the country of origin is a point of scholarly debate. Coles, like T. Sheppard in 1901,[47] has suggested a plausible Scandinavian origin. The contemporary Scandinavian evidence of animal-headed boats and conifers depicted on rocks, argued by her is persuasive. Dr Coles also noted a one-eyed aspect to some of the Roos Carr figures and that of the Ralaghan figure, being deliberate damage to left eye sockets, in each case a probable deliberate feature in antiquity. She associates these features with one-eyed Scandinavian legends (Plate 14).[48]

These one-eyed myths do, however, also occur with frequency in Irish mythology, as Balor and Fintan are one-eyed in various Irish stories. The earlier Ralaghan figure from Ireland, also made of yew, and with a similarly carved pubic hole, suggests an Irish precursor. Both the Ralaghan and Roos Carr yew figures are not weathered. Both were probably deliberately deposited in the condition they were found, in watery locations. It seems unlikely that Scandinavian archaeology could unearth as similar a figure as Ralaghan is to Roos Carr. Megaw and Megaw also present evidence for established trading links between Ireland and the Humberside region, based on excavated imported swords, dated to at least 200 BC.[49] Perhaps local Irish activity at the time the figures manufacture at Roos Carr, is as plausible as a Scandinavian origin.

The assembly and ethnic origin of the Roos Carr assemblage is still somewhat obscure. They encourage some speculation, as the prehistoric assembly of effort and materials is today physically incomplete, and therefore, incompletely understood. As suggested by N. Chadwick,[50] prehistoric figures like those from Roos Carr (and Ralaghan) may perhaps be the physical proof of what the first century classical source Lucan described as 'images of the gods, grim and rude, were uncouth blocks, formed of felled tree-trunks'. The Roos Carr assemblage was probably a kind of votive fertility deposit. Any secular purpose certainly seems difficult to conjure. Whatever their exact purpose or ethnic origin, their age and craftsmanship make this group unique and irreplaceable for the global archaeological community.

Records of prehistoric deities linked to yew

Many European countries have traditions that ascribe the status of deity to native trees. Many European countries have traditions involving the yew. The yew is a very rare tree in modern Scandinavia, so it is a surprise that there is a Scandinavian Iron Age god who is closely linked to the yew. The very early Scandinavian god, Ull, or 'Oller', whose name means 'glory', about whom little is known, was a god of the dwelling, hunting and justice. Turville-Petrie remarked on the cult of Ull, 'Their cult was so old as to be obscure by the time our records took shape.'[51] 'Ull, who lived in yew dales, among his other attributes was known to be a skilled skier, archer and hunter, and there may be a link here between living where yew trees grow and using a bow, although prehistoric bows were not exclusively made of yew.'[52] In fact, Neolithic Scandinavian bows are usually made of elm, emphasising the unlikely status of yew.[53]

Other early sources also show Ull living in a yew wood. In the Icelandic saga, The Elder Edda, Grimnir, who is the shape-changer Odin, says:

> Ull in yonder Yew-Dale
> Has made himself a mansion:
> Elf-Home for Frey in the old days
> The Gods gave us a tooth-fee.[54]

Ull was a powerful magician as well as a hunter and archer. 'Saxo talks of the god Oller (Ull) as 'such a cunning magician that instead of sailing in a ship he was able to cross the seas on a bone which he had engraved with fearful charms.' [55] At one point, Ull replaced Odin when the latter was banished for ten years by his fellow gods for having disguised himself as a woman. It is 'likely Ull was Odin in another guise, or rather that Odin was a later manifestation of the ancient god Ull'.[56] It is also recorded that Ull was a stepson of Thor in some traditions from Norway and Sweden.

This important early Scandinavian yew-related deity Ull is frustrating in its obscurity, but what remains seems to indicate a long history of respect and veneration in a wide area, perhaps indicating some circumstantial evidence for the evergreen Yggdrasil having been a yew, even though it is termed in texts as an evergreen ash:

> An ash stands, I know; its name Yggdrasil,
> A lofty tree sprinkled with bright water.
> Thence come the dews that fall on the dales.
> Evergreen it towers over the well of Urd.
> (Voluspa trans. Page 1995, 206).[57]

This is the famous tree of Scandinavian mythology that delivered Odin his enlightenment, after hanging from it for nine nights, he received the runes, having sacrificed an eye, to one of the wells beneath its roots, to gain wisdom.[58] Bryony Coles cites the writer R. Simek, an expert on Scandinavian mythology, who states that Yggdrasil has been interpreted by recent scholars as meaning 'yew pillar', as the evergreen mentioned in the above text, even though it is called an evergreen ash.[59] Interestingly, in Iceland, yew is often called *yr*.[60]

Another plausible yew-Ull-Odin link relates to the pagan temple of Odin, at Uppsala in Sweden, with its mysterious evergreen tree. It is described by J. Rattue: 'yew-tree which overhung the temple at Uppsala stood near a well in which human sacrifices were drowned'.[61] Ull was the key deity at this temple in Uppsala before worship moved to Thor and Odin. Ull place-names in Sweden were noted by Magnus Olsen, as exceeding those attributed to Thor.

Adam of Bremen described the Uppsala temple in the eleventh century:

> Near this temple is a huge tree, its branches spreading
> far and wide. It is always green, winter and summer alike.
> Nobody knows what species it is. There is also a well there
> where they have the practice of holding pagan sacrifices.
> A living man plunged into it. If he does not surface again,
> the people's desire will be fulfilled.[62]

Scandinavian archaeologist, Olsen is recorded as saying that the Uppsala temple was 'a late addition to the sanctuary. It had no natural connection with heathen religion', it was purely 'a house for the idols'.[63] John Blair suggests that the temple at Uppsala was an afterthought to the tree, and that 'here was a religion that might leave root-holes in the ground and little else'.[64] B. Griffiths adds 'a grove is recorded here, where animals and people were hung as sacrifices'.[65] This tree and well association compares well with Lucan's account of 'dark springs' at the unholy yew grove of Marseilles, destroyed by Caesar, where human sacrifices also occurred.[66]

The Roman writer Lucan recorded *circa* 39–65 AD an unholy grove of old yews that Caesar had felled near Massilia (Marseilles) in France.

> A grove there was untouched by men's hands from ancient times, whose interlacing boughs enclosed a space of darkness and cold shade ... gods were worshipped there with savage rites, the altars were heaped with hideous offerings, and every tree was sprinkled with human gore ... Water also fell there in abundance from dark springs. The images of the gods, grim and rude, were uncouth blocks, formed of felled tree-trunks. Legends also told that often the subterranean hollows quaked and bellowed, that yew-trees fell down and rose again, that the glare of conflagration came from trees that were not on fire, and that serpents twined and glided round the stems. The people never resorted thither to worship at close quarters, but left the place to the gods.[67]

Lucan's detailed information on ritual is borne out by European archaeology, which has confirmed the names of gods, the hewing of wooden idols and human sacrifice. Nora Chadwick described Lucan's testimony relating to Celtic deities as 'one of the few examples of specific agreement between classical writers and archaeological evidence'.[68] Given these excellent references we should probably accept the accuracy of his statement that these devotions took place specifically in a yew grove, for which he used the Latin word *taxus*.

These yews are described in a similar translation as, 'Fallen yew-trees often of themselves would rise; with seeming fire oft gleam'd the unburn'd trees.'[69] This process of decay and renewal in a yew wood is visible today at Newlands Corner. Yews seem to need at least several centuries of growth at least, to provide these effects in the wood, as described by Lucan. Lucan's site was probably of Iron or Bronze Age origin, like the Scandinavian god Ull, the Eburovices tribe and the prehistoric yew figures from Britain.

Lucan mentions that, 'The gods ... were uncouth blocks, formed out of hewn tree trunks.' The Ralaghan yew figure, the Roos Carr yew figures and the Euffigneix sculpture all seem to fit this description. The usage of wooden figures in ritual, described by Lucan, 'seems to be confirmed in the archaeological record'.[70] Evidence of early European Iron Age tribal shrines, such as at the Marseilles grove, has often been destroyed by later structures. 'Archaeological discoveries which relate directly to pre-Roman Celtic religion are still comparatively sparse and difficult to interpret. This is because Celtic temples were timber-built compared to the Roman structures of stone which replaced them. Even where the quantity of early finds is so great that the presence of an Iron Age shrine is certain, the massive nature of Roman building activity will frequently have destroyed, or badly damaged the earlier structure.'[71] This fact makes identifying timber remains in these archaeological contexts very difficult.

The sacred groves frequented by the Romans and Celts in Britain and France have been described by several documentary sources. These places were common features of religious life in Europe from at least 400 BC. The British population during the Roman era had a festival of Groves, the Lucaria. It was 'certainly native', suggesting a 'woodland cult and close links with the veneration of groves of the Celtic provinces'.[72] M. Green cites several European tribes with trees as symbols, including yew and alder.[73] The beech tree was worshipped as a god; altars were inscribed with 'the god Fagus' in the French Pyrenees.[74] We can postulate different tribes having different emblems based on regional features of importance, especially certain trees.

The town of Evreux, in Normandy, lies on the River Iton, a tributary of the Eure river in France. A Gaulish Iron Age tribe was based in Evreux, called

FIGURE 49
The Euffigneix
sculpture of a
probable deity of the
Aulerci Eburovices.

161

the Eburovices. It is well known that certain Gaulish tribal names, like Eburones or Eburovices, reflect a veneration for yews.[75] Evreux is still the *chef lieu* of the Eure region today. It was a Romano-Gallic temple site,[76] with which the Eburovices have links in place-name etymology. The coins of this local tribe, the Aulerci Eburovices, show motifs that 'link closely with'[77] the sandstone sculpture of a deity, combining man and boar found at Euffigneix, Haute Marne, France.

This ritual stone from northern France depicts a human figure with boar carved along its torso.[78] The coins of the Aulerci Eburovices also show a boar motif superimposed on the neck of an anthropomorphic representation. These both have been linked with the symbolism of the Eburovices tribe. (It is interesting in this context to mention that in Somerset, the village of Evercreech, has a place-name etymology of Celtic *Crug*, Hill with an uncertain first element, 'possibly Old English *eofor* "wild boar", or a Celtic word meaning yew-tree'.[79] The place-name York may equally exhibit some of this duality of meaning. Commentators suggest that the red sandstone Euffigneix sculpture represents the transition from wooden carving to stone.[80] The style suggesting familiarity with carving wood, at a site relevant to a yew tribe, is interesting. The Lucan observation of carving idols in the yew wood of Marseilles, when coupled with the several yew wood prehistoric sculptures found in British late Bronze Age ritual contexts, suggests some possible elements of continuity in prehistoric yew veneration across Europe.

Also reported as yew-based names are the Eburobriga tribe, located around Yonne (Aurolles). In Romano-Gallic inscriptions, yew appears in Ivo-magus, Ivo-rix.[81] Other places in Roman Gaul were possibly named after the yew, such as Ebromagus, or Eburomagus, now Bram (Aude), Ebeon (Charante-Maritime), and Eborolacum, now Ebreueil (Allier). These references make it no surprise that Caesar commented on the frequency of yew in Gaul.

The Eburones tribe, also named after the yew, were active in Europe at a similar time to the French Eburovices, and were based between the Maine and Rhine.[82] Evidence supplied by McCulloch suggests that the yew was the tree of death for them and that death had a certain role in its cult.[83] Caesar tells us that a king of the Eburones, Cativolcus, uncle of Arminius, ceremoniously poisoned himself with the juice of the yew.'[84] Since Eburones was the tribal name, there was symbolism in the departure of its chief using eponymous yew juice. This would be prepared from the leaves, as the berry would not have been as effective. It appears that this king's tribe was another European tribe with the yew as a tribal emblem. In Ireland there is also much medieval documentary evidence of local regional royalty also being aligned directly with European trees, especially the yew. These references to early yew place-names, tribal names and other evidence suggests that much of France and Britain in the Iron Age had great respect for the yew.

Iron Age yew artefacts from Britain

The Llanio yew head

The Llanio yew head, 3.3inches (84mm) high, was found in 1838 at a farm, when peat was being dug, in a field called Cae Gwerful, near the site of a Roman auxiliary fort.[85] The etching of this head shown here is surprisingly accurate. The Llanio head is owned by a local family. Unlike the earlier yew figures from Humberside and Ireland, this is clearly a female head, with finely plaited hair. Like the earlier Roos Carr figures, this yew head once had other portions, 'hands with part of an arm', now lost.[86] Like the other yew figures, the deep eye holes, 0.35 inches (8–9mm) deep, suggest 'some thorn-like pieces of bone or other substance, exactly fitting, or perhaps driven in'.[87] If the eyes had been made of bone, the peat would have taken them, as peat tends to consume bone almost as enthusiastically as it preserves yew wood.

M. Henig describes the style and possible use of the Llanio head, 'A female head with the coiffure of Crispina, wife of Commodius or Plautilla, wife of Caracalla. It is made of yew-wood, tough and durable, and if it was painted and set on a staff it must have been an impressive sight.'[88] The hairstyle of the Llanio head also matches quite closely the hair of a Romano-British sculpture found at Carrowburgh Roman site, also, like Crispina, dating from *circa* 200 AD. As it has not been radiocarbon dated, this is the accepted date for the head. This yew head seems as enigmatic as the Bronze Age yew figures. Other finds, excavated using modern techniques, may elicit further information concerning their exact roles of yew in Iron Age culture. It is interesting to note that the Ralaghan, Roos Carr and Llanio yew figures do not have any white sap wood.

A stone figure from this era, found at Caerwent, has sculptural similarities with the Llanio wooden head.[98] This 'seated mother' from Caerwent, in

FIGURE 50
The Romano-British ceremonial yew head from Llanio, reproduced in *Archaeologia Cambrensis* in 1850.

Wales, was discovered during a well excavation, at the bottom of the well. The figure clutches a sprig of foliage, likened by M. Green to a 'stylised conifer branch'.[90] The foliage has also been likened to palm, due to other exotic imported cultic evidence, yet the non exotic native style of sculpture may suggest that a native type of foliage is depicted. The Llanio yew head suggests that the species of wood it was carved from was carefully chosen, for a special purpose.

Yew in Iron Age Ireland

B. Raftery states that, 'while the perishable nature of timber has meant that few wooden artefacts have survived in the material record, we can assume that the inhabitants of Iron Age Ireland were intimately acquainted with the varying properties of the different tree species'.[91] Raftery comments in detail on rare evidence of Iron Age cart and chariot transport, including several yew finds associated with suspected cart-chariot apparatus, all found in wet locations, in or near Doogarymore (Roscommon).

The figure below shows one of the Doogarymore alder wood block wheels. It is unspoked, rounded alder boards are threaded by yew pins, through sleeves

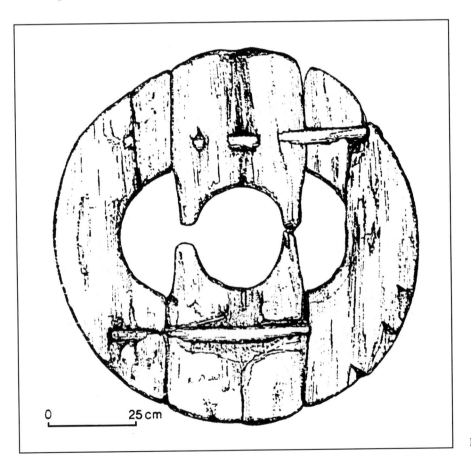

0   25 cm

FIGURE 51
An Iron Age wooden
wheel with yew
dowels from
Roscommon in Ireland.

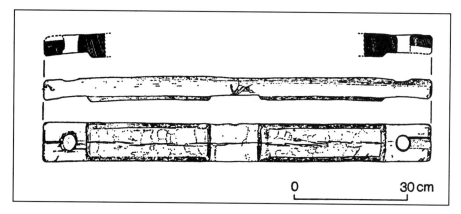

0   30 cm

of ash.[92] Alder is famous in Britain for growing with roots in water, its wood resisting decay admirably: an ideal, durable choice for wet location use.

The yew pins are described by Raftery as having been inserted with great skill.[93] These block-wheels are 'the earliest examples yet found in Ireland of wheeled transport', and are described as 'doubtless typical of wheels used in the later Bronze Age'.[94] These wheels have been radiocarbon dated to a calibrated date range of 410–260 BC.[95]

Yew dowels like these were used elsewhere in Iron Age Ireland. Raftery records the remains of a small carvel-built Iron Age boat found in Lough Lene, in County Westmeath, Ireland. It was oak planked, with transverse yew pegs through the oak planks holding mortice and tenon joints firm. Raftery expresses concerns that the age of the yew wood in the dowels, when living before being made into a peg, that may have influenced the radiocarbon dating of it. I would argue that this distortion is likely to be only between 20 and 50 years. A piece of yew from this boat was radiocarbon dated, at a normal range of 400–100 BC.[96]

Yew dowels in Irish wheels are not the only cart or chariot related yew finds from Ireland. B. Raftery records a yew bar 39 inches (99cms) long found near Doogarymore (Roscommon). Found in a wet location, it is thought to be a part of a chassis of a cart. This has been dated to *circa* 150 BC.[97]

Together, these yew finds, form a very significant proportion of the Iron Age chariot-cart evidence found in Ireland. The cart-chariots were possibly symbols of power themselves, as chariot burials in the La Tene culture in Britain and Europe suggest.[98] The use of yew may be significant not only for its physical strength, but also for its tribal symbolism. Raftery comments on the *bile*, the sacred trees of Ireland, as having been of especial importance at several key religious sites in Ireland.[99]

These numerous significant finds involving yew may perhaps be partly attributable to the exceptional resistance to decay of yew wood in wet locations. As other wood types may have decayed, the survival of yew chariot-cart materials, not showing much sign of heavy usage, rather small and deposited in wet locations, may indicate that these carts are not necessarily typical; they could have been ceremonial in purpose.

E. O'Curry cites some impressive references to the use of yew wood and suggests it had a unique status in Irish tribal society of this period. Master builders in Irish tribal society were known as *ollamh* builders, whose skills involved masonry, carpentry and other talents. These professors of crafts were accorded stipends in tribute to their skill, just as the chief professors of poetry, medicine, and law were similarly credited by the same hierarchical system. The master-builder was given great rewards, at least equal to those given to chief poets and chief teachers. In a Brehon Law tract preserved in the *Book of Ballymote* (also preserved in a manuscript dated 1391) [100] details of the traditional stipends of the master builders are recorded. Six cows were allotted for stone church building, six for wooden oratory building, six cows for mill building. The Master Builder was accorded 6 cows for '*iubroracht,* that is vessels and furniture from the wood of the yew-tree'.[101] The working of yew wood is therefore accorded an extraordinary value in this social milieu. No other woodworking skills are noted with so much value. *Iubroracht,* the working of yew wood, was considered equal to that of church building and more valuable than chariot building, which garnered two cows only. The working of yew must have embraced a wide range of objects, as it formed, with some exceptions, the material of all the most elegant articles of furniture in beds, bed-posts, buckets, cans, mugs, medars (or square mead-drinking mugs), cups and sometimes large vessels; as well as, we may fairly infer, various other articles of convenience and ornament for the houses of the higher classes of society. The stealing, breaking or defacing of this class of articles came within the range of the criminal law injury; articles made from any other kind of native wood did not.

The yew was also largely used in cornices, wainscoting, and the ornamentation of houses, from the very early times, as may be seen from the description of the palace of the Royal Branch at Emania.' [102] O'Curry states Emania stopped being a Royal house after the death of the last king in 331 AD, and therefore the tradition of ornamenting royal houses at raths in Ireland with carved yew, is clearly at least an early Iron Age tradition, already ancient in 331 AD. Another separately recorded example cites the yew as the main decoration for royal houses. Where the famous house of Rath Cruachain is described, it is said, 'an ornamental carving of red yew upon the entire of it'.

These diverse descriptions of the most spectacular legendary royal houses of all Ireland, suggest red yew was valued in many kingdoms as a symbol of wealth and tribal power.

Yew stave tankards and buckets

The prehistoric figures of Roos Carr and Ralaghan form a pair of sites that suggest a frequency of deliberate, specific yew wood use, over a wide time span and geographic distance. The Bronze Age Ferriby boats, and the Caldicot and Dover boats, suggest the repeated use together of yew withies and oak boards, over a wide geography and time scale. The Trawsfynydd bronze,

yew-lined tankard, is similarly mirrored by the Romano-British Prestatyn yew
stave, originally, but erroneously described as oak,[103] with twin holes, suggests
that fine bronze-lined wooden mugs, rarely found in the record, were often
lined with yew.

The Trawsfynydd tankard closely resembles a superior bronze, wood-lined
tankard found at Carrickfergus Castle, of similar date but unknown wood
type.[104] The rarity of such fine tankards in British archaeology is commented
on by B. Raftery. In describing the Carrickfergus tankard he stated, 'it is clearly
an imported drinking vessel, perhaps intended for the drinking of an alcoholic
beverage such as beer. It is unique in the country and is an imported piece
of the first Christian century, perhaps acquired to grace the table of a local
aristocrat.'[105] The aristocratic Carrickfergus tankard, of unknown wood type,
is described as unique in Ireland. The Trawsfynydd yew tankard must deserve
similar plaudits in Wales. Although simpler, the Trawsfynydd tankard, now
at the Museum of Liverpool, is very fine. It is 5.6inches (14.3cms) high, and
of late first-century date.[106]

An Iron Age yew stave and bronze-sheet bucket has been found in Luxem-
bourg.[107] The Welshpool pail is an example of a Romano-British yew bucket.[108]
The possibility of continuity of craftmanship skills into the early medieval
period exists as many wooden stave bronze-lined buckets made with yew have

been found in Anglo-Saxon graves at Linton Heath (Cambridgeshire) and Roundway Down (Wiltshire).[109] There are many more Anglo-Saxon examples of yew-stave buckets such as those from Sutton Hoo. At Swallowcliffe Down in Wiltshire, Finglesham in Kent and Portsdown II in Hampshire, Saxon funerary buckets made of yew were excavated from graves.[110] It is likely that other buckets, such as at Taplow, Buckinghamshire, were made of yew. H. Geake considers the yew wood and iron or bronze bound buckets found in conversion period Anglo-Saxon graves as identical in construction and style to earlier Roman era examples.[111] Most texts on the subject seem to consider wood type an unimportant feature; despite the consistency of materials. However, decay of the wood can render identification impossible. This yew usage was a widespread phenomenon, associating yew buckets and funerary ritual, over at least a ten century period across Western Europe.

Why was yew preferred for buckets and mugs? The resistance to decay of yew in damp conditions was celebrated by Gilpin, in 1791. 'Where your paling is most exposed either to winds, or springs; strengthen it with a post of old yew. That hardy veteran fears neither storms above, nor damps below.' A comment current in the New Forest, in 1838, was 'a post of yew will outlast a post of iron'.[112] This resistance to decay when wet is supported by these Romano-British, Anglo-Saxon, medieval and post-medieval stave tankard style applications for yew wood.

There were recorded in France, in 1892, 'water drinkers, who will have their water in a state of great perfection. Some native genius long ago invented a vessel which answers the requirements of the most fastidious. This is a pail-shaped receptacle of yewen wood, bound with brass bands, both inner and outer parts kept exquisitely clean. Water in such vessels remains cool throughout the hottest hours of the hottest summer and the wood is exceedingly durable, standing wear and tear, it is said, hundreds of years. The turning and encasing of yewen wood and brass-bound water-jars is a flourishing manufacture at Osse.'[113]

It is interesting to note in this context that the yew at Fortingall had pieces from it cut into traditional Scottish cups called '*quechs*'.[114] These practices all indirectly celebrate the resistance of yew to decay when wet. R. Graves refers to the yew in Ireland as making 'the coffin for the vine'.[115] The widespread early Irish legendary traditions of yew stave vats are also perhaps relevant here. S. H. O'Grady recorded some very early Irish traditions concerning the yew, 'Patriarch of long lasting woods is the yew, sacred to feasts, as is well known.'[116] The medieval Irish tale of the Settling of the Manor of Tara, involves a yew cut into many cups and vessels, perhaps used for feasts.

The uses of yew wood in the archaeological record depend on attributes of the wood for which the yew has always been appreciated: its durability, resistance to decay when wet and its elastic strength. These features enabled it to be used repeatedly for thousands of years, as a material for Palaeolithic spears, as a Neolithic and Bronze Age bow material and in the making of prehistoric boats. These roles in many prehistoric societies were absolutely crucial to survival, and represent cultural technologies of utmost importance. It is not therefore not surprising that several Bronze Age wooden figures made of yew, found in Britain, that date from before 550 BC, are believed to be religious in nature. Our prehistoric ancestors valued yew wood very highly, using it as a crucial material, to build boats, hunt with bows and drink from yew tankards. The evidence demonstrates that yew was a key timber in prehistoric Britain, for the entire Neolithic, Bronze and Iron Age periods, perhaps inspiring these cultures to make the religious yew figures, reflecting their respect for a timber that they found indispensable.

Notes

Preface

1. Rackham, O. (1976) *Trees and Woodland in the British Landscape*, J. M. Dent.

Chapter 1: Botanical Features of the Yew

1. Loudon, J. C. (1838), *Arboretum et Fruticetum Brittannicum, or the Trees and Shrubs of Britain*, vol. 4, Longman.
2. Tabbush, P. M. and White J. E. (1996), 'Estimation of tree age in ancient yew woodland at Kingley Vale', *Quarterly Forestry Journal*, 90, no. 3, pp. 197–206.
3. Wilks, J. H. (1972), *Trees of the British Isles in History and Legend*, London, Frederick and Muller.
4. Phillips, R. (1981), *Mushrooms and other Fungi of Great Britain and Europe*, Pan.
5. Hartzell, H. (1991), *The Yew Tree, a Thousand Whispers*, Hulogosi Press.
6. Hartzell, H. (1991), *The Yew Tree, a Thousand Whispers*, Hulogosi Press.
7. Graves, R. (1961), *The White Goddess*, Faber and Faber.
8. Loudon, J. C. (1838), *Arboretum et Fruticetum Brittannicum, or the Trees and Shrubs of Britain*, vol. 4, Longman.
9. Porter, N. ed. (1913), *Webster's Revised and Unabridged Dictionary*, G. and C. Merriam and Company.
10. Lowe, J. (1897), *Yew Trees of Great Britain and Ireland*, Macmillan.
11. Lowe, J. (1897), *Yew Trees of Great Britain and Ireland*, Macmillan.
12. Watson, W. J. (1926, 1986, 1993), *The History of the Celtic Place-names Of Scotland*, Blackwood.
13. Porter, N. ed. (1913), *Webster's Revised and Unabridged Dictionary*, G. and C. Merriam and Company.
14. Lowe, J. (1897), *Yew Trees of Great Britain and Ireland*, Macmillan.
15. Brueton, D. and Chetan, A. (1994), *The Sacred Yew*, Penguin Arkana.
16. Hampshire County Council Website (1999), Hampshire Treasures, www.hants.gov.uk.
17. Morton, A. (1986), *The Trees of Shropshire*, Airlife.
18. Mills, A. D. (1993, 1996), *Oxford Dictionary of English Place-names*, Oxford University Press.
19. Personal Communication, Melvyn Jones, Sheffield Hallam University, 2001.
20. Gelling, M. and Cole, A. (2000), *The Landscape of Place-names*, Shaun Tyas.
21. Aubury, J. (1719), *Natural History and Antiquities of the County of Surrey*.
22. Gelling, M. and Cole, A. (2000), *The Landscape of Place-names*, Shaun Tyas.
23. Watson, W. J. (1904, 1976, 1996) *Place-names of Ross and Cromarty*, Highland Heritage Books.
24. Mills, A. D. (1993, 1996), *Oxford Dictionary of English Place-names*, Oxford University Press.
25. Mills, A. D. (1993, 1996), *Oxford Dictionary of English Place-names*, Oxford University Press.

26. Wilson, B. and Mee, F. (1998), *The Medieval Parish Churches of York*, York Archaeological Trust.

27. Mills, A. D. (1993, 1996), *Oxford Dictionary of English Place-names*, Oxford University Press.

28. Mills, A. D. (1993, 1996), *Oxford Dictionary of English Place-names*, Oxford University Press.

29. Allcroft, A. H. (1908) *Earthworks of England*, Macmillan.

30. Mills, A. D. (1993, 1996), *Oxford Dictionary of English Place-names*, Oxford University Press.

31. Mills, A. D. (1993, 1996), *Oxford Dictionary of English Place-names*, Oxford University Press.

32. Woodward, A. and Leach, P. (1993), *The Uley Shrines*, English Heritage.

33. Watson, W. J. (1904, 1976, 1996) *Place-names of Ross and Cromarty*, Highland Heritage Books.

34. Cornish, Vaughan (1946), *The Churchyard Yew and Immortality*, Muller and Company.

35. Kermack, W. R., *Emblems of the Gael*, from Scottish Gaelic Studies.

36. Kermack, W. R., *Emblems of the Gael*, from Scottish Gaelic Studies.

37. Keating, *History of Ireland*, ed. P. S. Dinneen, Irish Texts Society, I, p. 223.

38. Lucas, A. T. (1963), 'The Sacred Trees of Ireland', *Journal of the Cork Historical and Archaeological Society*, 68, pp. 16–54.

39. Redmonds, G. and Hey. D., 'The Opening up of Scammonden', LANDSCAPES 2:1 (Spring 2001), Windgather Press.

40. Chetan, A. and Brueton, D. (1994), *The Sacred Yew*, Penguin Arkana.

41. Evans, J. D. (1988), *Churchyard Yews of Gwent*, Archangel Press.

42. Sparry, J. (1999), *Toasted Teacakes and Baked Potatoes, 31 Essays*, The Black Country Society Press.

43. Baines, D. (1822), *Directory of Yorkshire*, vol. 1: West Riding.

44. Hook, D. and Ambrose, R. (1999), *Boxley, The Story of An English Parish*, Modern Press Ltd.

45. Hampshire County Council Website (1999), *Hampshire Treasures*, www.hants.gov.uk.

46. Pigott, C. D. and Pigott, M. E. (1963) 'Late-glacial and post-glacial deposits at Malham, Yorkshire', *New Phytologist*, 62, 317–34.

47. Allen, M. J. and Gardiner, J. (2000), 'Neolithic Trees in Langstone Harbour, Hampshire', *Newsletter of The Prehistoric Society*, no. 34, April 2000.

48. Tittensor, R. M. (1980), 'Ecological history of yew, *Taxus baccata* in Southern England', *Biological Conservation*, no. 17, 243–265.

49. Godwin, Sir. H. (1975), *History of the British Flora*, Cambridge.

50. Switsur, R., Cambridge University Radiocarbon Laboratory personal communication.

51. Loudon, J. C (1838), *Arboretum et Fruticetum Brittannicum, or the Trees and Shrubs of Britain*, vol. 4, Longman.

52. Williamson, R. (1975), *The Great Yew Forest*, Readers Union.

53. Archaeology Data Service, Mansfield Depositors ID, 632013, Bolsover, Deposit ID, 650105, http//ads.ahds.ac.uk/catalogue/

54. Gough, R. ed. (1789); Camden's *Brittania* (1607).

55. Proceedings of the Worcestershire Naturalists Club (1881–1910).

56. Medical Toxicology Unit, Guy's and St Thomas's Hospital Trust, London.

57. H. Hartzell (1991) *The Yew Tree of a Thousand Whispers*, Hugolosi Press.

58. Medical Toxicology Unit, Guy's and St Thomas's Hospital Trust, London.

59. Lowe, J. (1897), *Yew-Trees of Great Britain and Ireland*, Macmillan.

60. Lowe, J. (1897), *Yew-Trees of Great Britain and Ireland*, Macmillan.

61. Lowe, J. (1897), *Yew-Trees of Great Britain and Ireland*, Macmillan.

62. Lowe, J. (1897), *Yew-Trees of Great Britain and Ireland*, Macmillan.

63. Williamson. R. (1978), *The Great Yew Forest*, Readers Union.

64. Tittensor, R. M. (1980), 'Ecological history of yew *Taxus baccata* in southern England', *Biological Conservation*, 17, pp. 243–265.
65. Lowe, J. (1897), *Yew Trees of Great Britain and Ireland*, Macmillan.
66. Loudon, J. C. (1838), *Arboretum et Fruticetum Brittannicum, or the Trees and Shrubs of Britain*, vol. 4, Longman.
67. Loudon, J. C. (1838), *Arboretum et Fruticetum Brittannicum, or the Trees and Shrubs of Britain*, vol. 4, Longman.
68. Personal communication Chris Stanley, Farmer of Camp Farm, Highgate Common, Staffs. February 2000.
69. Williams-Freeman, J. P. (1915), *Field Archaeology, As illustrated by Hampshire*.
70. Williamson, R. (1978), *The Great Yew Forest*, Readers Union.
71. Personal correspondence Appendino, G. (1998), Phytochemist, Torino University, Italy.
72. Personal correspondence Appendino, G. (1998), Phytochemist, Torino University, Italy.
73. Edlin, H. L. (1967), *Man and Plants*, Aldus Books, London.
74. Loudon, J. C. (1838), *Arboretum et Fruticetum Brittannicum, or the Trees and Shrubs of Britain*, vol. 4, Longman.
75. Personal correspondence (1998), Medical Toxicology Unit, Guy's and St Thomas's Hospital Trust, London.
76. Williamson. R. (1978), *The Great Yew Forest*, Readers Union.
77. Williamson. R. (1978), *The Great Yew Forest*, Readers Union.
78. Tittensor, R. M. (1980), 'Ecological history of yew, *Taxus baccata* in Southern England', *Biological Conservation*, 17, pp. 243–265.
79. Personal correspondence (1998), Medical Toxicology Unit, Guy's and St Thomas's Hospital Trust, Avonley rd, London.

Chapter 2: How Old are British Yews?

1. Johnson, W. (1912), *Byways in British Archaeology*, Cambridge University Press.
2. Johnson, W. (1912), *Byways in British Archaeology*, Cambridge University Press.
3. Lowe, J. (1897), The *Yew-Trees of Great Britain and Ireland*, Macmillan.
4. Lees, E. (1868), *Botany of the Malvern Hills etc.*, Simpson and Marshall.
5. Johnson, W. (1912), *Byways in British Archaeology*, Cambridge University Press.
6. Dallimore, W. (1908), *Holly, Yew and Box*, John Lane, The Bodley Head.
7. Johnson, W. (1912), *Byways in British Archaeology*, Cambridge University Press.
8. Cornish, V. (1946), *The Churchyard Yew and Immortality*, Muller.
9. Larson, D. W., Doubt, J. and Matthes-Sears, U. (1994), 'Radially sectored hydraulic pathways in the xylem of Thuja Occidentalis as revealed by the use of dyes', *International Journal of Plant Science*, 155(5), University of Chicago, pp. 569–582.
10. Edlin, H. L. (1958), *The Living Forest*, Thames and Hudson.
11. Swanton, E. W. (1958), *The Yew Trees of England*, Farnham.
12. Morton, A. (1986, 1995), *The Trees of Shropshire*, Airlife, Shrewsbury.
13. Morton, A. (1986, 1995), *The Trees of Shropshire*, Airlife, Shrewsbury.
14. Mee, A. (1944, 1966), *A King's England*, Shropshire volume.
15. Hartzell, H. Jr. (1991), *The Yew Tree, a Thousand Whispers*, Hulogosi Press.
16. Rackham, O. (1994), *The Illustrated History of the Countryside*, Weidenfield and Nicolson.
17. Anand, C. and Brueton, D. (1994), *The Sacred Yew*, Penguin Arkana.
18. Anand, C. and Brueton, D. (1994), *The Sacred Yew*, Penguin Arkana.
19. Mitchell, A. (1985, 1987), *The Complete Guide to Trees*, Parkgate Books.
20. Tabbush, P. M. and White, J. E. (1996), 'Estimation of tree age in ancient yew woodland at Kingley Vale', *Quarterly Forestry Journal*, 90, no. 3, pp. 197–206.
21. Tabbush, P. M. and White, J. E. (1996), 'Estimation of tree age in ancient yew woodland at Kingley Vale', *Quarterly Forestry Journal*, 90, no. 3, pp. 197–206.

22. Tabbush, P. M. and White, J. E. (1996), 'Estimation of tree age in ancient yew woodland at Kingley Vale', *Quarterly Forestry Journal*, 90, no. 3, pp. 197–206.
23. White, J. E. (1994), 'Estimating the age of large trees in Britain', Forestry Commission Research Information Note 250, Forestry Commission Farnham, Surrey.
24. Tabbush, P. M. and White, J. E. (1996), 'Estimation of tree age in ancient yew woodland at Kingley Vale', *Quarterly Forestry Journal*, 90, no. 3, pp. 197–206.
25. Dickson, J. H. (1994), 'The yew tree (Taxus baccata L.) in Scotland – Native or early introduction or both?', *Scottish Forestry*, 48(4), 253–261.
26. Tabbush. P. (1997), 'Veteran Trees: Habitat, Hazard or Heritage?' Paper delivered to Tuesday, 4 March 1997 meeting of Royal Agricultural Society of England and The Royal Forestry Society.
27. Tabbush, P. (1997), 'Veteran Trees: Habitat, Hazard or Heritage?' Paper delivered to Tuesday, 4 March 1997 meeting of Royal Agricultural Society of England and The Royal Forestry Society.
28. Tabbush, P. (1997), 'Veteran Trees: Habitat, Hazard or Heritage?' Paper delivered at Tuesday, 4 March 1997 meeting of Royal Agricultural Society of England and The Royal Forestry Society.
29. Tabbush, P. M. and White, J. E. (1996), 'Estimation of tree age in ancient yew woodland at Kingley Vale', *Quarterly Forestry Journal*, 90, no. 3, pp. 197–206.
30. Tabbush. P. (1998), 'Veteran Trees: Habitat, Hazard or Heritage?' Paper delivered to a meeting of Royal Agricultural Society of England and The Royal Forestry Society.
31. Hindson, T. R. (2000), 'The Growth Rate of Yew Trees: An Empirically Generated Growth Curve', The Dendrologist's Allen Mitchell Memorial Lecture, 4 November 2000 in association The Conservation Foundation.
32. Hindson, T. R. (2000), 'The Growth Rate of Yew Trees: An Empirically Generated Growth Curve', The Dendrologist's Allen Mitchell Memorial Lecture, 4 November 2000 in association The Conservation Foundation.
33. Personal correspondence Dr R. Switsur, Cambridge Radiocarbon Laboratory, October 1999.
34. Moir, A. K. (1999), 'The dendrochronological potential of modern yew (*taxus baccata*) with special reference to yew from Hampton Court Palace, UK', *New Phytologist*, 144, 479–488, Cambridge University Press.
35. Moir, A. K. (1999), 'The dendrochronological potential of modern yew (*taxus baccata*) with special reference to yew from Hampton Court Palace, UK', *New Phytologist*, 144, 479–488, Cambridge University Press.
36. Miles, D. H. and Bridge, M. C., *The Tree-ring Dating of Building Timbers, The Yew Tunnel and Other Trees at Aberglasney House and Gardens, Llandeilo, Carmarthenshire*, RCAHMW Report, 1999; Lowe, J. (1897), *The Yew-Trees of Great Britain and Ireland*, Macmillan.
37. Larson, D. W. (1999), 'Ancient Stunted Trees', *Nature Magazine*, vol. 398, April, 1999.
38. Personal correspondence Larson, D. W. (26.10.99), University of Guelph, Canada.
39. Mitchell. A. (1985), *The Complete Guide to Trees*, Collins and Brown.
40. *Bonsai Magazine* (1997), Issue 36, Winter 1997.
41. Anand, C. and Brueton, D. (1994), *The Sacred Yew*, Penguin Arkana.
42. Borrow, G. (1862), *Wild Wales*, John Murray.
43. Hartzell, H. Jr (1991), *The Yew Tree, a Thousand Whispers*, Hulogosi Press.
44. Anand, C. and Brueton, D. (1994), *The Sacred Yew*, Penguin Arkana.
45. Larson, D. W., Doubt, J. and Matthes-Sears, U. (1994), 'Radially sectored hydraulic pathways in the xylem of Thuja Occidentalis as revealed by the use of dyes', *International Journal of Plant Science*, 155(5):569–582, University of Chicago.
46. Mills, K. (1999), *The Cumbrian Yew Book*, Yew Trees for the Millennium in Cumbria.
47. Loudon, J. C. (1838), *Arboretum et Fruticetum Brittannicum, or the Trees and Shrubs of Britain*, vol. 4, Longman.
48. Mee, A. ed. (1944, 1966), *The King's England*, Hampshire volume.

49. Johnson, W. (1915), *Byways in British Archaeology*, Oxford University Press.
50. Williamson. R. (1978), *The Great Yew Forest*, Readers Union.
51. Johnson, W. (1915), *Byways in British Archaeology*, Oxford University Press.
52. Wilks, J. H. (1972), *Trees of the British Isles in History and Legend*, Muller.
53. Kinmonth, F. (1998), *Yews News*, The Conservation Foundation, Issue No. 2, February 1998.
54. *Archaeologia Cambrensis* (1876), p. 345.
55. Anand, C. and Brueton, D. (1994), *The Sacred Yew*, Penguin Arkana.
56. Anand, C. and Brueton, D. (1994), *The Sacred Yew*, Penguin Arkana.
57. Personal correspondence Hindson, T. R. (1999) founder, *Companions of the Yew*, Basingstoke.
58. Letters to the Editor, *The Irish Times*, 19 November 1992.
59. Personal correspondence Jeroen Pater, European native tree historian, Holland, 2001.

Chapter 3: The Churchyard Yew

1. Morton, A. (1986, 1995), *The Trees of Shropshire*, Airlife, Shrewsbury.
2. Morton, A. (1986, 1995), *The Trees of Shropshire*, Airlife, Shrewsbury.
3. Palmer, W. T., *Odd Corners in Derbyshire, Rambles, Scrambles, Climbs and Sport*, Skeffington and Son.
4. Greaves. C. S. (1880), 'The Darley Yew', *Derbyshire Archaeological Journal*, vol. 2, pp. 100–120.
5. Ussher, R. (1880), Addenda to Mr Greaves' paper on the Darley yew, *Derbyshire Archaeological Journal*, vol. 2.
6. Loudon, J. C. (1838), *Arboretum et Fruticetum Brittannicum, or the Trees and Shrubs of Britain*, vol. 4, Longman.
7. Loudon, J. C. (1838), *Arboretum et Fruticetum Brittannicum, or the Trees and Shrubs of Britain*, vol. 4, Longman.
8. Anand, C. and Brueton, D. (1994), *The Sacred Yew*, Penguin Arkana.
9. Watson, W. J. (1926, 1986, 1993) *Celtic Place-names of Scotland*, Birlinn Ltd.
10. Barrington, D. (1759), *Philosophical Transactions*, vol. LIX, December 1759, p. 37.
11. Barrington, D. (1759), *Philosophical Transactions*, vol. LIX, December 1759, p. 37.
12. De Candolle, A. (1831), *Physiologie Vegetale*, ii, p. 1002.
13. Loudon, J. C. (1838), *Arboretum et Fruticetum Brittannicum, or the Trees and Shrubs of Britain*, vol. 4, Longman.
14. Loudon, J. C. (1838), *Arboretum et Fruticetum Brittannicum, or the Trees and Shrubs of Britain*, vol. 4, Longman.
15. *Notes and Queries*, 5th series, v. p. 376. *Naturalists Journal*, 1896, p. 99.
16. Forestry Commission News Release, no. 2758.
17. Cornish, Vaughan (1946), *The Churchyard Yew and Immortality*, Muller.
18. Anand, C. and Brueton, D. (1994), *The Sacred Yew*, Penguin Arkana.
19. E. R. Yarham (1975), 'England's Churchyard Yews', *This England Magazine*, vol. 8, no. 3, Autumn 1975.
20. Mee, A. ed. (1944, 1966), *The King's England*, Sussex volume.
21. White, G. (1789), The Natural History of Selborne.
22. Anand, C. and Brueton, D. (1994), *The Sacred Yew*, Penguin Arkana.
23. Mitchell, A. (1985, 1997) *The Complete Guide to Trees*, Parkgate Books Ltd.
24. Hindson, *On the Growth rate of Taxus baccata, 1997–1999*.
25. *Proceedings from the Hampshire Field Club Archaeological Society*, 47, 1991, 153–170.
26. Johnson, W. (1912), *Byways in British Archaeology*, Cambridge University Press.
27. Dallimore, W. (1908), *Holly, Yew and Box*.
28. Cornish, V. (1946), *The Churchyard Yew and Immortality*, Muller.
29. Gregory, D. (1991), *Country Churchyards in Wales*, Gwasg Carreg Gwalch.

30. Gregory, D. (1991), *Country Churchyards in Wales*, Gwasg Carreg Gwalch.
31. Plomer, W. intro. and ed. (1977), *Kilvert's Diary, a selection*, Penguin.
32. Canterbury Probate Office register, Wingham, fol. 51, Will of Thomas Alday of Ash, Kent, dated 19 December 1520, printed in *Archaeologia Cantiana*, 34 (1922) pp. 48–9.
33. *Notes and Queries*, 2nd series (124), 15 May 1858.
34. *Notes and Queries*, vol. 10 (247), 22 July 1854.
35. *Notes and Queries*, vol. 1 (19), 9 March 1850, p. 294.
36. Tittensor, R. M. (1980), 'Ecological history of yew *Taxus baccata* in southern England', *Biological Conservation*, 17, pp. 243–265.
37. Johnson, W. (1912), *Byways in British Archaeology*, Cambridge University Press.
38. Morton, A. (1986, 1995), *The Trees of Shropshire*, Airlife.
39. *This England*, Quarterley Magazine, Autumn 1975.
40. Anand, C. and Brueton, D. (1994), *The Sacred Yew*, Penguin Arkana.
41. Greaves, C. S. (1905), 'The Darley Yew', *Derbyshire Archaeology Journal*, vol. 2, Citing Cox, *Derbyshire Churches*, vol. 2, p. 460.
42. Greaves, C. S. (1905), 'The Darley Yew', *Derbyshire Archaeology Journal*, vol. 2, Citing Cox, *Derbyshire Churches*, vol. 2, p. 460.
43. Greaves, C. S. (1905), 'The Darley Yew', *Derbyshire Archaeology Journal*, vol. 2, Citing Cox, *Derbyshire Churches*, vol. 2, p. 460.
44. Johnson, W. (1912), *Byways in British Archaeology*, Cambridge University Press.
45. *This England*, Quarterly Magazine, Autumn 1975.
46. A. Mee (1944), *The Kings England*, Sussex volume.
47. A. Mee, ed. (1944), *The Kings England*, Kent volume.
48. Lees, E. (1882), Worcestershire Naturalists' Club, *Minutes for Himley, Wichbury and Hagley*, 19 May.
49. Personal correspondence Pritchard, J., Local historian, Hagley, 2000.
50. Cornish, V. (1946), *The Churchyard Yew and Immortality*, Muller.
51. *The Guardian*, Saturday 11 December 1999.
52. Morton, A. (1986, 1995), *The Trees of Shropshire*, Airlife, Shrewsbury.
53. MacNeill, J. (1909), 'Notes on the distribution, history, grammar and import of the Irish Ogham inscriptions', *Proceedings of the Royal Irish Academy*, vol. XXVII, pp. 329–371.
54. Jones-Davies, J. (1970), *Brecknockshire and Radnorshire Museum News*.
55. Jones-Davies, J. (1970), *Brecknockshire and Radnorshire Museum News*.
56. Plomer, William, intro. and ed. (1997), *Kilvert's Diary, a Selection*, Penguin.
57. Kinmonth, F. (1998), *Yews News*, The Conservation Foundation, Issue no. 2, February 1998.
58. Canon Doble, G. H. (1971, 1984, 1993), *Lives of the Welsh Saints*, University of Wales Press.
59. Anand, C. and Brueton, D. (1994), *The Sacred Yew*, Penguin Arkana.
60. Sinclair, J.B. and Fenn, R.W.D. (1995), *Three Parish Churches, Glascwm, Rhulen & Cregrina*.
61. Andrew, J. (1992), *Churchyard Yew Trees in the Archdeaconry of Gower*, from Gower, XLIII, 1992.
62. Evans, J. Daryll (1988), *The Yew Trees of Gwent*, Archangel Publishing.
63. Harte, J. (1996), 'How old is that yew?', *At The Edge Magazine*, no. 4, December 1996.
64. Tabbush, P. M. and White, J. E. (1996), 'Estimation of tree age in ancient yew woodland at Kingley Vale', *Quarterly Journal of Forestry*, 90, no. 3, pp. 197–206.
65. Cornish, V. (1946), *The Churchyard Yew and Immortality*, Muller.
66. Gregory, D. (1991), *Country Churchyards in Wales*, Gwasg Carreg Gwalch.
67. Gregory, D. (1991), *Country Churchyards in Wales*, Gwasg Carreg Gwalch.
68. Gregory, D. (1991), *Country Churchyards in Wales*, Gwasg Carreg Gwalch.
69. Gregory, D. (1991), *Country Churchyards in Wales*, Gwasg Carreg Gwalch.
70. Cornish, V. (1946), *The Churchyard Yew and Immortality*, Muller.

71. Gregory, D. (1991), *Country Churchyards in Wales*, Gwasg Carreg Gwalch.
72. Kinmonth, F. (1998), *Yews News*, The Conservation Foundation, Issue no. 2, February 1998
73. Gregory, D. (1991), *Country Churchyards in Wales*, Gwasg Carreg Gwalch.
74. Cornish, V. (1946), *The Churchyard Yew and Immortality*, Muller.
75. Anand, C. and Brueton, D. (1994), *The Sacred Yew*, Penguin Arkana.
76. Jones-Davies, J. (1970), *Brecknockshire and Radnorshire Museum News*.
77. Hartzell, H. Jr (1991), *The Yew Tree, a Thousand Whispers*, Hulogosi Press.
78. Mills, K. (1999), *The Cumbrian Yew Book*, Yew Trees for the Millennium in Cumbria.
79. Andrew, J. (1992), *Churchyard Yew Trees in the Archdeaconry of Gower*, from Gower, XLIII, 1992.

Chapter 4: Abbey Yews

1. Baxter, T. (1992), *The Eternal Yew*, The Self-Publishing Association Ltd.
2. Mee, A. ed. (1944, 1966), *The Kings England*, Gloucestershire volume.
3. Anand, C. and Brueton, D. (1994), *The Sacred Yew*, Penguin Arkana.
4. Cornish, V. (1946), *The Churchyard Yew and Immortality*, Muller.
5. Piggott, S. (1950, 1985), *William Stukeley*, Thames and Hudson.
6. Rattue, J. (1995), *The Living Stream*, Boydell and Brewer.
7. Lowe, J. (1897), The *Yew-Trees of Great Britain and Ireland*, Macmillan.
8. Strutt, J. G. (1822), *Sylva Brittannica, or Portraits of Forest trees*.
9. Strutt, J. G. (1822), *Sylva Brittannica, or Portraits of Forest trees*.
10. Personal correspondence R. Switsur, Cambridge Radiocarbon Laboratory, 1999.
11. Dallimore, W. (1908), *Holly Yew and Box*, London.
12. Anand, C. and Brueton, D. (1994), *The Sacred Yew*, Penguin Arkana.
13. Loudon, J. C. (1838), *Arboretum et Fruticetum Brittannicum, or the Trees and Shrubs of Britain*, vol. 4, Longman.
14. Greene, J. Patrick (1992), *Medieval Monasteries*, Leicestershire University Press.
15. De Candolle, A. (1831), *Physiologie Vegetale*, ii, p. 1001.
16. Miles. A. (1999), *Silva: British Trees*, Ted Smart.
17. Personal correspondence Glyn Coppack, English Heritage.
18. Williams, S. W. (1889), *Strata Florida, Recent Excavations*.
19. Williams, S. W. (1889), *Strata Florida, Recent Excavations*.
20. Joshua Jones Davies, Brecknock Museum News, 1977.
21. Toulmin-Smith, L. (1964), *The Itinerary of John Leland, in or about, 1536–1539*, part iv, vol. 3, Centaur.
22. The Gardeners Chronicle, 30 May 1874.
23. Williams, S. W. (1889), *Strata Florida, Recent Excavations*.
24. Williams, S. W. (1889), *Strata Florida, Recent Excavations*.
25. Bromwich, R. (1982, 1987), *Dafydd ap Gwilym Poems*, Gomer Press.
26. Williams, S. W. (1889), *Strata Florida, Recent Excavations*.
27. Meyrick, S. R. (1810), *History and Antiquities of the County of Cardigan*.
28. Jones-Davies, J., *Brecknock and Radnor Express Museum News*, December 1970.
29. Personal correspondence Rachel Bromwich, 1997.
30. Jones-Davies, J., *Brecknock and Radnor Express*, December 1970.
31. Parry, T. (1962), *The Oxford Book of Welsh Verse*, Oxford University Press.
32. Jones-Davies, J., *Brecknock and Radnor Express*, December 1970, and *Museum News of Brecknock Museum*.
33. Borrow, G. (1862), *Wild Wales*, John Murray.
34. Borrow, G. (1862), *Wild Wales*, John Murray.
35. Borrow, G. (1862), *Wild Wales*, John Murray.
36. Borrow, G. (1862), *Wild Wales*, John Murray.

37. *The Gardeners Chronicle*, 30 May 1874.
38. *The Gardeners Chronicle*, 30 May 1874.
39. Moir, A. K. (1999), 'The dendrochronological potential of modern yew, with special reference to Hampton Court, UK', *New Phytologist*, 144, pp. 479–488.
40. Williams, S. W. (1889), *Strata Florida, Recent Excavations*.
41. Williams, S. W. (1889), *Strata Florida, Recent Excavations*.
42. Williams, S. W. (1889), *Strata Florida, Recent Excavations*.
43. Jones, F. (1954, 1992 and 1998), *Holy Wells of Wales*, University of Wales Press.
44. Williams, S. W. (1889), *Strata Florida, Recent Excavations*.
45. Williams, S. W. (1889), *Strata Florida, Recent Excavations*.
46. Robinson, D. (1996), *Cadw guide to Strata Florida*.
47. Greene, J. Patrick (1992), *Medieval Monasteries*, Leicester University Press.
48. Williams, S. W. (1889), *Strata Florida, Recent Excavations*.
49. Bromwich, R. (1982, 1987), *Dafydd ap Gwilym Poems*, Gomer Press.
50. Nash-Williams, V. E. (1950), *The Early Christian Monuments of Wales*, University of Wales Press.
51. Gregory, D. (1991), *Country Churchyards in Wales*, Gwasg Carreg Gwalch.
52. Morton, A. (1986, 1995), *The Trees of Shropshire*, Airlife.
53. *The Gardeners Chronicle*, May 1874.

Chapter 5: Yews at Wells and Springs

1. Fry, R. and Hulse, T. G. (1994), 'The Whistlebitch Well, Utkinton, Cheshire', *Source Magazine*, new series, issue 1, 1994.
2. Jones, F. (1954, 1992 and 1998), *Holy Wells of Wales*, University of Wales Press.
3. Jones, F. (1954, 1992 and 1998), *Holy Wells of Wales*, University of Wales Press.
4. Jones, F. (1954, 1992 and 1998), *Holy Wells of Wales*, University of Wales Press.
5. Jones, F. (1954, 1992 and 1998), *Holy Wells of Wales*, University of Wales Press.
6. Rattue, J. (1995), *The Living Stream, Holy Wells in Historical Context*, Boydell and Brewer.
7. Hodder, M. A. (1991), 'Excavations at Sandwell Priory, 1982–1988', *South Staffordshire Archaeological and Historical Society Transactions*, vol. XXXI (1991 for 1989–1990).
8. Jones, F. (1954, 1992 and 1998), *Holy Wells of Wales*, University of Wales Press.
9. Jones, F. (1954, 1992 and 1998), *Holy Wells of Wales*, University of Wales Press.
10. Lucas, A. T. (1962), 'The Sacred Trees Of Ireland', *Journal of the Cork Historical and Archaeological Society*, pp. 16–54.
11. Lucas, A. T. (1962), 'The Sacred Trees Of Ireland', *Journal of the Cork Historical and Archaeological Society*, pp. 16–54.
12. Rattue, J. (1995), *The Living Stream, Holy Wells in Historical Context*, Boydell and Brewer.
13. Richards, M. trans. (1954), *The Laws of Hywel Dda*, Willmer Brothers and Co.
14. Richards, M. trans. (1954), *The Laws of Hywel Dda*, Willmer Brothers and Co.
15. Lowe, J. (1897), *The Yew-Trees of Great Britain and Ireland*, Macmillan.
16. Lowe, J. (1897), *The Yew-Trees of Great Britain and Ireland*, Macmillan.
17. Personal correspondence Dr R. Bromwich, Aberystwyth, Ceredigion, 23.01.98
18. Jones, F. (1954, 1992 and 1998), *Holy Wells of Wales*, University of Wales Press.
19. Jones, F. (1954, 1992 and 1998), *Holy Wells of Wales*, University of Wales Press.
20. Jones, F. (1954, 1992 and 1998), *Holy Wells of Wales*, University of Wales Press.
21. Anand, C. and Brueton, D. (1994), *The Sacred Yew*, Penguin Arkana.
22. Personal correspondence McGeeney, A., Wildlife Author Photographer.
23. Jones, F. (1954, 1992 and 1998), *Holy Wells of Wales*, University of Wales Press.
24. Jones, F. (1954, 1992 and 1998), *Holy Wells of Wales*, University of Wales Press.
25. Rhys, J. (1880), *Celtic Folklore*, vol. ii, Manx and Welsh, p. 517.
26. Jackson, K. H. ed. (1951, 1971), *A Celtic Miscellany*, Penguin.

27. Rhys, J. (1880), *Celtic Folklore.*
28. Rhys, J. (1880), *Celtic Folklore.*
29. Toulmin-Smith, L. ed. (1964), *The Itinerary of John Leland, in 1536–1539*, part iv, vol. iii, Centaur.
30. Rhys, J. (1880), *Celtic Folklore.*
31. Rhys, J. (1880), *Celtic Folklore.*
32. Jones, F. (1954, 1992 and 1998), *Holy Wells of Wales*, University of Wales Press.
33. Henig, M. (1984), *Religion in Roman Britain*, Batsford.
34. Jones, F. (1954, 1992 and 1998), *Holy Wells of Wales*, University of Wales Press.
35. Jones, F. (1954, 1992 and 1998), *Holy Wells of Wales*, University of Wales Press.
36. Jones, Gwynn, T. (1930, 1979), *Welsh Customs and folklore*, Rowman and Littlefield.
37. Thorpe, L. (1978), trans. *Gerald of Wales, The Journey through Wales, Descriptions of Wales*, Penguin Classics.
38. Jones, F. (1954, 1992 and 1998), *Holy Wells of Wales*, University of Wales Press.
39. Jones, F. (1954, 1992 and 1998), *Holy Wells of Wales*, University of Wales Press.
40. Jones, F. (1954, 1992 and 1998), *Holy Wells of Wales*, University of Wales Press.
41. Fry, J. (1998), *Warriors at the Edge Of Time*, Capall Bann.
42. Fenton, R. (1804), *Tours in Wales.*
43. Gregory, D. (1991), *Country Churchyards in Wales*, Gwasg Carreg Gwalch.
44. Jones, F. (1954, 1992 and 1998), *Holy Wells of Wales*, University of Wales Press.
45. Hornsby, Ron (1999), Medieval Religion Mailbase Internet Archive.
46. Rattue, J. (1995), *The Living Stream, Holy Wells in Historical Context*, Boydell and Brewer.
47. Allen, E. W. (1871), *The Antiquary*, vol. 1, p. 44, London.
48. Hope Bagot Parish Paths Committee Leaflet, 1998.
49. Loudon, J. C. (1838), *Arboretum et Fruticetum Brittannicum, or the Trees and Shrubs of Britain*, vol. 4, Longman.
50. Loudon, J. C. (1838), *Arboretum et Fruticetum Brittannicum, or the Trees and Shrubs of Britain*, vol. 4, Longman.
51. Loudon, J. C. (1838), *Arboretum et Fruticetum Brittannicum, or the Trees and Shrubs of Britain*, vol. 4, Longman.
52. Mitchell, A. (1985, 1997), *The Complete Guide to Trees*, Parkgate Books Ltd.
53. Hope, R. C. (1893), *The Legendary Lore of the Holy Wells of England*, Elliot Stack.
54. Aubury, J. (1760), *A History of Surrey.*
55. Personal correspondence (1999) McGeeney, A.
56. Cornish, V. (1946), *The Churchyard Yew and Immortality*, Muller.
57. Rattue, J. (1995), *The Living Stream, Holy Wells in Historical Context*, Boydell and Brewer.
58. Personal correspondence (1999), McGeeney, A.
59. Watson, W. J. (1904, 1976, 1996), *Place-names of Ross and Cromarty*, Highland Heritage Books.
60. Watson, W. J. (1904, 1976, 1996), *Place-names of Ross and Cromarty*, Highland Heritage Books.
61. Lucas, A. T. (1963), 'The Sacred Trees of Ireland', *Journal of the Cork Historical and Archaeological Society*, 68, pp. 16–54.
62. Archaeology Data Service, Archsearch, http://ahds.ac.uk/catalogue. DepID FER154: 011.
63. Tabbush, P. (1998), 'Veteran Trees: Habitat, Hazard or Heritage?' paper delivered to a meeting of Royal Agricultural Society of England and The Royal Forestry Society.
64. Jones, F. (1954, 1992 and 1998), *Holy Wells of Wales*, University of Wales Press.

Chapter 6: Old Yews in the Wider Historic Landscape

1. Hoskins, W. D. (1955, 1985), *The Making of The English Landscape*, Reprinted, Penguin.
2. Taylor, C. (1975, 1987, 2000), *Fields in the English Landscape*, History Handbooks, Sutton.

3. Taylor, C. (1975, 1987, 2000), *Fields in the English Landscape*, History Handbooks, Sutton.

4. Tittensor, R. M. (1980), 'Ecological history of yew *Taxus baccata* in southern England', *Biological Conservation*, 17, pp. 243–265.

5. Personal correspondence (1999), A. Meredith.

6. James G. Wood (1904), 'Things to be observed between Ross and Chepstow', *The Proceedings of the Woolhope Naturalists Field Club Transactions*, p. 293.

7. Hooke, D. (1990), *Worcestershire Anglo-Saxon Charter-Bounds*, Boydell.

8. Davies, W. (1978), *An Early Welsh Microcosm*, Royal Historical Society.

9. Andrew, J. (1992), *Churchyard Yew Trees in the Archdeaconry of Gower*, from Gower, XLIII, 1992.

10. Hoskins, W. D. (1955, 1985), *The Making Of The English Landscape*, reprinted, Penguin.

11. Tittensor, R. M. (1980), 'Ecological history of yew *Taxus baccata* in southern England', *Biological Conservation*, 17, pp. 243–265.

12. Tittensor, R. M. (1980), 'Ecological history of yew *Taxus baccata* in southern England', *Biological Conservation*, 17, pp. 243–265.

13. Tittensor, R. M. (1980), 'Ecological history of yew *Taxus baccata* in southern England', *Biological Conservation*, 17, pp. 243–265.

14. Anand, C. and Brueton, D. (1994), *The Sacred Yew*, Penguin Arkana.

15. Richards, M. trans. (1954), *The Laws of Hywel Dda*, Willmer Brothers and Co.

16. Campbell, J. (1991), *The Anglo-Saxons*, Penguin.

17. Gomme, G. L. (1880), *Primitive Folk-Moots*, London.

18. Reynolds, A. (1999), *Later Anglo-Saxon England*, Tempus.

19. Reynolds, A. (1999), *Later Anglo-Saxon England*, Tempus.

20. Phythian-Adams, C. (1975), *Local History and Folklore: A New Framework*.

21. Rackham, O. (1994), *The History of the British Countryside*, Dent.

22. Anand, C. and Brueton, D. (1994), *The Sacred Yew*, Penguin Arkana.

23. Gelling, M. (1975), *Signposts to the Past*, Dent, London.

24. Paul Watkins, 'Hundred meeting-places in the Cambrideshire region' in Rumble, A. and Mills, A. eds (1997) *Names, Places and People, an Onomastic Miscellany for John McNeal Dodgson*, p. 195–240.

25. Wilks, J. H. (1972), *Trees of the British Isles in History and Legend*, Frederick and Muller.

26. Anand, C. and Brueton, D. (1994), *The Sacred Yew*, Penguin Arkana.

27. Gomme, G. L. (1880), *Primitive Folk-Moots*.

28. Personal correspondence (2001), Jones, Melvyn, Sheffield Hallam University.

29. Young, F. W. (1950), *Churchill and Blakeshall Parish Booklet*, an edited version of two lectures on local history given by Mr Frederick W. Young (1875–1966) in 1950 and 1957. Reproduced 1997–8, by P. S. Legat.

30. Gomme, G. L. (1880), *Primitive Folk-Moots*, Nash's Worcestershire, I, p. 57.

31. Gelling, M. (2000), *The Landscape of Place-names*, Shaun Tyas.

32. Rackham, O. (1976), *Trees and Woodland in the British landscape*, Dent.

33. Lowe, J. (1897), *The Yew-Trees of Great Britain and Ireland*, Macmillan.

34. Lowe, J. (1897), *The Yew-Trees of Great Britain and Ireland*, Macmillan.

35. Gould, I. C. (1908), *Victorian County History of Herefordshire*, vol. I, p. 230.

36. Johnson, W. (1912), *Byways in British Archaeology*, Cambridge University Press.

37. Wright, T. (1855), *Archaeologia Cambrensis*, 3rd series, I, pp. 168–174; *Notes and Queries*, 9th series, vi, p. 77.

38. Canon Doble, G. H. (1971, 1984, 1993), *Lives of the Welsh Saints*, University of Wales Press.

39. Gelling, M. and Cole. A. (2000), *The Landscape of Place-names*, Shaun Tyas.

40. Geake, H. (1997), *The Use of Grave-Goods in Conversion-Period England, c. 600-c. 850 AD.* BAR British Series, 261.

41. Geake, H. (1997), *The Use of Grave-Goods in Conversion-Period England, c. 600-c. 850AD.* BAR British Series, 261.

42. Johnson, W. (1912), *Byways in British Archaeology*, Cambridge University Press, citing J. Stevens, in *Journal of the British Archaeological Association* (1884), xi, p. 62.

43. Stocker, D. and Went, D. (1995), 'The evidence for a pre-Viking church adjacent to the Anglo-Saxon barrow at Taplow, Bucks', *Archaeology Journal*, 152, pp. 441–454.

44. Johnson, W. (1912), *Byways in British Archaeology*, Cambridge University Press.

45. Anand, C. and Brueton, D. (1994), *The Sacred Yew*, Penguin Arkana.

46. Hants County Council Website (1999), *Hampshire Treasures*, www.hants.gov.uk.

47. Williams-Freeman, J. P. (1915), *Field Archaeology, As Illustrated by Hampshire*.

48. Hants County Council Website (1999), *Hampshire Treasures*, www.hants.gov.uk.

49. Williams-Freeman, J. P. (1915), *Field Archaeology, As Illustrated by Hampshire*.

50. Lees, E. (1877), 'Bromsgrove, Fockbury Mill, Bourn Heath, The Bumble Hole, etc.', *Proceedings of Worcestershire Naturalists' Club*, 12 August 1877.

51. Lines, H. H. (1880), 'Bromyard, Thornbury, The Wall Hill, etc.', *Worcestershire Naturalists' Club*, 8 June 1880.

52. V. C. H. Hants (1908) vol. 3, pp. 417–8, citing Marsh (1808).

53. Williams-Freeman, J. P. (1915), *Field Archaeology, As Illustrated by Hampshire*.

54. Williams-Freeman, J. P. (1915), *Field Archaeology, As Illustrated by Hampshire*.

55. Williams-Freeman, J. P. (1915), *Field Archaeology, As Illustrated by Hampshire*.

56. Williams-Freeman, J. P. (1915), *Field Archaeology, As Illustrated by Hampshire*.

57. Williams-Freeman, J. P. (1915), *Field Archaeology, As Illustrated by Hampshire*.

58. Hindson, T. R. (1997–1998), *Merdon Castle Study, Companions of the Yew Archive*, vol. 1.

59. Personal correspondence (1998) Meredith, A.

60. Williams-Freeman, J. P. (1915), *Field Archaeology, As Illustrated by Hampshire*.

61. *Victorian County History of Hampshire* (1908), vol. 3, pp. 417–8.

62. Johnson, W. (1912), *Byways in British Archaeology*, Cambridge University Press.

63. Lees, E. (1870), 'Hagley, Pedmore, Wichbury Camp, etc.' *Proceedings of the Worcestershire Naturalists' Club*, Friday, 28 October 1870.

64. Brown, D. L., *Evaluation of Kidderminster, Blakedown & Hagley Bypass + A449 link*, Herefordshire & Worcestershire County Archaeological Service Report.

65. Reynolds, A. (1999), *Later Anglo-Saxon England*, Tempus.

66. Martin, P. (1999), 'The Historical Ecology of Old Oswestry', *Shropshire Botanical Society Newsletter*, pp. 10–11, Autumn 1999.

67. Duncomb, Rev. John, *History of Herefordshire, 1804–12*.

68. 'Monnington and Moccas', *Transactions of the Woolhope Field Club Volume for 1933–35*, Part 1, p. xxvi.

69. *The Gardener's Chronicle*, May 1874

70. *Transactions of the Woolhope Field Club, Volume for 1933–35*, p. xvii.

71. Williams-Freeman, J. P. (1915), *Field Archaeology, As Illustrated by Hampshire*.

Chapter 7: Yews in Woods, Hedges and Gardens

1. Tittensor, R. M. (1980), 'Ecological history of yew *Taxus baccata* in southern England', *Biological Conservation*, 17, pp. 243–265.

2. Tittensor, R. M. (1980), 'Ecological history of yew *Taxus baccata* in southern England', *Biological Conservation*, 17, pp. 243–265.

3. Tittensor, R. M. (1980), 'Ecological history of yew *Taxus baccata* in southern England', *Biological Conservation*, 17, pp. 243–265.

4. Tittensor, R. M. (1980), 'Ecological history of yew *Taxus baccata* in southern England', Biological Conservation 17, pp. 243–265.

5. Mitchell, F. J. G. (1990), 'The history and vegetation dynamics of a yew wood (*Taxus baccata L.*) in S.W. Ireland', *New Phytologist*, 115, pp. 573–577.

6. Spence, L. (1949, 1971), *The History and Origins of Druidism*, reprinted by Aquarian Press.

7. *Gentleman's Magazine* (1787), p. 313, cited in *Notes and Queries*, 2nd series, no. 37, 13 September 1856, p. 215.
8. Rackham, O. (1994), *The Illustrated History of the Countryside*, Widenfeld and Nicolson.
9. Personal correspondence Mr G. Manning, Norbury Park Ranger, Surrey County Council, Dorking 1999.
10. Williamson, R. (1978), *The Great Yew Forest*, Readers Union.
11. Johnson, W. (1912), *Byways in British Archaeology*, Cambridge University Press.
12. Lowe, J. (1897), *The Yew-Trees of Great Britain and Ireland*, Macmillan.
13. Williamson, R. (1978), *The Great Yew Forest*, Readers Union.
14. Watt, A. S. (1926), 'Yew Communities of the South Downs', *Journal of Ecology*, 14, pp. 282–316.
15. Tittensor, R. M. (1980), 'Ecological history of yew *Taxus baccata* in southern England', *Biological Conservation*, 17 pp. 243–265.
16. Williamson, R. (1978), *The Great Yew Forest*, Readers Union.
17. Tabbush, P. M. and White, J. (1996), 'Estimation of tree age in ancient yew woodland at Kingley Vale', in *Quarterly Journal of Forestry*, vol. 90, no. 3, July 1996.
18. Peterson, Rector, M. A. (1922), *A Short Guide to the Parish Church and Churchyard of Grasmere 1909–1922*.
19. Mills, K. (1999), *The Cumbrian Yew Book*, Yew Trees for the Millennium in Cumbria.
20. Tittensor, R. M. (1980), 'Ecological history of yew *Taxus baccata* in southern England', *Biological Conservation*, 17 pp. 243–265.
21. Jones, M. (1987), 'The Oldest Living Thing in Sheffield?' *The Hallamshire Historian*, vol. 1, no. 2, spring 1987, pp. 36–37.
22. Gelling, M. and Cole, A. (2000), *The Landscape of Place-names*, Shaun Tyas.
23. Jones, M. (1987), 'The Oldest Living Thing in Sheffield?', *The Hallamshire Historian*, vol. 1, no. 2, spring 1987, pp. 36–37.
24. Hartzell, H. Jr (1991), *The Yew Tree, a Thousand Whispers*, Hulogosi Press.
25. Lowe, J. (1897), *The Yew-Trees of Great Britain and Ireland*, Macmillan.
26. Mee, A. ed. (1944), *The Kings England*, Sussex volume.
27. Baxter, T. (1992), *The Eternal Yew*, The Self-Publishing Association Ltd.
28. Rackham, O. (1989, 1993), *The Last Forest, The Story of Hatfield Forest*, Dent.
29. Rackham, O. (1989, 1993), *The Last Forest, The Story of Hatfield Forest*, Dent.
30. Lowe, J. (1897), *The Yew-Trees of Great Britain and Ireland*, Macmillan.

Chapter 8: The Yew in Folklore Traditions

1. Rhys, Sir J. (1901), *Celtic Folklore*, Clarendon Press.
2. Doble, Canon, G. H. (1971, 1984, 1993), *Lives of the Welsh Saints*, University of Wales Press.
3. Graves, R. (1948, 1961), *The White Goddess*, Faber and Faber.
4. Jones-Baker, D. (1977), *The Folklore of Hertfordshire*, Batsford, pp. 61–3.
5. Gerish, W. B. (n.d., *c.* 1900), *Hertfordshire Folk Lore*, S. R. Publishers.
6. Gerish, W. B. (n.d.) *Hertfordshire Folk Lore*, S. R. Publishers.
7. Gerish, W. B. (n.d.) *Hertfordshire Folk Lore*, S. R. Publishers.
8. Plomer, W. intro. and ed. (1977), *Kilvert's Diary, a selection*, Penguin.
9. Westwood, J. (1985), *Albion*, Grenada.
10. Sikes, W. (1880), *British Goblins*, Sampson Lowe.
11. Sikes, W. (1880), *British Goblins*, Sampson Lowe.
12. Jones, F. (1998), *Holy Wells of Wales*, Uinversity of Wales Press.
13. Thorpe, L. trans. and intro. (1978) *Gerald of Wales, The Journey through Wales, descriptions of Wales*, Penguin Classics.
14. Rees, A. and B. (1961), *Celtic Heritage*, Thames and Hudson.
15. Jones, T. Gwynn (1930), *Welsh Folklore and Customs*, Roman and Littlefield.

16. Thorpe, L. trans. and intro. (1978) *Gerald of Wales, The Journey through Wales, descriptions of Wales*, Penguin Classics.
17. Lucas, A. T. (1963), 'The Sacred Trees of Ireland', *Journal of the Cork Historical and Archaeological Society*, 68, pp. 16–54.
18. O'Grady, S. H. (1892), *Silva Gadelica*, I-XXXI, Williams and Norgate.
19. O'Grady, S. H. (1892), *Silva Gadelica*, I-XXXI, Williams and Norgate.
20. Watson, W. J. (1926), *Celtic Place-names of Scotland*, Blackwood.
21. O'Grady, S. H. (1892), *Silva Gadelica*, I-XXXI, Williams and Norgate.
22. Matthews, C. and J. (1997), *The Encyclopaedia of Celtic Wisdom*, Element.
23. Matthews, C. and J. (1997), *The Encyclopaedia of Celtic Wisdom*, Element.
24. Matthews, C. and J. (1997), *The Encyclopaedia of Celtic Wisdom*, Element.
25. Campbell, John Gregorson, Minister of Tiree (published 1900, coll. *circa* 1860), *Superstitions of the Highlands and Islands of Scotland, Collected Entirely from Oral Sources*, James Maclehose and Sons, Glasgow University Press.
26. Wilks, J. H. (1972), *Trees of the British Isles in History and Legend*, Muller.
27. Wilks, J. H. (1972), *Trees of the British Isles in History and Legend*, Muller.
28. Wilks, J. H. (1972), *Trees of the British Isles in History and Legend*, Muller.
29. Anand, C. and Brueton, D. (1994), *The Sacred Yew*, Penguin Arkana.
30. Gough, R. ed. (1789), Camden's *Brittannia* (Originally published 1607).
31. Jones, T. Gwynn (1930), *Welsh Folklore and Customs*, Roman and Littlefield.
32. Rees, A. and B. (1961), *Celtic Heritage*, Thames and Hudson.
33. Griffiths, B. (1996), *Aspects of Anglo-Saxon Magic*, Anglo-Saxon Books.
34. Griffiths, B. (1996), *Aspects of Anglo-Saxon Magic*, Anglo-Saxon Books.
35. Griffiths, B. (1996), *Aspects of Anglo-Saxon Magic*, Anglo-Saxon Books.
36. Porter, J. (1995), *Aspects of Anglo-Saxon Riddles*, Anglo-Saxon Books.
37. Taylor, Keith, P. (1995), 'Mazers, Mead and the Wolf's Head Tree: A reconsideration of Old English Riddle 55', *Journal of English and Germanic Philology*, October 1995, University of Tennessee, pp. 497–512.
38. Griffiths, B. (1996), *Aspects of Anglo-Saxon Magic*, Anglo-Saxon Books.
39. Griffiths, B. (1996), *Aspects of Anglo-Saxon Magic*, Anglo-Saxon Books.
40. Watson, W. J. (1904, 1976, 1996), *Place-names of Ross and Cromarty*, Highland Heritage Books.
41. Mills, A. D. (1993, 1996), *Oxford Dictionary of English Place-names*, Oxford University Press.
42. Rees, A. and B. (1961), *Celtic Heritage*, Thames and Hudson.
43. Megaw, J. V. S. and M. R. (1989, 1990, 1996), *Celtic Art*, Thames and Hudson.
44. Green, M. J. ed. (1995), 'The Celtic World', Ch 38, Proinsias McCana, *Mythology and oral tradition*, Routledge.
45. Green, M. J. ed. (1995), 'The Celtic World', Ch 38, Proinsias McCana, *Mythology and Oral Tradition*, Routledge.
46. O'Curry, E. (1873), *Manners and Customs of the Ancient Irish*, Williams and Norgate, vol. ii, p. 226.
47. O'Curry, E. (1873), *Manners and Customs of the Ancient Irish*, Williams and Norgate, vol. ii.
48. Matthews, C. and J. (1997), *The Encyclopaedia of Celtic Wisdom*, Element.
49. Matthews, C. and J. (1997), *The Encyclopaedia of Celtic Wisdom*, Element.
50. Rees, A. and B. (1961), *Celtic Heritage*, Thames and Hudson.
51. Green, M. J. ed. (1995), 'The Celtic World', in Chapter 37, Redknap, M., *Early Christianity and its Monuments*, Routledge.
52. Mac Cana, P. (1968, 1983), *Celtic Mythology*, Hamlyn.
53. Lucas, A. T. (1963), 'The Sacred Trees of Ireland', *Journal of the Cork Historical and Archaeological Society*, 68, pp. 16–54.
54. Personal correspondence Bromwich, Rachel, 1997.
55. Matthews, C. and J. (1997), *The Encyclopaedia of Celtic Wisdom*, Element.

56. Rees, A. and B. (1961), *Celtic Heritage*, Thames and Hudson.

57. Raftery, B. (1994), *Pagan Celtic Ireland*, Thames and Hudson.

58. Hull, E. (1928), *Folklore of the British Isles*, Methuen.

59. Hull, E. (1928), *Folklore of the British Isles*, Methuen.

60. Stokes, W. ed. and trans. (1906), 'The Birth of Saint Moling', *Revue Celtique*, XXVII, p. 281.

61. O'Curry, E. (1873), *Manners and Customs of the Ancient Irish*, Williams and Norgate, vol. 3, p. 226.

62. Stokes, W. ed. and trans. (1895), 'The prose tales in the Rennes Dindshenchas', *Revue Celtique*, XVI (1894–5) pp. 277–8.

63. Lucas, A. T. (1963), 'The sacred trees of Ireland', *Journal of the Cork Historical and Archaeological Society*, 68, pp. 16–54.

64. Lucas, A. T. (1963), 'The sacred trees of Ireland', *Journal of the Cork Historical and Archaeological Society*, 68, pp. 16–54.

65. Lucas, A. T. (1963), 'The sacred trees of Ireland', *Journal of the Cork Historical and Archaeological Society*, 68, pp. 16–54.

66. Stokes, W. ed. and trans. (1893), 'The prose tales in the Rennes Dindshenchas', *Revue Celtique*, XV (1893) p. 420.

67. Lucas, A. T. (1963), 'The sacred trees of Ireland', *Journal of the Cork Historical and Archaeological Society*, 68, pp. 16–54.

68. Lucas, A. T. (1963), 'The sacred trees of Ireland', *Journal of the Cork Historical and Archaeological Society*, 68, pp. 16–54.

69. Jackson, K. H. (1964), *The Oldest Irish Tradition: A Window on the Iron Age*, Cambridge University Press.

70. Raftery, B. (1994, 1997), *Pagan Celtic Ireland*, Thames and Hudson.

71. Kinsella, T. (1969), *The Tain*, Oxford University Press.

72. Gwynn, E. 'Poems from the Dindshenchas, Text, Translation, and Vocabulary', *Todd Lecture Series*, vol. VII, Royal Irish Academy.

73. Kinsella, T. (1969), *The Tain*, Oxford University Press.

74. Rees, A. and B. (1961), *Celtic Heritage*, Thames and Hudson.

75. Spence, Lewis. (1913, 1962), *Dictionary of Medieval Romance and Romance Writers*, Humanities Press, p. 105.

76. Lucas, A. T. (1963), 'The sacred trees of ireland', *Journal of the Cork Historical and Archaeological Society*, 68, pp. 16–54.

77. Lucas, A. T. (1963), 'The sacred trees of Ireland', *Journal of the Cork Historical and Archaeological Society*, 68, pp. 16–54.

78. Rees, A. and B. (1961), *Celtic Heritage*, Thames and Hudson.

79. Lucas, A. T. (1963), 'The sacred trees of Ireland', *Journal of the Cork Historical and Archaeological Society*, 68, pp. 16–54.

80. Lucas, A. T. (1963), 'The sacred trees of ireland', *Journal of the Cork Historical and Archaeological Society*, 68, pp. 16–54.

81. Jackson, K. H. (1971), *A Celtic Miscellany*, Penguin.

82. Gantz, J. (1981), *Early Irish Myths and Sagas*, Penguin Classics.

83. Gantz, J. (1981), *Early Irish Myths and Sagas*, Penguin Classics.

84. Graves, R. (1961), *The White Goddess*, Faber and Faber.

85. Jackson, K. H. (1971), *A Celtic Miscellany*, Penguin.

86. Matthews, C. and J. (1997), *The Encyclopaedia of Celtic Wisdom*, Element.

87. Hull, E. (1928), *Folklore of the British Isles*, Methuen.

88. Lowe, J. (1897), *The Yew-trees of Great Britain and Ireland*, Macmillan.

89. Lowe, J. (1897), *The Yew-trees of Great Britain and Ireland*, Macmillan.

90. Chadwick, N. (1970), *The Celts*, Penguin.

91. Matthews, C. and J. (1997), *The Encyclopaedia of Celtic Wisdom*, Element.

92. Matthews, C. and J. (1997), *The Encyclopaedia of Celtic Wisdom*, Element.

93. Matthews, C. and J. (1997), *The Encyclopaedia of Celtic Wisdom*, Element.
94. Matthews, C. and J. (1997), *The Encyclopaedia of Celtic Wisdom*, Element.
95. Joyce, P. W. (1903), *A Social History of Ancient Ireland*, Longman.
96. Green, M. ed. (1995), *The Celtic World*, chapter 38, Proinsias McCana 'Mythology and oral tradition', Routledge.
97. Ross, A. and Robins, D. (1989), *The Life and Death of a Druid Prince*, Rider.
98. Matthews, C. and J. (1997), *The Encyclopaedia of Celtic Wisdom*, Element, USA.
99. O'Curry, E. (1873), *Manners and Customs of the Ancient Irish*, Williams and Norgate, vol. ii.
100. Joyce, P. W. (1903), *A Social History of Ancient Ireland*, Longman.
101. McCulloch, J. A. (1911), *The Religion of the Ancient Celts*, T. and T. Clark, Edinburgh.
102. O'Curry, E. (1873), *Manners and Customs of the Ancient Irish*, Williams and Norgate, vol. ii, p. 194.
103. Matthews, J. (1998), *The Druid Source Book*, Brockhampton, London.
104. Watson, W. J. (1926, 1986, 1993), *The History of the Celtic Place-names of Scotland*, Blackwood.
105. Green, M. ed. (1995), *The Celtic World*, in chapter 23, Ross, A., 'Ritual and the druids', Routledge.
106. Matthews, C. and J. (1997), *The Encyclopaedia of Celtic Wisdom*, Element.
107. Watson, W. J. (1926, 1986, 1993), *The History of the Celtic Place-names of Scotland*, Blackwood.
108. O'Curry, E., *Manuscript materials for Irish History*, appendix II, p. 466.
109. Lowe, J. (1897), *Yew Trees of Great Britain and Ireland*, Macmillan.
110. Personal correspondence Anne-Marie Moroney, Ireland, 2000.
111. Baxter, T. (1992), *The Eternal Yew*, Self-Publishing Association Ltd.
112. Loudon, J. C. (1838), *Arboretum et Fruticetum Brittannicum, or the Trees and Shrubs of Britain*, vol. 4, Longman.
113. Lucas, A. T. (1963), 'The sacred trees of Ireland', *Journal of the Cork Historical and Archaeological Society*, 68, pp. 16–54.
114. Lucas, A. T. (1963), 'The sacred trees of Ireland', *Journal of the Cork Historical and Archaeological Society*, 68, pp. 16–54.
115. Lucas, A. T. (1963), 'The sacred trees of Ireland', *Journal of the Cork Historical and Archaeological Society*, 68, pp. 16–54.
116. Lucas, A. T. (1963), 'The sacred trees of ireland', *Journal of the Cork Historical and Archaeological Society*, 68, pp. 16–54.
117. Lucas, A. T. (1963), 'The sacred trees of Ireland', *Journal of the Cork Historical and Archaeological Society*, 68, pp. 16–54.
118. Lucas, A. T. (1963), 'The sacred trees of Ireland', *Journal of the Cork Historical and Archaeological Society*, 68, pp. 16–54.
119. Joyce, P. W. (1875), *The Origin and History of Irish Names of Places*, first series, McGlashin and Gill, Dublin.
120. O'Grady, S. H. (1892), *Silva Gadelica*, I-XXXI, Williams and Norgate.
121. Lucas, A. T. (1963), 'The sacred trees of Ireland', *Journal of the Cork Historical and Archaeological Society*, 68, pp. 16–54.
122. O'Curry, Eugene (1873), *Manners and Customs of The Ancient Irish*, vol. 2, Williams and Norgate.
123. Matthews, C. and J. (1997), *The Encyclopaedia of Celtic Wisdom*, Element.
124. Matthews, C. and J. (1997), *The Encyclopaedia of Celtic Wisdom*, Element.

Chapter 9: Yew: An Archaeological Perspective

1. Thieme, H. (1997), 'Lower Palaeolithic hunting weapons from Shoningen, Germany, The oldest spears in the world', *The Newsletter of Prehistoric Society*, Number 26, July 1997.
2. Thieme, H. (1997), 'Lower Palaeolithic hunting weapons from Shoningen, Germany, The oldest spears in the world', *The Newsletter of Prehistoric Society*, Number 26, July 1997.
3. Mills, K. (1999), *The Cumbrian Yew Book*, Yew Trees for the Millennium in Cumbria.
4. Archaeology Data Service http://ads.ahds.ac.uk/catalogue, Sample OXA–3540.
5. Archaeology Data Service, http://ads.ahds.ac.uk/catalogue, Sample Q684.
6. Archaeology Data Service, http://ads.ahds.ac.uk/catalogue, Sample Q669.
7. Clark, J. G. D. (1961), 'Neolithic Bows from Somerset, England. Prehistoric Archery in N.W. Europe', *Proceedings of the Prehistoric Society*, 1961, Article No. 3.
8. Clark, J. G. D. (1961), 'Neolithic Bows from Somerset, England. Prehistoric Archery in N.W. Europe', *Proceedings of the Prehistoric Society*, 1961.
9. Clark, J. G. D. (1961), 'Neolithic Bows from Somerset, England. Prehistoric Archery in N.W. Europe', *Proceedings of the Prehistoric Society*, 1961.
10. Fowler, B. (2000), *Iceman*, Macmillan.
11. Fowler, B. (2000), *Iceman*, Macmillan.
12. Fowler, B. (2000), *Iceman*, Macmillan.
13. Renfrew, C. (1987, 1989), *Archaeology and Language: The Puzzle of Indo-European Origins*, Cambridge University Press.
14. Griffiths, B. (1996), *Aspects of Anglo-Saxon Magic*, Anglo-Saxon Books.
15. Thorpe, L. trans. and intro. (1978) *Gerald of Wales, The Journey through Wales, descriptions of Wales*, Penguin Classics.
16. Manley, John (1985), 'The Archer and the army in the late Saxon period', *Anglo-Saxon Studies in Archaeology and History*, vol. 4, Oxford University Committee for Archaeology.
17. Manley, John (1985), 'The Archer and the army in the late Saxon period.' *Anglo-Saxon Studies in Archaeology and History*, vol. 4, Oxford University Committee for Archaeology.
18. Hardy, R. (1992), *The Longbow, A Social and Military History*, Haynes.
19. Wilkinson-Latham, R. (1981), *Phaidon Guide to Antique Weapons and Weaponry*, Phaidon.
20. Lowe, J. (1897), *Yew Trees of Great Britain and Ireland*, Macmillan.
21. Lowe, J. (1897), *Yew Trees of Great Britain and Ireland*, Macmillan.
22. Lowe, J. (1897), *Yew Trees of Great Britain and Ireland*, Macmillan.
23. Lowe, J. (1897), *Yew Trees of Great Britain and Ireland*, Macmillan.
24. Lowe, J. (1897), *Yew Trees of Great Britain and Ireland*, Macmillan.
25. Archaeology Data Service, http://ads.ahds.ac.uk/catalogue Sample Q–1217
26. Archaeology Data Service http://ads.ahds.ac.uk/catalogue, Sample Q–3043
27. Archaeology Data Service http://ads.ahds.ac.uk/catalogue, Sample Q–3124.
28. *The Times*, 19 June 1997, citing British Archaeology, No. 24:7.
29. Green, M. J. ed. (1995), *The Celtic World*, in Chapter 15, *Celtic Seafaring and Transport*, Sean McGrail, Routledge.
30. Newall, A. S. (1930), 'Barrow 85, Amesbury (Goddard's list)', *Wiltshire Archaeological and Natural History Magazine*, vol. 45, pp. 432–58.
31. Newall, A. S. (1930), 'Barrow 85, Amesbury (Goddard's list)', *Wiltshire Archaeological and Natural History Magazine*, vol. 45, pp. 432–58.
32. Newall, A. S. (1930), 'Barrow 85, Amesbury (Goddard's list)', *Wiltshire Archaeological and Natural History Magazine*, vol. 45, pp. 432–58.
33. Newall, A. S. (1930), 'Barrow 85, Amesbury (Goddard's list)', *Wiltshire Archaeological and Natural History Magazine*, vol. 45, pp. 432–58.
34. Gibson, A. and Simpson, D. eds (1998), 'Prehistoric Ritual and Religion', Ch. 13, Coles, B. *Wood Species for Wooden Figures*, Sutton.

35. Raftery, B. (1994, 1997), *Pagan Celtic Ireland*, Thames and Hudson.

36. Gibson, A. and Simpson, D. eds (1998), 'Prehistoric Ritual and Religion', Ch. 13, Coles, B. *Wood Species for Wooden Figures*, Sutton.

37. Coles, J., Fenwick, V., and Hutchinson, G. eds (1993), *A Spirit of Enquiry, Essays for Ted Wright*, featuring article by Coles, B. 'Roos Carr and Co.', published by Wetland Archaeology Research Project, etc.

38. Gibson, A. and Simpson, D. eds (1998), 'Prehistoric Ritual and Religion', Ch. 13, Coles, B. *Wood Species for Wooden Figures*, Sutton.

39. Gibson, A. and Simpson, D. eds (1998), 'Prehistoric Ritual and Religion', Ch. 13. Coles, B. *Wood Species for Wooden Figures*, Sutton.

40. Sheppard, T. (1901), *Notes on Ancient Model of a Boat*, HMP4.

41. Gibson, A. and Simpson, D. eds (1998), 'Prehistoric Ritual and Religion', Ch. 13, Coles, B. *Wood Species for Wooden Figures*, Sutton.

42. Sheppard, T. (1901), *Notes on Ancient Model of a Boat*, HMP4.

43. Raftery, B. (1994, 1997), *Pagan Celtic Ireland*, Thames and Hudson.

44. Green, M. J. (1986, 1993, 1997), *The Gods of the Celts*, Sutton.

45. Green, M. J. ed. (1995), *The Celtic World*, in Chapter 15, *Wood and the Wheelwright*, S. Piggott, Routledge.

46. Coles, B. (1990), 'Anthropomorphic wooden figures', *Proceedings of the Prehistoric Society*, 56, pp. 315–333.

47. Sheppard, T. (1901), *Notes on Ancient Model of a Boat*, HMP4.

48. Gibson, A. and Simpson, D. eds (1998), 'Prehistoric Ritual and Religion', Ch. 13, Coles, B. *Wood Species for Wooden Figures*, Sutton.

49. Megaw, J. V. S and M. R. (1989, 1990, 1996), *Celtic Art*, Thames and Hudson.

50. Chadwick, N. (1970), *The Celts*, Penguin.

51. Griffiths, B. (1996), *Aspects of Anglo-Saxon Magic*, Anglo-Saxon Books.

52. Gibson, A. and Simpson, D. eds (1998), 'Prehistoric Ritual and Religion', Ch. 13, Coles, B. *Wood Species for Wooden Figures*, Sutton.

53. Clark, J. G. D. (1961), 'Neolithic bows from Somerset, England. Prehistoric Archery in N.W. Europe', *Proceedings of the Prehistoric Society*, no. 3, 1961.

54. Auden, W. H. trans. (1970), *The Elder Edda, a selection*, Vintage Books.

55. Griffiths, B. (1996), *Aspects of Anglo-Saxon Magic*, Anglo-Saxon Books.

56. Gibson, A. and Simpson, D. eds (1998), 'Prehistoric Ritual and Religion', Ch. 13, Coles, B. *Wood Species for Wooden Figures*, Sutton.

57. Gibson, A. and Simpson, D. eds (1998), 'Prehistoric Ritual and Religion', Ch. 13, Coles, B. *Wood Species for Wooden Figures*, Sutton.

58. Gibson, A. and Simpson, D. eds (1998), 'Prehistoric Ritual and Religion', Ch. 13, Coles, B. *Wood Species for Wooden Figures*, Sutton.

59. Gibson, A. and Simpson, D. eds (1998), 'Prehistoric Ritual and Religion', Ch. 13, Coles, B. *Wood Species for Wooden Figures*, Sutton.

60. Porter, N. (1913), *Websters Revised and Unabridged Dictionary*, G. and C. Merriam Co.

61. Rattue, J. (1995), *The Living Stream, Holy Wells in Historical Context*, The Boydell Press.

62. Gibson, A. and Simpson, D. eds (1998), 'Prehistoric Ritual and Religion', Ch. 13, Coles, B. *Wood Species for Wooden Figures*, Sutton.

63. Blair, J. (1995), 'Anglo-Saxon pagan shrines and their Prototypes, *A-S Studies in Archaeology and History*, no. 8, 1995, Oxford University committee for Archaeology.

64. Blair, J. (1995), 'Anglo-Saxon pagan shrines and their prototypes', *A-S Studies in Archaeology and History*, no. 8, 1995, Oxford University Committee for Archaeology.

65. Griffiths, B. (1996), *Anglo-Saxon Magic*, Anglo-Saxon Books.

66. Chadwick, N. (1970), *The Celts*, Penguin.

67. Chadwick, N. (1970), *The Celts*, Penguin.

68. Chadwick, N. (1970), *The Celts*, Penguin.

69. Lowe, J. (1897), *The Yew-trees of Great Britain and Ireland*, Macmillan.

70. Chadwick, N. (1970), *The Celts*, Penguin.
71. Henig, M. (1984, 1995), *Religion in Roman Britain*, Batsford.
72. Henig, M. (1984, 1995), *Religion in Roman Britain*, Batsford.
73. Green, M. J. (1986, 1993, 1997), *The Gods of the Celts*, Sutton.
74. Green, M. J. (1992), *The Dictionary of Celtic Myth and Legend*, Thames and Hudson.
75. Green, M. J. (1992), *The Dictionary of Celtic Myth and Legend*, Thames and Hudson.
76. Snailham. R. (1986), *Normandy and Brittany*, Weidenfield and Nicholson.
77. Green, M. J. (1986, 1993, 1997), *The Gods of The Celts*, Sutton.
78. Green, M. J. (1986, 1993, 1997), *The Gods of The Celts*, Sutton.
79. Mills, A. D. (1993, 1996), *Oxford Dictionary of English Place-names*, Oxford University Press.
80. Green, M. J. (1986, 1993, 1997), *The Gods of the Celts*, Sutton.
81. Watson, W. J. (1926, 1986, 1993), *The History of the Celtic Place-names of Scotland*, Blackwood and Berlinn.
82. Hubert, H. (1988), *The History of Civilisation: The Rise of the Celts*, Dorset Press.
83. McCulloch, J. A. (1911), *The Religion of the Ancient Celts*, T. and T. Clark, Edinburgh.
84. Caesar, *De Bello Gallico*, Liber VI, XXXI.
85. Boon, G. C. (1978), 'A Romano-British Wooden Carving from Llanio', *Bulletin of the Board of Celtic Studies*, XXVII, 1978, 619–624.
86. Boon, G. C. (1978), 'A Romano-British Wooden Carving from Llanio', *Bulletin of the Board of Celtic Studies*, XXVII, 1978, 619–624.
87. Boon, G. C. (1978), 'A Romano-British Wooden Carving from Llanio,' *Bulletin of the Board of Celtic Studies*, XXVII, 1978, 619–624.
88. Henig, M. (1984, 1995), *Religion in Roman Britain*, Batsford.
89. Boon, G. C. (1978), 'A Romano-British Wooden Carving from Llanio', *Bulletin of the Board of Celtic Studies*, XXVII, 1978, 619–624.
90. Green, M. J. (1986, 1993, 1997), *The Gods of the Celts*, Sutton.
91. Raftery, B. (1994, 1997), *Pagan Celtic Ireland*, Thames and Hudson.
92. Raftery, B. (1994, 1997), *Pagan Celtic Ireland*, Thames and Hudson.
93. Raftery, B. (1994, 1997), *Pagan Celtic Ireland*, Thames and Hudson.
94. Raftery, B. (1994, 1997), *Pagan Celtic Ireland*, Thames and Hudson.
95. Raftery, B. (1994, 1997), *Pagan Celtic Ireland*, Thames and Hudson.
96. Raftery, B. (1994, 1997), *Pagan Celtic Ireland*, Thames and Hudson.
97. Raftery, B. (1994, 1997), *Pagan Celtic Ireland*, Thames and Hudson.
98. Green, M. J. (1986, 1993, 1997), *The Gods of the Celts*, Sutton.
99. Raftery, B. (1994, 1997), *Pagan Celtic Ireland*, Thames and Hudson.
100. O'Curry, E. (1873), *Manners and Customs of the Ancient Irish*, Williams and Norgate.
101. O'Curry, E. (1873), *Manners and Customs of the Ancient Irish*, Williams and Norgate.
102. O'Curry, E. (1873), *Manners and Customs of the Ancient Irish*, Williams and Norgate.
103. *Bulletin of the Board of Celtic Studies*, XXVII, 1978, 619–624.
104. Raftery, B. (1994, 1997), *Pagan Celtic Ireland*, Thames and Hudson.
105. Raftery, B. (1994, 1997), *Pagan Celtic Ireland*, Thames and Hudson.
106. Megaw, J. V. S. and M. R. (1989, 1990, 1996), *Celtic Art*, Thames and Hudson.
107. Megaw, J. V. S. and M. R. (1989, 1990, 1996), *Celtic Art*, Thames and Hudson.
108. *Bulletin of the Board of Celtic Studies*, XXVII, 1978, 619–624.
109. Johnson, W. (1915), *Byways in British Archaeology*, Oxford University Press.
110. Geake, H. (1997), *The Use of Grave-Goods in Conversion-Period England, c. 600-c. 800*, BAR British Series 261.
111. Geake, H. (1997), *The Use of Grave-Goods in Conversion-Period England, c. 600-c. 800*, BAR British Series 261.
112. Loudon, J. C. (1838), *Arboretum et Fruticetum Brittannicum, or the Trees and Shrubs of Britain*, vol. 4, Longman.
113. Lowe, J. (1897), *Yew Trees of Great Britain and Ireland*, Macmillan.

114. Loudon, J. C. (1838), *Arboretum et Fruticetum Brittannicum, or the Trees and Shrubs of Britain*, vol. 4, Longman.
115. Graves, R. (1948, 1961), *The White Goddess*, Faber and Faber.
116. Watson, W. J. (1926, 1986, 1993), *The History of the Celtic Place-names of Scotland*, Blackwood.

A Gazetteer of Ancient Yews

The following gazetteer provides a selective list of older yews found in Britain today. Most of them are in churchyards, and can therefore be visited in most cases. The trees are in varying condition, with many having lost significant portions of trunk, and most of them are hollow. Though the largest trees are not always the oldest, most of the largest listed trees are easily in excess of a thousand years age and can, therefore, act as direct indicators of early settlement in their vicinity.

A more comprehensive database, is maintained by the Conservation Foundation (1 Kensington Gore London, sw7 2AR) as part of their Yew Tree Campaign. I am grateful to the Foundation for help compiling the gazetteer, to Andy McGeeney for the map references given below, to A. Meredith for some of his *Sacred Yew* Gazetteer data, also to T. Hills, T. Hindson and A. Morton for their information.

Place-name	County	Ordnance Survey Grid Reference	Estimated girth and comments
Bucklebury	Berkshire	SU 539 686	27ft
Ankerwyke	Berkshire	TQ 005 726	31ft
Cilycwm	Carmarthenshire	SN 753 400	23ft
Llanfair Clydogau	Ceredigion	SN 625 513	22ft
Strata Florida	Ceredigion	SN 746 658	23 ft (7m)
Overton-on-Dee	Clwyd	SJ 373 418	20ft yew circle
Llanarmon Dyffryn Ceiriog	Clwyd	SJ 314 332	25ft pair
Borrowdale	Cumbria	NY235 125	24ft no churchyard
Lorton	Cumbria	NY161254	19ft no existing churchyard
Allestree	Derbyshire	SK345395	17ft fragment
Darley Dale	Derbyshire	SK 267 615	33ft
Doveridge	Derbyshire	SK115 345	22ft
Muggington	Derbyshire	SK283 429	24ft
Farway	Devon	SY 186 954	25ft
Heavitree	Devon	SX 935 925	hundred court tree fragment

Place-name	County	Ordnance Survey Grid Reference	Estimated girth and comments
Kenn	Devon	SX 922 857	40ft
Mamhead	Devon	SX 931 808	31ft
Payhembury	Devon	ST 088 018	46ft shattered
Shirwell	Devon	SS 547 374	24ft
Broad Windsor	Dorset	ST 437 026	33ft
Knowlton Henge	Dorset	SU 024 103	25ft
Woolland	Dorset	ST 776 070	32ft
Glyncorrwg	Glamorgan	SS 874 99	24ft
Llanmihangel	Glamorgan	SS 981 719	22ft
St Bride's-Super-Ely	Glamorgan	ST 097 776	26ft
Awre	Gloucestershire	SO 709 081	22ft
Broadwell	Gloucestershire	SP 201 277	25ft
Forthampton	Gloucestershire	SO 858 326	7ft (was 27ft)
Staunton	Gloucestershire	SO 781 293	31ft
Harlington	Greater London	TQ 088 783	19ft
Totteridge	Greater London	TQ 247 943	26ft
Betws Newydd	Gwent	SO 363 058	33ft
Capel-y-ffin	Gwent	SO 255 316	20ft
Llanarth	Gwent	SO 375 109	26ft
Llanedeyrn	Gwent	ST 221 820	27ft
Llanfoist	Gwent	SO 290 138	25ft
Llangattock juxta Usk	Gwent	SO 330 096	24ft, forming part of boundary wall
Llanllowel	Gwent	ST 393 986	26ft
Llansoy	Gwent	SO 442 024	30ft
Mamhilad	Gwent	SO 305 034	31ft
Mynydislwyn	Gwent	ST 193 939	27ft
Ffynnon Bedr	Gwynedd	SH 763 693	24ft
Llanddeiniolen	Gwynedd	SH 545 659	28ft
Llanelltyd	Gwynedd	SH 717 195	21ft
Llangower	Gwynedd	SH 903 323	24ft
Llanymawddy	Gwynedd	SH 903 190	27ft
Mallwyd	Gwynedd	SH 863 125	31ft
Pennant Melangell	Gwynedd	SJ 024 265	27ft
Bishopstoke	Hampshire	SU 467 197	17ft, not churchyard
Boarhunt	Hampshire	SU 604 083	27ft
Corhampton	Hampshire	SU 610 203	24ft
Farringdon	Hampshire	SU 713 354	30ft
Itchen Abbas	Hampshire	SU 535 327	26ft
Lockerley	Hampshire	SU 299 246	25ft
Long Sutton	Hampshire	SU 738 474	18ft

Place-name	County	Ordnance Survey Grid Reference	Estimated girth and comments
Shipton Bellinger	Hampshire	SU 236 446	26ft, In a private field
South Hayling	Hampshire	SU 722 000	33ft
Tangley	Hampshire	SU 334 525	19ft
Warblington	Hampshire	SU 728 053	no measurement
Cusop	Herefordshire	SO 240 415	30ft
Kentchurch Court	Herefordshire	SO 422 258	35ft, not churchyard
Linton	Herefordshire	SO 665 254	33ft
Much Marcle	Herefordshire	SO 657 327	30ft
Peterchurch	Herefordshire	SO 345 384	28ft
Yazor	Herefordshire	SO 404 464	29ft
Benington	Hertfordshire	TL 293 235	23ft
Little Munden	Hertfordshire	TL335219	20ft
Thorley	Hertfordshire	TL 476 188	20ft
Bidborough	Kent	TQ 565 432	26ft
Buckland in Dover	Kent	TR 305 427	24ft
Cudham	Kent	TQ 445 600	28ft
Downe	Kent	TQ 433 616	25ft
Eastling	Kent	TQ 965 566	31ft
Godmersham	Kent	TR 062 505	24ft
Kemsing	Kent	TQ 578 596	23ft, no church
Leeds	Kent	TQ 826 533	30ft
Loose	Kent	TR 757 521	33ft
Molash	Kent	TR 024 522	29ft
Stansted	Kent	TQ 606 621	28ft
Stockbury	Kent	TQ 846 616	28ft
Tilmanstone	Kent	TR 303 515	30ft
Ulcombe	Kent	TR 116 449	26ft
Belvoir Castle	Leicestershire	SK 819 337	23ft
Warburton	Lancashire	SJ 696 896	10ft
Helmdon	Northamptonshire	SP 590 432	28ft
Britwell Salome	Oxfordshire	SU 675 936	23ft
Didcot	Oxfordshire	SU 529 899	22ft
Iffley	Oxfordshire	SU 526 025	25ft
Rycote Manor	Oxfordshire	SP 667 047	25ft
South Moreton	Oxfordshire	SU 557 880	23ft
Fortingall	Perthshire	NN 741 470	56ft; the largest recorded trunk girth in Britain
Cascob	Powys	SO 035 664	25ft
Llanafan Fawr	Powys	SN 969 558	32ft

Place-name	County	Ordnance Survey Grid Reference	Estimated girth and comments
Llanfaredd	Powys	SO 069 508	36ft
Llanerfyl	Powys	SJ 035 097	35ft
Llanfeugan	Powys	SO 087 246	32 ft, near yew circle
Llanfihangel nant melan	Powys	SO 180 581	30ft
Llansilin	Powys	SJ 375415	25ft
Llanspyddid	Powys	SO 012 282	27ft
Llanyre	Powys	SO 044 623	25ft
Buttington	Powys	SJ 249 088	26ft
Alltmawr	Powys	SO 073 468	30ft
Rhulen	Powys	SO 138 499	27ft
Aberedw	Powys	SO 080 473	22ft
Nantmel	Powys	SO 023 665	30ft
Discoed	Powys	SO 276 648	37ft
Whitton	Powys	SO 271 674	27ft
Craigends	Renfrewshire	NS415 665	21ft
Dundonnell	Ross-shire	NH 095 875	21ft, private garden
Hope Bagot	Shropshire	SO 589 741	23ft
Kenley	Shropshire	SJ 563 007	28ft
Milson	Shropshire	SO 639 728	20ft
Easthope	Shropshire	So 566 952	22ft
Ashford Carbonnel	Shropshire	SO 525 709	27ft
Acton Scott	Shropshire	SO 454 895	26ft
Acton Burnell Park	Shropshire	SJ 533 019	25ft
Church Preen	Shropshire	SO 543 982	22ft, was much larger
Ruyton XI Towns	Shropshire	SJ 395 223	26ft, shattered
Norbury	Shropshire	SO 364 928	35ft
Uppington	Shropshire	SJ 598 094	29ft
Clun	Shropshire	SO 301 805	33ft
Claverley	Shropshire	SO 793 935	28ft
Middleton Scriven	Shropshire	SO 681 875	29ft, in field away from existing church
Loughton	Shropshire	SO 616 831	33ft
Bicknoller	Somerset	ST 111 394	24ft
Compton Dundon	Somerset	ST 479 326	23ft
Abbots Leigh	Somerset	ST 544 740	25ft
Ashbrittle	Somerset	ST 052 214	38ft, split
Dinder	Somerset	ST 575 445	32 ft
Combe Florey	Somerset	ST 151 312	28ft
Elworthy	Somerset	ST 083 350	29ft

Place-name	County	Ordnance Survey Grid Reference	Estimated girth and comments
Bickenhall	Somerset	ST 282 185	28ft, no church remains
Tettenhall	Staffordshire	SJ 885 005	24ft, three boundary yews
Wintershall	Surrey	TQ 012 413	29ft, no church
Norbury Park (Druid's Grove)	Surrey	TQ 157 533	the largest is 24ft; many woodland yews
Peper Harrow	Surrey	SU 935 441	27ft
Newlands Corner (Merrow Down)	Surrey	TQ 030 490	24ft, many woodland yews
Dunsfold	Surrey	SU 998 363	24ft
Crowhurst	Surrey	TQ 390 475	32ft
Haslemere	Surrey	SU 907 346	30ft; no church by Keffolds Farm
Tandridge	Surrey	TQ 374 512	36ft
Old Enton	Surrey	SU 953 398	25ft; no existing church; near a hillfort
Hambledon	Surrey	SU 970 390	35ft
East Lavant	Sussex	SU 862 085	24ft
Barlavington	Sussex	SU 972 160	26ft; located near farm
Tangmere	Sussex	SU 902 062	24ft
Wilmington	Sussex	TQ 544 043	30ft
Crowhurst	Sussex	TQ 757 123	28ft
Kingley Vale	Sussex	SU 822 105	more than 23ft; yew woodlands
Coldwaltham	Sussex	TQ 024 166	31ft
Alton Priors	Wiltshire	SU 109 621	28ft
Lyneham	Wiltshire	SU 024 786	25ft
Tisbury	Wiltshire	ST 943 291	31ft
Longbridge Deverill	Wiltshire	ST 866 414	29ft
Churchill	Worcestershire	SO 879 793	19ft, fragment
Kyre Park	Worcestershire	SO 626 635	28ft split
Powick	Worcestershire	SO 834 515	20ft, fallen was larger
Thrift House Farm	South Yorkshire	SK 324 845	18ft, boundary yew no existing church
Fountains Abbey	North Yorkshire	SE 275 681 22ft	2 of the Seven Sisters survive

Bibliography

Allcroft, A. H. (1908), *Earthworks of England*, Macmillan and Co.

Allen, M. J. and Gardiner, J. (2000), *Neolithic Trees in Langstone Harbour.*

Andrew, J. (1992), *Churchyard Yew Trees in the Archdeaconry of Gower*, from Gower, XLIII, 1992.

Archaeologia Cambrensis (1876), p. 345.

Aubury, J. (1719), *Natural History and Antiquities of the County of Surrey.*

Auden, W. H. (1970), translation *The Elder Edda, a selection*, Vintage Books, NY.

Baines, D. (1822), *Directory of Yorkshire*, vol. 1, West Riding.

Barrington, D., *Philosophical Transactions*, LIX, December 1759, p. 37

Baxter, T. (1992), *The Eternal Yew*, Self Publishing Association.

Blair, J. (1995), 'Anglo-Saxon pagan shrines and their prototypes', *Anglo-Saxon Studies in Archaeology and History*, 8, 1995, Oxford University Committee for Archaeology.

Bonsai Magazine (1997), Issue 36, Winter 1997.

Borrow, G. (1862), *Wild Wales*, John Murray, London.

Bromwich, R. (1982, 1987), *Dafydd ap Gwilym Poems*, Gomer Press, Llandysul.

Boon, G. C. (1978), *A Romano-British Wooden Carving from Llanio*

Brown, D. L., *Evaluation of Kidderminster, Blakedown & Hagley Bypass + A449 link*, Herefordshire & Worcestershire County Archaeological Service Report.

Brueton, D. and Chetan, A. (1994), *The Sacred Yew*, Penguin Arkana.

Bulletin of the Board of Celtic Studies, XXVII, 1978, 619–624.

Canterbury Probate Office Register, Wingham, fol. 51, Will of Thomas Alday of Ash, Kent, dated 19 December 1520, printed in *Archaeologia Cantiana*, 34 (1922) pp. 48–9.

Caesar, *De Bello Gallico*, Liber. VI, XXXI.

Campbell, J. (1991), *The Anglo-Saxons*, Penguin.

Campbell, John Gregorson, Minister of Tiree (1900) *Superstitions of the Highlands and Islands of Scotland, Collected Entirely from Oral Sources*, James Maclehose and Sons, Glasgow University Press.

Chadwick, N. (1970), *The Celts*, Penguin.

Clark, J. G. D. (1961), 'Neolithic bows from Somerset, England. Prehistoric Archery in N.W. Europe', *Proceedings of the Prehistoric Society*, 3, 1961.

Coles, B. (1990), 'Anthropomorphic wooden figures'. *Proceedings of the Prehistoric Society*, 56, pp. 315–333.

Coles, J., Fenwick, V., and Hutchinson, G. (1993), eds, *A Spirit of Enquiry, Essays for Ted Wright*, Wetland Archaeology Research Project.

Cornish, Vaughan (1946), *The Churchyard Yew and Immortality*, Muller and Company.

Dickson, J. H. (1994), 'The yew tree (Taxus baccata L.) in Scotland – native or early introduction or both?' *Scottish Forestry*, 48 (4), 253–261.

Dickson, J. H. and Dickson, C. (2000), *Plants and People in Ancient Scotland*, Tempus, Stroud.

Dallimore, W. (1908), *Holly, Yew and Box*, John Lane, The Bodley Head.

Davies, W. (1978), *An Early Welsh Microcosm*, Royal Historical Society.

De Candolle, A. (1831), *Physiologie Vegetale*.

Doble, Canon G. H. (1971, 1984, 1993), *Lives of the Welsh Saints*, University of Wales Press.

Duncomb, Rev. John, *History of Herefordshire*, 1804–12.

Edlin, H. L. (1958), *The Living Forest*, Thames and Hudson.

Edlin, H. L. (1967), *Man and Plants*, Aldus Books, London.

Evans, J. D. (1988), *Churchyard Yews of Gwent*, Archangel Press.

Fenton, R. (1804), *Tours in Wales*.

Fowler, B. (2000), *Iceman*, Macmillan.

Fry, J. (1998), *Warriors at the Edge Of Time*, Capall Bann.

Fry, R. and Hulse, T. G. (1994), 'The Whistlebitch Well, Utkinton, Cheshire', *Source Magazine*, New Series, Issue 1, 1994.

Gadeau de Kerville, H., *Les Vieux Arbres de la Normandie*, 1895, 1930, 1932.

Gantz. J. (1981), *Early Irish Myths and Sagas*, Penguin Classics.

The Gardeners Chronicle, 30 May 1874.

Geake, H. (1997), *The Use of Grave-Goods in Conversion-Period England, c. 600-c. 850 AD*, BAR British Series, 261.

Gelling, M. and Cole, A. (2000), *The Landscape of Place-names*, Shaun Tyas, Stamford.

Gelling. M. (1975), *Signposts to the Past*, Dent, London.

Gentleman's Magazine (1787), p. 313, cited in *Notes and Queries*, 2nd series, no. 37, 13 September (1856), p. 215.

Gerish, W. B. (n.d.), *Hertfordshire Folk Lore*, S. R. Publishers.

Gibson, A. and Simpson, D. eds (1998), *Prehistoric Ritual and Religion*.

Godwin, Sir. H. (1975), *History of the British Flora*, Cambridge.

Gomme, G. L. (1880), *Primitive Folk-Moots*, Nash's Worcestershire, I, p. 57.

Gough, R. ed. (1789), Camden's *Brittannia* (1607).

Gould, I. C. (1908), *Victoria County History of Herefordshire*, vol. I, p. 230.

Graves, R. (1961), *The White Goddess*, Faber and Faber.

Greaves, C. S. (1880), 'The Darley Yew', *Derbyshire Archaeological Journal*, vol. 2, pp. 100–120.

Green, M. J. (1986, 1993, 1997), *The Gods of the Celts*, Sutton.

Green, M. J. ed. (1995), *The Celtic World*, Routledge.

Greene, J. Patrick (1992), *Medieval Monasteries*, Leicester University Press.

Gregory, D. (1991), *Country Churchyards in Wales*, Gwasg Carreg Gwalch.

Griffiths, B. (1996), *Aspects of Anglo-Saxon Magic*, Anglo-Saxon Books.

Hampshire Newsletter of The Prehistoric Society, no. 34, April 2000.

Hampshire County Council Website (1999), Hampshire Treasures, www.hants.gov.uk.

Harte, J. (1996), 'How Old is That Yew?' *At The Edge Magazine*, no. 4, December 1996.

Hartzell, H. (1991), *The Yew Tree, a Thousand Whispers*, Hulogosi Press, Oregon, USA.

Hardy, R. (1992), *The Longbow, A Social and Military History*, Haynes.

Henig, M. (1984, 1995), *Religion in Roman Britain*, Batsford.

Highland and Agricultural Society of Scotland, *Old and Remarkable Trees of Scotland*, Edinburgh, Blackwood and Sons, 1867.

Bibliography   Hindson, T. R. (2000), 'The Growth Rate of Yew Trees: An Empirically Generated Growth Curve,' The Dendrologist's Allen Mitchell Memorial Lecture, 4 November 2000, in association with The Conservation Foundation.

Hindson, T. R. (1997–1998), *Merdon Castle Study*, Companions of the Yew Archive, vol. 1.

Hodder, M. A. (1991), 'Excavations at Sandwell Priory, 1982–1988', *South Staffordshire Archaeological and Historical Society Transactions*, XXXI (1991 for 1989–1990).

Hooke, D. (1990), *Worcestershire Anglo-Saxon Charter Bounds*, Boydell.

Hooke, D. and Ambrose, R. (1999), *Boxley, The Story of An English Parish*, Modern Press Ltd.

Hope Bagot Parish Paths Committee Leaflet, 1998.

Hope, R. C. (1893), *The Llegendary Lore of the Holy Wells of England*, Elliot Stack.

Hoskins, W. D. (1955, 1985), *The Making Of The English Landscape*, Penguin.

Hubert, H. (1988), *The History of Civilisation: The Rise of the Celts*, Dorset Press.

Hull, E. (1928), *Folklore of the British Isles*, Methuen.

International Journal of Plant Science, 155(5), University of Chicago, pp. 569–582.

Jackson, K. H. (1964), *The Oldest Irish Tradition: A Window on the Iron Age*, Cambridge University Press.

Jackson, K. H. (1971), *A Celtic Miscellany*, Penguin.

Johnson, W. (1912), *Byways in British Archaeology*, Cambridge University Press.

Jones, F. (1954, 1992 and 1998), *Holy Wells of Wales*, University of Wales Press.

Jones, T. Gwynn (1930, 1979), *Welsh Customs and Folklore*, Rowman and Littlefield.

Jones, M. (1987), 'The Oldest living thing in Sheffield?' in *The Hallamshire Historian*, vol. 1, no. 2, Spring 1987, pp. 36–37.

Jones-Baker, D. (1977), *The Folklore of Hertfordshire*, Batsford, pp. 61–3.

Jones-Davies, J. (1970), Brecknockshire and Radnorshire Museum News.

Joyce, P. W. (1875), *The Origin and History of Irish Names of Places*, first series, McGlashin and Gill, Dublin.

Joyce, P. W. (1903), *A Social History of Ancient Ireland*, Longman.

Keating, *History of Ireland*, ed. P. S. Dinneen, *Irish Texts Society*, I, p. 223.

Kermack, W. R., *Emblems of the Gael*, Scottish Gaelic Studies.

Kinmonth, F. (1998), *Yews News*, The Conservation Foundation, Issue No. 2, February 1998.

Kinsella, T. (1969), *The Tain*, Oxford University Press.

Larson, D. W., Doubt, J. and Matthes-Sears, U. (1994), *Radially Sectored Hydraulic Pathways in the Xylem of Thuja occidentalis as Revealed by the use of Dyes*.

Larson, D. W. (1999), 'Ancient Stunted Trees', *Nature Magazine*, vol. 398, April, 1999.

Lees, E. (1868), *Botany of the Malvern Hills etc.*, Simpson and Marshall.

Lees, E. (1870), 'Hagley, Pedmore, Wichbury Camp, etc'. *Proceedings of the Worcestershire Naturalists' Club*, Friday, 28 October 1870.

Lees, E. (1877), 'Bromsgrove, Fockbury Mill, Bourn Heath, The Bumble Hole, etc', *Proceedings of Worcestershire Naturalists' Club*, 12 August 1877.

Lines, H. H. (1880), 'Bromyard, Thornbury, The Wall Hill, etc.', *Worcestershire Naturalists' Club*, 8 June 1880.

Lees, E. (1882), Worcestershire Naturalists' Club *Minutes for Himley, Wichbury and Hagley*, 19 May.

Loudon, J. C. (1838), *Arboretum et Fruticetum Brittannicum, or the Trees and Shrubs of Britain*, vol. 4, Longman.

Lowe, J. (1897), *Yew Trees of Great Britain and Ireland*, Macmillan.

Lucas, A. T. (1963), 'The sacred trees of Ireland', *Journal of the Cork Historical and Archaeological Society*, 68, pp. 16–54.

MacCana, P. (1968, 1983), *Celtic Mythology*, Hamlyn.

McCulloch, J. A. (1911), *The Religion of the Ancient Celts*, T. and T. Clark.

MacNeill, J. (1909), 'Notes on the distribution, history, grammar and import of the Irish Ogham inscriptions', *Proceedings of the Royal Irish Academy*, XXVII, pp. 329–371.

Manley, John (1985), 'The Archer and the army in the late Saxon period', *Anglo-Saxon Studies in Archaeology and History*, vol. 4, Oxford Uniiversity Committee for Archaeology.

Martin, P. (1999), 'The Historical Ecology of Old Oswestry', *Shropshire Botanical Society Newsletter*, Autumn 1999, pp. 10–11.

Matthews, C. and J. (1997), *The Encyclopaedia of Celtic Wisdom*, Element.

Mee, A. (1944), *The King's England*, Shropshire volume.

Mee, A. ed. (1944), *The King's England*, Hampshire volume.

Mee, A. ed. (1944), *The King's England*, Sussex volume.

Mee, A. ed. (1944), *The King's England*, Kent volume.

Mee, A. ed. (1944), *The King's England*, Gloucestershire volume.

Megaw, J. V. S. and M. R. (1989, 1990, 1996), *Celtic Art*, Thames and Hudson.

Meyrick, S. R. (1810), *History and Antiquities of the County of Cardigan*.

Miles. A. (1999), *Silva: British Trees*, Ted Smart.

Miles, D. H. and Bridge, M. C., *The Tree-ring Dating of Building Timbers, The Yew Tunnel and Other Trees at Aberglasney House and Gardens, Llandeilo, Carmarthenshire*, RCAHMW Report, 1999.

Mills, A. D. (1993, 1996), *Oxford Dictionary of English Place-names*, Oxford University Press.

Mills, K. (1999), *The Cumbrian Yew Book*, Yew Trees for the Millennium in Cumbria.

Mitchell, A. (1985, 1987), *The Complete Guide to Trees*, Parkgate Books.

Mitchell, F. J. G. (1990), 'The history and vegetation dynamics of a yew wood (Taxus baccata L.) in S.W. Ireland', *New Phytologist*, 115, pp. 573–577.

Moir, A. K. (1999), 'The dendrochronological potential of modern yew (taxus baccata) with special reference to yew from Hampton Court Palace, UK', *New Phytologist*, 144, 479–488, Cambridge University Press.

Morton, A. (1986, 1995), *The Trees of Shropshire*, Airlife.

Nash-Williams, V. E. (1950), *The Early Christian Monuments of Wales*, University of Wales Press.

Newall, A. S. (1930), 'Barrow 85, Amesbury (Goddard's list)', *Wiltshire Archaeological and Natural History Magazine*, vol. 45, pp. 432–58.

Notes and Queries, vol. 1 (19), 9 March 1850 p. 294.

Notes and Queries, 2nd series (124), 15 May 1858.

Notes and Queries, vol. 10 (247), 22 July 1854.

Notes and Queries, 5th series, v, p. 376.

Naturalists Journal, 1896, p. 99.

O'Curry, E. (1873), *Manners and Customs of the Ancient Irish*, Williams and Norgate, vol. 2.

O'Curry, E., *Manuscript materials for Irish History*, appendix II, p. 466.

O'Grady, S. H. (1892), *Silva Gadelica*, I-XXXI, Williams and Norgate.

Bibliography

Palmer, W. T., *Odd Corners in Derbyshire, Rambles, Scrambles, Climbs and Sport*, Skeffington and Son.

Parry, T. (1962), *The Oxford Book of Welsh Verse*, Oxford University Press.

Peterson, Rector, M. A. (1922), *A Short Guide to the Parish Church and Churchyard of Grasmere 1909–1922*.

Phillips, R. (1981), *Mushrooms and other Fungi of Great Britain and Europe*, Pan.

Phythian-Adams, C. (1975), *Local History and Folklore: A new framework*.

Piggott, S. (1950, 1985), *William Stukeley*, Thames and Hudson.

Pigott, C. D. and Pigott, M. E. (1963), 'Late-glacial and post-glacial deposits at Malham, Yorkshire', *New Phytologist*, 62, 317–34.

Plomer, W. ed. (1977), *Kilvert's Diary, a selection*, Penguin.

Porter, N. ed. (1913), *Webster's Revised and Unabridged Dictionary*, G and C Merriam and Co.

Porter, J. (1995), *Aspects of Anglo-Saxon Riddles*, Anglo-Saxon Books.

Proceedings from the Hampshire Field Club and Archaeological Society, 47, 1991, 153–170.

Proceedings of the Worcestershire Naturalists Club (1881–1910).

Rackham, O. (1994), *The Illustrated History of the Countryside*, Weidenfield and Nicholson.

Rackham, O. (1976), *Trees and Woodland in the British landscape*, J. M. Dent

Rackham, O. (1989, 1993), *The Last Forest, The Story of Hatfield Forest*, J. M. Dent.

Raftery, B. (1994, 1997), *Pagan Celtic Ireland*, Thames and Hudson.

Rattue, J. (1995), *The Living Stream, Holy Wells in Historical Context*, The Boydell Press.

Redmonds, G. and Hey. D., 'The Opening-up of Scammonden', LANDSCAPES 2:1 (Spring 2001), Windgather Press.

Rees, A. and B. (1961), *Celtic Heritage*, Thames and Hudson.

Renfrew, C. (1987, 1989), *Archaeology and Language, the Puzzle of Indo-European Origins*, Cambridge University Press.

Revue Celtique, XV (1893) p. 420.

Reynolds, A. (1999), *Later Anglo-Saxon England*, Tempus.

Rhys, Sir J. (1901), *Celtic Folklore*, Clarendon Press.

Richards, M. trans. (1954), *The Laws of Hywel Dda*, Willmer Brothers and Co.

Robinson, D. (1996), *Cadw guide to Strata Florida*.

Ross, A. and Robins, D. (1989), *The Life and Death of a Druid Prince*, Rider.

Rumble, A. and Mills, A. eds (1997), *Names, Places and People, an Onomastic Miscellany for John McNeal Dodgson*.

Sheppard, T. (1901), *Notes on Ancient Model of a Boat*, HMP4.

Sikes, W. (1880), *British Goblins*, Sampson Lowe, London.

Sinclair, J. B. and Fenn, R. W. D. (1995), *Three Parish Churches, Glascwm, Rhulen & Cregrina*.

Snailham, R. (1986), *Normandy and Brittany*, Weidenfield and Nicholson.

Sparry, J. (1999), *Toasted Teacakes and Baked Potatoes*, 31 Essays, The Black Country Society Press.

Spence, Lewis. (1913, 1962), *Dictionary of Medieval Romance and Romance Writers*, Humanities Press.

Stokes, W. ed. and trans. (1893), *The Prose Tales in the Rennes Dindshenchas*.

Spence, L. (1949, 1971), *The History and Origins of Druidism*, Lon, Rider & Co., reprinted Aquarian Press.

199

Stocker, D. and Went, D. (1995), 'The evidence for a pre-Viking church adjacent to the Anglo-Saxon barrow at Taplow', Bucks, *Archaeology Journal*, 152, pp. 441–454.

Stokes, W. ed. and trans. (1906), 'The Birth of Saint Moling,' *Revue Celtique*, XXVII, p. 281.

Swanton, E. W. (1958), *The Yew Trees of England*, Farnham.

Tabbush, P. M. and White, J. E. (1996), 'Estimation of tree age in ancient yew woodland at Kingley Vale', *Quarterly Forestry Journal*, 90, no. 3, pp. 197–206.

Tabbush, P. (1997), 'Veteran Trees: Habitat, Hazard or Heritage?' paper delivered to Tuesday, 4 March 1997 meeting of Royal Agricultural Society of England and The Royal Forestry Society.

Taylor, C. (1975, 1987, 2000), *Fields in the English Landscape*, History Handbooks, Sutton.

Taylor, Keith, P. (1995), 'Mazers, mead and the wolf's Head Tree: A reconsideration of Old English Riddle 55', *Journal of English and Germanic Philology*, October 1995, University of Tennessee, pp. 497–512.

This England, Quarterley Magazine, Autumn 1975.

Thieme, H. (1997), 'Lower Palaeolithic Hunting Weapons from Shoningen, Germany, The Oldest Spears in the World', *The Newsletter of Prehistoric Society*, no. 26, July 1997.

Thorpe, L. ed. and trans. (1978), *Gerald of Wales: The Journey through Wales, descriptions of Wales*, Penguin Classics.

Tittensor, R. M. (1980), 'Ecological history of yew, Taxus baccata in southern England', *Biological Conservation*, no. 17, 243–265.

Transactions of the Woolhope Field Club, Volume for 1933–35, Page XVII.

Toulmin-Smith, L. ed. (1964), *The Itinerary of John Leland*, in, 1536–1539, part iv, vol. iii, Centaur, London.

Ussher, R. (1880), 'Addenda to Mr Greaves' paper on the Darley Yew', *Derbyshire Archaeological Journal*, vol. 2.

Victoria County History of Hampshire (1908), vol. 3, pp. 417–8.

Watson, W. J. (1904, 1976, 1996) *Place-names of Ross and Cromarty*, Highland Heritage Books.

Watson, W. J. (1926, 1986, 1993), *The History of the Celtic Place-names Of Scotland*, Blackwood.

Watson, W. J. (1926, 1986, 1993) *Celtic Place-names of Scotland*, Birlinn Ltd.

Watt, A. S. (1926), 'Yew Communities of the South Downs', *Journal of Ecology*, 14, pp. 282–316.

Westwood, J. (1985), *Albion*, Grenada.

White, J. E. (1994), *Estimating the age of large trees in Britain*, Forestry Commission

Wilkinson-Latham, R. (1981), *Phaidon Guide to Antique Weapons and Weaponry*, Phaidon.

Wilks, J. H. (1972), *Trees of the British Isles in History and Legend*, Muller.

Williams, S. W. (1889), *Strata Florida, Recent Excavations*, London.

Williams-Freeman, J. P. (1915), *Field Archaeology, As Illustrated by Hampshire*.

Williamson, R. (1975), *The Great Yew Forest*, Readers Union.

Wilson, B. and Mee, F. (1998), *The Medieval Parish Churches of York*, Yorkshire Archaeological Trust.

James G. Wood (1904), *Things to be Observed between Ross and Chepstow*.

The Proceedings of the Woolhope Naturalists Field Club Transactions, p. 293.

Bibliography   Woodward, A. and Leach, P. (1993), *The Uley Shrines*, English Heritage.

Wright, T. (1855), *Archaeologia Cambrensis*, 3rd series 1, pp. 168–174; *Notes and Queries*, 9th series, vi, p. 77.

Yarham, E. R. (1975), 'England's Churchyard Yews', *This England Magazine*, vol. 8, no. 3, Autumn 1975.

Young, F. W. (1950), *Churchill and Blakeshall Parish Booklet*, An edited version of two lectures on local history given by Mr Frederick W. Young (1875–1966) in 1950 and 1957. Reproduced 1997–8, by P. S. Legat.

The Gardeners Chronicle, 30 May, 1874.

Index

ON THE TRAIL OF THE WORLD'S TOUGHEST MOUNTAIN RACE

FAILURE IS AN OPTION

MATT WHYMAN

Vertebrate Publishing, Sheffield
www.v-publishing.co.uk

FAILURE
IS AN
OPTION

MATT WHYMAN

 First published in 2022 by Vertebrate Publishing.

Vertebrate Publishing
Omega Court, 352 Cemetery Road, Sheffield S11 8FT, United Kingdom.
www.v-publishing.co.uk

Cover illustration © Laurie King. www.laurieking.co.uk
Author photogragh © Phill Rodham (MyBibNumber).

This book is a work of non-fiction based on the life of Matt Whyman. The author has stated to the publishers that,
except in such minor respects not affecting the substantial accuracy of the work, the contents of the book are true.

A CIP catalogue record for this book is available from the British Library.

ISBN: 9781839811333 (Paperback)
ISBN: 9781839811340 (Ebook)
ISBN: 9781839811357 (Audiobook)

10 9 8 7 6 5 4 3 2 1

Design by Jane Beagley, Vertebrate Publishing.
Production by Cameron Bonser, Vertebrate Publishing.
www.v-publishing.co.uk

Vertebrate Publishing is committed to printing on paper from sustainable sources.

Printed and bound in the UK by TJ Books Limited, Padstow, Cornwall.

In memory of my mother, Rosemary,
who started something to find a moment of peace.

CONTENTS

PROLOGUE

Anyone who has crossed Crib Goch will be wiser for the experience. Some might also find themselves prematurely older than the years they have lived.

This vertiginous ridge is the most challenging means of summiting Snowdon (Yr Wyddfa), the highest peak in Wales. It's a long knife-edge of a route, 923 metres above sea level at the highest point, with steep-sloping drops on each side. Whether you're a rock hopper or a rank amateur, setting out to reach the far end touches you. I still have some way to go, but already I've learnt a valuable lesson: the toughest challenges are those we face when we've come too far to turn back.

'We're not at parkrun any more,' I mutter to myself, quietly longing for the presence of nice marshals in high-visibility vests. I am just over midway across the ridge, and frankly amazed that any member of the public can have a crack at this if they think they've got what it takes. Even without my glasses, which does little for my nerves, I am pretty sure I can see the curvature of the earth. Crib Goch is classified as a grade 1 scramble, which sounds quite fun until you're here. Then the experience redefines itself for many as a code-brown crawl.

Far below me, inside this mountainous horseshoe with Snowdon at its apex, a lake glitters in the sunshine. A scenic path winds around the water's edge in places. It's smooth, flat, sheltered and would make a lovely stretch for a light jog. From there, I would perhaps pause to peer up at the scattered, ant-like procession of thrill-seekers on the ridge and shake my head disapprovingly. Instead, here I am in a cross-wind, having sweated exclusively through my palms since I ascended the giant curtain of rock to reach the ridge, with questions about my own decision-making.

In a bid to face my fears, I know this is the right thing to do. It's part of my training for a race that expects competitors to take this section in their stride. As a reflection of what's in store, however, it leaves me wondering what the hell I was thinking when I signed up.

In the world of endurance running, the Dragon's Back Race is a monster. Across six days and 380 kilometres, this legendary, intimidating and punishing event traverses the knuckled spine of Wales. Runners begin in the grounds of Conwy Castle in the north, heading south across the wild and rugged landscape to the ramparts of Cardiff Castle. In crossing the entire country from coast to coast, they face 17,400 metres of elevation, which is almost twice the height of Everest. The terrain is largely trackless and challenging at every turn, from steep climbs to tumbling descents, soul-sapping bogs and rock-strewn fells. There are no course markings. The whole thing is self-navigated, with regular checkpoints and tight cut-off times. Then there's the weather, which can be unpredictable and elemental, while competitors must keep one eye on the skies as if they're vulnerable to being picked off by winged, fire-breathing beasts. This last bit might be a stretch, but could come as a blessing for some in a mountain race with a reputation as the toughest and most brutal in the world.

To level with you here, I am not naturally cut out for this calibre of racing. If you're looking for a story about an elite runner pushing for the win, I can safely predict before the race has even started that this story won't end with a massive trophy on my mantelpiece. My map-reading skills are basic and long-forgotten, like French at school. I hate heights, and if there's one thing I loathe more than that, it's camping. I'm from the south of England, which is all but made from cotton wool and a long way from fell-running country. My exposure to brooding, craggy mountains is mostly limited to stock photos on my computer screensaver, and yet here I am. Why? It all comes down to a love of putting one foot in front of the other, which lies at the heart of this race and then takes it to an extreme.

There is a reason why I have paused at this point on the ridge. It's not because I'm frozen in fear, which does strike the unfortunate as they make this crossing. Behind me, I had come across one poor guy crouched tight against the rock face with his back to the wind. His companion stood over him, seemingly immune to danger, and sounded like he was trying out reassuring words in the hope that something might lift this spell. He had exchanged a look with me as if to say everything was under control, which was a relief because I'd have been no help at all. I might look like I'm comfortable in all the gear I intend to wear for the race, but until I've broken myself into this environment it just feels like fancy dress. All I could do was offer him a smile as I manoeuvred around them, well aware that it wouldn't take much for my own composure to slip and turn me into a statue. I just had to keep progressing, hand over hand, foot over foot, and even taking my anchor points to five with my backside where possible. Despite inching along like a dog with worms, I had even dared to think that I might nail this. Ahead, a tombstone of rock obscured what I had believed would be the home run to the other side. I had duly clambered to that point feeling like I was over the worst, only to stop in my tracks before a break in the ridge behind it shaped like the socket for a missing tooth.

'Oh, come on,' I said in exasperation, mostly to myself but also to Mother Nature.

In my research, conducted from the comfort of my sofa back home, I had seen photographs of the rock formation I now faced. Relaxing with a biscuit in one hand and my phone in the other, I just hadn't appreciated the sheer scale of what was known as Crib Goch's Third Pinnacle. Behind me, the preceding two pinnacles had presented no surprises. They were about as challenging to traverse as speed bumps, which had hardly served to slow my ponderous crawl. Taking into account the fact that this one was preceded by quite a deep pocket in the ridge line, the towering slabs on the other side rose up like a scene from Lord of the Rings.

Up until a few minutes ago, when the tombstone had obscured my view, I'd been able to keep one eye on some people ahead. Two women had simply picked their way across the ridge as if they were out for a stroll, and clearly not from this world. Most others, like me, had considered every move they made as if it might be their last. I'd followed the line taken by the pair, constantly on the lookout for the 'polish in the rock', as one of them had suggested when they passed me on the clamber up. Despite feeling like one of those idiots who go up on to the roof in a storm to fix the TV aerial, I found that sticking to the well-worn lines across the top had provided me with some confidence.

Then the third pinnacle had revealed itself to me, and all that fell away.

I see no sign of the two women. I can only conclude that somehow they've negotiated this monolith in my way and are pushing for the point where the ridge joins the tourist footpath to the summit. There is an alternative reason for their disappearance, of course. I just don't want to give it space in my mind. Through my untrained eyes, there appears to be just one way to progress. After gingerly clambering down to the platform in front of the pinnacle, and basically seeking any excuse that I can to postpone the inevitable, I decide to call my wife, Emma. We had last spoken before I started the climb. I'd left her at home for the weekend, promising to take good care of myself. Despite my assurances, I know she'll be worrying. It'll also be good for me to hear her voice, I think to myself, while summoning the favourites on my phone.

Without my glasses, which I use for screen work, I find the list of family members is just a blur. Having stabbed at what I believe to be my other half's number, I catch my breath when our eldest daughter picks up. Grace has just qualified as a doctor, living and working away from home, though she mastered the requisite no-nonsense outlook on life before her fourth birthday.

'Sorry,' I say. 'I meant to call Mum.'

'What's wrong?' she asks me after a moment. 'You sound stressed.'

'I'm not stressed,' I protest, in an octave that suggests otherwise.

Just then, a gust of wind whistles through the gap in the rocks where I'm standing. The silence on the line tells me it didn't go unnoticed.

'Where are you?' Grace has been purposely excluded from my plan to push my fifty-something body through hell later this year. I'm aware this race is something I should've done in my prime. Now it's a question of taking it on before time runs out on me. Given my daughter's medical insight, and the fact that I'm her dear old dad, I didn't think it would be wise to put her in the picture. 'Are you at home?' she presses me. 'You don't sound like you're at home.'

'Just out getting some fresh air,' I say and then attempt to steer her from the cliff edge of truth by asking about her week on the wards.

Fortunately, I've accidentally rung her at a busy time. I've no doubt she'll call her mother in due course and extract what's really going on. For now, I say good-bye as casually as I can for a man on a precipice with his heart in his mouth, and finish the call. Next, with the phone pressed to my nose so I can read the names, I successfully ring my wife. When Emma's answerphone kicks in, I leave her the *kind of jaunty message I imagine I'd share from the other side, and then drop in that I love her just in case.*

Before stowing my phone, I take one last precautionary measure. Clutching an outcrop of rock with my free hand, I take a selfie with Snowdon's majestic east face behind me rising from the lake shore. It's just the shot I want because after putting myself through all this I plan to absolutely milk it on Strava.

Then, mindful that I must keep moving in case the fear finds me here, I step across to the foot of the pinnacle. The only line I can see involves climbing upwards and then swinging out on to a ledge to the right. I've read enough to know that this is the bad side, with a plunging drop if it all goes wrong. From where I'm standing, it's impossible for me to see what follows above and beyond the ledge. I just have to trust that following the shiny, worn stones will lead me safely over. There are plenty of handholds in the wall of the rock. I just can't ignore the abyss on that flank.

With my heart kicking, I shake my arms down to my hands and fingertips and then breathe out long and hard.

'Unless you do this,' I tell myself, 'it's all over.'

PART

01

READY? GO . . .

Everybody runs for different reasons. There's always a motivation, and this can be defined in one of two ways: either we're running *towards* a goal or *away* from something as a means of escape.

For the most part, during his early years as a parent, my dad fell into the latter category. Within minutes of his return home from the daily grind at his London office, he would shed the suit for a polyester T-shirt tucked into shorts cut so high they showed the tan lines from a pair of Speedos.

It was a signature look for the seventies jogger. At a time when the sport wasn't considered to be a way of life but a crank's shortcut to knackered knees, runners like my father had limited choice when it came to kit. As a little boy, I'd watch him hurriedly lace up his tennis shoes by the front door. Then he'd set off into what I could only process as an unknown world.

One hour later, he'd return a different dad. This one had time for me, my younger brother and sister, and my mum. Puffed and perspiring, he'd sit with us at the kitchen table as we finished our tea and ask about our day. Somehow, that time on his feet, alone with his thoughts, had a transformative effect on him.

It was only as I became more tuned in to my surroundings, somewhere around six years old, that I realised Mum was less than happy with him about it.

'I've been at home all day,' she'd remind him on his way out. 'I'll save the washing up for you.'

Looking back, Mum saw my dad's desire to run after work as an excuse to duck the childcare equivalent of rush hour. I was too young to see it like that, of course, but once when I asked Dad if he could take me with him, she answered before he even drew breath.

'What an excellent idea,' she said gleefully. 'I'll get him ready.'

I wore my school shorts and gym shoes for that first run, which went no further than the junction to a cul-de-sac twenty metres up the road. I'd set out in great excitement and then quickly pulled up breathlessly with my heart throbbing. It didn't occur to me that my dad liked to run a loop for a couple of miles around the country lanes that fringed this commuter-belt town where I grew up.

'Can you manage a little more?' he asked hopefully.

Dad didn't seem too disappointed when I dug in my heels and we headed back home. He probably figured I'd had enough of running and would leave him alone from there on out.

The next day after work, he came home to find me ready to set out once more. Within a week, my younger brother and sister had joined us, leaving Mum to enjoy a well-deserved break. For my dad, running had gone from a means to get away from the family to compulsory time with his kids.

While my siblings were just a little too young to make it a daily event, I looked forward to our run. It meant I could be with my dad, and to be fair to him he encouraged me to keep pushing. As a small boy, a couple of minutes on the move felt like we'd covered a million miles. Eventually, in an era when an understanding of the Green Cross Code was enough for children to make their own way in the world, I reached an age and distance where I pulled up and Dad would continue. Then I'd stand by the side of the road and wait for him to come back, thinking somehow he was superhuman.

Running wasn't central to my life in those formative years, but it was a feature. I grew up with it. When I first went out on my own, to the point where I usually stopped and my dad pressed on, it felt both scary and exciting. It gave me a little taste of independence and seemed like I was expanding the boundaries of my world, one step at a time. I didn't think of running as a sport, however. I never considered myself sporty at all. That was something my friends embraced in the form of football. Most of them had older siblings or parents who supported a team. I had no such influence. Through my dad's eyes, kicking a ball about for however long a game lasted just lacked any purpose. What's more, it attracted fans who roared and chanted, and that just wasn't on. If the theme tune to *Match of the Day* ever struck up on the TV, he would be on his feet to switch channels as if he had a duty to protect us from a pursuit better suited to the prison yard.

In a bid to fit in with my friends at school, I traded football stickers with a passion. I just couldn't find the same thing on the pitch. Everyone seemed to be more tuned in to the game than me. I was one of those kids who'd find himself last to be picked for a kickabout, and only then as part of some complex trade negotiation that meant I'd join the stronger side to hold them back a little. Running didn't bring that kind of awkwardness or humiliation. It needed no particular skill set or teamwork. There was no pass or shot for me to fumble.

While my dad saw running as a solitary activity, Mum possessed a competitive streak. She played in goal for a local women's lacrosse squad. All I remember about that is the game in which she stopped a ball with her teeth, the blood-drenched hurry to hospital that followed, and my sense that perhaps team sports weren't for me.

My mum also loved to swim. She encouraged me to get in the water from a very early age, and that was supported at primary school. Together with the Green Cross Code and the Cycling Proficiency Test, the Holy Trinity of Survival Skills for Small Children in the Seventies was completed by the Five-Metre Shallow Water Certificate. For those kids who had been left traumatised by the short public information films warning of the dangers of climbing electricity pylons and locking themselves into old and airtight fridges, entering the water without any qualification held a special terror. With the certificate to our name, the Grim Reaper would no longer hang around in river shallows with hidden currents. We would be free to ride our bikes out to the banks unsupervised and have fun.

Gathered outside with my classmates on one side of the tatty school pool, one that basically wasn't green with algae for two months during the summer, I faced what seemed like a yawning aquatic abyss. It was only a width, but the other side just seemed too far away for me to process. The only thing filling the space in between was a sense of overwhelming dread. I had absolutely zero confidence that I would complete the distance. With no way to back out, however, all I could do was go for it when my turn came around. The cold water shock swiftly brought me to my senses, and once I'd finished thrashing about, I began to paddle.

Three metres across, a transformation occurred. As I continued to splutter and splash, all the negative thoughts that had been weighing me down began to float away. I had got this far because frankly I didn't want to sink, and yet I was making progress. What's more, the end was in sight. I could do this, my little mind registered, and when I touched that pool wall I felt a rush of pure elation.

I still recall the episode clearly, from the cracked tiles to the chlorine in the air and the teacher with the clipboard who congratulated me, but most of all I remember the emotional journey. Today, whenever I line up for a race that feels beyond me, I'm always transported back to the moment when I faced the width of that pool.

In the water, just as I found when plodding along the pavement from our house, I liked the fact that I was alone. I had no idea whether I was any good as a swimmer, but that didn't matter to me. I just enjoyed being active on my own terms. When I was old enough to compete in school galas, however, it became clear that I was quite average in the pool. I could swim well but lacked the dolphin-like speed and power of some kids my age. In the short sprints, I would finish to find the top three had already climbed out of the pool. It didn't bother me as such, but then nor did it fire me up.

Then came an early incarnation of what would become the annual Swimathon. This was an endurance event hosted in pools across the country, raising money for charity and promising competitors a finishing photograph with an Olympic swimmer. Today, participants can choose from a range of distances from 400 metres to three 5K sessions. I have no idea how far I attempted to swim. I don't suppose my mum would've let me take on more than twenty lengths. I just remember feeling out of my depth but determined not to give in. Completing the distance earned me a pool-side photograph with the moustachioed swimming legend David Wilkie.

I had a bowl haircut and puffy eyes from being in the water for so long, but that had to be my proudest moment. It wasn't about time but distance. With no pressure on me, I realised I could make up for being a plodder by persevering.

I had just turned thirteen when the opportunity arose for me to run at school. I didn't consider sports-day races to be my thing. Even though we'd left the eggs and spoons behind a few years earlier, I just wasn't much of a sprinter. So, when a teacher set up an after-school cross-country running club, I jumped at the chance. There was no way I'd ever feature in the line-up for the school football team. Being slim-built, I found rugby frankly scary, while cricket came with rules I just failed to understand. So, rather than standing on the outside edge with no clue who was winning, I had a chance to do something where I felt I might fit in.

Nowadays, we talk about hitting the *trails*. It sounds exciting, sexy and adventurous, conjuring images of hard-packed winding routes with splendid vistas at every turn. For those who ran before the term became mainstream, its predecessor cooks up an altogether different vibe.

When I think about cross-country running, mud is the first thing that comes to mind. At school, we would begin each session by lining up along the side of an absolutely massive ploughed field. The furrows ran deep, churning into soil with a heavy clay content, and we were expected to run across it. The club was only an option during the autumn term, which meant it was usually raining horizontally.

'The faster you run, the quicker you'll warm up,' our teacher and coach would remark, wrapped up in a thick coat and scarf as we lined up along the field. 'OK, go!'

Surging across the furrows, which stretched out like choppy ocean waves, our first footfalls sank in deep. Extracting ourselves required some force and brought up great sods on the soles of our shoes. Within seconds, we had all pretty much doubled in body weight. Maintaining any kind of form was impossible. We just began to look more like staggering zombies. By the time we reached the other side of the field, in fact, every single young runner was dead on their feet.

'I hate this,' mumbled my friend Moby, who had awarded himself this nickname to back up his boasts and then pushed it until most of us forgot what he was really called. 'Let's walk it.'

In the mid-pack of any ultramarathon, when competitors are battling with exhaustion, it doesn't take much to trigger a downshift in gear. If someone ahead hits the slightest incline and stops running, or even eases up without reason, it can lead to a domino effect of mooching. We weren't long-distance athletes by any means, but the ordeal of that ploughed field had taken our legs from under us.

As soon as Moby stopped running, the entire pack around him followed suit.

'Pick up the pace!' came the order from across the field. 'If anyone walks, they'll have to go round again!'

The course followed a ditch along the length of the orchard before leading us away from the view of our teacher. As soon as we were safely behind trees, my fellow clubmates and I pulled up smartly once again. Some rested their hands on their knees, coughing as they fought for breath. Others simply tipped their faces skywards as if hoping to find more oxygen there. Having completed less than half a mile, across terrain that would beach a tank, every one of us was completely broken. From there, once we'd figured out all the sightlines from the school grounds, the cross-country run became a ramble.

The route criss-crossed through a patchwork of ploughed fields and apple orchards. In October and November, stripped of leaves and life, even the trees looked miserable. Despite following the same course every week, which took us across ground with the consistency of wet cement, I turned up every time. Why? Because it was a shared experience that brought us together, and at that age the banter could be so sharp we'd spend more time laughing than anything else.

In many ways, I felt safe in that pack. A seam of bullying ran unchecked through the school, which wasn't uncommon in the late seventies and early eighties. You could be targeted for the slightest weakness, and if you didn't fight back or assert dominance, that made the target bigger on your back. I was first picked on for the crime of being too smiley, and that escalated because I just wasn't the sort to wipe the grin from the faces of my tormentors. One of them was in the running club, but things were different between us from the moment we floundered across that first field. We were in this together, after all; united in our bid to outsmart our coach and his stopwatch.

'I'm not seeing much improvement,' he would grumble at the finish line each week, unaware that we could all shave at least five minutes off our times if we just stopped fooling around.

Back then, my running performance wasn't as important to me as the sense that it offered me something. Not only did it level the playing field socially, briefly turning enemies into friends, I found the time out on my own helped me to recharge, as it did for my dad. If I'd been picked on at school, a plod to the end of the road and back would make me feel better. By then, I'd outgrown running with my father. I just followed his loop on my own terms. I didn't push myself to go further or faster, and that was enough for me.

Then, towards the end of one autumn term, our teacher decided to enter the cross-country team into a competition. It was an inter-schools meeting, the first of its kind in the region, and for some unknown reason it generated a buzz of excitement that reached far beyond our niche little club. Suddenly, everyone in class was talking about it. For once, the focus shifted from the football team to the runners. Becoming legends in a lunch break took us all by surprise. It even spelled an amnesty on the bullying front. For the first time in ages, I didn't dread the moment that the bell rang for break.

The race was staged on a Saturday. Rather than spend their time loitering in shiny new shopping malls, it seemed like everyone from school had turned up to support us. On a crisp and bright morning, we arrived at the host school to find every other team was equally mob-handed.

'The course goes around the playing fields and then follows a footpath through the woods,' we were informed by the organiser at the mass briefing. 'It's a lovely day. The ground is firm throughout. Just go out and enjoy yourselves!'

I glanced at Moby. There had been no mention of ploughed fields, flooded ditches or the risk of trench foot. In today's terms, it sounded suspiciously like ... trail.

Moby nodded confidently, as did several of my teammates. Having slogged across the worst possible landscape in training, it felt like we had got this.

I had never taken part in a competitive, mass start. As we gathered at the line, I bounced on my toes with nervous energy. Ahead, the course followed the edge of well-tended grounds with not a furrow in sight.

'On your marks ... get set ... '

I didn't register the signal that marked the start of the stampede that followed. I'm not sure anyone did. In a heartbeat, every runner just went for it, and that included me.

With crowds of schoolkids and even parents screaming at us from each side, what followed was a fast-moving brawl as we all jostled for position. Elbows connected with chests and faces, and I took a blow to the ear. All I could do was find a space and then hold on to it as we thundered around the playing field. In any running race, it takes a while for things to settle down. You've gone from standing around to breathing hard and feeling uncomfortable, and then slowly everyone gets into a rhythm.

Sure enough, the pace began to settle. That's when I discovered, much to my dismay, that it was far quicker than anything I could sustain.

'Keep up,' grunted Moby, who promptly eased away.

'I'll try,' I called back, but in truth I knew it was hopeless.

The route was marked and marshalled at every turn. These were at least adults, who knew how to offer positive encouragement to the stragglers at the back. I wasn't completely last, until we left the playing field for the woods. Then the final runner slipped by and I was on my own.

Following the path between the trees, pushing as hard as I could but effectively getting nowhere, I panicked. I had never been in a race before, let alone dead last, and the pressure was all too much for me. I couldn't breathe properly, I discovered, and my legs felt like they might short-circuit at any moment. I wanted to stop. I also wished we could restart the race. It had never occurred to me that I might be worst in show, and in that moment I clung to the belief that it was pure bad luck.

As the minutes ticked by, if not the miles, I realised I had been seriously dropped by the pack. The path through the woods was illuminated by slanted bars of sunshine and fringed by golden bracken. I had never experienced cross-country running like it, and yet with every step this was beginning to feel like one of those nightmares where the branches start clawing towards you.

By the time I left the trees behind me, floundering across a heath that brought the school grounds back into my sights, the applause from the marshals was beginning to sound strained.

'Well done,' some called out, in a tone I had last heard from a reception class teacher after presenting her with a stickman picture of my family. 'Don't give up!'

I was still in shock as I reached the school gates. What brought me to my senses was the sight of all the spectators. They were gathered on the banks and behind the railings. When my appearance was met by more jeers than cheers, I decided to feign injury.

'My foot,' I cried, limping theatrically but with genuine tears. 'I think I've broken it!'

It was then I laid eyes on one of my teammates. He stood at the gates with a medal round his neck and the kind of look he reserved for me outside of club time.

'You're dead,' he growled. 'What an embarrassment.'

It was a race I wanted to forget. I didn't have the maturity to feel like I could learn from the experience. I just felt completely humiliated, a failure at a sport I had enjoyed and a little bit scared that I would pay a price in the school corridors. I couldn't make sense of what had gone wrong. Looking back, I had let my adrenaline turn to anxiety. At the time, however, it seemed to me that I simply wasn't very good at running compared to everyone else.

By then, of course, it was in my bones. I couldn't give it up altogether. Even at that tender age, I knew it worked like a kind of battery charger for the soul. Back home from school one day the following week, despite weathering jibes all day about being slow, I even took myself up the road and back to clear my head.

Running could still take me to a happy place, and that wasn't something I wanted to leave behind.

And so, I decided, I would continue to run in my own way. I wasn't fast. I also had no urge to be competitive. Like swimming, I just enjoyed the time out rather than pushing to get over the line, and the route my dad first forged suited me fine. What I lacked in pace, I made up for in enthusiasm. Lost in my own little world on those lanes, with nobody around to see me, I could even run with a smile on my face.

02

THE PEBBLE IN MY SHOE

As a free climber with approximately ninety minutes of experience behind me, I am relying on instinct and not expertise to negotiate Crib Goch's third and final pinnacle. Having established two handholds, and one for my foot, I scan the rock face for the next step. The voice in my head that urges me to get this done is very small. I just can't afford to listen to the louder, hysterical one.

'Follow the polish,' I remind myself, and take some comfort from the breadcrumb trail of worn rock above me. People do this all the time, and that includes some Dragon's Back competitors who can cross this section of the first day of the race with the grace and speed of geckos. These men and women tend to be at the sharp end, and though I'll never count myself among them I need to recognise that tight cut-off times mean I will have to keep moving at all costs.

With a focus on my breathing, I lift myself upwards. I find the next anchor points and repeat the process, only now the next moves don't seem so straightforward. At the same time, having lifted myself out of the relative shelter of the pocket in the rock in front of the pinnacle, I find myself in a considerable crosswind. All the adrenaline in my system distils into a drop of pure terror. I feel like it might be inflammable. With a half-mile drop to my right, and the smooth, shinier rocks forcing me out that way, I just cannot allow it to ignite into panic.

* * *

When it comes to mindset, there isn't much in common between the ultrarunner and the adolescent. One looks forward to time on the sofa as a reward for their efforts. The other cuts out the hard work and just kicks back happily with crisps all down their front.

As a teenager, I lacked the single-mindedness, resilience and commitment it takes to run very long distances. Frankly, who does have what it takes at that time of life? Even if ultramarathons had been a thing back then, I would've shown no interest. Not only are young athletes rightly encouraged to consider their developing bodies when it comes to endurance races, my fifteen-year-old self would've failed to see the point. Back then, five miles on my own was quite far enough, and about twice the distance we had covered at cross-country club.

I liked running, but I wasn't stupid about it.

Inevitably as a youth switching on to the world around me, I was easily distracted. First it was parties that started popping up on an otherwise empty social calendar. Then came the challenge of creating a convincing ID to access pubs and 18-certificate films. These things didn't stop me going for a run a few afternoons each week. It's just that the prospect of lacing up my trainers didn't excite me as much as ordering a pint of snakebite and black without being questioned about my age.

There was perhaps just one social activity that had an impact on my running. In some ways the two were intertwined. After a year or so in the running wilderness, I rejoined cross-country club. I had no intention of entering the annual inter-schools race, and as numbers had grown a little, the selection process was on my side. The club continued to meet on a weekly basis and I missed that time with my friends. I looked forward to the chat on my first session with them, which made the mud-suck a bit more bearable. Moby was among the first runners who pulled up once we were out of sight. Quite a few pressed on, but I was reassured to see the original crew had not changed their ways. I slowed to a walk with my chest heaving, and then a catch in my throat when Moby whipped out a carton of cigarettes.

'Smoke?' he asked me as others produced their own packs and even pouches of rolling tobacco and papers.

In my absence, I realised that my cross-country club colleagues had developed new pursuits.

I could hardly say no. Well, I could have done so but I just wanted to be part of the pack once more. Even though the volley of coughing that followed my first lungful of smoke was met by laughter, it felt good to fit in once again.

When we finally made it to the finishing stretch, reeking of guilt and mints, our teacher looked less than impressed.

'I know you can do better,' he muttered, stopwatch in hand, and he was right in so many ways.

With no drive to improve as a runner, on my own and with cross-country club, I focused my efforts on becoming a better smoker. My parents were strongly against the habit. As lighting up at home was unthinkable, I needed an excuse to get out and about. I'd always enjoyed the time and space that came with lacing up my trainers and heading out of the front door, and this was the opportunity I needed. Off-road, it became a way for me to enjoy a cigarette or even two without fear of being caught. As my tobacco dependency grew, so I became a more frequent runner. My afternoon outings after school went from a handful of times a week to a daily event, while the weekends saw me evolve a training technique that involved literally a dozen very short shakedowns that would take me no further than the copse beside the cul-de-sac. Any health benefit from the exercise was of course completely cancelled out by the fact that I was only doing it so I could smoke. I was running for completely the wrong reasons, and yet that thread continued to form a stitch through my years towards adulthood.

At university, I did at least break free from the self-defeating habit of lighting up during a run. Free to smoke in my bedsit, I got back in touch with taking time out from my studies to pound the pavements and treat my lungs to fresh air. Inevitably, I would be coughing within minutes and forced to pull up shortly afterwards with a chest so tight it felt fitted with drawstrings. Even I knew that smoking and running were completely incompatible. I just found either one impossible to give up.

It was only as a graduate in a grown-up world of the early nineties that I recognised it was time to take responsibility for myself. Unlike my friends, who were pursuing sensible and structured careers, I had set out to write a novel. To fund it, I found a part-time job in a call centre and settled into life on the breadline. I couldn't afford the luxury of smoking, while running cost me nothing, and that was all I needed to stub out my last cigarette. Living in a Bristol bedsit, I spent nine months writing every morning before trudging into work to don a headset and deal with customer complaints all afternoon. I would run after work simply so I could tune out. I wasn't at all inventive with my routes. I just followed the same pavements around Montpelier and St Pauls and used the time to mentally plot the story taking shape on the page.

When I reached the final full stop of my novel, I could barely believe I'd had the perseverance to pull it off. Instead of jumping on the hamster wheel of work, I had set out to forge my own path. While I had nothing to contribute about salaries and summer breaks when it came to pub chat with my mates, I felt sure the manuscript I posted off to publishers would bring me fame and fortune.

Six months later, the final rejection arrived in the post. I had submitted a manuscript with my blood, sweat and tears infused in every word. In return for my efforts, I received nothing but knock-backs. Once I'd got over the shock and horror, it dawned on me that my part-time job in a call centre was no longer a means to an end. It *was* the end. I had taken a gamble to pursue something I loved, and lost. Any fire to write that I had left in me just fizzled out. I spent my mornings in bed before drifting into work to jockey a phone, listen to customers blowing off steam and apologise to them for everything. Within weeks of resigning myself to this life, I saw no point in running each evening when I could be in my bedsit feeling sorry for myself.

The call centre was in the heart of the city. To get there, I would cut through a shopping arcade and then torture myself by weaving through the big bookshop for the side door into the street. When I was writing, it served as a reminder that this soulless job of mine was funding what I really wanted to do, and that one day my book might grace the tables in there. Then reality struck and the titles on display just taunted me. It didn't stop me looking, of course, and even losing myself for a short while in the pages of work by proper novelists. Just standing there with a bestseller open in my hands was painful, but it meant I could avoid thinking about my shift ahead.

As good times go, this didn't even come close to qualifying. In fact, it was a chapter in my life I would've filed as 'wasted' had I not stopped off at the bookshop to torture myself on my way to work one drizzly day. With most of the offices yet to break for lunch, the store was practically empty. A cluster of people were talking quietly at the till. Apart from that, I was alone in the company of work by better writers than me. Or so I thought until I heard the slow, steady creak of shoes nearby. Very quickly, it became apparent that someone was approaching. I pretended not to notice, focusing on the books on the shelves, but that became all but impossible when the individual in question drew level with me. In such a big store, it felt like my personal space was being completely invaded. More immediately, I sensed they had turned to face me. I glanced across, wondering if I was under suspicion for shoplifting or something, and froze.

Directly in front of me stood a broad-built, smartly dressed figure whose face would've been almost expressionless were it not for his eyes. They were pin-sharp and pinched at the corners, as if I was about to become the punchline to a joke that I'd also find funny. He was no more than a foot away from me, but I'd have recognised him from a mile off, as would anyone on this planet. He even looked like he knew me, which would've been impossible, for I was just a failure at everything and this was the heavyweight boxing champion of the world, Muhammad Ali.

'Sorry,' I said, barely audibly, with no clue why I was apologising.

In response, one of sport's most celebrated living legends beckoned me even closer.

On this wet lunchtime in the West Country, in front of the fiction A–D section of a bookshop, I wouldn't have been more surprised had I just run into Neil Armstrong in full astronaut gear or even Elvis incognito. Slowly, trembling slightly, but with his eyes still gleaming and a hint of a grin, Ali took a handkerchief from his top pocket and showed it to me. Next he closed his great fist. For a second I thought he might wallop me, but then he opened his hand again and the handkerchief had seemingly disappeared.

Just as I remembered to blink and take a breath, The People's Champion produced the vanished item from behind my ear. With an expression of pure mischief, as if daring me to see through the magic, Ali returned the handkerchief to his pocket and shuffled away. I wanted to say something, *anything*, but having lived in a shell of my own making for so long I just stood there with tears streaming down my cheeks.

Naturally, at work, nobody believed me. Muhammad Ali? Here in Bristol? Oh, come on! No wonder I couldn't get published if I tried to pass off that kind of fantasy as fact, they crowed. As my shift wore on, taking one tedious call after another, I began to doubt myself. It seemed ridiculous, after all. What would a player in world history be doing here? I really needed to get out more, I thought to myself. Preferably as far from this soul-destroying job as possible.

Once I'd taken my final call of the day, I removed my headset and decided to go back to the bookshop. It was about as quiet as it had been at lunchtime, though the staff were busy repositioning tables and gathering in a velvet rope cordon. Something big had happened here, judging by the crowd-control barriers outside the shop, while the posters on the pillars told me exactly what I had missed. As part of a whistle-stop tour of the country to promote his autobiography, Muhammad Ali had made a guest appearance at the store that afternoon. I *hadn't* been mistaken, and yet I still struggled to make sense of how he made time for me.

'I'm sorry to bother you,' I said awkwardly to one of the booksellers, and then pointed at a picture of Ali. 'Did he have a handkerchief in his pocket?'

The bookseller took a step back, considering me for a moment. Then she seemed to solve a mystery in her mind.

'So it was you!' she said, loud enough for other members of staff to look across. 'I hope you're feeling brighter now.'

According to the bookseller, Ali and his entourage had arrived surprisingly early. His team had been expected at three o'clock and yet for some unknown reason they rocked up before lunchtime. While the signing had seen crowds of fans flock to this once-in-a-lifetime opportunity to set eyes on the great man, Ali had found himself in a near-empty store. So, while the team were discussing security for the forthcoming event, Ali had drifted off to look at books and unwittingly transformed the life of a young man who had all but thrown in the towel.

With what little money I had, I left with a copy of Ali's autobiography. Having shared a moment in time with him, I wanted to remember it somehow. The book turned out to be as engaging as the man himself. As well as being a gifted boxer, Ali had a way with words. Floating like a butterfly and stinging like a bee might have been his most recognisable phrase, but other words of wisdom spoke to me as someone who had set out to achieve something and then given up.

A man who lacked imagination, according to Ali, was a man with no wings, and that gave me pause for thought. I was in possession of an imagination, after all, and yet I had folded away those wings when the novel it helped me to write didn't take off. Alone in my bedsit, I asked myself what Muhammad Ali would have done. I was in no doubt that as he fought to the top he had taken all kinds of punches, and yet he never gave up. If anything, he had drawn strength from those setbacks. Reflecting on my experience, I realised that despite the sense of rejection, I had at least completed a novel. People often talk about writing one if only they had the time, but very few see it through. I had set out to pursue an impossible dream. Some 350 pages later, I had made it happen. The end result may not have won any prizes, or even a publishing contract, but it had taken commitment and perseverance to get there.

Then I came across another pearl of wisdom in his book that left me in no doubt about the way forward. Not just as a writer, I would discover, but as a runner when that became as central to my life as the drive to write a novel from start to finish. It isn't the mountains that wear you out, believed Ali, and I am reminded of this whenever the going gets tough, it's the pebble in your shoe.

Within a year, having rekindled my enjoyment of both writing and running after my shifts at the call centre, I completed another novel. That never saw the light of day either, but this time was different. In some ways, the end result wasn't as important as the journey, which I had really enjoyed. What's more, I recognised that the experience was equipping me with the skills to get better at something I loved, deal with self-doubt and stay resilient.

On my third attempt, everything changed. The publishing deal didn't earn me enough to take early retirement by the pool, but it paid for me to pack in my job talking angry customers off the walls and pursue my career as a novelist. I moved out of my bedsit, relocating to London and the next chapter in my life that saw me get married and start a family. Thanks to Muhammad Ali's intervention, I had learnt to pick myself up, shake out my shoes and set off up the mountain. Without doubt, that briefest of encounters with The Greatest encouraged me to take on any challenge – even if I took a pasting in the process.

03

FLOELLA, THE TOMATO AND ME

Negotiating the flank of Crib Goch's infernal final pinnacle, I find myself in a position where the serious drop is no longer to my right. It's directly beneath me. The polish in the rock had been quite apparent for the initial clamber. Then I just busked it out and around to a ledge because I couldn't see any other way. All of a sudden, with the sky above and the ground far below, I feel like the loneliest human being in the world.

I daren't even glance around to see if anyone else is following in my attempt. I'd feel much better knowing that someone else thought my line was worth following, but right now I just have to keep moving.

'Don't look down. Keep going. Come on.'

By now, my hands are soaked in cold sweat. I'm not sure if it's possible to dehydrate through the palms alone, but it feels like it might be a thing. It's just one more factor to consider when I reach for the next rock. I don't want to risk trying to dry my fingers on my shirt. If I slip and fall at this point, quite simply I will die. I just have to put up with it and make sure my grasp is solid before I move my feet.

It's purely the height that is testing me here. If this pinnacle was at sea level, around a rocky cove, perhaps, I wouldn't think twice about taking it on. The manoeuvre itself isn't difficult. There's nothing too technical. It just feels that way when compounded by the fear of falling. It's inescapable. A universal dread that can creep into our core when we're far from our comfort zones. All I can do is accept it's going to keep me in its grip until I reach safer ground.

For now, the only way is up towards the pinnacle summit. It's too steep for me to see what's actually there, and if I find it offers no respite, I think I might just cry.

* * *

Regardless of ability or experience, every amateur runner dreams of completing a marathon. Over time, those 26.2 miles have become the default distance that attracts so many to set up charity fundraisers and start training in earnest for what could be the greatest challenge of their lives.

For those who make it to the start line for the first time, very few see beyond the finish. It's just such an all-consuming prospect. In 2004, sardined into a legion of nervous hopefuls for the London Marathon, I counted myself among that number. So many thousands of competitors filled Blackheath's broad and open public space that I couldn't even make out what was going on beyond the big guy in front of me. It didn't help that he abandoned all sense of dignity to join in with the mass warm-up, as did almost everyone else. As he reached for the sky in his too-tight shirt and shorts, I focused on my feet like I imagined the elites were doing up at the front.

'Sorry, mate,' he offered, on realising my personal space was all but gone.

'No worries,' I said, and to be honest it wasn't bothering me as much as the fog of Deep Heat that hung in the air.

I was so far back I didn't hear the start gun. I just sensed movement up ahead and within seconds we were off. I had no idea what I was heading into. Pumped up by excitement and nerves, and completely carried away by the moment, I felt like I could run forever.

Sometimes it seems like everyone who runs a marathon has a story behind it. I was no exception. I just couldn't bring myself to talk about it at the time. Three years earlier, both my mother and younger sister had died of cancer. That they'd both been diagnosed with a terminal illness within a short space of time had left our family in disbelief. It seemed so cruel, and we watched helplessly as they fought and then ultimately faded. By then, I had my own family. Emma and our three young daughters, Grace, Bluebell and Ethel, became a source of comfort and commitment. I could lose myself in writing novels and then avoid confronting difficult feelings with the responsibilities that come with raising kids.

During that period, running served as a kind of emotional pressure relief. Two or three times a week, I'd take myself around Victoria Park in the capital's East End where we lived. Often I'd take a buggy with me. Back then, no models existed for people who sought to combine running with parenthood. With one youngster after another learning that a rattle over the pavements in the pushchair meant it was time to stop wailing and go to sleep, I just ran with ours until the wheels quite literally fell off. I didn't use the time to process my loss. I simply didn't think. I just tuned out and found some sense of freedom from grief.

Watching the London Marathon on television one year, I paid close attention to the coverage of those runners who had been moved to race for charity as a means of giving back. With the children sitting alongside me, fired up by the spectacle and asking lots of questions, it became quite clear what I needed to do. I had never run further than a couple of casual miles. A marathon seemed beyond my comprehension, but something I had to try at the very least. So many everyday people were out there pounding the streets in the name of good causes, it felt like this could be my opportunity to do something for those I had lost.

'You can't,' said Emma supportively when I told her I had registered. 'There's no way you can run that far.'

'We won't find out unless I try,' I reasoned.

'What if you die trying? The girls need a father.'

It had taken me a while to find a good moment to put my wife in the picture. I knew she wouldn't react well to begin with, simply because she could be quite risk-averse. I was also aware that after thinking things through she would come on board and provide all the support I could possibly want.

As I passed the first mile marker, I knew that I would soon see Emma and the girls. She had planned to be at several vantage points, and this extended to the very end. Over the year since I had signed up, raising money for Macmillan in recognition of the care and compassion their nurses had shown my mother and sister, her confidence in me had grown. This was largely down to the fact that I had taken my training schedule seriously.

At the time, I felt like I had assembled and executed a comprehensive programme that would ensure I was in peak physical shape when I ran the marathon. In hindsight, with experience as a distance runner on my side, it was an utter shambles.

With no running friends or mentors I could consult, and in an era when dial-up internet beyond the walls of a service provider like AOL or Freeserve felt more like the Wild West, my training resources were limited. Yes, there were bound to be books on the subject, and I dare say with a little digging I could've found solid guidance on building towards the distance. Instead, I decided that it wasn't rocket science. I simply needed to increase my number of weekly runs from three to, well … four. I'd never heard of training intensity, peak loads or tapering. My longest run in preparation took me to a full ten miles, and after that I needed the week off. Meanwhile, my designated charity was sending me encouraging messages and a branded vest that helped me to feel the part. The way I saw things, my efforts to raise money would carry me over the line.

It meant that when the big day arrived, driven by the generosity of friends and family, I ticked off the opening miles feeling like I was in the form of my life. I didn't bother stopping for water at the trestle tables filled with cups. Hydration was something I'd taken care of at breakfast with a glass of juice, while expanding my usual breakfast routine from two slices of toast to three. As far as I was concerned, I had followed a plan and this was the pay-off. Flanked by cheering crowds, the experience of running through streets normally at a standstill with traffic was exhilarating. Such a joyful atmosphere only encouraged me to pick up the pace. When I first heard Emma shouting my name just before the *Cutty Sark,* I even wondered if I might outrun their efforts to see me in the later stages.

'How is it going?' she asked, raising her voice over the din.

'Great!' I told her, slowing to high-five my excited daughters.

'Daddy, you're amazing,' said Bluebell with a look of wide-eyed wonder.

'I know,' I said, only half joking.

Declining Emma's offer of food and drink from the cool bag she had prepared for me, I continued to move with the steady flow of marathon hopefuls. In a current of high spirits, we wound through Rotherhithe on our way to the halfway mark. I hadn't run in a pack since my school cross-country days, but this was different. Firstly, it wasn't an excuse for a smoke. More importantly, it didn't feel like a race. Nobody was jostling for position or threatening to drop me. If anything, this event was demonstrating to me that running didn't just have to be a solo activity. With no pressure to win or avoid coming last, it could also be a great shared experience. The collective tempo was perhaps a little quicker than I might have maintained on my own, but then I was having the time of my life.

'Come on, Matt! Well done! You can do it!'

With my name emblazoned across my race vest, the support from strangers was really quite moving. As we turned on to the approach to Tower Bridge, midway into the marathon, I felt like I didn't want this day to end.

By the time I had reached the other side of the Thames, less than 250 metres across, I couldn't wait for it to finish.

'Matt … are you OK? Take it easy, buddy.'

If I had hit the bridge in fighting form, I left it looking utterly defeated. The transformation had been shockingly quick. One moment I was soaking in the atmosphere, the next all the blood in my system felt like it had drained away.

In terms of an energy crash, I had totally tanked. It had never happened to me before. I was also completely unaware of the concept. Back then, bonking was a tabloid newspaper term. It had no association with running on empty, and my needle was well into the red. I'd neglected to consider any kind of fuelling strategy, and – at pace – run further than I'd ever gone before.

In unknown territory, rather than regroup and consider what I needed to do overcome it, I just assumed that I was dying.

In a tailspin of panic, my vision began to blur. I was trembling and in a mortal sweat, and yet with such mass momentum all around me I didn't feel that I could stop and ask for help. In some ways my sense of embarrassment at suddenly thinking I might faint compelled me to keep running. I just didn't want to be *that* guy. In my view, it was fine to be the one staggering heroically in the final stages, powered by a look of grim determination before collapsing over the line. At this point in the marathon, however, I didn't feel I'd earned that right.

In a fog of weakness and fragility, I fumbled for the zip belt around my waist. It contained my phone and a bag of jelly beans, which Emma had made me carry. I was still running, even though my legs felt like they were made from twigs. Tearing open the bag, I shovelled in the contents like a drug dealer faced with a sniffer dog. Quite a few beans missed my mouth, but enough went in for me to discover I would now have to breathe through my nose alone. I chewed furiously, until the beans turned to the kind of paste that just cemented my jaw shut.

It was, in short, an awful experience. I felt completely disorientated, while the din from the supporters turned from a source of encouragement to a noise with no escape. I tried to be more like Muhammad Ali, but that was a struggle when I felt like I might hit the deck at any moment. By now, my pace had dropped considerably. I couldn't bring myself to walk, but when I next saw the family it was clear by my pitiful shuffle that I was in trouble.

'Oh my God!' Emma made a vague attempt to shield the girls from the sight of their father. 'There are medics … ' she added, looking around, but that was out of the question.

'Don't worry,' I said through teeth that weren't so much gritted as pasted together by a multicoloured mash. 'I've got this.'

The second half of that marathon was an exercise in extended torture. I lost all sense of time and progress, and only briefly came to my senses as the capital's familiar landmarks inched into view. By the time I had fixed my sights on the London Eye and Big Ben, I knew it couldn't be much further. A steady stream of runners continued to wash by me, which made me feel like I was going backwards, but by then I could sniff an end to this torture. Even as the course banked around and Buckingham Palace switched into view, I wasn't convinced that I would make it.

'Don't give up now, Matt!' cried some well-meaning random, which only served to make me think I must totally look like I was ready to quit. 'Run!'

Somehow, I had managed to stay on my feet. My legs hadn't buckled so the television cameras zoned in on me, but my soul was completely crushed. As for my pace … well, I was moving.

In my head, the sight of the finishing gantry spurred me to shake free from my woes and sprint. In reality, it made no difference at all. Runners were still swarming around me. In the build-up I had dreamt of this moment in which the ordinary Joe becomes a hero. I would cross the timing mat with my fists aloft, I had decided, into the arms of my adoring family. Not only were members of the public banned from the space beyond the line, where officials doled out medals and encouraged finishers to disperse safely, I had been fuelling my little fantasy on the basis that this marathon was all about me. Not once did I anticipate that I might be beaten in those closing metres by some guy in a massive tomato outfit, who barged by so forcefully that he almost spun me around. It happened so fast that I barely had time to acknowledge the female runner, *Play School* presenter and national treasure coming in hot behind me.

Floella Benjamin was a face from my childhood. As a small boy, I had sat cross-legged in front of the screen and sung songs along with her. Now, here she was, looking composed and in control while beasting me to the line alongside an oversized fruit. It would be a commemorative photograph that I declined to purchase. Not that it was uppermost in my mind when I staggered over the mat behind them. Having run for what felt like an eternity, I suddenly found myself too fearful to stop altogether in case I passed out. So, with my medal around my neck and foil blanket over my shoulders, I just shuffled onwards to find some space, peace and quiet.

I can't say how much time passed before the helpful lady from St John's Ambulance found me drifting aimlessly, as if in shellshock from the experience. Drawn by the fact that I seemed oblivious to the fact that my phone was ringing, and then answering it on my behalf, she kindly spoke to my wife and then stayed with me until I was in her care. To be honest, my memory of that part of the day is still missing. I just remember being so glad to see Emma and the girls, weeping in a huddle with them, and then making a promise I had every intention of keeping.

'It's done,' I said with absolute certainty. 'I never have to run a marathon again.'

04

THE DOWNHILL SECTION

With one final push, I reach the summit of Crib Goch's third pinnacle.

I'm on my hands and knees, thankful for this moment where I can just loosen my focus. I look up and around, feeling like I'm in some kind of windblown crow's nest made from rock. I have an unobstructed view of the long ridge behind me, and a somewhat sketchy but manageable descent off the pinnacle. This one leads to a tabletop of grass about ten metres below. A few people are sitting around down there, enjoying the view from a safe vantage and just regrouping before the next assault to reach the summit of Snowdon.

All I want to do, I realise, is join them.

We all have our own limits, and I am well aware that the test I've just come through might not seem like a big deal to others. Just then, however, my experience had pushed me further than anticipated. I had done my research. I knew this traverse can be challenging for those uncomfortable with heights. I just hadn't appreciated quite how it would leave me feeling.

My hope, before I came here, was that I would complete the crossing and conquer my fears. This would give me three clear months before the Dragon's Back Race to focus on all the other aspects of the challenge, from navigating an unmarked course across an entire country to mastering a degree of mountain craft that's quite hard to achieve in the south-east of England.

Even though the worst of this ridge is almost behind me, I don't feel the sense of closure I had hoped for. Instead, I can't escape the fact that I'm going to have to put myself through this again. In some ways, I think to myself as I begin to tentatively pick my way down the other side of the pinnacle, crossing Crib Goch has just made things worse. I can no longer say it's all in the mind for those who are frightened by this sort of thing. Yes, I have done it, and lived to tell the tale, but it has left me in no doubt that it's a bloody stupid thing to do.

∗ ∗ ∗

Athletes come out of retirement for all sorts of reasons. Some miss the discipline and demands of their chosen sport. Others need the attention or even the money. With no legacy at stake, I laced up my running shoes once more for a very different reason.

Pushing forty years of age, comfortable as a writer and frazzled as a father of four following the arrival of our son, Wilf, I was worried about my waistline.

Following the London Marathon, I didn't run a single step for several years. The event itself had been incredible. I came away from it feeling like I had experienced London in a unique way. I also had a medal to show for it. I felt no huge pride in the achievement, because frankly it had been a slow-moving train wreck from the halfway mark, but it was done. I had completed the 26.2 mile distance. In my view, there could be no greater goal in running. It meant I was free to focus on my writing career while juggling childcare with Emma, who had her own work commitments. The demands on our time were relentless, but also rewarding. We were raising a family, after all, which is the ultimate endurance event. With three daughters and a son, it sometimes felt like the intense parenting phase would never end. Everyone finds their own way through it, of course, which for me meant an increasingly large glass of wine to mark what little downtime was available.

I was constantly tired – the kind of dad who would flop into the flip seat at gymnastics classes and nod off before the kids had even assembled for the warm-up – but content. Work was going well, we were happy as a family, and yet I found myself looking forward to the end of bedtime stories so I could open a bottle. It wasn't a major problem, I often told myself while quietly refreshing my glass alone in the kitchen. Nobody would notice.

'Surprise!' said Emma one day, and presented me with a box-fresh collared shirt. 'I thought you could do with a new one.'

'That's nice.' I held it to my chest, admiring the cut and the colour, and then examined the label. 'It's a size bigger than I normally take.'

'I know,' said Emma after a moment.

Later, facing myself in the bathroom mirror with a towel around my waist, I realised it was time I had a conversation with myself. Throughout my life, I'd been naturally slim-built. I'd never really paid much attention to staying in shape. In the years since I'd given up running and pursued drinking as a pastime, however, it seemed my body had decided to relax considerably. I looked like I had sighed long and hard, and then failed to inhale again. I wasn't the only middle-aged man on the way to a sedentary lifestyle, but when I factored in the habitual boozing, that gave me pause for thought.

Just then, I could see where this was heading. I wasn't so young that I could take my health for granted any more. I didn't want to run out of road.

The next morning, after school drop-off, I retrieved my running shoes from the back of the cupboard. Enough time had passed since the marathon for my memory of the event to soften. It had been a great day, I reminded myself, with no flashbacks to those moments when it felt like the Grim Reaper had come along for the ride on my shoulders. Admittedly, the short outing that marked my return to aerobic exercise proved quite a wake-up call. I wasn't completely unfit, but a couple of kilometres was more than enough. In the past, it might have taken me a week or so to get up to speed. This time, I had to work at it for a month at least before a run felt like a rewarding use of my time.

On the upside, my return to solo running made me feel a whole lot better about the drinking. Now, when I poured myself that glass just after bedtime stories – and sometimes before if the picture book was long – I decided I had earned it.

In terms of routine and distance, I just went back to my old ways. I jogged along at an unhurried pace in my lunch break simply because I liked how it left me feeling. There was no goal beyond that. During my extended hiatus from running, however, we had moved from London's East End to the wilds of West Sussex, which meant switching from the pavements to trail. On the one hand, I loved getting out in the countryside. On the other, being fresh from the city, I didn't like getting my trail shoes muddy. I would rather pick my way around a stretch of farm track slop than charge on through, and with nobody looking that was fine by me. I wore no watch, because at that time they resembled a brick on a wrist strap, and so pace, time and heart rate were irrelevant. My sole aim in running was to justify my drinking while keeping my shoes clean. Both pursuits were completely habitual and mostly carried out in private so nobody could take me to task.

At least that's how I saw things.

'What do you think about this?' asked Emma one summer. Our youngest had scooped up a flyer after swimming at the sports centre, which his mother had folded into her back pocket and then remembered back home. 'Apparently it's really popular among local runners.'

I took the flyer from her. It was for the Barns Green Half Marathon, which was an annual race around country lanes staged in a nearby village.

'But it's got the word "marathon" in it,' I said, as if to remind her.

'Only half the distance,' said Emma. 'Half the pain.'

I smiled despite myself, and then returned the flyer to her.

'I'm happy as I am,' I told her.

Emma held my gaze, which left me feeling a little uncomfortable. Then Wilf came in from the garden to protest about one of his sisters.

'Well, if you're not up to it … ' said Emma, leaving the flyer on the kitchen table before following our son outside to play peacemaker.

If I was going to run this race, I told myself, having completed the form I'd printed out and then sealed it into an envelope along with a cheque for entry, it would be on my terms. This wasn't just about recognising that my wife knew exactly how to play me. After my humbling at the London Marathon, I would go into this event having learnt from the experience. It was 2012, and the internet had evolved from the lawless badlands of old. With three months to go before the race, I found a half-marathon training plan that suited me. I'd never considered putting some shape into my running routine to this extent, but I was keen to give it my best shot. With a digital wristwatch to make sure I hit my marks, I took the plunge in more ways than one.

Within a week, I was happily returning from tempo runs and interval workouts with my trail shoes and calves splattered in mud. With a goal in mind, this was a small price to pay. Kicking back in the evenings, with a glass of wine in hand that felt truly earned, I began to feel as if my running had a purpose.

A month into my programme, I decided to enter a low-key little event that was once hosted on an annual basis in the village where we live. Starting at the cricket pitch, the Alf Shrubb Memorial Race consisted of five miles around the countryside surrounding the birthplace in 1879 of one of the UK's greatest middle-distance runners. By the turn of the century, Shrubb was winning bets that he could outrun horses and entire relay teams. I imagine he had even mastered the ploughed-field traverse to become a national cross-country champion. At his height, Shrubb held world records for the half-mile, one-, two-, three- and four-mile distances. Although full details of his life remain hazy, perhaps my favourite known facts about our local hero are that he made the natural progression from running to become a tobacconist by trade, before emigrating briefly to Canada to work as a zookeeper.

In celebrating a life well lived, the Alf Shrubb Memorial Race attracted a small cohort of elite local club runners, as well as a handful of enthusiastic locals. It was staged early in the morning that Sunday, before the cricket took over, and seemed like a low-key, fun event that I could treat as a training run under race conditions. With fuelling in mind this time, I pre-loaded the night before with a large gin and tonic ahead of my carb-heavy pasta meal, which I washed down with an entire bottle of wine. I was ready for this, I told myself, on flopping into bed having laid out my running gear for the morning.

When my alarm went off, I don't recall reaching out to slap it down. I just remember my brain registering that I was way too hungover to face daylight. Naturally, I was annoyed at myself for missing the race when I finally surfaced towards mid-morning, but it wasn't until the Monday morning that I took myself to task about it.

'Apparently the start was delayed by fifteen minutes,' Emma told me, having dropped the kids at school and picked up on the gossip at the gates. 'The race director was calling your name out over the public address system.'

A moment passed as I pictured the scene. I was at my desk when Emma put her head around the door. With nowhere to turn, I could feel my face warming.

'Well, that was ... good of him,' I said. 'I didn't think I needed to call in sick.'

Emma shot me a look that told me I was only fooling myself here.

'Let's hope you can recover in time for the half,' she added, before leaving me to face my computer screen along with the cold, hard truth.

I was drinking too much. My relationship with alcohol had shifted so I was no longer in control. I felt ashamed that the man behind the Alf Shrubb Memorial Race, a decent guy, had delayed the start for me. I was also embarrassed that my wife quite clearly considered it to be an issue, and grateful in a way that she was giving me this chance to deal with it on my own terms. What really bothered me, however, was the fact that I had got into this fix simply by following the path of least resistance. It was just an end-of-the-day habit that had slowly taken hold until it became a compulsion, and I didn't like that one bit. My life hadn't crumbled around me as a result. I wasn't picking fights with bins or waking up in skips, but I had ignored the warning signs. The fact that I was appalled with myself for even getting here told me that I had come far enough down this route.

That morning, I decided there could be only one way forward. With just weeks before my half marathon, I had the perfect motivation to put my drinking on hold. The truth was I had been enjoying my training. I liked the structure that I had imposed on each session, even if I was also running to clear my thick head. By taking a break from the booze, I decided, I could possibly improve my performance in the race and then celebrate with a drink that didn't automatically lead to another.

I ran early the next day, simply because I'd gone to bed sober and had a restless night. It felt weird, but also like a small milestone. That I even had to think in these terms came as a shock. As I jogged home from a tempo session, it felt like I was awaking from a sleepwalk that had lasted several years.

A week or so into being on the wagon, I found that I no longer broke into an unpleasant sweat just minutes into a run. I had no idea if that had been my body expelling alcohol toxins from my system. It just left me feeling horrified if that was the case and slightly proud of the fact that I was trying to make a change for the better. At the same time, my sleep pattern began to settle and my concentration improved at work. I even found I could remember conversations from the previous evening, or moments on television, that otherwise would have been lost. After the horror show of the London Marathon, my sole aim in running a half was to enjoy it. I wanted to feel in control from start to finish, and even in a position to push it towards the end. I still had no real appreciation of pace or any kind of time in mind. I just wanted to feel like I had given it my best shot, and that was enough to help me overcome temptation when it came to medicating myself with a bottle of Médoc.

'Dad,' said Ethel on the day of the race, 'promise you won't be sick on the way home this time.'

Given that my seven-year-old and her five-year-old brother beside her weren't even born when we drove home from the London Marathon, I could only assume their older sisters had handed down their account of that fateful day like a family heirloom. As Grace and Bluebell were now well into their teens, they had wisely opted to stay at home this time.

'I'll try my best not to disappoint,' I promised them both. 'This time will be different.'

'You've done well,' said Emma, who had planned a picnic with the children while I took on just over thirteen miles of undulating lanes in this pocket of West Sussex. For such a small village, it was a popular event. All around us, just over 1,300 runners and their friends and family were assembling on the green. After a month of not drinking, I was hydrated for all the right reasons, and in decent shape as a result. With a breakfast of porridge, an energy gel in my pocket for the halfway mark and a plan to grab a water from each aid station on the way, I felt properly prepared.

I was also looking forward to one ice-cold beer to celebrate. By proving to myself that I had my drinking back under control, I would savour every drop.

This time, when the starter horn sounded and the tightly packed corridor of runners ahead began to shuffle forwards, I dictated my own pace. Unwilling to place any pressure on myself to go with a fast flow, I had positioned myself quite near the back. It was a good call. I started out at a trot, and for the first 10K I found myself slowly picking my way up the field. Admittedly, most of the runners at this point were in their senior years or too busy chatting to notice, but I was making progress.

The second half of the Barns Green Half Marathon takes in several long road climbs. Here, runners begin to ebb more than flow, and I was no exception. I was far from crashing, and yet I still needed to focus hard on achieving my goal.

'Get to the finish,' I muttered to myself, 'and you can have that beer.'

With three miles left in the race, that mantra came to dominate my thoughts. I had nothing left to push as planned. In fact the temptation to walk it in like so many others was proving almost impossible to ignore, but having come this far I couldn't allow it. The prospect of a beer was all that propelled me along. Everything from the droplets of condensation snaking down the label of the bottle to that momentous first sip played out in my mind. Just how sweet would it taste after four weeks of fizzy water and early nights? With every step, and in warm conditions, I came closer to finding out for myself. On approaching the village outskirts, I could hear the muffled strains of the commentator over the public address system. By now, crossing the finish line was meaningless. I just wanted to press on for the bar inside the clubhouse before catching my breath and the attention of the first person who could serve me.

And then, as I laid eyes on the gantry, with a crowd on each side of the approach and what looked like a decent time on the clock, I was hit by the reality of the situation. Having come this far, and worked so hard for it, I realised that a drink was the last thing I wanted. As the thought registered in my brain, with just metres to go, it felt like a liberation as much as a complete surprise. I even sprinted over the line, and there the desire for a beer that had carried me through the race just vaporised.

For a month, I had walked away from my relationship with booze. In that time, I realised, I had fallen in love with running. Instead of looking forward to a glass of wine at sundown, I had focused on getting out at sunrise and then seizing the day. Physically I felt in better condition. Mentally, to my surprise, I felt much better about myself. Every aspect of my life, in fact, from being a writer to a husband and a father, had improved beyond measure.

I had completed that half marathon in a shade over two hours. Immediately, it gave me a new target to beat. In this light, I realised that giving up alcohol wasn't a sacrifice. It was a *liberation*. It meant I was free to embrace running with the same dedication and commitment that I had shown to drinking, but with a more rewarding outcome on every level. As a volunteer placed a medal around my neck, I felt quite clear in my mind that this race marked a turning point. Since then, almost a decade has passed and not once have I felt the desire to touch another drop. Instead, as a runner reborn – far from elite but driven by enthusiasm – I've found I have everything to live for.

'Daddy, are you going to be sick?'

Wilf and Ethel were the first to find me. I had stopped to sit on the grass and just gather my thoughts. I looked up to see my two youngest children eyeing me warily.

'Not a chance,' I said, rising to my feet as their mother crossed the village green to join us. 'Those days are gone.'

PART

2

05

A RUN, NOT A RACE

'So, where is the stream on the map exactly?'

One day after my solo crossing of Crib Goch, I had joined a small party of Dragons in Training. This is the nickname given to those who feel compelled for their own reasons to put themselves through hell for six days in September. We are twelve strong here. A moment ago, we had paused by a waterway to get our bearings. This is our first break on a day-long recce of part of the route south of Snowdon. It's led by the cheery and capable Kate Worthington of RAW Adventures. Kate is also taking part in the Dragon's Back Race this year. Based on what I've seen so far of her impeccable mountain craft and navigation skills, I expect she might find herself with several hundred hangers-on. Once again, I consult my map in search of the blue thread representing the waterway that Kate used to pinpoint our position.

'It's just here,' she says helpfully, refolding it for me so I'm on the correct panel in a way that doesn't make me feel like a massive amateur.

Kate is the kind of guide you'd want by your side if forced to run to the hills to flee a zombie apocalypse. She knows how to stay alive out here, always remaining positive under pressure, and could clearly navigate her way to the safety of the stadium or wherever survivors are gathering for the airlift. Today, Kate is assisted by two sure-footed mountain guides. She has also been joined by a legend of the Dragon's Back, Joe Faulkner, a seasoned fell runner with a face chiselled from granite and a willingness to share his knowledge and expertise every step of the way. Right now, Joe has straddled the stream with his great feet as if preparing to wrestle a fish from the water for our lunch.

'Who thinks it's safe to drink from here?' he asks us all instead.

We consider our surroundings: a sodden moor wreathed in mist and studded by long-stemmed reeds. It's the grazing sheep, however, and by extension the waste they produce that might get into the water, that provide many of us with an answer.

'Not here,' offers one Dragon in Training, and I nod along sagely.

'Well, I'd go for it.' Joe conjures up a soft Perspex flask out of nowhere and proceeds to fill it.

'Do you sterilise the water before you drink it?' I ask.

Joe stands tall, a giant of a man, and considers the crystal-clear water in his flask.

'I never add chemicals,' he says before taking a swig.

I am carrying two full flasks on the front of my race vest, which I had filled with a litre of Volvic in my hotel room that morning as I wasn't sure about the tap.

'So, Joe has considered the risks here,' says Kate, perhaps mindful that most of us don't share his decades of experience. 'The water is fast-flowing, which is good, and we can see from here that there are no sheep carcasses upstream.'

'Just be aware that on race day you might find runners stop to piss in it,' warns Joe, and then takes another swig from his flask. 'Or worse.'

'So, maybe steer off the course to draw water,' Kate adds tactfully.

I recognise the importance of this lesson. On each of the six days of the Dragon's Back, water is only provided at the halfway points. In between, we must make judgements like this that could wind up being critical.

As we move on, I make a mental note to find out how often we will be passing near a shop.

We are each clutching an official race map. It's waterproof, folded into a concertina, and features a line snaking relentlessly across the terrain that covers the stages of each day. With no markers or signs on the ground to guide us, I am keenly aware that this single item could make or break my week. Yes, I have a GPS watch that can guide me. I just can't completely rely on it. Any communication failure with the satellite signal could send me into a tailspin. Aware that I might be one drained battery away from disaster, I simply must master my navigational skills. I don't consider myself to be stupid, but I have a lot to learn.

In a haphazard caravan, we run across exposed ground for a while. The going isn't easy, but that pretty much sums up this backbone of Wales. The landscape looks dramatic from a distance, while the terrain demands focus and foresight. Every foot placement requires a moment of consideration before committing, which is quite likely to become exhausting. With each step, I am reminded that my running experience to date has never taken me into this kind of territory.

A few minutes later, approaching a slope of strewn boulders from a ridge above, we slow to a walk once more. The young guy ahead of me consults his map, and even goes so far as to deploy his mandatory baseplate compass.

'Wow,' I say, genuinely impressed, and figure perhaps I too should use the one currently hanging uselessly around my neck just to see if I can get to grips with it. I know my north from south, but if I'm going to divine the right direction it would help to know where I am. 'Does it make any sense?' I ask.

The guy glances up from the map.

'It's coming back to me,' he says, as we pick up the pace once more. 'From my army days.'

* * *

When my daughter Ethel first described it to me, having seen a bunch of people rotate around the local park one frosty Saturday morning in the winter of 2015, parkrun did not sound like my kind of thing.

'Everyone was chatting before and afterwards,' she said. 'It just looked really sociable.'

'Sounds great,' I said. 'I'm out.'

It was this final detail that had sealed it for me. In the years since I quit drinking, I had placed running at the centre of my routine. I ran four times a week, usually for half an hour or so, apart from Sunday, which was reserved for a full sixty minutes. Now the children had grown up, with two departed for university, I could head out and just enjoy the peace and quiet.

In late summer, I would put in extra training ahead of the annual Barns Green Half Marathon. Overall, my finishing times were improving, and though I enjoyed the experience of a big race, I reserved the rest of my time for doing my own thing. So, the prospect of joining some collective activity every Saturday went against what running represented for me.

'It's free and open to everyone,' said Emma, who had also heard of this growing weekly gathering taking place in parks around the UK. 'You don't need to be particularly fast.'

I pretended not to hear her. Nobody else in the family ran except for me. All of a sudden, it felt like they were telling me what to do.

'One race a year is enough for me,' I said all the same.

'But it's not a race,' Ethel protested. 'Some of my friends do it, and their parents. You bring a barcode that you get swiped afterwards and the results go up online.'

I looked at my twelve-year-old as if hoping she might recognise the contradiction in what she'd just said.

'Sweetheart, if you get a time and a position then it's a race.'

'It's a *run*.' Emma sounded quite firm now. 'It takes away all the pressure so that anyone can join in.'

'Well, I'd like to do it,' said Ethel, and in that same moment I knew exactly how my father had felt all those years ago.

The morning after New Year's Day, leaving Emma behind with Wilf – because it was just more efficient this way in terms of getting it done so we could go home – I found myself shivering with our daughter beside the duck pond at Horsham Park. Ethel and I had joined a motley band of runners in leggings, layers and beanie hats, all of whom had arrived to take part in the first parkrun of 2016. The nearest event to where we lived, it had been established just over a year earlier and was attracting almost 150 participants each week. We had signed up online, printed out our barcodes, and were now in danger of losing the feeling in our fingertips.

'Are you sure you want to do this?' I asked.

As the cold started to bite, Ethel was looking less than enthusiastic. She was an accomplished junior swimmer with a strong competitive spirit and club trophies to show for it. I just wasn't sure how comfortable she would be out of the water.

'I was hoping my friends would be here,' she said while looking around.

'If you just wanted to hang out with your mates, they could've come to our house,' I said, and paused to blow on my hands. 'Where it's warm.'

Ethel didn't seem to hear me. Just then, her face lit up as she appeared to recognise someone in the crowd.

'Dad, can I run with Amelie?' Ethel gestured towards a girl about her age. 'You'll be all right on your own, won't you?'

As everyone fell quiet for the briefing, I toyed with the idea of just stepping aside altogether. I had come here to run with my daughter, but she had taken up a better offer. The prospect of jogging in a non-competitive way around a park with a bunch of strangers really didn't appeal. It was only when the run director invited us to applaud the volunteers for giving up their time that I realised it was probably easier if I just got into the spirit of the event. I could stretch to five kilometres of goodwill, I told myself. Just about.

'Get set ... Go!'

For a run, not a race, the guys taking part at the front set off in a suspiciously competitive way. I hadn't paid any particular attention to my starting position because I was under the impression no such tactics would be necessary. Instead, I'd given Ethel some space from an embarrassing dad by squeezing into the middle of the pack. By the time we reached the other side of the park, as runners jostled for position, I had effectively found myself going backwards. Still, I wasn't going to rise to the bait. What was the point in gunning it, I thought to myself as we completed the first two loops, if we were supposed to be here for a social?

Then I heard a familiar voice closing in behind me. As my daughter traded gossip with her friend, sounding like she was out for a stroll, I sensed the blinkers close in over my eyes.

There was no way, I decided in that moment, that she could beat me. I waited until we reached the next corner of the park, where everyone was thanking the marshal on duty, and then abandoned all sense that this was just a run. As casually as I could, despite the upswing in my breathing, I attempted to create some distance between myself and the two girls chattering behind me. With less than half a loop to go, I overtook several parkrunners and fully expected to be told to slow down. Instead, one responded by matching me for pace.

With the finishing funnel in sight, as I pelted towards it in full flight with absolutely no intention of allowing the guy I was holding off to take me at the line, I conceded that this non-competitive jogging thing had a certain appeal.

Later that morning, when Ethel showed me the results online, I decided that parkrun really was quite a decent experience. I had finished mid-pack in just under twenty-six minutes, with my daughter only a minute behind me. Having considered it to be a one-off just to keep her sweet, and like so many hundreds of thousands of people who have taken part over the years since parkrun began in 2004, I felt sure that I could do better.

Before January ended that year, I had taken two minutes off my 5K time. Worryingly, Ethel had done the same thing. Only she was barely breaking sweat.

'Yeah, but consider the age grading,' I pointed out, alerting her to the scores beside our names that levelled the playing field for men, women, young and ancient. 'Your old man is holding his own.'

'For now.'

Ethel narrowed her eyes at me over the kitchen table. We were just finishing breakfast before heading down to the park ahead of the nine o'clock start. I had enjoyed this weekly fixture with my daughter. Even though we ran apart from each other, it was giving us shared time together.

'If I can dip under twenty-three minutes today,' I said, 'I'll be happy.'

'You're never happy with your time,' she said. 'Every time the results come in, you tut.'

Just then, Emma swept into the kitchen with our young son in tow. Both Ethel and I turned to look at them and then glanced at one another.

'You're in running gear,' I said to Emma, with the same air of surprise I might have used had she presented herself in a milkmaid's outfit. Beside her, our ten-year-old was also dressed in shorts and what looked like his school PE top. 'But neither of you do running.'

'We do now,' said Emma, and showed me the barcodes she had just printed. 'We thought we'd join you both. I'll probably walk most of it but Wilf can run with you.'

'Of course,' I said, and cleared my throat to try again with more en-thusiasm as my target time receded into the distance. 'It'll be ... great.'

That morning, despite my young son complaining that his knees were locking up, we completed the three laps of the course. For a boy who would happily play video games all day if left to his own devices, I recognised the effort he had made here. Several times I suggested that we wait for his mother so he could amble along with her and let me take off, but Wilf was determined to get round in the same manner as his sister. Even though Ethel finished before us with enough time in hand to buy a hot chocolate with her friend and drink it, he wouldn't allow himself to bail. It was a painful experience, but I was proud of him. I just didn't expect he would want to come back for more.

'It's the T-shirt,' said Emma later. 'Kids get one for doing ten parkruns.'

By mid-spring, with Grace and Bluebell finding their own local venues at university, parkrun became a central feature of the weekend for all the family. Emma progressed from a walk to a run by enrolling in a Couch to 5K programme, while Ethel set out to close in on my time and Wilf counted down to his coveted prize. I thought he would call it a day on completing ten Saturdays and earning himself the white top that was issued to minors at the time. Instead, he set his sights on running fifty to bag the red shirt.

In that same week, quietly to my relief, Wilf also turned eleven years of age. It would be a few years before he could be prosecuted as an adult or free to buy alcohol from a supermarket, but it did mean he now qualified to do parkrun unaccompanied by a grown-up.

'It's been lovely running with you, but the time has come,' I said to him as we made our way into the park on the first Saturday that followed. I glanced at Emma, who rolled her eyes at the mock solemnity of the occasion. 'Son, you're on your own.'

'Really?' Wilf looked at his parents like I'd just presented him with a surprise birthday present. I had expected some resistance, but he just looked like a free man. 'I'll wait for you at the end!' he said before drifting off to enjoy his newfound parkrun independence.

'Like you'll get there before me,' I scoffed to myself, or so I thought.

'Don't you think you're taking this a little too seriously?' asked Emma as we joined the ever-growing numbers who congregated by the duck pond for the parkrun service to begin. 'You've never shown a competitive side before.'

'So, I'm a late developer,' I said in my defence, and there was some truth to this since coming last so traumatically as a kid. Now I had found myself back in the mix, at a weekly event with a focus on participation over pushing for the win. I just happened to be among those runners who liked to participate so hard that my eyeballs threatened to burst. 'I like to feel that I've done my best.'

'Yes, but where does it end?' asked Emma.

I gestured towards the finishing funnel.

'Hopefully in a quicker time than last week.'

I was wearing a brand new pair of running shoes. According to the running magazine I had now subscribed to, they were specifically geared for the hard-packed trails and municipal pathway that formed the loop around this park. Just then I noted my daughter dip down to tie a loose shoelace. I glanced at my footwear, confident that the YouTube clip I'd watched about lacing for races wouldn't let me down. I realised I ought to share the tip with her, and then figured perhaps it could wait.

'Is this about staying ahead of Ethel?' asked Emma, who after decades of marriage had a direct line to my thoughts.

'Of course not.' Avoiding her gaze, I remembered a line from a running blog I'd read that sounded like the sort of thing she'd want to hear. 'You should only ever be in competition with yourself.'

My times were still improving, though I was no longer taking off minutes but seconds. On my last solo parkrun, I had come tantalisingly close to dipping under twenty-two and a half minutes. With cool conditions and barely a breeze, I hoped to get off fast to avoid an early pinch point. There, the open field we swept across from the start line throttled into a sharp turn on to the park's perimeter path. If I could get through before the main body of runners, I planned to maintain a set pace on the running watch I'd considered to be worth the price if it led to a personal best.

'Are you going to start near the front?' asked Ethel as we parked our stuff by the fence around the pond.

'Maybe.' I eyed my daughter suspiciously. 'Are you?'

I had intended to get in position before the masses, and numbers were growing by the week. Now I worried that Ethel might come with me, get ahead and potentially slow my passage through the pinch point.

'I'm not even trying today,' she said, as if having inherited her mother's gift of being able to read my mind. 'Don't worry.'

'Fast runner coming through!'

The volunteer marshal who saw me coming, and unwittingly made my day by alerting those I was about to lap, clapped encouragingly as I passed. With three loops to complete, this last one often saw the front runners overtake those at the back, which was a completely new experience for me. Up ahead, two senior parkrunners steered to one side, which earned my breathless thanks and left me feeling like a middle-aged Mo Farah. By my reckoning, I was just inside the top twenty. On the back straight of the park, I could see several runners some distance ahead. Compared to me, they made it look effortless, but I was in no mood to be discouraged. I glanced at my watch. If I kept up this pace, I stood a chance of beating my best time. Nothing could stop me now, I told myself, despite feeling like my lungs were about to blow a gasket.

'*Good work!*'

'Thank you, marshal!'

At full tilt, the final kilometre of any parkrun is always the hardest. Even though this was the third time I had followed the path here, the slight but steady incline felt like it had become steeper. With plenty of space to clear those still on their second loop, I just dug in deep. In that moment, delirious on adrenaline, it seemed to me that nobody on earth could possibly match my raw pace. Such was my focus on the finish line in the distance that I didn't register the runner work her way alongside me and then slowly inch ahead.

'Well done,' I muttered through gritted teeth, but she was too deep in her own zone to respond.

All I could do was watch the woman pull away and then focus on not falling apart. That Saturday, I took several seconds off my personal best. I should have been elated. I just couldn't shake the feeling of deflation that had weighed in on me in those closing moments.

Seven days later, the same runner took me down once more. On the third occasion, I was ready to respond to this late surge, only for her to push even harder and leave me trailing in her wake. On finishing behind her once again, I needed to know her secret.

'I can't keep up with you,' I said, sounding like I also couldn't catch my own breath.

We were both crossing to the barcode scanners when I approached her, unaware that she was in fact heading for a small band of runners who had finished ahead of us both.

'Well, I can't keep up with this lot,' she said on joining them.

'It's payback for beating us at track night,' one said, and the others laughed.

It was then I realised that all of them were wearing matching vests. I had heard of Horsham Joggers, the local running club. They were responsible for my wife's Couch to 5K programme, which she had completed by running a parkrun from start to finish. Given the friends she'd made in the process, I had also marked it down as something that sounded far too sociable for a solo runner like me. Only now this Saturday-morning fixture had unlocked a drive in me to improve. Feeling like I lacked some kind of magic ingredient, I was keen to find out more.

The runner's name was Emma Walters, so her first name was easy to remember. She introduced me to her clubmates in turn, one of whom appeared to be on commission, judging by the enthusiasm with which he pitched the benefits of joining.

'So, what goes on at track night?' I asked specifically, because that sounded way more interesting to me than the quiz nights and group runs he had just told me about.

He looked at me like it was obvious.

'We learn to run faster,' he told me, before taking his turn to have his barcode scanned.

By my own admission, I had reached that critical stage in the evolution of so many parkrunners. Now, come nine o'clock every Saturday morning, I hungrily sought any means to improve my time. I was visualising the course in the bath on a Friday night, fuelling with porridge in the morning for that carbohydrate hit, and even hitting the apex of the corners like this was Formula One and not a fun run. The concept of training at a running track had just not occurred to me, but it felt like a step up and in the right direction.

One evening the following week, having established that anyone could book time at the local track behind the Tesco without having to be part of an organised club session, I stepped out from the grandstand and surveyed my surroundings. Individual runners were revolving around the lanes at speed, which formed the boundary to an athletics field. Some slowed to a walk for a section, while others were cantering in the opposite direction. There was clearly some kind of unspoken code at work here, as nobody was getting in each other's way.

'Be cool,' I said under my breath, and decided to do some stretching while I figured out how to join in.

After a minute of touching my toes and randomly twisting at the waist, I had established that most runners were congregating beside the long jump pit near the start line. A few other athletes were huddled inside some very tall semi-circular cage at the top end of the field, while a couple of lanky teenagers were sizing up a high jump beside it. Aiming to go under the radar while I acclimatised to this new world, I set my sights on a bench. It was just across the field on the outside perimeter of the back straight. That would be my base, I decided. Casually, I set out across the grass towards it. Once I had dumped my car keys, top and bottle of water, I intended to fall in behind runners who looked like they knew what they were doing and then quietly copy their session.

'OI! HEY ... DONKEY-BRAINS! WHAT ARE YOU DOING?'

I was midway across the grass when the voice bellowed out from the far end of the field. It was only when she repeated the question, sounding even more enraged, that I realised it was directed at me. With a start, I looked across towards the cage. There, a formidable-looking female athlete clutching a hammer throw in both fists was glaring at me. A moment later, I realised I had just blundered across her landing zone.

'Oh God, sorry!' I called out, shifting into a trot.

'DON'T KEEP GOING, YOU IDIOT! NEVER CROSS A LIVE FIELD!'

The about-turn I performed, followed by a walk of shame, was one I never wish to repeat. Not only had I interrupted the hammer-throw session, but I also appeared to have brought every activity on the track and field to a halt. Just to make things worse, the woman who had called me out appeared to be in the grip of quite an elevated rage.

'THAT'S IT! GO ON! KEEP MOVING! GET OUT OF HERE! HOW STUPID CAN YOU BE?'

By now, even though the runners were beginning to resume their workout, I felt as if I had shrunk to the same height as the clipped grass blades. Clearly I had broken some cardinal rule of athletics, but this response was bordering on one of those bad dreams in which you go on to realise you're also naked. All I wanted to do was cross the track back to the grandstand and head for home. While I was here because I had found a passion for pushing myself at parkrun, it was now the last place I wanted to be.

'DON'T EVER LET ME CATCH YOU DOING THAT AGAIN!'

'All right, Steroid Mary,' I grumbled to myself, and then panicked that in the silence she could hear me.

Instead, as I looked up to be sure I wasn't about to impede anyone by crossing the lanes, I recognised several runners in Horsham Jogger hoodies who had just come through the main gates.

'Are you here for the club session?' asked the guy who had sold it to me at parkrun.

'You're welcome to join us,' said Emma, the woman with the pace I envied. She gestured towards a tall, silver-haired man among their number with the lean and graceful air of a retired greyhound. He looked like he'd never be caught dead crossing the field. 'Keith is going to put us through our paces.'

06

RUNNING DOWN THE CLOCK

I don't need a map to tell me that I have a mountain to climb. Standing in the shadow of the mighty Rhinog Fawr, which comes as a relief from the afternoon sun behind it, we have paused as a group to steel ourselves for the next ascent.

'The suggested line is straight up,' says Kate, 'but on the day you'll find Dragons choosing alternative routes. Just be aware that although some lines might save time, they can be far more technical.'

I am looking at a steep-sided slope, which Joe Falkner puts at just over 700 metres high after one of my fellow Dragons in Training asks about the elevation. More immediately to my eye, this side looks like it has suffered its fair share of rock tumbles. In fact, the entire face is one perilous pile-up of boulders. It spills to the edge of an upland lake where we've gathered to regroup. I just have no experience in judging whether the last fall happened a hundred years ago or five minutes before lunchtime. There's no doubt it's strikingly beautiful, here in the wilderness of the Rhinogydd mountain range. It just all feels a little alien to me. Right now, I wouldn't be surprised if Joe told me to keep away from the edge of the water on account of the piranhas. I try not to feel frustrated, reminding myself that I'm a capable distance runner. It's just this is a course like nothing I have experienced before. For one thing, I can't even see it.

'Where is the line exactly?' I ask to clarify, squinting at the slope because any kind of way up it is invisible to me.

'Just there.' With her forefinger, Kate traces a winding route from the foothill to the summit. I nod appreciatively, despite being none the wiser.

Had I found myself here for the first time without a guide to hand, there is no way that I would consider ascending this side of the mountain. I'm not scared. It just doesn't strike me as passable. To my unseasoned but wary eye, one rogue step or even a sneeze looks like it could bring the rocks crashing down. The suggested route for the entire race has been tried and tested many times over, which means it must be fine, and yet I know that if I encountered this sort of thing alone I would assume I had gone a little astray. With nobody to tell me otherwise, I'd be off-piste in no time and hunting for a way up that I could come to regret. Even if I had a bad feeling about it, I also know that on the day I can't simply skirt around a mountain like this and crack on. The fact is almost every summit on the course serves as a checkpoint. Whatever path we choose to get up there, we runners are expected to punch in to confirm that we have made it.

I keep staring at Rhinog Fawr as I ponder the situation, hoping the path might materialise like a Magic Eye dolphin. Before I can blink, however, Kate begins the clamber and everyone falls in behind.

As we begin the ascent, I glance at my watch, which I have pre-loaded with the route for the day. A black dot swings around the watch face, as if magnetically drawn by the mountain. This is the heading indicator. Together with direction prompts, it should keep me on course from start to finish. I'm just not sure how comfortable I am with placing all my faith in a sports watch with buttons that can still surprise me when I press them. Having watched Kate and Joe at work with their maps, along with several more capable Dragons in Training than me, I promise myself that navigation must go to the top of my to-do list. I am map literate, just not in a fully joined-up way yet. Increasingly, as I climb into the latter half of this second and final day of my recce, that list feels like a compilation of skills I really need to master if I am to avoid being airlifted from this race by mountain-rescue helicopter.

* * *

Six months into my new running regime, as a club member and weekly track regular, I developed an affliction nobody could ignore. The symptoms would present when pelting along as hard as I could, drawing attention from both spectators and my fellow runners.

The Honk, as it became known, was completely beyond my control.

One moment I could be running in relative silence, with my legs and lungs working overtime. The next, a noise would develop in my throat on every exhalation and build to a hideous shriek. To the unsuspecting, particularly those one loop back at Horsham parkrun, it must have sounded like a low-flying goose was coming at them in a state of acute hysteria. On the upside, it cleared a path for me. I just had to put up with remarks as I passed.

'*What the —*'

'*Is he OK?*'

Try as I might, I could not curb the noise. It tended to kick in during the closing stages of a track workout or race. With the finishing line in sight, I'd dig in deep only to find myself unleashing my inner banshee. Someone suggested it could be a product of low-level panic; an alarm call from my body that could only be shut down by stopping. Others took pity and said it was the sound of passion as I pushed myself so hard. Most just took the mickey. It should have been completely mortifying, but by then I was in deep. All I could do was see it as a small price to pay as a slave to pace.

Thanks to the structured track sessions offered by the club, building strength and efficiency, I found myself in a honeymoon period at parkrun. Every Thursday evening, I would learn to run just out of my comfort zone in sets of 400 to 1,600 metres. A typical session would extend to 5K, with each hard interval followed by a thirty-second recovery jog. It was both exhausting and exhilarating. It also paid off handsomely on a Saturday morning. Granted, I could clear the duck pond of all waterfowl with the noise I made, but it was worth it to dip under twenty minutes for the very first time.

'I'm happy for you,' my wife said towards the end of that year, having heard me in my closing stages from the other side of the park, 'but you don't have to race every parkrun for a personal best.'

Her comment left me baffled.

'What other way is there?'

Emma directed my attention to our two youngest children. They had both just meandered through the funnel, having used the time to chat in a way that they wouldn't dream of doing back home.

'They could go faster,' I reasoned.

'Ethel could probably take you down,' said Emma. 'It's just she's not obsessed.'

It was a throwaway comment, but somehow it stuck. Over the course of nine months, I had gone from an antisocial solo runner to a parkrun disciple with a band of club friends. With a calendar of events in circulation, I also took on several 10K races and a half marathon on flat roads that had promised a PB beyond anything I could hope to achieve at Barns Green. In advance, I'd work out what pace I could sustain and just detached myself from the hideous honking that would accompany my closing stages.

With increasing enthusiasm throughout that time, I devoured every article I could find about improving and sustaining pace. At my next attempt at a half, I even claimed a top-ten placing in a field of 1,500 runners. Admittedly, the race took place through a vineyard, with competitors encouraged to wear fancy dress and get increasingly smashed on the free wine at every aid station. As someone who didn't drink, dress up or admittedly know how to have fun, I set about earnestly working my way through swathes of half-cut middle-aged men in tutus and women sporting fairy wings singing bawdy songs. While most of the field were too hammered to re-mark upon the honk when it happened, I wasn't too ashamed of myself to complete what was a fun run with an all-out sprint finish.

As my calendar began to fill with races, I reinforced my belief that run-ning was all about performance by signing up to Strava. With one click, this carved up my surroundings into segments and leaderboards I could not ignore. I even bought into the barefoot buzz and invested in a pair of running sandals. I had hoped they would improve my form, only for expectation and reality to clash one Saturday morning when I just looked like a holidaymaker failing to make the last call for his flight. Through my eyes, it was worth experimenting if it meant I ran faster. I even lobbied the family to become parkrun tourists at venues with next to no elevation in a bid to skin a second off my 5K time. The wretched noise I made at the tail end of each race continued to cause amusement and alarm, but none of that mattered to me as much as a coveted PB.

Then my wife called my focus into question. I hadn't considered my newfound interest in running to be an obsession, but her comment caused me to pause for breath. If I looked at my parkrun performance graph over time, which I did on a regular basis, all the rapid early growth had effectively levelled off. There I was, bumping along in a respectable way for my age category, achieving the same times every week while earning myself a reputation as a running scream queen.

For once, the fact that I had sacrificed my dignity for the sake of speed cut through. As much as I had grown to love the weekly attempt to topple my time, we all have an inbuilt limiter. My focus had been on going faster from one weekend to the next. If I extended that to months, years and even decades, the line on that graph wouldn't just level off. Eventually, it had to go into decline. I could see the same direction of travel in my 10K times and the half marathons I'd been pursuing. As a motivational moment, it really sucked. In my mid-forties, age was not on my side when it came to speed. As an epiphany that reminded me running had so much more to offer, however, I saw a way forward.

If I couldn't go much quicker without the aid of a professional coach or performance-enhancing drugs, I could go further. The key, I realised, was to slow the pace considerably, focus on distance over time, get off-road and wake up to the world around me. I should also add that I didn't just recalibrate my aims and ambitions from the sum of my wisdom and experience. To be completely honest, I had read *Born to Run*.

Granted, West Sussex offered little in the way of the Mexican canyon trails that serve as the stage for Christopher McDougall's seminal book about ultrarunning. Even so, the idea of discarding the cushioned shoes, dropping down several gears and feeling at one with the landscape for hours on end proved deeply seductive. My barefoot flirtation hadn't lasted, thanks to my bruised heels and the heightened dread of dog shit between the toes, but I could buy into the concept of gently pushing myself towards a steady state of bliss. Having raced through the book, I decided that the future lay in running long.

'Let's not forget London,' was all Emma had to say when I shared my plans. 'We had to scrape you off the pavement.'

'This goes far beyond a marathon,' I said loftily, still buzzing from just finishing the final chapter. By then, I had blanked out all memory of my one experience at this distance. In my enthusiasm for discovering the world of ultrarunning, I told myself that my inaugural 26.2 miles was just a gateway I had opened prematurely. 'It's about taking to the trails at a comfortable pace, and also eating and drinking on the go,' I added. 'I've even found a race that passes through the village. You can come and watch if you like.'

'Last time we did that was kind of traumatic.'

'Trust me,' I assured her, 'this will be different.'

The Downs Link Ultra does what it says on the tin. The route follows a former railway line – now converted into a green corridor for walkers, cyclists, horse riders and runners – and joins a parallel range of chalk hills in the south-east of England known as the North and South Downs. This thirty-eight-mile challenge is staged annually by Jay, Danny and Chris of Sussex Trail Events, who possess the rare ability as race directors to be both impeccably professional and massively laid-back.

'Who hasn't done this before?' asked Jay through his megaphone, addressing several hundred runners at the top of St Martha's Hill in Surrey. I raised my hand as a newbie to this ultra, and it was reassuring to see over half the crowd do the same thing.

'You see Paul here?' Jay said next, encouraging a runner at the front to make his presence known. 'Paul won it last year. He knows the way. Follow him.'

It was a moment of good humour that helped to take the edge off my nerves. The organisers had in fact marked the length of the course with red and white tape. I was also looking forward to experiencing my first aid station, laid on at regular intervals to help runners stay fuelled and hydrated on their journey south to Shoreham on the West Sussex coast. Despite feeling like I was in good hands, I couldn't shake the fact that this course was so long it could be seen from space.

I had made the discovery the week before, slowly zooming out on Google Maps with a rising sense of dread. Was I capable of running this distance? I just couldn't get my head around it. All I could do was remind myself that I had some experience on my side compared to my marathon debut. Since signing up eight weeks earlier, I had adapted my training for distance over pace. I slowed things down and worked on extending my time out on runs. With the Downs Link on my doorstep, I repeatedly ran sections to the north and south. I deliberately didn't take things too far as I wanted this race to feel like an adventure. That had been a big part of the draw when I first considered running an ultra. From our elevated position at the start line, looking across seemingly endless folds of forest and fields wreathed in mist, I just felt like I was about to run into the great unknown.

'Look after each other,' said Jay, in one of those quiet but reassuring voices, and signalled for the race to begin.

Starting at the very top of an impressive, steep-sided hill, the opening descent unfolded as one joyful bundle. Running heel to toe, we followed tracks and dry stream beds before the course levelled out and finally joined the former railway line. From there, with space to find a rhythm, the pack began to stretch considerably.

'Run your own race,' I reminded myself, mindful not to let others dictate my pace as they had in the capital.

It wasn't hard to keep things slow. For one thing, I was wearing a hydration vest. With two old-school hard bottles stowed at the front, the sloshing sound emphasised the frequency of my footfalls. Keeping to a delicate rinse cycle was fine, I told myself, while the noise was also a constant reminder to stay hydrated.

The Downs Link offers little by way of twists and turns. Many local runners write it off as monotonous, and yet I found something endearingly hypnotic about following a long, straight route. I may not have been born to run with the Tarahumara tribe, but I was quite happy rocking along with a bunch of cheery, funny and encouraging competitors from all walks of life and one shared goal for the day.

As the early stages ticked by, it seemed to me that a rubber-band effect controlled the cohort I was in. A runner would cruise up beside me for a chat before pulling away, and a little later I would find myself alongside them again as they eased off the pace. I took this as licence to do the same thing, and simply ran to feel rather than fretting about my position in the pack. Strikingly, I felt no sense that I was in a race against these runners. For one thing, there weren't that many of us and I came to relish the space.

No doubt things were different for the elite competitors like Paul, who I had last seen take off at the start. Downstream from the front end, it seemed to me that managing the miles was the central focus for each of us. It was good to know I wasn't alone in this respect. In some ways, facing that daunting distance was a bonding experience. By the time I arrived at my first ever aid station, I felt like I had earned my place at the trestle table.

'What can I get you?' The volunteer on duty greeted me with a smile and flourish of her hand to showcase the spread on offer. 'We have sandwiches, flapjacks, watermelon, jelly babies ... '

As she ran through the menu, I felt less like an ultramarathon runner and more like a child who had just shown up at a birthday party.

'Is there cake?' I joked.

'Save that for the finish,' she told me, and offered to refill my bottles. 'How are you feeling?'

'Good,' I told her, picking off some fruit and a fun-sized Mars Bar to take with me. 'I'm loving it.'

Later, when I passed through our village around the midway point, Emma was waiting to ask me the same question.

'Great,' I lied. 'Strong.'

I wasn't broken this time. Unlike the London Marathon, I hadn't crashed so hard that every second felt like a bad dream. After running all morning, I was just becoming very tired. My shoulders were aching and a general fatigue had set in some way back. I wasn't alone in feeling this way. Pretty much everyone around me was beginning to find it tough, while those with experience on their side pointed out that it was supposed to be like this.

'What do you need?' asked Emma, walking quickly to match what I had thought was a decent ultra pace.

'A lift?' I suggested.

Emma found my hand, squeezed it, and let me go.

'You can do this,' she told me. 'Only another seventeen miles left!'

It was the best thing she could've said, and the worst. I was still running, but as soon as she put a figure on the distance it seemed an impossible task. If I was struggling now, I fretted to myself, what would I be like in five, ten or even fifteen miles?

'Don't think about it.' The voice seemed to come out of nowhere. I glanced around to see a runner appear at my side. We had stopped at the last aid station together. She wore a sun visor and a T-shirt declaring her membership of the 100 Marathon Club, which marked her out through my eyes as someone who knew what she was talking about. 'Just focus on getting through the next mile.'

I smiled to myself, feeling a small charge of positivity thanks to her.

'I work in kilometres,' I told her.

'Then you don't have so far between each one,' she said, which made complete sense to me in spirit.

Throughout the early afternoon, as the temptation to just walk the rest of the way began to wrap its arms around me, I set myself a string of small, achievable goals. Sometimes I would set my sights no further than the next kilometre, but often I would shorten that to some feature up ahead like a tree, a fingerpost or one of the many tunnels that took the Downs Link under the roads. It was, I found, a discipline, but one that helped me to progress. In a way, I realised, with so much time on my hands to think as I plodded along, running an ultra was a lot like writing a book. When I sat down in front of my keyboard, I didn't think I had 300 pages to fill. I just broke it down into manageable sections, and sometimes that went no further than the next paragraph or page. As long as I stuck to the plan, and always put in my best effort, I would reach The End.

When I approached that moment on the Downs Link Ultra, almost thirty-eight miles and seven hours after setting off, I felt as if I was emerging from a dream. The race hadn't quite been the transcendental awakening I had read so much about. If anything, it had been bloody hard, but not in that lung-busting way that I had come to associate with short runs. This had been about running through physical fatigue and into exhaustion, and then switching to a psychological motor to keep moving. I had never experienced anything like it, and that included several moments where the urge to give up had been hard to ignore. Towards the closing stages, however, as the shadows around me turned like a clock hand, I had begun to feel less intimidated by the remaining distance. My legs were trashed but

I had found a drop of confidence in an otherwise empty tank. On the home stretch, the path follows a wide river course as it flows to the sea. Finally, it crosses a footbridge and then follows open ground bordering Shoreham's airfield. That's when I saw the inflatable finishing arch. Still I focused on taking one step at a time, because by then even 500 metres seemed too much for me.

'I've done it,' I breathed to myself, feeling choked in the final moments of my first ultramarathon. The elation, relief and even shock that I had succeeded felt like it might spill into tears as I crossed the line. The moment I stopped running, however, all my emotions fell away. Instead, I just felt completely at peace.

'Well done, mate.' Placing a medal around my neck, it was Jay who welcomed me in like I'd just graduated from a self-help academy. In a way, I'd done exactly that. What's more, I realised as I spotted Emma coming through the throng of anointed ultrarunners and their families, I had run all day without a single honk.

07

THE ENGLISHMAN WHO WENT UP A HILL

We climb towards the summit of Rhinog Fawr without word. This isn't running, I think to myself, as I wait for the person above me to feel confident in finding their next hand- and foothold. It isn't quite mountaineering either, but goes above and beyond my concept of rock scrambling. In my mind, that's the kind of carefree thing kids do on their summer holidays when the tide goes out. Right now, on this steep spill of boulders and scree, I'm acutely aware that there are Dragons in Training below me as well as above. I don't want to stop a loose rock with my face. Nor do I want to be responsible for taking someone out with clumsy footwork.

All I can do is compare this ascent to my experience on Crib Goch the day before. At least this time my heart hasn't transplanted to my mouth. I am moving at the same steady pace as everyone else, and while I still feel like I have a lot to learn, I am riding that curve nonetheless. Mindful not to look down at the lake, or consider how far we have left to go, I revert to that ultramarathon mind state of putting one foot in front of the other. In this case, however, my hands feel kind of critical here as well. I just choose not to dwell on the fact that I'm grasping at heather as I ascend and hoping it will hold me.

'So, from here we can see what's in store for us next,' declares Kate when we finally gather at the trig point on the summit that will serve as a checkpoint in the race. While the views are sublime, it is basically nothing but mountains. 'I guess that may or may not be a good thing,' she adds, perhaps mindful of the silence that has descended over the group.

We pick our way towards the other side of the mountaintop, and I'm hoping it's just perspective that makes it look more like the platform for a base jump. Even so, having conquered this climb, I feel quite positive. We're making progress through a beautiful part of the world. It's incredibly rugged and remote, but also strikingly tranquil. In some ways the peace feels quite precious, because all day it's been drilled into us how treacherous this region can be should conditions turn. If we didn't have to find our way down safely, I have no doubt I could just spend time here feeling deeply appreciative of the moment.

'What's this grey stuff?' I ask Kate as we leave the trig point behind, mindful that I've just trudged through yet another patch of fine, clay-coloured powder. 'It's sticking to my trail shoes.'

'Well, if you think about where we are,' Kate answers, and I realise she has followed a course that keeps her soles clean, 'I would suggest it's scattered ashes.'

* * *

Several days after completing my first ultramarathon, so broken that I was forced to negotiate the stairs on all fours like a toddler, I signed up for another one. The race was part of a coastal 50K series. It meant from the moment I came home with that second ultra medal around my neck, I knew exactly what would follow.

From there on out, I ran one ultra for every season. My final 50K in that series took place on the Sussex coast in March 2018. Conditions had been bracing in a cold and breezy way, and then during the course of the race the Beast from the East swept in. In the teeth of a howling blizzard and sub-zero temperatures, my pace in the final phase was reduced to a feeble trudge. Form-wise, as I entered the frame of the official race photographer lurking on the white cliffs, I didn't so much resemble a runner as that emoji of the forlorn walking man. It was an arduous experience, and yet even before I fully regained the feeling in my fingertips that evening I had set my sights on the next start line.

'It might sell out,' I reasoned with Emma, having asked her to tap in my details while I dealt with chilblains. 'And it's not for a few months,' I added, like that would sell it to her. 'Better weather.'

Emma asked for my bank card so she could complete the transaction.

'I just don't get it,' she said when I found it for her. 'What's the draw?'

Her question was hard for me to answer. My first experience on the Downs Link pushed me to a place I had never experienced before. I knew it would be deeply challenging, but it was only afterwards that I appreciated how much of it came down to sheer determination. There had been nothing to stop me just pulling up, physically exhausted, and calling for a lift home. There would have been no punishment. I dare say people would have commended me for giving it a shot, but in my mind that was not something I could consider. Instead, running on empty, I was forced to exist in the moment. I might have set myself short targets, reducing my focus to one kilometre after the next for hours on end, but in reality my focus had gone no further than blinking, breathing and putting one foot in front of the other.

Whenever I reflected on what running long meant to me after the event – spanked on endorphins and possibly not thinking straight – it came down to the sense of purpose. I could find that in other areas of my life, of course, but out there it was so simple. All I had to do was keep moving, no matter what obstacles I faced en route or within myself, until I crossed a line. There was no trophy, prize money or press awaiting me. At least not at my level. I might get a medal like every other finisher, and a T-shirt if I had opted in for one, but that was it. The reward was in the experience, which reveals who you really are, and in the afterglow. I liked how it left me feeling. The sense of accomplishment was hard to beat, along with a renewed appreciation for home comforts we might otherwise take for granted. So, when it came to answering my wife, all I could say quite simply was that I wanted more.

'It's just such a buzz,' I said by way of explanation.

'So is buying a Porsche or a motorbike,' said Emma. 'What's wrong with a normal midlife meltdown?'

'Is that what you think this is?'

Emma shrugged as she tapped in my card number; half smiling as if she had a point to make while playing with me.

'You're middle-aged and the kids are growing up. Isn't that when most men ask themselves what it's all about?'

'There could be worse ways,' I said in my defence, and Emma didn't disagree.

It was only a brief exchange, completed with some head-shaking over the fact that I now had another new date in the diary, but it gave me pause for thought. If I was being completely honest with myself, this wasn't about searching for something I lacked in my life. I'd done all the drinking. I'd also plastered myself in tattoos throughout my twenties. Even if the urge returned for a midlife club badge on my bicep, I'd run out of room. Above all, I was quite content at both home and in work. In some ways, now that I was emerging from a phase of parenthood that offered little scope for anything else, this was the ideal moment for ultrarunning. I had time on my hands for training that just would not have been available to me with small children. In short, I was only doing something I had always loved. It's just that now running had become a means of taking me places.

Over the course of a year, I felt like I had gained a decent understanding of how to run 50K. I had gone from just hoping to survive to the finish line to homespun strategies that helped me to improve. I was no longer obsessed by the pursuit of a fastest time, as I had been at parkrun. Pace still played a role in my running, but then so did managing the terrain and elevation, along with the question of what I could feasibly sustain from start to finish. In finding my way, I began to appreciate that I needed to be moving as efficiently as possible at any given moment. A flat stretch of tarmac might serve as an opportunity for me to push things a little, while a hill climb was often better tackled at a march. Throw exhaustion into the mix – the enemy of good intentions – and often my objective would be just to finish over the line and not in a ditch.

Ultimately, I wanted to feel like I was learning from experience. It was like a never-ending work in progress. There was so much to consider, from choice of food, drink and footwear to a growing awareness that a strong core was key for me to keep my back and shoulders trouble-free. Pilates proved to be a revelation in making sure I was fit for purpose, and I found plenty of video tutorials on YouTube. Once I'd ditched the frenetic sessions hosted by impossibly pretty things in bikinis on the beach, and resigned myself to more sedate workouts for seniors in slacks, I began to enjoy the benefits.

Around the same time, feeling like I had found my feet as a distance runner, I set my sights on an event that seemed like a world away from anything I'd done before. Taking a break from cruising YouTube for Pilates tutorials, in search of something that didn't look like it was staged in the communal area of a retirement village, I fell upon a documentary about a unique race that took my breath away.

Until recently, the island of La Palma was perhaps best known for hosting a legendary ultramarathon that traverses the ruins of a volcano. This jagged rock in the ocean is part of the Canaries, the Spanish archipelago just off the coast of North Africa. Starting and finishing at sea level, with seventy-six kilometres of challenging trails in between, Transvulcania invites runners to ascend almost 2,500 metres to the summit before crossing the giant, crescent rim and then winding down the other side. As the volcano had been dormant for half a century, I figured I'd be fine for a weekend. Had I known that it was in fact relatively close to erupting out of nowhere, disrupting island life for the foreseeable future including the annual race, I might have been more risk-averse. What seduced me at the time was the fact that La Palma was often at the centre of a vast cloud inversion. It meant much of the ultramarathon took place on trails that quite literally seemed to cross the heavens. Having watched one video and then consumed all the footage of the event that I could find, I prepared a sales pitch for a mini-break that Emma could not refuse.

'Just look at the facilities this hotel has to offer,' I said, placing my laptop in front of her so she could check out the page I had loaded. The pictures showed a chic resort surrounded by banana groves and a commanding view of the Atlantic Ocean. I figured it was best to present her with the upside before mentioning that it would be a kind of activity holiday for me. 'You have a choice of seven pools, five restaurants and all the food and drink you can manage over the weekend. Grace has even agreed to hold the fort here,' I added, before she could suggest that I was forgetting Wilf and Ethel. 'It's a chance to unwind. You know? Just us.'

'What's the catch?' she asked.

From a distance, on the sea crossing that served as the last leg of the journey, La Palma looks a lot like Skull Island. I had made my way to the front of the ferry, trying hard to hold on to my lunch, so I could take a good look at our destination. Steep forested foothills reached up from the coastline, ringed by halos of cloud, with a jagged summit that was quite possibly home to an enormous, chest-beating ape called Kong.

'There it is,' I said to Emma, hoping she would soon forget the tortuous, multi-stage trip that I had slung together on a shoestring to get here.

'That looks … ' She faltered and turned from the window to face me. 'Matt, are you sure you're up to this race?'

'We'll soon find out,' I said buoyantly, and invited her to look at the passengers around us. 'We're all in the same boat.'

Earlier, from the moment we had disembarked from our budget flight to Tenerife, walking through the terminal en route to catch a bus to the port, it was clear that many travellers were heading to our destination. Athletic young men and women wearing expensive trainers and race shirts hustled their baggage on to connecting flights and into taxis as we waited at the stand. Judging by the chatter, most of them had travelled from Spain, where the race is considered to be the most prestigious on the national calendar, although the entry list reflected a truly international field.

'I don't want to be rude,' said Emma, 'but most of these people look like they have a sponsorship deal, and you … don't.'

There was no doubt that we were among professionals. Unlike so many sports, at an ultramarathon you could find yourself in the same field as the very best in the world. I was excited to learn that several stars of the trail-running circuit would be running, with Sweden's Ida Nilsson and Xavier Thévenard from France among many others. The organisers had published an 'elite list', in fact, and yes, I had held out for a miracle on dropping down to scan the surnames beginning with W.

At the time, three years before the volcano woke up and made headlines around the world, La Palma was known as one of the quieter outposts in the Canaries. Come race weekend, however, the island transformed into a celebration of trail running. On arrival, we found banners and bunting fluttering in the Atlantic breeze from every street corner, while our taxi driver chatted in broken English about the steady stream of participants that he had ferried to the hotel complex. The island itself is a 700-kilometre-square national park. It's a rugged mountain wilderness with abundant plant life and a thin skirt of civilisation at sea level. The uplands are also home to significant astronomical observatories. When darkness fell that night, the sky above swelled with vast banks of stars.

I barely slept a wink, and just dozed in fits through the registration day that followed. This involved collecting a bib that sported my number, name and a Union Jack flag in the corner.

'I feel like a poor man's Paula Radcliffe,' I said while going through my kit for the sixteenth time. 'The nation's hopes rest on my shoulders.'

'I counted about 100 Brits on the entry list,' said Emma, who was sitting in the sunshine on the balcony. 'You can shoulder the load together.'

It was hard to relax, despite being spoilt for choice for swimming pools. I just couldn't escape the enormity of what the next day would bring. I even began to feel like I had no right to be here. While everyone else looked like they were living their best lives as twenty-something trail runners, here I was just one year away from turning fifty. At their age, I'd considered a loop of the park with the pram to be a success. Who was I kidding, thinking now was the time to take this sport seriously?

Behind the hotel and the plantations, the lower slopes of the volcano dominated the skyline. It was impossible to ignore, and while I was excited about the race ahead I felt far from home in different ways. I wanted to be cool and collected like the human gazelles who floated around the complex. The female athletes almost exclusively sported high-banded ponytails that would swish the next day to embody their perfect pace, while the guys kicked back at poolside tables with supercool sunglasses, baseball caps on backwards and indecently short shorts that barely contained their quads. They all looked so relaxed and in control, while I stuck to the shade like a vampire on vacation and worried about whether there would be a queue for the toilets at the start line.

When it comes to managing my race anxiety, I tend to use it as a driver to get organised. It meant the next morning I arrived in plenty of time at the lighthouse where proceedings would kick off, which was a wise move on discovering a massive line for the Portaloos. It was still dark as over 2,000 trail runners poured in from coaches laid on across the island in readiness for the 6 a.m. start. I had left Emma sleeping as I crept out of the complex and climbed on my bus, and then wondered how long it would be before I stopped feeling sick with nerves.

With a sound system in full swing, and a countdown clock projected on to the cliffs above the start gantry, it began to feel more like we were gathered for a pre-dawn rave than a run. As the time approached, I took my customary place near the back and then waited with everyone else for the signal to switch on our head torches. This came as the clock ticked through the final ten seconds to the deafening musical assault of 'Thunderstruck' by AC/DC. The mass illumination was marked by a roar of excitement from the throng, which was subsequently eclipsed as we surged forward by the crackle and boom of a firework arsenal. In the shock and awe of the spectacle, for a moment I thought we were being shelled. I was always braced for a DNF in a race. Now it seemed I ran the risk of PTSD.

'*Ánimo! Ánimo!*' yelled supporters in the crowd, which meant nothing to me but sounded stirring. '*Venga! Venga! Venga!*'

Within a kilometre, as we pushed along the mountain road up and away from the lighthouse, I witnessed the first of many astonishing sights that day. With the elites surging ahead, and plenty of runners who had been in front of me just walking out to high-five the crowds and pose for selfies, I found myself in an extraordinary snake of light from all the head torches. This bobbing string of illuminations seemingly zigzagged towards the stars in the sky and left me in no doubt that I was facing one hell of an adventure.

Almost one hour into a steady but relentless climb, as darkness began to lift, we left the scrubland and dusty farm tracks behind to pass through Los Canarios. This was no sleepy Spanish village, however. Either the residents had got up early to cheer through the runners from behind crowd-control barriers or they had been partying through the night. The atmosphere was wild, with supporters screaming encouragement on each side as we climbed through streets and up ancient steps. Some were wearing pyjamas, others had dressed up for the event, but everyone was in the mood for a wild fiesta.

Leaving the party behind, we continued for some time along a pine-forest trail. Some runners jostled for position but largely we kept in a train, and as the first bars of sunshine began to poke through the trees, the head torches came off. Shortly afterwards, instead of being united by lights, every runner up ahead and behind me became disarmed by the emerging view. I could glimpse it where the forest seemingly fell away to the sky, but it wasn't until we left the pines behind for open slopes of loose black sand that I paused to appreciate the moment. For as I looked east towards the ocean, all I could see before the rising sun on the horizon was a seemingly infinite carpet of cloud.

Amid such a serene and breathtaking landscape, it was hard to complain about tiring legs and the building heat. I refilled my bottles at each aid station, developing a taste for the blue liquid on offer that might've been windscreen washer but also seemed to oil the wheels. Some of the sections were technical, and involved a little scrambling, but nothing ever felt perilous. The greatest hazard proved to be the sharp volcanic rocks that littered the path. I witnessed many bloody palms and knees. As a precaution, I even deployed the poles that I carried with me to ensure I didn't face-plant whenever I caught my footing.

By the time the relentless climbing began to plateau before the final ascent to the summit, the sun was high in the sky. What I hadn't anticipated, however, was the number of microclimates we would pass through. Just as I felt like I was melting in the heat, the path dipped on to an exposed ridge line that served as a breaker for the clouds that pressed into that side of the island. The resulting fog swirl caused both the temperature and my field of vision to drop considerably. Minutes later, I passed through a rainforest dripping with moisture and filled with the sound of exotic birdsong and plunging waterfalls. At one point, following the path around a ravine that took us into the wind, I was pretty sure I felt hail on my face. Then, when the climbing resumed, we left behind these weird weather pockets for the dry heat that would dominate the rest of the day.

It was only as the elevation, trees and vegetation dwindled to become a broad amphitheatre of red rock under blue sky that I registered we had reached the remains of the crater rim. At almost two and a half kilometres above sea level, the views from this long and lofty crescent were incredible. Above clouds that stretched to the four corners, it felt as if this trail-running paradise was in a world of its own. Worn down by hours of largely runnable ascent, however, I forced myself to stay focused on trotting along the path that weaved between jagged rocks.

I had no idea of my position, but gradually it felt like I was gaining places. Mostly, I passed competitors who were feeling the heat, or simply looked burnt out after fifty challenging kilometres. While it seemed like I was on top of the world, I didn't feel that way on the inside, and slowly began to sense that I might soon suffer myself. I had been warned that altitude sickness could creep in as we crossed this Martian landscape studded with the white domes of telescope observatories. Scrambling towards the aid station at the highest point, Roque de los Muchachos, my legs began to feel like they were made from lead, while each breath of air I took in felt like it wasn't enough. Despite wanting to break for a minute or two like so many others, I realised the exit led to the beginning of the descent. Grabbing a slice of watermelon and magic blue fluid that turned out to be Gatorade, I forced myself not to hang around.

What followed was a downhill half marathon. Through the early stages, in the thin air and mid-afternoon heat, however, this came as more of a struggle than the ascent. What lifted my spirits as I picked my way down this mountainous horseshoe was the realisation that I could see my destination. It was far below me, a seemingly miniaturised patchwork of rooftops, roads and squares, and its position tallied with the map of the course I unfolded from the pocket of my race vest. I could even hear vague strains from a folk music troupe celebrating the arrival of those fine specimens who had no doubt been lolling casually by the hotel pool the day before. I was exhausted, but still running and the end was in sight. Coupled with a return of the tree canopies, into air that felt both cooler and distinctly more breathable, I even picked up the pace.

In my head, on passing under the finishing gantry at what had been my first ever mountain race, I felt like a running god who had just come down from Olympus. In reality, covered as I was in twelve hours' worth of volcanic dirt, I looked more like some left-for-dead miner emerging into the land of the living. Having started at the back, uncertain of my right to be here, I had traversed a volcano to finish mid-pack, and that was enough to make me feel like I belonged. As the realisation dawned on me, I found a space on a bench beside a spent-looking runner with a German flag on his bib. I intended to call Emma so she could find me, but on sitting down I suddenly felt quite overwhelmed. A moment later, I felt his hand on my shoulder.

'All done,' he said as I sobbed into my palms. 'All good.'

08

IF THEY'RE UPRIGHT, KICK THEM OUT

For much of the Dragon's Back Race, runners are free to choose their own lines from one checkpoint to the next. Given that I barely know where I am in Wales, let alone on the race map, the suggested route is my only realistic option.

'There are plenty of ways to reach the next summit,' advises Joe Faulkner all the same. 'Working them out in advance could save you time.'

Six hours into this guided recce, Joe is still drinking from his flask filled with stream water and has yet to bleed out from his eye sockets. Together with Kate, his presence fills me with confidence. I'm just aware that he won't be here when it matters.

'Is the route marked on the map always the easiest?' asks one of the Dragons in Training.

Joe shrugs like he's not the route planner here, which serves as another reminder of the personal responsibilities that every runner must bring to this race. According to the map, if I'm on the right panel, we're faced with yet another steep climb. I compare the contour lines with the view in front of me. Both confirm another testing time.

'This is a very technical section of the race,' says Kate, perhaps sensing that most of her flock are feeling a little intimidated by their surroundings. 'Don't let yourselves get hungry or thirsty when you need your wits about you.'

We've just descended from Rhinog Fawr. I achieved this mostly on my heels in loose scree and with very little control. Now we're crossing a sodden stretch of wild grassland towards the foothills of Rhinog Fach. Still scarred by my crossing *of Crib Goch the day before, I fall back to walk alongside Kate for a moment.*

'Can I ask you a question about the third pinnacle?' I ask her.

'Sure,' she says, like she wouldn't be surprised if I ask her to hold my hand across it during the race itself.

'I'll be honest,' I admit, 'it freaked me out. That ledge out to the right? The one over the drop? It just seemed really sketchy.'

'Oh, the main line doesn't quite go that far round,' she says breezily, and a chill passes right through me. 'Most folk who choose that side of the pinnacle take more of a vertical line. Others find even that's just a bit too exposed for them and go round the other side.'

I take a moment to consider what this means. Alone on Crib Goch, I had thought there was only one line I could take. Not only have I just learnt there are options, but it also seems I inched out on to a route reserved for hardcore thrill seekers or sensible climbers with ropes. While I'm relieved I came to no harm, I feel rattled that my judgement placed me at some risk.

'So, you're saying there's an alternative?' I follow up with her.

'Of course!' says Kate, and I don't know whether to sigh in relief or beat myself up for missing it. 'We often show people another feasible way that takes them down to the left and around the base of the pinnacle.'

'When you say feasible,' I say, 'do you mean less terrifying?'

A veteran mentor of Dragons in Training, placing safety before a subjective issue like expectation, Kate responds to my question with a smile. As we march onwards, I promise myself that at the very least when I face that pinnacle again, I will have conquered it in my head.

* * *

There are no limits. That's the kind of motivational slogan we often see emblazoned over images of heroic-looking runners looking out at some infinite horizon. Now, I don't want to be a downer, but at some stage in our lives we all reach a point where we cannot go both faster and further. Ultimately, as runners and human beings we all have our limits. On the upside, finding them can define us. If failure is an option in any challenge we choose to face, we can only look back knowing that we pushed ourselves as hard as we could go.

At the same time, all of us must start from somewhere. Whether it's trotting to the end of the pavement as a kid, finding our feet at 5K or pushing for a best time at a half marathon, these are milestones that can be used to steadily expand our running boundaries. Where it ends is entirely up to the individual.

Having entered the world of ultrarunning to focus on distance over speed, I slowly stopped feeling like an imposter and began to question where it could take me. The more time I spent in this world, chatting to runners during races or looking online for events that appealed to me, the clearer the answer became. If I wanted to truly test myself, there was one distance I had to attempt. Given my age, I didn't think it was something I could delay for too long. If anything, approaching fifty served as an incentive for me to act while I still had the opportunity. Even so, the prospect of taking on a race of this length filled me with dread. It was enough to stop me from just signing up the moment I found an event that I could train towards. First, I had to remind myself that feeling was no different from when I first faced five metres of a shallow swimming pool. Then I decided that if I was really going to do this, I would have to be properly prepared.

One hundred miles is a long way to run by any stretch of the imagination. I just couldn't get my head around it. Even travelling that far by road or rail requires some planning. How on earth did people achieve it on foot and in one hit?

At the time, I had been cutting my teeth on 50K coastal races. It was by no means easy, but slowly I was learning how to manage moving for five to six hours upwards so I could be pleased with my performance. To earn a buckle, which is the prestigious badge of honour awarded to those who complete 100 miles and what seemed to be a true test of an endurance, I would have to run over three times that distance.

If Centurion Running were in the business of waging wholesale military warfare instead of staging ultramarathons, you'd want to be on their side. The brainchild of commander-in-chief James Elson, Centurion's 50- and 100-mile events are highly organised, precisely executed campaigns from start to finish. They're also accessible to all who can stay within tight cut-off times at checkpoints along the way. The rules of engagement are crystal clear, completely fair, and totally uncompromising. If you're a second outside the permitted time at any stage of the race, then your race is over, which means competitors know what to expect and then make every effort to rise to the challenge. Notably, Centurion have fostered a loyal, thriving, good-humoured and supportive Facebook community, which is where I chose to lurk while I worked out if I could really push myself this far.

It took a while for me to recognise that some of the most prolific posters weren't elite ultrarunners with Olympic-grade times. They were ordinary people from all walks of life who had discovered a shared passion for running what seemed an unthinkable distance. On Facebook, as a group member who felt he had nothing to contribute but everything to learn, I witnessed the build-up to one of the four Centurion 100-mile trail races staged each year. Individuals shared anxieties and kit recommendations, sought advice, posted memes and enjoyed good-natured chat. It felt like a club in which everyone was welcome, and yet I hesitated in joining in case I had misjudged it completely and my novice presence sparked an outbreak of tumbleweed.

On the day of the race itself, the community page was marked by an eerie silence for an obvious reason, and I could not stop thinking about what those runners were going through. The live timer, available to view online, became a focal point for my fascination. I watched names rise and fall through the field, or simply hold steady as the miles ticked over and over. Just before I went to bed, I checked in to see that a handful of elites had already finished the race. Incredibly, the winner had clocked in at just under sixteen hours. In awe and admiration, I made a vague attempt to calculate his pace in my head. Settling on something far beyond my wildest dreams, I switched off the bedside light looking forward to seeing how the foot soldiers fared.

'People are still running,' I said to Emma over coffee the next morning. 'Imagine being over twenty-four hours on your feet.'

'I wouldn't know where to begin,' she said, and considered me from over the rim of her cup. 'But something tells me you've given it some thought.'

'Not me.' I felt my cheeks heating up. 'Well, a bit.'

Emma sipped at her coffee. I felt as if I had just alluded to wanting to dress up in adult babygrows.

'How long has this been a thing?' she asked, which didn't help. 'One hundred miles? In a single run? *Why?*'

'I'm not rushing into this,' was all I could say, and though I had no answer to her question, I chose that moment to share my plan.

Two months later, dressed for a long night ahead, I parked my car at Kent's most popular spot for dogging. I had no idea this kind of thing went on here until I joined my fellow volunteers at the Blue Bell Hill checkpoint for the North Downs Way 100. The moment someone mentioned it, as we set up tables of food and drink under a gazebo, we bonded over jokes about how our after-hours presence in this corner of the secluded beauty spot would be a welcome sight for some and a source of horror for others.

'We're here for the runners,' said the volunteer who had been tasked with the responsibility of captaining this checkpoint from the moment it opened at four o'clock that afternoon until its closure twelve hours later. An ultra veteran herself, she shot us a wry grin. 'Anyone else goes to the back of the queue.'

At dawn that day, some seventy-five miles to the west, almost 300 runners had set off from Farnham in Surrey. We were expecting the leader to arrive before sundown, with a steady trickle of competitors following into the night. Our central role, I learnt at the briefing, was to welcome in these weary souls as they arrived to refill flasks and bottles and pick off food from the table, and then encourage them on the way. A stop of just five minutes, if repeated at each of the thirteen aid stations that marked the route, could add over an hour to someone's finishing time. Runners needed to be efficient, we were told, but many would arrive in a state of some exhaustion.

'These guys won't want to leave,' our captain suggested. 'Just be aware this is not a hotel. Nor are we here to lance blisters. It's fine if anyone needs time to sort themselves out. Just make them aware of cut-offs. If they can't go on, take their race numbers. If they're upright, kick them out.'

I listened, feeling both excited and a little apprehensive. Primarily I had signed up as a volunteer because I wanted to get a sense of what was involved in running 100 miles. I figured at this three-quarter distance I would see competitors in the teeth of their challenge. Now our station captain had spelled out what was in store, I realised I also held some responsibility in making or breaking their race. I just hoped that I could make myself useful on a night shift that came with a bonus. Should I decide that 100 miles was a distance I couldn't ignore, my time here would earn me a free place on the start line the following year.

'Here he comes!'

My first role was to spot incoming runners and register their arrival. When the leader first appeared, making his way along the ridge towards us having completed the long field climb from the Medway Viaduct, I was struck by the intensity of his focus. He had the kind of face on that I reserved for the last kilometre at parkrun before expiring in a heap. I just couldn't comprehend how anyone could maintain that kind of single-minded determination all day. This guy was on his way out of the aid station before I had finished clapping him in.

By the time the sun dropped behind the horizon, and after several cars had pulled through the main gates and then performed hasty three-point turns, we were dealing with a strengthening influx of runners. Some arrived looking bright and alert, engaging in chat as they restocked with the efficiency of a motorsport pit stop. We helped to fill bottles as they picked off gels, sweets and sandwiches from the tables, before seeing them out with a cheer. It had been a very hot day, however. Increasingly, many shuffled in having clearly suffered from the heat as much as the distance. These were the runners who required closer attention. Quite a few came in with a thousand-yard stare and a loose grip on their reason for soldiering through the night. We created an annexe to the gazebo, furnishing it with plastic chairs around the edge. By the time darkness had set in, the place was rammed with broken runners attempting a short recharge. Few of them spoke, though everyone was under orders to step outside to the hedgerow if they wanted to throw up. Had any doggers been lurking out there, their night could only have gone from bad to worse.

As volunteers, we went from rotating through roles to hands-on help for whoever needed us. Whatever state the runners were in, I had nothing but admiration for just how far they had come. While a handful were forced to withdraw through injury or severe dehydration, some in tears but all vowing to return, everyone else found the willpower to push on into darkness and the final marathon before the finish line. Some joked through their pain and fatigue, others suffered it out loud or had simply withdrawn into themselves to get the job done. Quite a few arrived accompanied by a pacer. This was within the rules, providing those tasked with the responsibility joined from a checkpoint no earlier than the fifty-mile mark. Several pacers met their runners at Blue Bell Hill, in fact. I really admired the fact that they had given up their Saturday night to help a friend or acquaintance achieve their goal. The camaraderie was clear in every scene I witnessed as everyday people sought to run an incredible distance. It wasn't pretty in places, but everyone shared the same aim. Through to the early hours, our busy little checkpoint felt more like a field hospital for the soul, and I loved every moment. As I drove home at dusk, thinking about those men and women as they went beyond anything I had experienced, I knew that I wanted to follow in their footsteps.

Having earned my place by volunteering, I had a plan for the following year. With the North Downs Way 100 as my main event in the running calendar, I had twelve months in which to prepare. I still enjoyed track sessions and events with my club, as well as the weekly parkrun, but now my focus turned to time on feet. As a nod to the fact that I'd just made life hard for myself, I switched my weekly Saturday morning 5K from the flat, fast paths of Horsham to another local venue with a reputation for being frequently ankle-deep in mud. Cranleigh parkrun offers stretches of pure slop as well as fields punctured with rabbit holes to keep everyone on their toes. It also boasts a short, sharp and wholly unnecessary hill that turns legs to jelly not once but twice before runners flop over the finish line and hope they haven't got trench foot. The small community there take great pride in the fact that it's not a fast parkrun by any means, and cheerfully embrace the ordeal as an end-of-the-week cleansing ritual. As a means of taking away that all-consuming drive for a PB, and then fighting not to lose the will to continue after just one of two godforsaken laps, I found what felt like the perfect circuit for my purposes. I even began to run to and from the event, adding 20K of Downs Link to the equation, and got involved in volunteering to help set up the course or pack it up afterwards.

'What's the draw?' asked Emma when I came home one time, after having ordered me to strip out of my running gear by the back door and load it straight it into the washing machine. 'You keep moaning about it.'

'In a good way,' I said to clarify. 'It's like a cut-down endurance event. Just getting through it makes it more rewarding. Come with me next time!'

By now, our son had completed his fiftieth parkrun. Every Saturday morning, Wilf had defied my expectation to get up early and slog his way towards earning the red shirt. When that moment finally came, he declared his intention to swap his running shoes for football boots and join the local youth team. For a while I pushed him to put his speed to good use on the wing, before finally recognising that my encouragement could be counterproductive. My son needed to find his own way, in defence as it turned out, but there was no doubt that running had got him this far. I loved the fact that everyone in my family had forged a relationship with the same activity. In many ways it brought us together, while allowing each of us to follow our own path. For our eldest daughters, away at university, it was a means of taking time out from the pressures of study, while both Emma and Ethel cursed me for introducing them to Cranleigh before leaving the tarmac paths behind and embracing trail as their central passion.

To qualify for running any one of the 100-mile trail ultras in the Centurion series, I was required to file a time for a fifty-mile race. Earlier that year, I had completed Race to the King, which is an annual double marathon across the South Downs Way. It's a fully supported event that actively encourages walkers as much as runners, imposing no cut-offs and offering a hot meal and giant beanbags at the halfway point. It's a great way to enter the world of ultramarathons, as reflected by the numbers who take part. I had entered it feeling no pressure and learnt a great deal about perseverance. This was largely down to the fact that I had picked up an injury exactly two seconds into the race. As we moved forward over the timing mat, I had bent down to retrieve a gel dropped by the runner in front of me and duly pulled my hamstring. It wasn't serious, but hurt enough to keep my pace in check, and that had worked in my favour. I didn't overcook it, or find myself death-marching the final stage, and while my finish time was unspectacular it was within the limit set by Centurion to earn my place at the North Downs Way 100.

From the day my name appeared on the entry list, looking like it was there in error, the race loomed large on my horizon. Recruiting Google as my trainer, and staying abreast of other runners' progress posted on the Centurion Facebook page, I stuck to my structured plan during the week while reserving Sundays to slow things down and enjoy the long plods. Setting off at dawn with fuel and hydration to see me through the morning, it felt more like an adventure than a workout. I placed myself under no pressure. With a vague trail route in mind, my aim was to keep moving across the landscape as efficiently as possible for hours on end.

I had no doubt that a running coach would take one look at my training plan, suck the air between their teeth and then order me to perform a bunch of push-ups as punishment. At the same time, I felt confident enough to find my own way. I knew enough to be well aware that I had lots to learn, and would always gladly incorporate advice that I felt could help me. I just felt sure from growing experience that I had a base to at least look 100 miles in the eye.

At Transvulcania, I had gone in feeling fit and come away from climbing 2,500 metres thinking I could have been in better shape. With the prospect of just over 3,000 metres of elevation between the start and finish of the North Downs Way 100 – even if the longer distance smoothed things out – I decided to add hill work to my weekly workout. It was tough, but I took it on with a purpose. If I was going to run for a day and a night, there was no way that I could hope to wing it.

With just over a month to go, it felt like the sole purpose of my existence had come to focus on this race. I thought about it from dawn to dusk, during work and after hours. I invested in a standing desk, and put in hours of barefoot writing. I also bolstered my diet to cater for the fact that I was running upwards of eighty kilometres a week. While I often strung together back-to-back runs at that time, amounting to a marathon over two days, I didn't feel the need to run further in one hit. I'd gone a long way in La Palma, and bought into the concept that while the first fifty miles of a hundred are physical, the demands of the second half are predominantly psychological.

'I feel ready,' I said to Emma one Monday morning. I was giving her a lift back from the local garage, where she had left her car for a service. That weekend, I'd completed what would be my last long run before the taper kicked in. I'd been looking forward to this phase. It felt as if I had earned the right to relax a little before the race.

'Does that mean we'll be seeing more of you?' asked Emma as we pulled up in traffic. Both of us had to get back home for work, and though we were only minutes away the sheer volume on this road at rush hour gave us time to talk.

'I'll be swapping Lycra for lounge pants,' I said. 'And carb-loading to test the elastic waistband.'

Emma laughed despite herself, and then sighed at the fact that we remained at a standstill in a short queue. Up ahead, a car was waiting for a gap to turn right.

'You've done well,' she said next. 'I thought you might've had second thoughts about signing up and then found some excuse to slide out of it.'

'No way,' I said. 'I really want to give this my best shot. Whatever happens, I need to be able to look back knowing I tried my best.'

I glanced across at Emma, half expecting her to suggest I try harder, only for the rear-view mirror to catch my attention. Instead of reflecting open road, which had been there the last time I looked, an oncoming radiator grille now filled the frame. All I remember thinking was how giant it appeared to be, and how quickly it closed in. Then, before either of us could register what was about to happen, an articulated lorry carrying a sea container ploughed into the back of the car and our world simply detonated.

PART

3

09

SPRINT FINISH

I have never been dragged through a hedge backwards. Nor have I done twelve rounds with Mike Tyson. So far, I've avoided a tonne of bricks landing on my head, but among all the commonplace expressions we use to describe feeling absolutely dreadful, I do know how it feels to be hit by a truck.

'Welcome to your second life,' said the paramedic who assessed us both at the roadside. 'You've both been incredibly fortunate.'

Emma and I climbed out of the wreckage without any apparent physical injury, as did the driver behind the wheel of the lorry who had been so catastrophically late on the brakes. By some miracle, even the crate of homing pigeons survived in the back of the van ahead of us that was also written off in the crash.

In shock, as the emergency services descended, we both just wanted to go home. It all felt quite unreal, and somehow exhausting. I spent the rest of the day lying on the bed with Emma beside me feeling equally dazed and washed out. Even so, we were both aware that it could have been so much worse.

If this was how it felt to be hit by a truck, I remember thinking, it was probably preferable to being showered by a measure of building materials.

Twenty-four hours later, once the adrenaline subsided, I began to think the bricks might have been a better option. At first it was the ringing in my ears that emerged. The high-pitch tone sounded like a short-wave radio approaching a station and proved to be inescapable. Emma heard it too, and while the world hadn't stopped turning for either of us I found myself beginning to spin on a new, internal axis.

Increasingly throughout that next week, a nauseating giddiness began to accompany every move I made. If I so much as looked to one side, it triggered a feeling that I was spinning. I also discovered that whenever I closed my eyes, a tumbling sensation kicked in that could floor me. It was as if all the stabilisers that keep us on a steady course through the day had come adrift for me. I found it hard to concentrate at my desk, while simple parenting and domestic duties demanded effort that brought a fog of dizziness down upon me. My doctor, who I visited repeatedly, assured me it would pass. When a huge lorry hits a stationary vehicle from behind, he explained, that energy transfer has got to go somewhere. While the seat belts and airbags saved us, the force of the impact would have swept through our skulls.

'Things will settle,' he assured me, but wouldn't be drawn on a timeframe.

Normally, when pressure mounted in my life, I found running to be a means of release. Now it just stirred up the feeling of unsteadiness and nausea. Within minutes, just as I thought I could tough it out, I'd be throwing up by the roadside. After three attempts, each of which left me feeling floored for the day, I resigned myself to the reality of my situation. Given that I could barely make it beyond my house before feeling sick, running the race of my life was out of the question.

After months of training, and with my sole focus on preparing myself both physically and mentally, I recognised that I was in no fit state to attempt the North Downs Way 100. I was gutted, of course, but also felt so miserable with the constant dizziness that other concerns came into play. I was struggling to stay focused at work, while everyday tasks like supermarket shopping could leave me feeling as if my brain was vibrating like a tuning fork. While Emma had escaped feeling like she was at sea, she struggled with the constant hum as well as recurring nightmares about the crash. Together we drifted through the summer and into the autumn, while Wilf and Ethel stepped up for us, as young people so often do when their safety net disappears.

Runners like to know where they are. The distance to their destination is important. It helps them to get through low moments and figure out what needs to be done to make it over the line. I had no end in sight. For the rest of that year, I waited in vain for the turbulence to settle. Eventually, following a bunch of brain scans and in the care of a specialist who made sense of what I was experiencing, I learnt that I was living with a form of vertigo. This had been caused by disruption to my vestibular system, which is a delicate array of sensors within the inner ear that informs our sense of spatial orientation. He compared my head to a snow globe, and the sensors to the glitter swirling within it following a shake. The condition had a name, and treatment effectively involved controlled exposure to the triggers that could spin me out. As I only needed to stand up to feel floored, it became quite clear that I had a long way to go before I could hope to feel human again.

At the same time, so I was warned, there could be no guarantee that I would ever fully recover. The constant hum in my ears was a case in point, and likely to last a lifetime. It was a lot to take in. I had a road map to help me move on, involving regular sessions with a neurological physio-therapist, but also recognition that I would need to find my own way to adapt to the lasting symptoms.

Back home, I did the one thing that had always helped me to process my thoughts. For the first time in months, I went for a run.

The specialist had assured me that – unless I fell over – it wouldn't cause me any physical harm. Refreshingly, he also recognised that it wasn't a shortcut to a coronary but an activity that helped people maintain good physical and mental health. He just cautioned me not to be an idiot and asked that I simply eased back into something I so clearly enjoyed without exceeding the boundaries of what I could tolerate.

For my first outing, I ran to the end of our lane and back. A total of two kilometres. I returned home feeling like I'd just climbed off a roller coaster. I was also elated, because while the nausea came as no surprise, I had fully expected to bail. I had felt rough within a minute of setting off, but as I pushed on it didn't worsen. I kept my head level, with my eyes loosely fixed on the road ahead, and just monitored myself with every step.

'Was it really worth it?' Emma asked me later that day, when she found me flopped on my sofa in the office with my hand over my eyes.

'It will be.' I tried to sit up. 'Eventually.'

Following the crash, Emma had pursued the same course as me with her running. She had tested the water, and then elected to stay on the side until she felt better. I had been really pleased for her when she eased back into parkrun with Ethel, but also frustrated at my own lack of progress. Outwardly, I looked fine. In my head, the constant giddiness, low-level nausea and inescapable ringing in my ears became a source of frustration. I could run, but in stirring up the symptoms it came at a price.

Slowly but steadily, the one pursuit I loved in life began to wear me down. It wasn't just that running literally left me feeling travel-sick. In low light, it threw me out of kilter completely. On the Downs Link, where I tended to go because it was a straight path, I only had to head through one of the string of tunnels to find myself malfunctioning. In the gloom, instead of maintaining a steady line, I'd suddenly feel so disorientated that I'd veer to one side. Once I even clipped the wall. It only took a couple of seconds to reach daylight on the other side but served as a wake-up call to me that all was not well.

It was the specialist who made sense of this for me. He explained that when it comes to balance, we rely on three sensory inputs: our connection with the ground beneath our feet, our vision and our vestibular system. We can survive quite comfortably on two, as demonstrated by walking with our eyes closed, but knock that back to one and the world turns topsy-turvy.

My feet were fine, but with a compromised vestibular system my eyes had become forced to work overtime. It explained why I could be so tired at the end of each day, and made sense of the fact that in darkness or very low light I lost my sense of balance completely. It was just one more challenge that chipped away at my resolve. Since the crash, I had taken to running alone because I needed to concentrate so hard. I could also be quite withdrawn afterwards for the simple reason that the peace, quiet and stillness I found there was the only way that I could really function. At the time, I was the last person to register that this path was taking me into a tunnel of my own making. In fact, it only really became apparent to me that I had become a source of concern when Emma got me a dog.

'Surprise!' she said on revealing the new addition to our family. 'We thought you needed a running companion.'

The puppy skittered towards me, only to turn at a right angle at the last moment and give chase to the shadow of his own tail. Having followed him with my eyes, the room promptly took off around me and I needed to sit down.

I called him Sprint because he only had one speed. An English springer spaniel who didn't stop until he dropped at night, he was the product of a very kind gesture and possibly also the last thing that I needed at the time. Indoors, I just couldn't keep up with the constant canine activity without feeling ill. Fortunately, Emma, Wilf and Ethel were on hand to help me out, which meant he'd happily found his place at the heart of the family by the time he was old enough to join me on a run.

'Please don't go sideways or circle around me,' I instructed him as we prepared to set off along the Downs Link. 'Think like an assist dog, OK?'

I let Sprint off the leash with low expectations. While he possessed a lovely placid nature and had settled in at home without issues, he often went wild outside. Sprint wasn't aggressive in any way. He just threw himself into chasing scents and squirrels in a wide circumference around me that I would now have to try hard to ignore. I could just about handle it on a walk. Running simply dialled up my sensitivity levels to the extent that bad luck would befall me if a hyperactive spaniel repeatedly crossed my path.

To my surprise, Sprint didn't scramble up the bank and mess with my peripheral vision. He just ran in front of me, as if tied to an invisible leash.

A minute later, my spirits sank somewhat when a mountain biker cycled towards us. I fully expected Sprint to get in his way or decide that chasing him would be fun. Instead, my four-legged companion stayed in his lane and continued to lead the way. Sprint didn't even glance at the guy as he passed. I could barely afford to do that myself, but hoped he registered me as one of those people who could basically train a dog to cook a roast just by clicking his fingers. Sprint was still in lockstep just ahead of me as we plunged into a tunnel. Rather than hope for the best and then ricochet off the brickwork, I trained my gaze on the four-legged silhouette of my new-found faithful friend as he led me towards the light.

'It felt like I've just found his reason for existing,' I reported breathlessly to Emma on my return home. 'Sprint wasn't interested in other dogs or people. Even horses didn't faze him. All he wanted to do was run.'

'Well, that makes two of you,' said Emma, who sounded completely unsurprised.

We had been home for thirty seconds before Sprint registered that Ethel held a tennis ball in her hand and followed her excitedly into the garden for a game.

'He never stops,' I said, 'but it was brilliant. That's the best run I've had in ages.'

'Good.' Emma seemed to tick off something from a mental list just then. 'It's nice to hear you sounding positive again.'

By the time I had grown tired of running in a straight line, Sprint was ready to take me off the Downs Link and into the woods and vales. The more frequently we went out together, and for longer distances, the better I understood the snow globe in my head. I found that if I ran at a relaxed pace, I didn't feel so shaken that I had to stop, and while I could pick up speed it was for a limited period. Given that I had started from a place where I couldn't walk around my own house without wanting to lie down, I was thankful for the progress.

Now, with Sprint as a positive force to stop me from feeling sorry for myself, I had reached a point of no return. I joined Emma and Ethel at parkrun once again, and sessions with my friends at the club. Even though I felt rough after each run, I was fortunate that my work was a solitary occupation. It also didn't involve a great deal of moving around. In some ways, writing stories for a living was as much a form of escapism as running. Following the crash, I just had to work harder to achieve the same results, but that was a small price to pay for being able to do it all.

In March that year I turned fifty. As a milestone, it was a chance to reflect on where I'd come from and consider where I was heading. Family had always been my foundation stone, and it was a joy for Emma and me to watch our children growing up. I was happy with my lot in life, and yet I still felt like I hadn't fully moved on from the accident. I was constantly reminded of it from dawn to dusk, with sleep being the only place where the snow globe settled and the hum in my ears ceased to register. Thanks to Emma and an unstoppable springer spaniel, I'd learnt to find a way through it as a runner. I even started entering races again. I had to choose carefully, of course, because ultimately, I knew how it would leave me feeling. Providing I set aside a day afterwards for my head to settle, I could chase my old times at 10Ks and half marathons. I even took part in the Brighton Marathon, finishing without a *Play School* presenter in sight but with a decent time under my belt. The nausea that accompanied the final six miles lasted a week, but despite it all I felt more in tune with what I could tolerate.

If I had chosen not to run at all, I would have felt better in some ways but worse in others. While I was grateful to still be able to put one foot in front of the other, I couldn't ignore the fact that things were different for me now. If I hoped to be on a level with everyone at the start line, then the race would have to take place around the perimeter of a cruise ship in unsettled seas. As it was, I just put up with the unwelcome sway on dry land and reminded myself that everyone has their own challenges.

Despite it all, however, I couldn't lose sight of the fact that the accident had put paid to my plans to attempt 100 miles. I had trained for that race and reached the final weeks of preparation. The truck had taken that away in a heartbeat, but increasingly as I got back on track, I felt the need to chase that goal again.

'You might as well just save yourself the effort and stick your fingers down your throat,' Emma suggested when I shared my intention of signing up once more. 'It'll achieve the same outcome.'

'I just need to keep things slow and steady,' I said. 'No heroics.'

'But you'll also have to run after dark,' she pointed out, reminding me that I quickly went adrift without visual markers. 'You can't take Sprint with you.'

'Trust me,' I said, keen to demonstrate that I wasn't deluding myself here. 'I have a plan.'

10

THE FIRST HALF IS PHYSICAL . . .

The North Downs Way combines ancient trade routes and pilgrim path-ways across Surrey and Kent. Slipping almost unnoticed under the capital, it crosses pastoral farmlands, winds through ancient woodland and spans ridges that provide unrivalled views across England's High Weald.

For a trail that takes you into the heart of this area of outstanding natural beauty, it feels odd that the official gateway is just a gloomy alley off the Farnham ring road. As I funnelled in among just over 300 runners, it seemed more like a place for provincial youths to deal dope than a historical departure point for drovers and Chaucerian travellers. Still, it served as the start line for a non-stop ultramarathon across 100 miles, which was all that mattered to me. As Centurion's Race Director, James Elson, stood on the bank with his air horn aloft, a hush spread all the way to the back of the pack.

'Have a good race, everyone. Look after each other . . . '

As a first-timer attempting this distance, it didn't feel like the beginning of something that might prove too far for me. In many ways, the mental undertaking had begun some time before. For the preceding fortnight, I had been forced to process so much self-doubt and anxiety that reaching this point felt like a victory in its own right. As the big day had approached, I knew that I would feel nervous. I just hadn't anticipated that I would come close to a panic attack on several occasions. It all boiled down to the enormity of the undertaking. It was just too much to process. Converting what I faced into kilometres didn't help matters. One hundred and sixty of the damned things just seemed ridiculous. As I had learnt in James's race briefing, the twists and turns of the North Downs Way 100 translated on the ground to about 104 miles. I had thought about recalculating what that meant in real money, but it seemed a bit pointless when it all lay ahead of me. As soon as I tried to imagine running towards triple mileage figures, my chest would tighten and a voice inside my head asked me what the hell I had been thinking. That voice only fell quiet on setting off, as if perhaps there was nothing more to be said. All week it had encouraged me to skip the race and move on with my life. Now there was no other option left for me but to find out the hard way whether I had taken my running too far.

'What's been the best bit?' asked Emma when she called me as arranged five hours into the race. A keen cyclist as well as a runner, my wife was away that weekend with her two-wheel friends. While I'd never been drawn to climb into the saddle, too scarred by all the kids' bikes clogging the hall, just then it seemed like quite an inviting way to move. 'And what's been the worst?' she added.

I drew breath to say that it was becoming quite muggy and that one of the hard lids from my new soft flasks kept bumping against my collarbone. I was also tired, having just passed the marathon mark, and the dizziness and ringing ears were constant companions. Then I paused for thought, having broken from my run to walk so I could talk, and realised that I had nothing to complain about. I had promised Emma that I'd take good care of myself, aware that she was worried, and duly revised what I had to share. I'd run new trails, linking places I'd only ever travelled to by road. The course had also been painstakingly marked, which was reassuring. Every thirty metres or so, strips of red and white tape fluttered from branches or gateposts like some kind of treasure hunt without end. I'd even made new friends along the way, including an endearingly talkative Bulgarian yoga instructor called Dimi whose husband, Andrew, was waiting at every crew stop with an array of refreshments on offer for her. I hadn't even been aware that crewing was a thing until I passed across a common and found clusters of family and friends awaiting their runners with food and drink. At Dimi's insistence, even though I was happy to refuel at checkpoints only, I had helped myself to bananas, flapjacks and Lucozade from the back of Andrew's car. Even after I had lost sight of her when the elastic-band effect took shape along the length of the field, Andrew continued to push snacks on me whenever I saw him. He had nothing but kind words, good humour and encouragement for me, and that summed up the spirit of my race to that point.

'It's tough,' I told Emma, passing yet another strip of tape, 'but I'm not alone.'

Run at every opportunity and walk when there's no other choice. That was the broad mantra I had read so much about in my quest to become a half decent ultrarunner. On paper, it makes complete sense. Approaching fifty miles, however, it's very easy to justify simplifying things even further, shrug in resignation and just *walk*. As tempting as that might be, however, it defeats the purpose of the race somewhat and puts you at risk of timing out.

There is a place for walking, of course, and that tends to come down to hills. At the beginning of my day, I had followed in the footsteps of every competitor ahead of me and only dropped to a power march on the steepest of climbs. As the race wore on, however, it seemed as if the collective assessment of what constituted an ascent broadened out to include gentle rises.

'Is this a hill?' I asked a runner beside me as I sensed the slightest of inclines underfoot, though I didn't need to wait for confirmation. 'It's a hill.'

Without word, we both downshifted from a tired trot to a resigned walk, only to pick up the pace as the path levelled off once more.

'We're controlling the walks,' he said to me after a moment, as if perhaps saying it out loud would confirm it in his mind. 'We just can't let the walks control us.'

It might have been a throwaway comment, but I was still thinking about it as I jogged along the road to the village hall that marked the halfway checkpoint. As much as I wanted to walk, I had such a long way to go that I needed to stay in control. When my approach inadvertently triggered a vehicle-activated speed sign, praising me for entering the village at a responsible speed of five miles per hour, I responded to the green, happy face with a smile of my own.

I was tired. My body ached and my ears were howling. I had to be careful to keep my gaze loose, with no sudden head movements, but frankly I'd reached a point where everything I did was slow but steady. I hadn't paid attention to my pace. I just knew I was sufficiently ahead of the cut-offs not to panic. In total, I had thirty hours available to me. It had taken me eleven hours to complete fifty miles, but I had heard that it wasn't wise to simply double that to predict a finish time.

If the first half was a physical ordeal, so it was said, the next was psychological. In that phase of a 100-mile race, the wheels would at least come loose in all manner of ways. As I set out from the village hall, having texted my wife while managing a few mouthfuls of the hot meal on offer, I just hoped it wouldn't derail me completely. When I factored in my vestibular issues, all I could say for sure was that my head would make or break me on this race.

I had anticipated that the challenges I faced as a runner would increase for me as the daylight faded. Sure enough, as the time approached for me to fire up my head torch, I found myself feeling a little unstable on my feet. That tree roots had spread across the woodland path like varicose veins didn't help. Nor did the camber of the North Downs Way, which I had discovered to be on the wonk in one direction or another since I'd set off that morning. By now, I was forcing myself to keep drinking, aware that the electrolyte mixed with water in my flasks was key to making sure I took in sufficient salts and minerals to keep my body ticking over. I had a small bag of banana chips in the pocket of my race vest. I picked at them intermittently, but as night descended, so too did that off-kilter feeling that killed my appetite completely.

On any run in which the finish is far out of sight, we all must dig deep. Even at parkrun, when going all out, we reach a moment when it all just feels a bit much. What matters, I had learnt over time, is how we respond to it. There's always an easy way out, but that short-term relief can only lead to lingering feelings that we let ourselves down. Running through that night, with almost seventy miles on the clock, I found those troughs of self-doubt came in waves. Whether it was down to feeling dizzy or a sense of doom over just how much further I had to run, I was forced to talk myself back from the brink on a regular basis.

At the same time, mindful that I was in unknown territory now, the low moments were often followed by crests of confidence that seemed completely misplaced. In the space of a kilometre, I could go from wanting to retire to fantasising about how it must feel to win the entire race. Approaching midnight, eighteen hours after setting off, I knew the front runners had already finished. I still had a long way to go, but in those brief moments where things seemed to be going well, I felt like a winner.

I also knew that if I could make it to the next checkpoint, where I had served as a volunteer, I stood a fighting chance of earning that coveted buckle. I began to count down the miles, converting them into parkruns, but with just a few loops left in my head I found the peaks of positivity petered out to one long slump. By the time I reached the Medway Viaduct, which is a kilometre-long concrete walkway over the river with motor-way lanes on one side and suicide-prevention fencing on the other, I had revised my definition of what constitutes a hill to include this stretch.

Having emerged from narrow woodland paths and crossed vast, moonlit cornfields, it was weird to find myself under flood lamps with traffic rush-ing by. At the same time, it was one more jigsaw join of ancient and mod-ern that seemed to sum up the North Downs Way. One moment I could be following the red and white tape along a track with ruts which likely dated back to a time when goods were moved by horse and cart, only for it to lead me through an underpass reeking of wee and daubed with acid-colour graffiti. Unexpectedly, this ultramarathon had offered me an intimate appreciation of the landscape that we can only truly experience when travelling on foot.

As I left the viaduct behind, however, along with the constant exhalation of lorries and cars on the motorway, the path seemed to disappear into the night. Along the side of another great field, the dots of light from runners' head torches told me I had a proper hill to climb before I reached the next checkpoint. I also knew from my memory of the faces of those I had wel-comed up there twelve months earlier that it was set to be a challenge. As well as all the jokes we had swapped back then about nocturnal adult activity, I remembered talk about this section being the location for para-normal activity. The ghostly tales had all been very entertaining to hear under the fairy lights strung across the gazebo. As I registered it in my mind, I was relieved to feel far too tired to be spooked by the fact that a low, thin mist had begun to form. I was only midway up the side of the field, but I attacked it at a march in line with the guy in front. I realised I was closing in on him, in fact, and that stirred me to pick up my pace a little more.

'How are you getting on?' I asked as I caught up behind.

'I'll tell you when I get to the top.'

The guy didn't look around. He just carried on marching, and I followed suit. The silence between us was only broken a minute later, in fact, when I heard him say hello. I glanced up and around. When my head lamp picked out a young woman in the dark, sitting cross-legged in the field with a hoodie pulled over her brow, I repeated the same greeting. Like the guy in front of me, I didn't stop. We were too close to the ridge line now, and within faint earshot of the checkpoint. It was only when we reached the top of the field that he turned to look behind us.

'All OK?' I asked, as he seemed a little unsettled.

'Just now,' he said as we followed the path alongside a hedgerow, 'we did pass a girl, didn't we?'

'I wonder what she was doing out so late,' I said to confirm. 'She looked quite chilled, to be fair.'

The runner considered me for a moment before looking back at the slope we had climbed.

'It's just I can't see her any more,' he said, before shrugging and focusing his attention on the stile ahead. 'After seventy-five miles, I wouldn't be surprised if my mind started playing tricks.'

'Same,' I said, and chose to put the matter behind me. Had I been less knackered, I might have questioned what a silent figure in a hood was doing out here gone midnight. Instead, as I followed the guy over the stile, I realised that I had reached a stage in this race where the darkness and its mysteries could no longer defeat me.

11

ASLEEP AT THE DISCO

There it was, shining like a beacon of hope from the corner of the car park. Fronted by two Centurion feather flags, the gazebo had been planted with glow sticks around the perimeter and illuminated inside by camping lamps. Just then, the Blue Bell Hill checkpoint felt like the most welcoming place in the world. Crossing the timing mat, I interpreted the beep as confirmation that I was cleared for entry.

'Welcome,' said the volunteer who had adopted my role this time as a sort of concierge for crushed runners. 'What can we get for you?'

Just as it had been when I manned this checkpoint, the place was littered with runners who appeared to have powered down. All the plastic chairs under the gazebo were occupied. Some individuals were dealing with blisters on their feet. Others deployed a dead-eyed stare into the night. Only a few chatted with sandwiches in hand like someone would be round with the rosé at any moment.

'I'm just looking for something,' I said.

I glanced at the food on the table, and the kettle whistling on a camping stove to make tea and coffee. The volunteer offered me both, but I was only here for one thing. This had been a pivotal part of my race strategy from the moment I signed up, in fact.

As a marshal, I had seen many runners pick up pacers here. Aware that I might well be feeling wobbly at this point, I had recruited one for myself to steer me through the rest of the night.

'Finally,' declared a voice from the gloom. 'I thought I'd get here earlier than planned just in case.'

I faced the car park to see my running club friend, Emma, clipping her race-pack straps together. When I had thought about who could pace me, it made sense to approach her. Emma was an experienced trail-marathon runner with similar times to me. She was also aware of my vestibular issues, and as she worked as a physio I figured I would be in good care should I start going sideways. Aware that I was asking her to sacrifice her Saturday night, and leave her husband to take care of their two small children, I had shown my appreciation when she agreed by presenting them both with a bottle of gin. Having stressed that it wasn't a run-for-booze arrangement, but just a token of my gratitude, I knew that I could rely on her.

'Sorry to make you wait,' I said. 'To be honest, my hopes of making the podium are fading.'

The marshal laughed.

'If you've made it this far then you're a winner,' he said. 'Just one more marathon to go!'

Seeing a familiar face had a briefly energising effect on me. Having arrived at the checkpoint at a low ebb, exhausted and aware that my efforts to fight the dizzying effects of running in darkness were beginning to grind me down, I set off with Emma at a jog with stories to share from my day on the trail.

'You didn't see a ghost,' she said dismissively, after I had hoped to dine out on that tale. 'You've been running for nearly twenty hours, Matt, and to be honest you don't sound too with it. Make sure you drink and eat, and let's leave that kind of thing for when we're out of the woods, OK?'

'All right,' I said, feeling as if I had just been firmly put in my place, and to be honest that was fine. I was so deep into this act of endurance, and so far gone, I realised, that I was happy to be told what to do. 'Sorry.'

'Don't apologise,' said Emma, who was leading the way with her head torch shining bright. I was finding it much easier to just follow like this rather than concentrate on my own beam, and my pacer was clearly taking her role quite seriously. That she had twisted her hair into professional trail-runner plaits should have told me she meant business. Now I was finding out from her relentless forward progress. While it had come as a surprise, from a clubmate who excelled at endurance chatting, it meant I was moving with more sense of purpose than when I had arrived at the checkpoint. 'Let's just focus on getting to the finish.'

Plugging onwards, we followed a path through dense forest. The darkness was absolute in places, with just the reflective strip in the red and white tape lighting up in our torch beams to guide us through. Here, our casual conversation about life at home and work kept at bay the fact that we were effectively running through the set for some backwoods slasher movie. Eventually, the path began to climb until it reached a series of steps made from wooden sleepers. They were so challenging I had to push on my thighs to help my aching quads. Had I been alone, despite the seemingly real possibility that an arrow, axe or poisoned dart could thwack into a nearby tree at any moment, I might well have stopped to rest. The fleeting high of running with a friend was certainly beginning to pass. As my legs grew heavier, no kind words of encouragement could distract me from the fact that I was in the teeth of an ordeal here. With a pacer who had come out this far to help me, however, I didn't want to be the runner who just gave up. Maybe Emma knew that if she indulged my grumbling it would all be over, because whenever I so much as muttered to myself she didn't sugar-coat the situation.

'Emma.'

'Yes?'

'How much further to the next checkpoint?'

'Far enough.'

We all know how it feels to be tired. If we stay up late or work too hard, that feeling of fatigue weighs heavily upon us. Sometimes we can find ourselves nodding off for nanoseconds, which is usually the mind's way of telling us to turn in. Eighty miles into an ultramarathon, having been too keyed up to properly rest the night before, those brief snatches of sleep on my feet evolved into something more disconcerting. Running in silence along a rutted path behind my pacer, literally following in Emma's footsteps in the hope that she had picked the right line, I registered a shape in the glade to my right and processed it as a dinosaur.

'Wow!' I said under my breath.

'What is it?'

'Nothing!'

Just as soon as the thought had entered my head, I knew I was imagining it. Unlike the girl in the field, who was likely to have been out with friends after a party or whatever, this was mostly definitely not real. Teenagers often hung out after dark. A triceratops was history. I had read a great deal about long-distance runners experiencing hallucinations. I just hadn't anticipated that it would happen to me. Then I saw another, one of the nice ones with the long neck, calmly grazing from the treetops. I had no doubt it was just an illusion, but as these great beasts continued to form out of the darkness it was also out of my control.

I wasn't scared of imaginary creatures, but the fact that fantasy was now merging with reality unnerved me. For a while I dealt with it by talking about dino-free subjects like track etiquette and TV shows we had each been watching. While it passed the time, and slowly ticked through the distance, it did nothing to stop me from feeling like this ultramarathon had morphed into late-night Jurassic parkrun.

'I was looking at the live results while I waited in the car,' Emma told me, unaware that I was tripping exhaustion-induced ultra-balls. 'Quite a few runners have pulled out along the way, so you're doing brilliantly.'

I heard her loud and clear but said nothing in response. This was because I didn't perceive that my pacer was doing the talking here. It was the baby facing me that was strapped to her back. In my mind, I knew it was just a communication breakdown between the reflective strips on Emma's race pack, my tired eyes and my scrambled brain. Nevertheless, in that heart of darkness the infant was seeking to motivate me so earnestly that I registered it as real. I watched its little hands curl into fists of encouragement and logged it as just another unforgettable moment on a run that felt more like an odyssey with every step.

Decades passed before we dropped out of the woods to reach the next checkpoint. At least that's how it seemed to me as we finally cleared the trees and arrived outside a village hall. With the doors pinned open, I could hear the rousing strains of 'Gold' by Spandau Ballet. The volume was low, given that it was about three in the morning, but with the lights shining brightly it felt like we weren't too late for the party.

'Two minutes,' Emma instructed me as I negotiated the single step. 'Grab what you need and let's crack on.'

I was in no doubt that my clubmate's presence and positive words had provided a focus for me to keep moving forward rather than spinning out. Emma also knew about the cut-offs, which she seemed to be treating like some apex predator with my scent in its nostrils. By my fuzzy calculations, we had plenty of time to cover the remaining twenty miles or so. I figured we could even afford to slacken off a little. Nevertheless, with every mile we put behind us, the more my pacer was beginning to turn militant on me.

'I'm not sure I can eat anything,' I said to her, as a volunteer in a Centurion Marshal T-shirt, complete with plastic floral garland and grass skirt, invited us inside with a flourish of her hand. 'In fact, I just want to sleep.'

The urge overtook me with frightening ease. On being greeted by another eighties belter, and registering that in fact every marshal present was dressed for a Hawaiian night out, I no longer knew what was real or imagined. Either these guys had gone to great lengths to dress up the place and lift the spirits of weary runners, or I had lost it completely. It felt as if my brain was shutting down, and that was enough for me to plead with my pacer to give me a break.

'Fifteen minutes?' I asked. 'Just let me lie down for a quarter of an hour.'

Emma considered me for a moment. Before she responded, I could see she had noted that I was on the verge of passing out.

'Ten minutes.'

'Twelve?' I asked.

'Ten. And then we go.'

Slumping on a straw mat, I closed my eyes and effectively disappeared from existence. The music ceased. The light turned to darkness. Silence reigned. What felt like a second later, I heard someone calling my name with great alarm.

'Matt! Matt! What has happened to Matt?'

As my head rebooted, and the sound of a party in full swing returned, I opened my eyes once more. The first thing I noted was Emma standing over me. She was dancing happily by herself to Wham's 'Club Tropicana' while eating a Twix. She only stopped when Dimi – the runner I had met earlier in the race – crossed the floor from the food table with a cup in hand and concern in her expression.

'I'm fine,' I said, groaning as I hauled myself into an upright position. 'Just stretching.'

'Oh!' Dimi sounded both relieved and amused, and swapped a grin with Emma. 'I thought he was dead.'

My pacer consulted her watch.

'Time's up,' she said. 'Strictly speaking, you have another two minutes but seeing that you're awake … '

As part of my strategy for this race, sleep was not something I had factored in. It had turned out to be nothing more than a power nap, but as we set out once more it proved to be exactly what I needed. In those first moments after waking, it had been a struggle to get my head around the fact that I still faced another eighteen miles. Once I'd shaken off the stiffness that had set into my limbs, however, and gulped the tea that Emma had made for me, I began to feel annoyingly fresh.

'I feel *great!*' I said, perhaps a little too brightly as we passed a runner reduced to a pitiful shuffle. 'How are you doing?'

'Better now we're on the move again,' said Emma, who was carrying her phone in one hand. 'I was looking at the live timings while you were out,' she continued, consulting the screen once more. 'There have been so many dropouts. The field is down to about 200 now, but you're doing all right, Matt. In fact, as long as you don't lie down again, there's a chance you could finish in the top 100.'

My position in this race wasn't something I'd considered since fantasising about coming first. My sole focus was on running 100 miles. Nothing else mattered to me, but clearly my pacer had other ideas.

'What position am I now?' I asked anyway.

'Oh, quite far back,' she said breezily, 'but we're not that far behind a lot of runners. We can do this, but you can't mess around any more.'

I didn't have the energy to spell out just how much I had needed that nap. While I was enjoying fresh wind in my sails, my legs were already beginning to remind me that it couldn't last. As Emma set a pace that felt punishing because it wasn't a walk, I fell in behind her once more and just got my head down.

We ran in silence for quite some time. It was a relief to find I had left the hallucinations behind, and a dawning joy to register that the sky was beginning to brighten and colour. I had never run through the night, nor believed it was something I could do, but when the first golden bars of sunshine broke over the horizon, I felt like I had arrived in a whole new world. I was beyond tired as I switched off my head torch and stowed it in my race pack. Left to my own devices, I had no doubt that I would be shuffling along in the early morning light like the trickle of competitors we passed. We exchanged greetings with everyone, along with words of encouragement because it really did feel like every runner in the race was in this together. Emma was first to remind them that they didn't have far to go now, wishing them well as she dragged me onwards.

It was only when the next competitor in turn came into her cross hairs that her commitment to my cause came into play.

'Ten more to go,' she muttered.

'Miles?' I asked, a little confused because I was still working in kilometres and my brain was too tired for maths.

'No,' she said, like it was obvious, 'the runners you need to take down.'

I looked across at my pacer, unsure if I had heard her correctly. Emma had always struck me as pleasantly well-mannered and easy going. Now here she was displaying a competitive edge that practically glinted in the early light.

'We're not out to kill them,' I said. 'I mean, we've all come a long way.'

Emma tutted sharply on the trot.

'Do you want to make the top 100 or not?'

With just a parkrun to go in distance, I had set my sights on a cup of sweet tea. I never normally took sugar, but it was the only form of fuel I had been able to manage over the previous ten miles. Just peeling off for the final aid station in the farm courtyard had required some negotiation with my pacer. Quite simply, the closer we got to the finish, the sharper her focus became. At first, on having to shift up a gear, I had come close to resenting the relentless pushing. As the end became a realistic proposition, and with just a few more runners to pass to place as planned, I was surprised to find it turn into a motivating force. I had to break for short walks on a regular basis, but they didn't control me. By extension, my pacer oversaw everything, and was living up to her job description. I had to dig deep to get by quite a few runners, but by then I was sold on the goal. The prospect of a top-100 finish, having pushed harder when I wanted to coast, was something that suddenly seemed of the utmost importance.

I was just in the process of sharing my experience with the volunteer who had kindly brewed my tea when Emma cut in that we didn't have time.

'But it's too hot for me to drink,' I said, blowing madly at the steaming liquid in my cup.

'You can have as much tea as you want at the finish!' Emma had stayed on the farm track when I trotted across to the trestle table. She looked back along the stretch we had completed. I could tell from her anxious expression that the runners we had overtaken to get here were on their way. 'Just grab a water and *hurry up!*'

The final leg of the race breaks from the North Downs Way, cutting through a field of sunflowers. As we ran between the giant dials, closing in on a pair of runners who were walking intermittently, the enormity of what I looked set to complete weighed upon me. With just a few kilometres left, I just felt intensely emotional. I thought about the moment I could Facetime my wife and show her the buckle I had earned. I wasn't there yet but it was close at hand. Physically, I was functioning on fumes. Mentally, I had no defences left as tears flowed freely down my cheeks.

'Sorry,' I said, wiping my face with the heel of my hand. 'I'm so grateful for what you've done, but it's broken me.'

'Of course it has!' Emma checked I wasn't about to lose it completely. We still had to join the country lane into Ashford and then follow the tape to the stadium. By her reckoning, providing I pushed to get beyond the two runners we were closing in on, I would make the top 100 from a starting field three times that number. 'You're going to do this, but isn't it better to look back knowing you gave it everything?'

She was right. I knew that. It's just this race was so vast in scale that I had only been able to approach it by putting one step in front of the other. Even estimating a finish time had left me feeling like I was tempting fate. What's more, I knew that from the halfway mark I might well have let things slide without a pacer. With time in hand, I'd have been content to allow the walks to control me. Instead, as we finally hit the tarmac, swapping encouragement with the two runners as we passed, I found myself pushing with the same commitment to shaving off seconds as I did at much shorter races. Powered purely by a rush of adrenaline, and in the wake of my pacer's motivational ploy of targeting people to overtake, I held my head up in defiance of the dizziness that had accompanied me this far. It hadn't defeated me as I had feared. Yes, it had made this race more challenging, but then I had no doubt that every competitor faced down demons of their own to reach this point.

'One hundred miles,' I said out loud because it felt like I owned it.

'One hundred and four,' said Emma to correct me. 'You missed the triple-figure moment before the last checkpoint. I didn't want to say anything in case you decided to stop and celebrate.'

The North Downs Way 100 finishes with three quarters of a victory lap of Ashford's Julie Rose Stadium athletics track. With less than 400 metres to go, as the morning sun strengthened, I joined the inside lane feeling like my race had only just started. On the other side of the field, which nobody would dream of crossing by foot, I could see and hear volunteers at the finish line clapping and cheering alongside the Centurion staff. Another runner had just reached the line, arms aloft but then dropping his hands to his knees. The sight served to spur me on. I wanted to be able to stop as he had, with no urgency to keep moving. Like him, I needed to put that trail of red and white tape behind me. After just over twenty-six hours since setting off, I could not wait to just be still.

'Are you sure this track is 400 metres?' I asked Emma breathlessly. 'It feels longer.'

'Just go,' was all she said in response, before dropping back as I approached the home straight.

For the first time since the concept of running a 100-mile-long race came on to my radar, I realised I could do it. I had to see the finishing arch to believe it, and that felt like a landmark moment in my life. I'd had my doubts throughout, from signing up to setting off to seeing the sun set and then questioning if I'd still be running when it rose again. As a boy, skittering to the end of the pavement with my dad, this distance would've seemed like a journey to another planet. Finishing last at the inter-schools cross-country race, holding back tears at being so useless at something I enjoyed, it would've been comforting to know that one day I would earn a buckle recognising that I had run further than I could ever imagine.

12

A MASTERCLASS IN MISTAKES

Running injuries can be painful, and not just physically. It can come as quite a blow if a strain, pain, ache or break stops you from taking part in a race or even hobbles your chances on the day. Just having to take time out from a training schedule, or even a regular jog, can feel like a setback that stings.

An overuse injury is the worst. It's basically the body's way of reminding runners that we can have too much of a good thing. In my progression from parkrun to 100 miles, it sometimes felt like I was picking up one complaint after another. Notwithstanding the issues with my head, from my shoulders to my ankles, knees and toes, there was almost always some issue causing me grief. I could deal with the accidents, from rolling my foot to the grazes if I tripped and fell. It was the slow-building discomfort that ceased when I stopped that meant just one thing: I needed to rest to recover.

In these instances, stewing at home when I wanted to be on the trails, I vowed to learn from whatever mistake I had made. Online, I sought out stretches and strengthening exercises that would help me back on track in new and improved ways. I visited a sports-injury clinic so frequently that poor Cheryl who treated me with ruthless efficiency probably thought I was harming myself deliberately just to spend time wincing through the face hole at the top of her table. Possibly in a bid to get rid of me, Cheryl showed me a series of routines I could do to ensure my body was fit for purpose. It meant finding time to prostrate myself on a mat and remind myself that if I was going to age well as a runner then I could no longer take my body for granted.

Over time, as I swooped in on the slightest niggle as if it was a crack in a dam, I reached a point where injuries became a rarity rather than a regular feature of my running life. There's always a risk it'll come crashing down, of course, but with care and attention to the slightest ache I have learnt to minimise my time out. It would be very easy to claim that I subsequently sailed into completing progressively longer races without drama. The truth is distance running is not quite as straightforward as it sometimes seems. Yes, it's a simple act of putting one foot in front of the other, but there are more than just physical and psychological challenges at play. When it comes to any act of endurance, fuelling is critical. This might seem obvious, but the fact is every runner must establish an intimate understanding of their food and hydration needs, and this comes down to trial and error.

In my case, usually around the 40K mark and seemingly without solution, the errors took the form of slowly losing my appetite and taste for any kind of drink. I would turn pale and clammy while running, and cold sweat would prick my brow. If I happened to be alongside anyone at the time, they'd be forgiven for thinking I was one of those guys trying to hide a fresh zombie bite under his shirt. While I never turned, the rising sense that bad things were about to happen to me became unavoidable. This usually culminated in me grinding to a shuffle and then throwing up in a verge. As if to compound the situation, I'd feel much better as a result, only for the process to repeat itself again over the coming hours but with diminishing returns in my performance.

As much as I loved running long, the experience was always tarnished somewhat by my propensity to feel unwell along the way. On rare occasions, such as the North Downs Way 100 where I was more concerned about losing my balance than my breakfast, I managed to keep it together to the finish. It didn't help that I'd been hit by a truck, of course, but there was a difference between the dizziness I experienced because of my vestibular issues, and the urge deep into an ultramarathon to just curl up and die.

Much like dealing with injuries, I sought solutions for the sake of my running enjoyment. I knew that adding electrolyte tablets or powders to the water in my race-vest flasks was a key part of the hydration process. My issue, I realised, was in drinking enough to make it effective. At first, I figured it would be fine to just stretch out two flasks across whatever distance I was taking on. I had to learn the hard way that a runner of my weight and height needed to sink one of those per hour. Even then, however, I found my appetite fading. Perhaps my most humiliating moment in this respect occurred when I was recruited as a pacer by another club runner on her bid to complete a double trail marathon in under ten hours. I set out with my friend, Geri, relying on me to get her over the line on time, only to ruin her chances that afternoon as I yacked up into the brambles.

'It doesn't matter,' she said, holding back my race-vest straps, though it totally did to me.

As this phase became a regular feature of my racing, and sometimes continued to the finish, I would reflect on what had gone wrong. I tried a variety of electrolyte mixes as well as different types of food, until eventually I just resigned myself to the fact that I was one of those runners who would reach a point in an ultramarathon where he couldn't even look at a jelly baby without wanting to lie in a verge.

Running is a simple sport. That's the appeal for so many. It's a fundamental form of human movement, and yet there's always something new to learn. We can read books and blogs, seek guidance and advice from experts and peers, but ultimately, running well for long distances comes down to fully understanding ourselves. What might work for some could be unthinkable for others. While most ultrarunners are evangelical about fuelling with real food, for example, I am one of those monsters who still carries a few gels to consume when nobody is looking. During the seemingly endless period when I'd struggle to keep anything down after a few hours of running, I'd open one as a last-ditch and almost always futile effort to get my body back on course. At the tail end of a 50K, which I had hoped to complete before the curse kicked in, I only had to pull one from my pocket for the sight of it to tip me over the edge.

It was then, as I stared at the grass on my hands and knees while drooling like a dog, that a kind gesture from a Samaritan runner changed everything for me.

'Try this.' The woman placed a white capsule on the grass in front of me before continuing along the path.

The way I was feeling at the time, had it been cyanide that would've been a blessing.

'What's in it?' I called after her.

'Salt,' she said simply.

While I recognised that accepting medication from strangers probably wasn't going to earn me a Cub Scout badge, I really wanted to finish that race. So I picked myself up, along with the pill, plodded to the next check-point and swigged it down with a cup of water.

And the transformation was miraculous.

Within minutes, I felt better. I also felt a little thirsty. I even found that I could sip at the electrolyte mix in my bottles without bringing it straight back up. Crucially, I was running, and though my time didn't win any prizes I finished in good shape.

'Thank you so much,' I said to the runner, on spotting her sitting on the grass behind the finish line. 'You literally saved me back then.'

'I used to be like you,' she told me. 'I'd drink and eat but it always ended badly. Turns out I wasn't taking in enough sodium.'

Listening to her explain its role in regulating the body's fluid balance and absorption, and how quickly we can feel like death warmed up without sufficient levels, I felt like I had discovered some holy grail of running.

'You sound like an expert,' I said.

'Well, I had to become one.' She paused to sip at a recovery milkshake, which told me she knew what she was doing. I just wished that I had remembered to pack one myself.

'Salt capsules,' I said, nodding as I made a mental note. 'I'm all in from here on out.'

'Just be careful,' she advised. 'Too much salt can be as bad as not enough. We're all built differently, and you need to get it right.'

In the same way that I tried to fast-track recovery from physical injuries, I went home and did my homework. Then, I set about incorporating the capsules into my long runs with care and attention. I used them as a supplement to the sodium content in my food and drink, and with practice found they helped me considerably. Some of my club friends regarded me like I'd started doping, but then they were lucky enough not to have experienced the same issues. Just as I've never had a problem with chafing, but still deal with a truck-induced dizziness that is particular to me, we all face different challenges in running to the best of our abilities.

If anything, carrying salt capsules on my long runs and races served as both a security measure and confidence boost. It meant I could look at the buckle perched on the corner of a shelf in my office and consider where to go next. I had run 100 miles, which can only feel like a lifelong achievement for anyone who has completed the distance in one single, continuous hit. In reaching this point, I had slowly expanded my distance from the end of the pavement to 5K, and then 10K to a half marathon and onwards. Now I'd hit what was once an unthinkable number, I didn't feel any immediate need to go longer. I'd found a distance that could be both challenging and rewarding on so many levels. My first attempt had been both a race and an adventure, and a journey that shaped up to be as emotional as it was physical.

So, I signed up to run it again. Not just the North Downs Way, but all four 100-mile races in the Centurion trail series.

A few days went by before I told my wife that I had entered the 100 Grand Slam, as it's known. I knew she would support me, despite the upswing in my ambitions. What led me to hold back was the fact that I had failed to curb the urge to also sign up for the four additional races that make up Centurion's fifty-mile series.

'The Double Grand Slam,' she said when I finally confessed. 'That's 600 miles, over eight races, in one year.'

'You get a cool T-shirt,' I said, like that would help, before recognising that I needed to show my workings more clearly. 'Look, I realise this is a huge undertaking, but it's spread out so there's roughly six weeks between races. The way I see it, once I've done the training then each race sets me up for the next.'

I didn't share this purely to justify what I was doing. It really did seem like a sensible way to approach such an ambitious undertaking. As long as

I took things easy between each event, I pointed out, I would have plenty of time to rest and recover.

From there on out, my sole focus was in preparing for the Double Grand Slam. Now that I'd found a better handle on my fuel and hydration, I knew that I could run fifty-mile races without too much drama. As each one preceded an event of double the distance, where the second half was largely down to grit, I figured I'd be in decent shape when I arrived on that start line. As the first race in the series approached, I began to think this might be the climax to my running career. I might not have done much with it for decades, but if anything that fuelled my desire to push at the boundaries before they began to close in on me. If I managed to complete the Double Grand Slam, I would look back on the year as being truly memorable.

As it turned out, before spring had begun to dry out the ground, 2020 became the one we all wanted to forget.

Throughout the Covid pandemic, amid all the restrictions imposed on us by lockdown, runners escaped with some semblance of normality. All races were postponed, of course, but as a form of daily exercise I continued to explore local trails with Sprint. With the lanes stripped of traffic, the skies clear of planes and a long period of beautiful sunshine, I really enjoyed my time out with the dog. It helped me to get away from the insecurities and uncertainty we all faced about our future. With no immediate goals to chase, and the company of a springer spaniel who stuck to me like Velcro, I really came to appreciate the sense of escape. Over the months, I opened my eyes to my surroundings rather than squinting at my watch for data.

It meant that when the world began to open up a little in the summer, I felt somewhat torn. In my everyday life, I was ready. As a runner getting to grips with a rescheduled race calendar, the Double Grand Slam looked even more daunting than before.

Rather than take place across the course of a year, most of the races had been compressed into a matter of months. Centurion had gone to great lengths to salvage their events and stage them safely. For the handful of runners who had signed up to them all, however, it meant several would now take place in frighteningly quick succession.

'All I can do is take one race at a time,' I told Emma, ahead of the revised season. 'What's the worst that can happen?'

On several levels, I regarded it as fortuitous that the first race was the North Downs Way 100. I knew the course and was hungry to improve on my first experience. This time, my wife and daughter had kindly volunteered to crew me at set points across the first fifty miles, which was encouraged by Centurion to cut down on congestion at the checkpoints. My pacer from the previous year, and the other Emma on my team, had generously agreed to lead me through the darkest phase once more. I had hesitated about asking her again, but when I braved it she told me that pacing had turned out to be a rewarding way to get involved in an ultramarathon she wouldn't dream of taking on from start to finish.

'I really enjoyed it,' she said, 'apart from the babysitting.'

This time, I promised her that I would do my utmost to save at least fifteen minutes of time by not lying down and passing out under the guise of a power nap.

'I am ready for this,' I assured her, and would repeat to everyone in my team in the week preceding the race. 'Nothing is going to stop me from giving this Double Grand Slam my best shot.'

I had experience on my side. I'd enjoyed a decent spell without injury. With a strategy to minimise the chances of being sick or falling asleep, I went into that 100-miler feeling like I had covered every base.

In doing so, I overlooked the fact that no amount of preparation can guarantee a successful race. Sometimes, it's simply not your day. In the case of this one, which fell in early August, the south-east of England was beginning to cook.

I knew it was going to be hot. The forecast predicted that the temperature would climb into the high twenties before noon. As the first quarter of the North Downs Way crossed largely open ground, my plan was to move quickly towards the shadier, woodland stage. With a two-hour window in which competitors could begin, to maintain social distancing on the run, I set off at the earliest opportunity at a pace that was frankly pushing my luck. I was baking before the sun had fully climbed into the sky. Runners were flagging within the first few hours, and I counted myself among that number. Still, I pressed on for my first crew stop around the twenty-mile mark, where Emma and Ethel were waiting with what I considered to be a masterstroke of forethought.

'The bucket!' I called out in advance, on finally setting eyes on them. 'That's all I need!'

As briefed, my wife was ready. She'd set up a camping chair in front of a plastic container containing a couple of inches of water and ice from the cool box. Falling into the chair, I ignored the inevitable sensory tumble as I leant over and plunged my head inside.

'Well, it's a look,' I heard Ethel say behind me.

'I don't care,' I said from inside. 'I am literally melting.'

'I'll fill your flasks,' Emma said next, and then observed that I had sucked them dry so hard they were crinkled into a vacuum. 'Are you drinking enough?'

In my desperation to submerge as much of my head and face as possible, I was practically waterboarding myself as she pressed me again for an answer. The truth was I had vastly underestimated how much fluid I would need, while doubling my salt capsule count from one to two per hour had just left me thirsty.

'Everything will be fine as soon as I get to some shade,' I told her after having surfaced for air. 'I'll call you once I reach the woods.'

In what felt like a race against time, along with many other runners who had the same idea, my sole target was to reach tree cover. From a rise sweeping down to the River Mole, Surrey's Box Hill loomed in the distance. While the steep climb ahead might have looked intimidating, the dense canopy of treetops served to spur me onwards. Pausing at the checkpoint at the foot of the hill purely for the timing post to register me, I pressed on with a rising sense of relief. Across the road, with the sun burning the back of my neck despite coating myself in factor 50, I plunged into the woodland trail as if it were the finish line.

There, within the space of a minute, I was on the phone to my wife.

'Bad news,' I said on plugging my way up the climb. 'It's *cooking* in here. The trees have just trapped all the heat. There's no air. It's like a greenhouse.'

'Maybe it'll cool off,' she said unconvincingly.

The next time I saw my wife and daughter, the remaining ice in the cool box had melted. I dropped my head into the bucket to find the water had reached air temperature. By then, I had got into a complete mess with my hydration. Had I stood a chance of keeping on top of it, I realised I should have been carrying another two soft flasks. My salt capsules weren't a huge amount of use, what with my raging thirst. Already, I was experiencing the first signs that the transformation from runner to reanimated corpse was underway.

I was in no doubt that I would be death-marching at some stage. It's a feature of so many ultramarathons. Not everyone is reduced to what is effectively a pitiful power walk, which can happen for all sorts of reasons. For some, it's a phase they can recover from. Others find their legs defy orders and refuse to run any further, which means the only option is to plough on like a pedestrian with a purpose. In my experience, runners often deteriorate into this grim parade in the closing stages of a race. That afternoon, slow-roasting in a woodland corridor, I found myself walking before the halfway mark while feeling increasingly unwell. I couldn't blame the heat, which the forecasters had been warning about all week. Had I set out with extra water and at a slower pace, I realised, rather than racing for useless cover, I would've endured the day in better condition.

Once again, I was learning in the field. Not that I went on to see things in such a positive light as I left the fifty-mile checkpoint having failed to manage even a sip of flat cola. All I'd managed to do, in fact, was stare at a crisp for ten minutes. One hour later, dry-heaving for the umpteenth time, I realised I was in trouble. By this point, in a late sun that had no right to be so hot, I was aware that I was close to chasing cut-offs. Having been unable to keep anything down for thirty miles, all my remaining energy was directed at staying upright. Other competitors were in a bad way as well, but most were moving quicker than me. If I could make it to nightfall, I told myself, perhaps then I would finally cool off and find my race legs.

Stumbling over the landscape, I was reduced to ugly running for short bursts and then stopping to sit because I felt so weak. By the time the sun finally quit punishing me by sinking away, I was dead on my feet. I had another two miles to go before I reached the next crew point, and at least another fifteen before my clubmate, Emma, picked me up. My progress was so pathetic that I had even texted my pacer-in-waiting and asked her not to set off from home too early. She replied with encouragement, but also asked me to give her the green light once I reached my wife and daughter. At any other time, with a two-hour drive ahead of her, I would've suggested she was cutting things fine. Now I just worried that even with this revised plan in place she'd still have to wait for me to show up.

I felt terrible. Not just physically, with stomach cramps that made me worry that my kidneys were shutting down, but also mentally. My first attempt at this race had been tough but memorable. This just felt like an ordeal. I'd all but given up on running, and that took away my purpose for being there. Trudging through the settling darkness, following the beam from my head torch around the perimeter of a horse paddock, the first tendrils of doubt that I could do this began to wrap around my resolve. I hadn't quite covered sixty miles. I still had forty left to go, with no sign that the cooling temperature was going to spark a Lazarus-like revival. If anything, I didn't just feel wretched now. I felt wretched and little bit close to fainting. For about twenty seconds, which was all I could manage, I broke into a stumble that vaguely resembled a jog, and that's when I heard a voice, calling across a field at me.

'Well done! Keep going! You can do it!'

I looked around, seeing nothing on the other side of the paddock but vague shapes of hedgerow and trees. The voice called out to me again, accompanied this time by a clapping of hands. I hadn't quite reached the point where hallucinations crept in, but I questioned if there was anyone out there at all.

'Thanks! I'll try!' On hearing the lack of conviction in my voice, I reached a decision on the spot. There was no need for me to allow that sense of doubt to flourish, which was inevitable now. It would just be wasting Emma and Ethel's time. If I acted on it now, rather than waiting until I either timed out or passed out from dehydration, my pacer could also stand down and enjoy the rest of her evening.

'I'm done,' I told my wife, calling her without further thought. 'There's no point in carrying on.'

'Are you sure?' asked Emma, who had been worrying about my deteriorating state all afternoon. 'What about the Double Grand Slam?'

Just then, it meant nothing to me. I was only being realistic, I told her. Either the cut-offs would lay claim to me or I risked some kind of organ damage. I was no medical expert, but it felt like there could be consequences for pressing on in this state.

'I can live with the decision,' I told her, and I meant it. Handing in my number at the next checkpoint, by which time the cut-off was snapping at my heels, I felt like a great weight had lifted from my shoulders. I had developed a deep-seated passion for running to extremes, but part of the never-ending learning process was recognising when I had taken things as far as I could go.

13

ENTER THE DRAGON

It was unfortunate that my first DNF put paid to my Double Grand Slam, but I wasn't alone. In the heat, the attrition rate had been huge across the entire field. It left me with a great deal of admiration for those runners who found a way through. I was quietly thankful that I hadn't made a big song and dance on social media about my attempt to complete 600 miles in eight races, only to falter at the first hurdle. I just went back to my life with a newfound respect for taking on an ultramarathon in very hot conditions. It didn't guarantee I'd make a success of it next time, but as a runner there is wisdom to be had from experience.

In my case, I recognised in retrospect that entering eight connecting ultramarathons carried a very high chance of ending in disappointment.

With my slam hopes sidelined, and so much uncertainty built into the year due to the pandemic, I decided to cherry-pick those races left in the series that I really wanted to run. This amounted to just two events. I had four weeks to recover before the Thames Path 100, which took runners from London to Oxford. This one appealed to me because it was flat. What's more, by September the sun was less likely to incinerate my chances. I figured by ironing out all the ups and downs that characterised the North Downs Way, I could perhaps control my pace and even see if I could complete it in under twenty-four hours. It would also earn me the coveted buckle given to runners who complete 100 miles in one day. As it had taken me two hours longer to complete the same distance the year before, but with just over 3,000 metres of elevation, this didn't seem like an impossible task. The second event was a fifty-miler around a particularly idyllic loop of the Chilterns, which was close to where I'd grown up. The downside was that it took place just six days later. It wasn't ideal, but I figured that at least this stripped-back challenge would salvage my race year.

With a fifty per cent success rate behind me, I set off on my third attempt at 100 miles with my wife and daughter at crew points for the first half of the race and my pacer on call for the last quarter should I look like I might need her. As Emma Walters hadn't left her front room for my last ultra-marathon, my clubmate considered this race to be a transfer of services. It was very kind of her, even if I did feel like a charity case this time.

'I appreciate that you need to do this,' she told me. 'In order to move on.'

'Well, I'm really grateful,' I said. 'I'd do the same for you.'

'Oh, I'm never going to go that far,' said Emma, like anyone who did so was crazy.

As the day of the race approached, I tried to tell myself that my DNF on the North Downs Way could only work to my advantage. I'd analysed what had gone wrong, and hoped I had learnt lessons. At the same time, it was still quite raw in my mind. As I set off, I was in no doubt that it had rocked my confidence. I wasn't scared of the distance, as I had been the first time. I just didn't want to mess up. As a result, I carried some tension into the day.

Despite feeling uptight when I should've been relaxed, other factors came into play along that long and winding path. By the time I reached Emma and Ethel at Henley-on-Thames, for the last crew stop before they headed home, I had resigned myself to missing out on a sub-twenty-four-hour finish. I was doing OK, but experiencing what I sometimes called a 'bad vestibular day'. There was no particular cause. I just found the sense of being adrift and a little unstable could sometimes creep up on me. At the same time, attempting to run 100 miles was likely to be a massive factor in shaking up my balance and leaving me feeling out of kilter. I could hardly complain, seeing that I was putting myself through this by choice. Even so, it meant I felt about as flat as the path that was proving to be unexpectedly testing.

With this mindset, little things that went wrong during the race felt like big setbacks. When it was time for my head torch, I accidentally flicked it to full power. Two hours later, when the lights went out, I was reduced to a backup that felt like I was running by match flame. Alongside the challenge I then faced in not veering into the water, the absence of any hills meant I was constantly calling on the muscles in my legs to work without variation. By the time my pacer escorted me over the line in Oxford, having recognised I was in no fit state to be pushed this time, I had been reduced to a slow-moving scuttle. It wasn't pretty, but I earned another buckle and increased my success rate at running 100-milers to two out of three.

'I'm glad I did it,' I told my wife back home. 'It's a beautiful course and a great atmosphere. I just felt like I could have done better.'

Emma sat down beside me on the garden bench. Given that I had arrived home barely able to put one foot in front of the other, she had brought two mugs of tea with her. I had been looking through the results to see how the remaining Double Grand Slammers were getting on. Several, I had noted before setting my phone down to take the cup, were putting in impressive performances.

'Why don't you give running a rest for a while?' she suggested, and I sensed that perhaps she knew that I was comparing myself to others. 'If it's not making you happy.'

'It's not making me *un*happy,' I said to clarify. 'I've got another one next weekend.'

'It's still a lot.' Nursing her mug, Emma considered the state of the lawn I had failed to cut recently on account of all the training. 'Maybe it's time to just rest soon. You know? Recharge your batteries with the family and figure out what you want to do next.'

I sipped at my tea for a moment.

'I was thinking we could rewild the garden,' I said eventually.

'By neglecting it?'

We shared a smile.

'Less time mowing the lawn is more time doing things we love.'

During lockdown, our daughter Ethel began to grow as a trail runner. She had inherited her mother's determination and my wilful ambition when it came to seeing how far I could take things. She divided her time between studying at home for her A levels and running with Sprint across the trails for hours at a time. That she hadn't quite turned eighteen became a source of frustration for her, mainly because that was the minimum age to enter several long races she had her eye on. Emma and I both admired her spirit, while reminding her that she had plenty of time ahead for that sort of thing.

'There's no rush,' I advised her that evening. Ethel had been talking about the leading ladies she'd seen on the Thames Path while waiting with Emma to crew me. 'Age is on your side.'

I said this with good intentions, despite serving to remind me that it most definitely wasn't on mine. I took a moment to ease on to the sofa; grimacing at the fact that since finishing, my thigh muscles had undergone what felt like a rigor mortis process over the course of the day.

'What are we watching?' asked Emma beside me.

'A running film.' Ethel had the remote. 'What else is there?'

Like many families throughout the pandemic, we had found ourselves doing more things together. One such feature of our week fell on a Sunday evening, when Ethel would root out some race documentary to stream on the TV. It had been good. We had watched everything from homemade shorts of local races to polished films about iconic ultras in exotic locations or individual bids to claim a fastest known time. Sometimes our son, Wilf, would join us, expressing no such interest in running long distances but sitting with us to the finish all the same.

'So, what's this one?' he asked, sauntering in five minutes after we started. 'It looks grim.'

Ethel had made her choice earlier in the week, and then scheduled it for this viewing.

'Shh!' She glared at her younger brother. 'It's called the Dragon's Back Race.'

To be honest, having just completed 100 miles and strangely feeling like I needed to put it behind me, a running film was the last thing I wanted to watch. Unwilling to break the family tradition, however, I settled in and hoped it didn't employ too much jumpy hand-held camera action.

My fragile vestibular system had seen enough action for one weekend.

From what I could gather, having idly switched my attention from my phone to the TV screen, the film told the story of a mountain race through Wales that I had heard about but never properly investigated. Judging by the look of pain and anguish etched across the face of almost every competitor picked out by the camera, the close-ups of gruesome blisters and the late-night sequence featuring some poor guy in a ditch receiving medical attention for hypothermia and exhaustion, it looked far too extreme for me.

'Does anyone even finish?' asked Emma, for everything we had seen so far only covered the first day of the race. With five in total across almost 200 miles, it certainly seemed like an impossible task. 'Why would anyone put themselves through this?'

'Let's find out,' said Ethel pointedly, which stopped me from adding that I had yet to see any course markings. Having relied on the comforting breadcrumb trail of red and white tape to guide me from London to Oxford, I even found myself looking for it on the screen.

At the same time, I watched with rising interest as the race moved southwards, shedding numbers with every day. Frankly, it looked brutal. From steep ascents and rocky pinnacles to exposed ridges and vast rolling fells, the landscape appeared both epic and beautiful but no doubt savagely hostile for those attempting to run across it. With each day, the camera continued to pick out competitors clearly hiding fresh zombie bites; jaws clenched and eyes unblinking as they soldiered on. At one point we lingered for so long on one poor soul whose fate was written clearly in his expression that I started feeling uncomfortable.

'It's like he's just been told his dog's died,' observed Wilf.

'Or he's lost his will to live,' Ethel suggested.

'He's just tired,' said Emma, which we all agreed was an understatement.

By the fifth and final day of the race, traversing the Brecon Beacons, over half the field had dropped out. Increasingly, the remaining runners seemed to draw strength from each other. They varied in age and pace, but shared an unspoken understanding that they had each uncovered the same elemental quality inside themselves to get this far. Sustained by pure determination, nothing was going to stop them from reaching that finish line.

The competitors who survived the race looked broken. There was no champagne spray or wild celebration. These men and women had extracted every ounce of mental and physical strength they possessed to get there. With nothing left but smiles on their faces and tears in their eyes, the Dragon's Back had challenged them like no other race. In effect, they'd been into battle and come through it with a true understanding of themselves. From what I had seen, they weren't just accomplished runners. They were warriors.

'Don't get any ideas,' Ethel said to me as the credits rolled.

'Me?' I said in surprise, or at least what I hoped sounded that way. 'I'm not completely stupid.'

By rights, anyone on a post-ultra high should be banned from entering another race for at least a week. Intoxicated by endorphins, the sense of elation that follows the completion of any kind of endurance event can lead to poor decisions. You're tired and emotional in a nice way, but a return to civilian life beckons. That's when the temptation arises to chase another hit without really thinking things through.

Since its inception in 1992, the Dragon's Back Race had been staged on just five occasions. When I checked, first thing the next morning, I learnt that a sixth edition of the race was exactly a year away. I also found the entry list had just gone live. When I clicked on the button, part of me was hoping to find it completely sold out. That way I could assure myself I'd had the courage to at least look into it and then move on. Unfortunately, the online form made it quite clear that the opportunity was available for me to prove I was up for the challenge.

'Really?' I muttered to myself, as if some part of me couldn't believe I was even considering entering. All the evidence I had seen so far suggested I would be way out of my depth on this race, and yet there I was filling out the form.

From the moment the idea materialised in my mind, as I went to bed after watching the film, I just had not been able to make it vanish. If anything, it came to dominate my thoughts. Instead of being unable to sleep because I was still flying high from running 100 miles, I fretted about how I'd feel if I ignored the urge to take on basically double that distance over extreme terrain. For a long time I'd considered dream races such as UTMB, the Glastonbury Festival of European trail-running races, or the Western States 100, which was America's Woodstock equivalent. I'd earned sufficient qualifying points to enter the ballot for both events, but with the restrictions imposed by Covid – and a rising awareness that travel came at a price – those international destinations no longer appealed so much. The Dragon's Back was a homegrown race, and served as a reminder that challenging and breathtaking landscapes were on our doorstep.

Facing the jury in my mind, I went on to reason that this race would also free me from the curse of overbooking. It was just so ambitious that I couldn't afford to enter any more events on a whim, even if I was doing exactly that here.

Normally, I would chew over my race plans with Emma. Mindful of how she was likely to respond, and aware that it would not at all be unreasonable, I decided I should at least do some research first.

When I sat down at my keyboard with a morning coffee, I hadn't anticipated doing anything more than searching for more footage of a mountain race that had entranced me the night before. Having gone on to practically auto-complete the entry for the next edition, the little part of me that was questioning what I was doing had raised every red flag available.

What happened next was about as impulsive as reacting to amber lights at a railway crossing by pressing the accelerator. I hadn't consulted the family or considered what training for a race so far above my pay grade might demand. Quite simply, I got caught up in the moment. It was a panic buy in some ways. With no means of knowing whether the remaining places might get snapped up in seconds – and not the weeks that subsequently passed, which would be quite normal for a race of this scale – I just floored that pedal.

And then, as the confirmation email came through, I went cold.

I had secured a place for the Dragon's Back. An event billed as the world's toughest mountain race. With no apparent cooling-off period on offer – and I did look – I realised I would have to take responsibility for my actions and put my wife in the picture. Which I did after work so as not to ruin her entire day.

'I knew you would,' was Emma's first response that evening, which completely took me by surprise. 'The last time you signed up to something this ridiculous you'd been drinking.'

'That was different,' I said, aware that she was talking about a morning in my former life as a functioning alcoholic. Back then, I woke up to discover I had applied online to become an astronaut with the Mars One programme. I couldn't recall registering my interest the night before. More immediately, in the searching light of day I had questions to answer as to why I thought it would be OK with the family for me to join a one-way mission to colonise the red planet. Ultimately, the venture failed to launch – as predicted by Emma and no doubt the partners of hundreds of thousands of subsequently grounded pioneers – and yet it proved a useful personal stepping stone on my pathway to sobriety. This time, I wasn't planning on travelling to another world. It's just we both knew that at the Dragon's Back the terrain in question would be equally inhospitable to someone with my lack of experience. 'I know it's ambitious but I'm serious,' I added.

'Why didn't you just tell me?' she asked.

'Well … ' I paused to think of the long list of reasons, and then read the room. 'Are you not cross?'

'We all make mistakes.'

'I just assumed you'd talk me out of it,' I said, 'but I still should have discussed it with you, and I'm sorry.'

'You would have signed up anyway,' she said, sounding horribly like she had prepared for this conversation. 'Regardless of the consequences.'

For one horrible moment, I thought she meant that entering the race was grounds for divorce.

'You think it's too much?' I asked just to check.

Emma had just climbed out of the bath when I broke the news to her. I had figured she'd be at her most relaxed. Even so, she was being unnervingly calm about it.

'Too much?' Wrapped in a bathrobe, Emma sat down at her mirror to brush her hair. I had followed her in to stand behind her. It was then I caught her eye in the mirror. 'Were you paying attention when we watched the film?' she asked.

'I know it's a step up.'

'It's six days in the mountains, Matt! You can't even brush your teeth without feeling dizzy.'

Even if I hoped she was only venting, I felt I needed to challenge Emma on this. I was ready for her reminder about my vestibular issues, which admittedly I had shut away in my own mind when I signed up. I just felt I should set her straight on what was involved so she didn't overstate the case.

'Five,' I said to correct her. 'It's a five-day race.'

'Six,' she said again, calmly now but in total control of the conversation. 'Next year, it's been extended by a day so it runs from coast to coast. I know because I had no doubt you'd check it out, so I looked to find out for myself. I just assumed that would be enough to put you off.'

'I must have missed that detail,' I said in a hollow voice.

'So you can add another sixty kilometres of hell to the equation,' she added. 'Taking you on a north-to-south traverse of an *entire country*!'

'OK,' I said and raised my hands. 'It's a very long way, but I have a year to prepare. I'll make time for training so it doesn't impact on the family, and be ready to tackle this properly.'

'I know you will,' she said, cooling just as quickly as she had fired up. 'I'm not questioning your determination. I just wonder where it'll end.'

I considered her in the mirror glass for a second.

'It finishes with knowing that I tried while I still had the opportunity.'

'Even if you fail?'

'Absolutely.'

Emma began to rake the brush through her hair.

'What are you trying to prove here?' she asked me.

It was a good question. I couldn't respond simply by saying that in a world of constant noise in my ears, I loved the solitude such a race would bring. There was more to it than that, even though since the accident I had found peace on long runs, and we both knew it. I certainly didn't feel driven by ego or the desire for status. If anything, my experience in running ultra-marathons had been humbling. I found them hard, with a DNF under my belt to remind me that I could never take them for granted. They could strip me down to raw emotion, in fact, but in doing so the journey was always enlightening.

'I'm not lost or anything,' I said, keen to put her mind at ease in case she thought this was the sign of a personal crisis.

'Not yet,' she said pointedly. Emma leant over to pick up her hairdryer, leaving me with a clear view of myself in the mirror. 'It's just the Dragon's Back is self-navigated from start to finish, and let's not forget the record you set last time you ran an unmarked race.'

14

LONGEST KNOWN TIME

Race briefings are a little bit like pre-flight safety demonstrations. You've heard it all before, and yet that one time you ignore it and there you are floundering for the exits.

Assembling in front of the race director as requested, ahead of the South Downs Way 100 Miles Relay, I felt confident that I knew what he would have to say: share the public paths and bridleways responsibly and observe the Countryside Code. Even though he stretched it out for fifteen minutes, I nodded responsibly while trying not to dwell on the fact that all the other runners for this first leg looked like human/hare hybrids.

Every year, by invitation only to running clubs across the south-east of England, sixty teams of six runners race across eighteen legs of this ancient trail from the Sussex coast to the outskirts of Winchester. The summer before the Dragon's Back came into my life, Horsham Joggers had entered a male and a female team. I had been unsure about accepting the call to take part. At the time, I was still finding my way after the lorry crash. As it was sold to me as one of the best days out a club runner could have, I decided that it was another chance for me to get back on the horse. With a staggered start based on estimated finish times, and each runner taking on three legs apiece, the women's team set off ninety minutes before the men. What followed was a thrilling day of racing and chasing in sweltering conditions, along with time in two minibuses rattling along country lanes like we'd just done a bank job in matching race vests.

By mid-afternoon, we had closed in on a very fast women's team. It was by no means a certainty that we would catch them with just a few legs left. So, when the two minivans pulled in at the next handover point ahead of our incoming runners, all we could do was wait and see. When our man came in and we took the lead, it seemed like the boys had it in the bag.

We just hadn't reckoned on two factors. Firstly, the raw speed of the women's team on the penultimate leg, who reeled in our team captain to regain the lead for the final handover, and secondly, the wisdom in selecting me to give chase.

By the time I took the baton, five minutes after the women's team cheered their final runner into the distance, I had just under six miles in which to snatch victory from the jaws of defeat. With the sun setting directly into my eyes, all I could do was get my head down and hope for the best.

A sweeping and more exposed route than the ridge thirty miles to the north, the South Downs Way has been in existence for over 8,000 years. A ribbon of chalk and flint track over elevated, undulating terrain, it's been a pretty good way through history to traverse the south of England without getting wet feet. It's also largely straight, with just a few forks and turns to catch out the unwary traveller. For this event, the course was unmarked. Ahead of the race, and again in the briefing, the organisers had stressed the importance of running designated legs in advance. Unwilling to make the two-hour journey from my home to recce the final stretch – and because I wasn't that much of a try-hard – I was relying on common sense and the printout of the leg map rolled up inside my baton. We were running along a pathway that was popular with families out to stretch their legs. This was hardly deepest Patagonia.

At some point, with my lungs burning and heavy legs, I caught sight of a runner in the distance. It took a while for me to recognise Kate, my club-mate from the women's team. It wasn't just the fact that she was cast in silhouette but the fact that I was without my glasses. Since I turned forty, when my eyesight took early retirement, I've pretty much worn them all the time. It's just I can't quite bring myself to do so when I'm running. I totally rate those who are comfortable with it, but through my failing eyes it would feel like one more thing to worry about. As a result, it was only when I drew behind the blurry figure, and she turned to say 'Hi, Matt!' that I knew it wasn't a competitor from another team.

I ran alongside Kate to exchange a few words, torn as to whether I should stay abreast or pass. Part of me thought it would be nice for our two teams to finish together, but I was mindful of the grief I might get from my side. I also worried that it looked really patronising. Plus there was always the possibility that Kate was holding back to outrun me at the end. With no right outcome, I decided to press on.

I should pause here to admit that, yes, I am aware that I have been getting my excuses in early. I had skipped the advice to run the leg in advance, tuned out of the race briefing and left my glasses with my stuff in the minivan. At that moment, however, all I could see in front of me was a high point of my running career.

There is a road crossing, less than half a mile from the finish line, where the teams often gather to watch their runners before racing down the road to see them in. When I appeared in their view, having regained the lead, a jubilant cheer went up. I responded by squeezing the pace a little harder. As they'd finished their work for the day, my team even raised a guard of honour with their beer cans. I pushed on through for the field across the road, exhausted but elated, before slipping into the mists of club mythology.

On the minibus before my final stint, I had studied the map just to see what was in store. It was all quite straightforward. Once I'd crossed the field, I'd drop down a long, gentle descent. Soon afterwards, as our designated driver confirmed, having run this leg one year before, the race left the South Downs Way and then joined a footpath. From there, he told me, it was a short sprint to the cricket grounds that hosted the finish.

In the weakening light, at the foot of the descent, I had to squint to confirm I was approaching a fingerpost. I slowed to a walk, hoping all the signs would come into focus, which they didn't. Even up close, with tired, dry eyes, they were just a blur. I was also keenly aware that I hadn't made that much ground over my clubmate. Whenever I had passed through a gate, rigged with a weight to draw it back, I would hear a clang behind me. When this same sound repeated no more than a minute later, I knew that Kate wasn't far behind.

Aware that she could appear at any moment, and with a distinct movement advantage over me given that I was stationary, I hurried to extract the printout rolled inside my baton. Without my glasses, I discovered, it might as well have been a map of the moon. As I just hadn't expected to find the sign so soon after the descent, I made a split decision to stay on the South Downs Way. I was still in a race here, and couldn't afford to dither again. It felt good to press on and hold my advantage. I even pushed myself to go harder, knowing that it would soon be over. The shorter the distance, the more pain I could endure, and yet the signpost I anticipated never came. All I could do was hang on, refusing to slow by a step in the belief that I would switch for the finish line at any moment. It wasn't until the path crossed open land, with no post pricking the horizon, that I registered I might have gone too far.

My downfall, on wheeling around to look back, was that I thought I had only just made the mistake. As I would discover, that horse had bolted long before. Breathlessly, I retraced my steps until I found an overgrown crossroads in the path that I had missed. On one side, obscured by tree branches, stood a fingerpost. Even though I couldn't read it, having narrowed my eyes and stared at the lettering, I duly took the turn. After a minute or so, that led me to a country road, and a gate on the other side with a warning sign about live ammunition. With nothing in the race brief about a risk of being shot, which would've certainly commanded my attention, and in a spin as everything that had been going so right was now going wrong, I hurried back to the path crossroads. There, turning the map one way and the other, and with the damned thing practically pressed to my nose, I determined that I should have taken the turn on the other side. At the same time, in the settling dusk I convinced myself I could see a runner fast approaching from the way I had come – even if it was just a low swaying tree branch. And so I broke into a mad dash along my second choice of turn-off, winding through woodland alongside a huge field that never ended. When it did ten minutes later, I conceded I was lost.

Hurrying over a stile, I followed the path around the perimeter of the field. With no desire to work my way back to the crossroads that had confused me, and in denial that I could have gone so wrong, this *felt* like the right direction.

If I just circled around I would find it, I thought to myself. At the same time, I tried to listen out for the sound of a race finish. With so many teams awaiting their final runners at the cricket grounds, I strained to hear any hint of cheering and clapping from open grounds. A few minutes later, as I pressed on as if expecting to finish at any moment, a man out walking with his dog appeared on a ridge in front of me. Breathlessly I stopped to explain my situation ... quite badly, as it turned out.

'Oh, yes,' he declared, much to my relief, and turned to gesture the way he had come. 'Just follow the path all the way down, go over the bridge and take a right.'

'You're a lifesaver!' I said, unable to determine quite what I was looking at. In the distance, all I could really make out was a blurred spread of lights. It might have been a cricket clubhouse down there in the distance. It could have been an Asda. Without my glasses, I placed blind faith in the kindness of this stranger, and ran on.

The bridge, as it turned out, spanned the M3 into Winchester, which was a world away from where I needed to be. And the right turn he had recommended led me through an alleyway to a travellers' camp. At this point, confronted by caravans, washing lines, kids and dogs, and aware that heads had turned at the appearance of a runner in a race bib with a baton in one hand, I found a new burst of energy.

Now, I knew that I had gone horribly wrong. I was just in that panicky mindset where every decision I made on the fly only worsened things for me. Having crossed the motorway, it was clear to me that I had gone about three miles beyond where I needed to be – wherever that was. I should have turned around, but somehow thought I could still save this. I approached a knot of youths by a car outside a Kwik Fit, who quickly pulled apart as if I was some undercover cop in a spicy outfit. Asking for their help, I showed them the map. Having held it scrunched in one sweaty fist since losing my way, the damp, crumpled printout looked like it would require a forensics team to decipher. One of the lads nodded sagely nevertheless, and with great confidence set me off in the wrong direction.

I continued to run as if I was still in a race. I don't know why. It was partly denial that I had messed up so badly, and the desperate hope that it would mean less time being lost. It wasn't until I reached the other side of Winchester that I realised I'd been fooled. Finding myself on yet another bridge over the M3, while thinking military service really ought to be reintroduced to sort out the youth of today, I conceded that I was now lost and also disorientated. I knew the motorway skirted the fringes of the cathedral city, but if I thought of it as a clock face I had no idea of the time.

Crossing the bridge, I faced a long, straight road out of town flanked by trees and fields. It looked like the kind of landscape I needed to be in, but that wasn't much consolation. Overhead, stars pricked the sky. I had gone far beyond my projected finish time. At first it left me worrying about the grief I must be causing the two teams. Eventually, I began to despair. Having negotiated a seventy-six-kilometre ultramarathon over a volcano in the Canaries, here I was lost and alone in leafy Hampshire.

I found a stile leading across heathland overlooking distant hills. I was pretty sure I needed to be heading in that direction, and ran on. A moment of elation followed when I saw a couple on a late evening walk. I jogged towards the pair, noting them both tense a little, and hoped a smile would help soften the image of a heavily tattooed man wielding what looked like a stovepipe in one hand. Understandably, they claimed not to have a phone I might use, but kindly pointed me towards a church in the distance. Behind it, the man told me, I'd find a path that would take me in the direction of a village he believed had a cricket ground.

'Are you sure?' his partner asked him. 'Isn't it just playing fields?'

I didn't care. It sounded better than nothing. Thanks to them, I found the church, and the path, which took me on a steep decent in near darkness ... to the wrong side of a roaring dual carriageway.

I don't think I cried, but I wanted to. I was wearing running shoes, shorts and a distinctly non-fluorescent race vest. With no headlamp, I had become an underdressed road hazard. All I could do was pick my way along one overgrown verge and then the other, before sprinting through any lull in the traffic until I found a turn-off to a village. It was now pitch black. With no street lighting, and a waning moon, the distant hills that had at least given me some reference point were gone. I was cold, but still clinging to my relay baton as if somehow that would guide me home. Relieved at least to be on a country lane, I plodded along for a couple of miles only to find myself spat back out on the dual carriageway at the other end.

Just then, shivering and dehydrated, I wanted to give up; just flop into a ditch and hope I might wake up in my bed. At the same time, squinting hard to get some focus, I spotted an ambulance parked further up the carriageway. It had broken down, and while the driver was busy summoning help his partner kindly fired up Google Maps on his phone for me.

'You want to be around that corner,' he said, and I almost sobbed with joy. 'Just cross the roundabout and keep going.'

'You really are an angel!' I declared, sensing this hideous unravelling of my race was about to end, and broke off at a trot so I at least looked the part.

'No, wait!' he called after me. I turned to face him once again. 'I'm looking at the map upside down. What an idiot, eh?!'

Let me just say that my confidence had all but crashed as I followed his revised directions. I was running on the verge into the traffic this time, dropping into the ditch at each passing car and lorry and thinking at some point soon I was going to see a police chopper in the sky with a searchlight combing the fields and woodland. When I found myself back on the same lane to a village that didn't seem to exist, I decided the game was up. I was quite literally going around in circles. I would've happily knocked on a door to ask for help, but every place I passed was set back in huge grounds with security gates that were probably electrified for good measure. Even if the intercoms weren't booby-trapped, I realised that thanks to years of technological advances and shortcuts I didn't actually know our home telephone number or my wife's mobile.

Passing yet another palatial pile, I found myself slowing to a plod. A moment later I stopped running altogether. Since setting off to complete the final short leg of the relay, I had only paused to ask for directions. This time, I had no desire to continue. According to my activity watch, I had gone beyond the six miles to cover almost a marathon in distance. Add in the twelve miles I had run at pace on my first two legs, and this was shaping up to be the world's worst ultra. I was lost, alone, disorientated and exhausted, as dizzy as I had ever been, thirsty, hungry, frozen to the bone and utterly humiliated. I was also looking for someone to blame apart from myself, of course, and began to wonder if the organisers would serve a jail term for neglecting to mark the course.

Some minutes later, when I heard the hum of an engine, and then saw the flicker of headlights on the hedgerow ahead, I prepared to do some flagging down. With the vehicle's beams on full as it came into view, I stepped back and cupped my eyes. I realised I was looking at a minivan just a moment before it pulled up beside me. The passenger side window went down and I found myself facing the women's captain.

'Fuck sake,' I swore I heard her mutter in greeting, which was fair enough given that the entire team should have been tucked up long ago. 'Get in.'

The side door opened from the inside. I stepped up into the back of the minivan, shocked in some ways that this moment had just happened after so long in the dark. In the weak glow from the interior lighting, and from every seat, members of the women's team just stared at me as if perhaps I'd been the target of an alien abduction.

Following a three-point turn in the lane, and then a one-mile drive of shame to cricket grounds that seemed wilfully out of the way, all I could do was apologise repeatedly. Everyone kept assuring me it was fine, as if it was just one of those things to vanish two minutes from the finish line and go missing for the night. It could've happened to any of them, they said, but it hadn't.

'I'm just so grateful to you for not giving up on me,' I said at one point, and then promptly wondered why the entire ladies' team had jumped on board with all their stuff for this search by van. From the passenger seat, the captain glanced over her shoulder as if to signal that there was no need for anyone to respond.

At first, I learnt, my disappearance had been treated as a joke. I'd clearly taken a wrong turn, forfeiting our in-club race and indeed a decent position in the relay. As the other runners on the final leg came over the line to join the big barbecue, crack a beer and enjoy the prize-giving, my clubmates had become increasingly concerned. This was party time, after all. In order not to miss out, they had equipped themselves with six-packs and formed a search party. Some tracked back to my last known sighting, half joking that I had suffered a coronary and was lying face down in undergrowth.

The others had headed in the opposite direction until the lights of Winchester loomed in the distance and they figured nobody would feasibly go that far. By the time everyone regrouped at the cricket grounds, refreshed but without me, the embers of the barbecue had all but gone out and just two minivans remained in the car park. Sometime afterwards, in the grip of the night chill, it was agreed that one team should head home. The other would hold vigil until the booze in the back ran out, and if I failed to show up by then it would be time to report me to the police as a missing person.

It was one of the designated drivers who put in a hesitant but diplomatic call to my wife. It made sense to see if I had phoned home, even if it did create a domestic drama that I would go on to face when I finally got back. Needless to say, I faced a few more hurdles that night before I finally hit my bed, and naturally my teammates ensured that I wouldn't forget about what happened for some time. It was fair enough. Collectively, we had devoted an entire day to racing close to 100 miles across the South Downs Way, only to be disqualified for failing to finish. Lest anyone forgot, on the journey home in the early hours my watch automatically uploaded my ordeal to Strava. It recorded a valiant effort in the opening stage, followed by a series of stupidly wide but every decreasing spirals of sadness across town and country to a point in the middle of nowhere.

The right thing to do, so everyone said when they stopped laughing and started feeling sorry for me, was to represent the team the following year. I had created a demon of my own making, which I could only lay to rest by running that last leg in full. It made sense, of course, but one thing stopped me from accepting the club's kind invitation: the race briefing. There was no way I could look the same race director in the eye as he stressed the importance of a reconnaissance run, or endure the distinct possibility that he would announce that the final stint to the finish line had been renamed the Matt Whyman Memorial Leg. For out there in the dark, stumbling around having blown it for my team, I had totally died on the inside.

Now, one year after my return from the wilderness of the Winchester suburbs, I had signed up to head into a proper one with very clear and present dangers. As a runner who had effectively failed to navigate a straight line, my wife made a good point when she flagged up that I might not thrive on the Dragon's Back. There, I'd face some 240 miles of mountainous terrain without a single race marking.

'Search and Rescue won't reach for the beers if they get called out,' she suggested on the evening I confessed to entering. 'There are costs.'

'I know that,' I said, well aware that over the course of the next twelve months they could become overwhelming.

15

TWO STEPS BACK

'I am capable of being self-sufficient and making safe decisions in remote mountainous terrain.'

Emma read the line out loud to me from the terms and conditions at the foot of the entry page for the Dragon's Back Race. Twenty-four hours had passed since I told her I'd signed up for the next edition. Now she was over the shock, it appeared to have become the joke that kept on giving.

'What about it?' I asked. 'I mean, I doubt I could saw off my own leg if it was trapped under a rock, but nobody is asking me to go to that kind of extreme.'

'Did you tick the box beside the statement?' she asked, showing me her phone screen. 'You're supposed to tick it.'

'Of course I ticked it.' My patience was thinning considerably. 'I can navigate an entry page.'

'That's something,' she said under her breath, which is when I snapped.

'What happened on the South Downs Way was unfortunate, but with a decent map I can find my way from A to B.'

'All right, Marco Polo.'

I was loading the dishwasher at the time, while Emma waited for the kettle to boil to make tea. Over supper, she had made no mention of the race. Admittedly, I had steered the conversation far from anything related to Wales.

'I'm not treating this lightly,' I conceded.

'Seriously, Matt, you'll need to practise.'

'Navigating is on my list of things I need to master in the next year,' I told her. 'I'm actually quite excited about the idea of running with a map and compass.'

'How about the tent-sharing,' asked Emma, referring to the fact that in the film runners were grouped collectively under canvas at the end of each day, 'given that you hate camping holidays?'

'That's not true.'

'Then name a holiday in this country that you enjoyed.'

When the kids were little, we would often head to a Cornish campsite for a fortnight in the summer. Under canvas, the weather frequently reflected my mood.

'OK, camping with small children can be challenging,' I admitted. 'They need entertaining and that's hard when water is pooling across the groundsheet. This is different.'

'I imagine it'll be worse,' said Emma as she made the tea. 'You'll be sharing an eight-person tent with sweaty, snoring runners. Imagine the smell after a few days!'

'So, I didn't sign up for the camping,' I said, as she pretended to gag, and took both cups through to the sitting room. 'But I'll put up with it for the chance to run across the most challenging landscape imaginable. Right now, that terrifies me. But it's fine. I have time to prepare, and that makes it more exciting. For me, the Dragon's Back Race starts today.'

'So, does that mean you'll skip the Chilterns next weekend?' Emma took her seat beside me on the sofa. 'Seeing that you're all about the mountains now.'

In the excitement of setting my sights on the following year's running plans, I had temporarily forgotten about the second and final race I salvaged from the Centurion Double Grand Slam. Now that Emma had reminded me, I felt even more determined to take on my choice from the fifty-mile series. Even though my legs had yet to loosen from the weekend's 100-miler, this felt like the kind of test that proved I was up for the challenge of a gruelling six-day ultramarathon.

'I'll be at the start line,' I told her. 'It's my first training run.'

One week made a massive difference in my mood. From the start line on-wards, I just hadn't quite engaged with the Thames Path 100. I only had myself to blame. It's a great event. There is something very special about running out of the capital, across an ever-changing landscape, with the waterway as a constant companion. Heading into Henley-on-Thames at sunset, I was hooted on by posh boys in striped jackets. Ten miles upriver, on an isolated and run-down section through Reading after dark, a bunch of down-at-heel drunks on a bench broke into cheers and applause. These were vastly different sections of society. In taking on a distance that guar-anteed a response from people when they asked how far we were running, it felt like we were the stitches that drew them together.

Despite the special moments, and there were plenty, I just didn't feel as if I had thrown my heart and soul into the race. Now, as I prepared to take on half the distance after just six days of recovery, I felt transformed. Signing up for the Dragon's Back had rebooted my sense of drive and motivation. It meant Centurion's Chiltern Wonderland 50 no longer felt like a consolation event from a grand slam series that had defeated me. Long before sunrise, I had set off from home in West Sussex with high hopes for a trail race that formed a challenging loop around one of southern England's Areas of Natural Beauty. As I waited in turn for the marshal at the start line to point a temperature gun at my forehead and confirm I wasn't primed to turn this into a very long super-spreader event, I could not wait to get going.

Mentally, at any rate.

From the moment I set off, having taken it easy all week, my legs made it quite clear that this was the last thing they wanted to do. My hamstrings felt so tight that I started with the same uncomfortable shuffle that had seen me over the line at Oxford.

'Oh well,' I said to myself, and tried to recall all the motivational running quotes about pain being part of the journey.

After just fifteen miles, I concluded that whoever came up with that crap had never truly hurt themselves.

What had begun as a generalised stiffness slowly concentrated as an ache just below my left ankle. There was no obvious cause. I didn't flinch when I pushed or prodded it. At first, it was one of those things that felt like it would fade if I continued running. Instead, it just got worse. Every footstep saw me grit my teeth, and later switch to walks just to ease the discomfort. It also distracted me from the fact that the route wove through stunning pockets of English countryside. As we clambered our way towards a handsome white windmill, other runners cooed while I just cursed and glared at my foot. In retrospect, I should have retired. After thirty miles of running and hobbling, accompanied by the insidious feeling that this was just a taste of worse things to come, the smart move would have been to stop at a checkpoint and wait for the sweeper bus. Instead, having decided I had what it took to pit myself against all of Wales the following year, I felt obliged to prove that I could tough it out.

'You've earned yourself a stress fracture,' said the A&E doctor the next morning on examining the X-ray. 'You're lucky, because sometimes if you ignore these things the bone can just snap.'

I had been one of the last to finish the race, with just minutes to spare before the final cut-off. Even as I limped over the line, I knew that I had taken things too far. On the drive home, I found myself avoiding too many gear changes just so I didn't have to depress the clutch. That night I had gone straight to bed feeling deeply sorry for myself, and then woken to find my calf ballooned so acutely it appeared to have swallowed half my foot.

'I'm guessing that means I can't run for a while.'

The doctor switched her attention to me. As soon as I had asked a question with such an obvious answer, I hoped she realised I was just in shock.

'Six to eight weeks won't kill you,' she said, though under the circumstances it came as a crushing blow.

With a year to go before the Dragon's Back, I still had plenty of time to prepare. That's what I told myself as I adjusted to life on the sidelines. Wasn't overcoming setbacks all part of being a good ultrarunner? I aimed to keep this in mind, but in truth I was gutted. In some ways, it felt like the running gods were seeking to put me in my place.

While I had a couple of months of bone recovery ahead of me, it only took a few days for me to get over this bout of self-pity. It helped that nobody at home had time for it. Accidents happen, they reminded me. Even if I had brought it upon myself. And they were right.

Having finally accepted that stewing was not the solution, I set out to use the recovery period productively. I purchased a compass, subscribed to the Ordnance Survey app and learnt to familiarise myself with my surroundings. I realised that living here for so long meant I could probably find my way around blindfold, but it was a start. I also subscribed to a comprehensive YouTube channel offering short tutorials on navigation skills for fell runners. Each one finished with a challenge that invited the viewer to orientate themselves based on clues provided by a split screen containing a still photograph and a map. For my first five tutorials, which I got wrong, I told myself that most students like me would struggle to work out their location on a barren moor. Then the exercises began to feature landmarks like drystone walls, quarries and restricted byways, and I reasoned that all would become clear if I just learnt what all the different lines and symbols meant.

After a month of extensive self-tuition in map reading and navigation, I upgraded to a fancy GPS watch that would do it all for me.

Despite running around the entire alphabet at the tail end of the South Downs Way 100 Miles Relay, I didn't consider myself to be hopeless at getting from A to B. I knew my way across the basics of a map. I had also learnt a lot from the tutorials. I was just keenly aware that I wouldn't be starting the Dragon's Back Race with longstanding experience of fell and mountain running to guide me. Determined to cover for my shortcomings, I invested in a watch that talked to all manner of satellites in the sky. I had no intention of relying on it completely. With the route uploaded, however, it was just one more means of making sure I was heading in the right direction. I also picked up a pair of cheap reading glasses that could fold away into my race vest but allowed me to read the screen rather than guess at what was going on.

By the time I was ready to return to running, I felt I had also made progress in other areas of my preparation. I hadn't just focused on navigation. I'd begun to obsess about what shoes would best suit me for the six-day challenge. This largely stemmed from reading blogs and run reports from previous Dragons and noting how many had suffered from problems with their feet. My concern was further compounded when the mandatory blister kit arrived. The event team had put together everything required in one handy package. I had unclipped the lid with some excitement, only to reveal what looked more like the tools required for a mouse autopsy.

'That's a lot of blades,' said Ethel, peering over my shoulder. 'I hope you know what you're doing.'

To reinforce the horror, the lid of the kit sported a photographic guide to the severity of blisters we could expect, along with appropriate care advice.

'Jesus,' I said to myself, sensing my toes curl as I examined the parade of raw and oozing wounds. 'Some of those look fit for amputation.'

Ethel picked up one of the blades between her thumb and forefinger.

'I would just learn to dress them like it suggests.'

Unlike the navigation, I wasn't entirely sure how I could set about practising my first-aid skills to this extent. As a runner who still didn't really like to get his trail shoes muddy, my feet tended to stay in good shape. In Wales, I knew I'd have to take the plunge, which meant wet feet and the likelihood that blisters would develop. Once again, YouTube performed a valuable if somewhat queasy service by serving up tutorials for dealing with worst-case scenarios. At the same time, I figured prevention was as good as a cure. So, I set out on a search for footwear I could rely on to comfortably protect my feet while keeping me grounded.

And like any runner in search of the perfect race shoe, that became a searching quest.

From heel cup to toe box and everything in between, there were just so many components to consider. Ideally, I was looking for a pair of light-weight, minimalist shoes so I could feel the ground, but which provided masses of cushioning over a punishing week. I needed something that would drain well from all the wet terrain, but which would stop my precious feet from getting soaked. I liked a shoe that could provide maximum traction in slippery mud and a smooth ride across the long tarmac stretches. Ultimately, until shoe technology evolved to harness magic, I was asking for the impossible. Still, that didn't stop me from believing that some-where there existed a pair that were perfect for me.

Even my research stage lasted way beyond the time it took me to learn to run again. Following advice from the doctor who signed off my leg as fit for purpose, I had to go back to basics. To make sure I allowed time for the repair work on the bone to strengthen, my first run lasted for thirty seconds followed by a walk of two minutes. I repeated the process four times and then called it a day just to check my leg could handle the load. Throughout that brief return to running, the prospect of covering 240 miles seemed like a world away.

'One step at a time,' Emma assured me. She could see that I was worrying, even after I had worked my way into the new year in a bid to get back up to speed. By the end of February, I was running for an hour at a stretch with no problems. The Dragon's Back took place in September, which gave me six months to prepare.

'What if the next step hurts?' I asked, not entirely seriously, though I still hadn't quite regained full confidence in my leg.

'Then you take two steps back, but you'll get there.'

Despite Emma's initial doubts about my ability to take on the Dragon's Back Race, she had slowly got behind me. As I made every effort to prepare, so her comments that I had lost the plot turned to words of encouragement. It struck me that her early concerns were rooted in fear. She didn't want me to get hurt, by which I mean she was scared I might fail. Through my eyes, if I fell short despite my training, then I had at least ventured to the edge of my abilities. Unless I gave it my best shot, I'd never know what that might be. Eventually, when my wife made plans to be at the finish line at Cardiff Castle, I knew that I had her full support. With this in mind, I had yet to share the footage of Dragon's Back competitors from a previous edition traversing a dicey-looking ridge in Snowdonia. That could wait, I decided, until I crossed it on a recce that I had planned. Crib Goch couldn't be that difficult, I told myself. Even with my balance issues.

Before I set foot in Wales, however, I had set myself a training schedule with targets too challenging for me to just skip across.

16

WHY WE RUN

It started with a spreadsheet, which I consigned to the trash can on my desktop when it became clear that I could basically memorise the plan. It wasn't difficult. With half a year before the Dragon's Back Race, I intended to divide my training time into two blocks.

For the first three months, I would focus on endurance running. I wanted to make sure that I had learnt from experience so I could stay in good shape across long distances. To put that to the test, I decided to enter just one race ahead of my main event for the year. Not only did I see it as a useful stepping stone, but I also felt that I had something to prove to myself.

I had completed two 100-mile ultramarathons. Every time I looked at the buckles on my office shelf, however, I only really felt as if I'd earned the first one. As I came back from the stress fracture that had no doubt taken shape on the Thames Path 100, it seemed that time out had also helped me to reset my aims and objectives. Maybe I had just needed the break, because when I looked back over recent years they had been dominated by one race after the next.

In hindsight, I'd run the Thames Path 100 because I hadn't quite come to terms with crashing out of the Double Grand Slam. I retired from the first race in the season because it had been the sensible thing to do. Even so, I hadn't allowed myself time to process the disappointment. It meant I went into the next 100-miler with my head in the wrong place. With a period of enforced rest after the fifty-mile fiasco that followed, I looked back with a renewed appreciation for how important it was to be prepared not just physically but psychologically.

So, if I was going to be ready for the Dragon's Back Race, I decided, I needed to return to the Thames Path 100 and run it as I had intended. That meant being engaged with every step and focused on seeking to complete the race in one day. There was no guarantee that I was good enough to earn a sub-twenty-four buckle, but if I could look back knowing that I had run with both my head and heart, that could only set me up for the second phase of my training schedule.

So, for three months, I made sure that I ran with a purpose. Rather than defaulting to my natural, comfortable plod when I felt like it, I set out for sixty minutes of kilometre intervals, or a progressive run that slowly dialled up the speed to a pace I could only just sustain. I ran four to five times each week, finishing with a long, easy Sunday outing with Sprint and sometimes friends. In a bid to be more efficient on the move, I even enrolled on a day-long workshop with the movement specialist and Running Reborn founder Shane Benzie. After enduring Shane's video playback that showed me merrily heel-striking like a Morris dancer, I hung on every word of his advice as he encouraged me to stand tall and renew my relationship with the ground. I left feeling transformed and absolutely knackered, with the understanding that it could take some time and effort before any conscious changes to my form felt natural. Still, I was determined to put in the work, and dreamt of unleashing the kind of effortless flow state at Thames Path that would turn heads enviously.

As the pandemic had put paid to my Pilates classes, I pursued my own workouts on a mat with the cat watching over me. While I devised my own plan, I felt like I had established a structured and holistic approach to my running. I even made sure my diet supported the upswing in my efforts, and finally gave up my lifelong habit of staying up late watching rubbish for the sake of it.

In terms of time and energy, I had stepped up my commitment to a sport that meant so much to me. Having got things into perspective as I waited for a bone to mend, however, I found that I was also enjoying the preparation process. Following the reset that came with being on crutches,

I didn't feel I had to squeeze in one race after another to make the most of my time on the trails. Granted, I had rushed into signing up for the Dragon's Back, and then paid for it with a sustained period of panic. With time to come to terms with such a hasty move, however, and a sensible approach to training, I felt as if I had matured as a runner.

It was a little late in the day, given I had reached my fifties. I just told myself that a pinch of wisdom couldn't hurt in the build-up to the toughest race of my life. With no intention of running into another stress fracture, I made sure that if I pushed my ageing bones then I gave them time to recover.

It meant instead of lining up at the start line for races that didn't fit with my plan, I could spend time with my family and support them at events of their own. Wilf didn't share my passion for running, but I admired the time and energy he invested in playing football for a local team. I enjoyed watching him from the touchline, and never stopped suggesting that a track session could improve his stamina, even if it did fall on deaf ears. While Ethel counted down to her eighteenth birthday, and the chance to enter long trail races, her mother stepped up her own ambitions. It's just that I was the last to find out.

'The South Downs Way 50 is a Centurion event,' I said, after I'd asked Emma about a day that was mysteriously blocked off in the calendar.

'Yes, I know,' she said. 'With cut-off times.'

'And you're OK with that?'

'No,' she freely admitted, 'but I've worked out a pace plan and hope I can stick to it.'

Despite the surprise, I really admired my wife for stepping up like this. As much as she enjoyed running, Emma had always considered herself to be limited by ability. Through lockdown, she had worked on her form and regularly ran with Ethel, but I never thought she would consider a race of this nature. The South Downs Way is a beautiful trail, but quite a roller coaster in terms of ascent and descent. It was only as I began to advise her on the best way to tackle some of the hills that I realised why she had kept it to herself.

'Just let me do this,' she said, having cut me off mid-sentence. 'I need to find my own way.'

'Can we come and support you?' I asked as Ethel appeared, having overheard our conversation.

Emma smiled at us both.

'I was hoping you would crew me,' she said.

Dropping Emma at Worthing College for the race start, on the cusp of what would be a gloriously clear and sunny spring day, I reminded myself just how nervous I had been ahead of my first ultra distance. I knew not to ask how she was feeling, or offer any advice. Still, when I saw Dimi lacing her shoes alongside her husband, who also wore a race number, I made an introduction. It just meant I knew that Emma would be in good care on the course if she needed it. I wasn't surprised when my offer to crew them both as well was politely declined. As a master in the art, Andrew was carrying enough provisions to see them to the finish line.

'Whatever happens,' I said to Emma before she set off, 'it takes courage to start.'

Emma looked ashen.

'Why am I doing this?'

'I ask myself the same thing every time,' I said. 'I still can't answer it.'

Privately, I anticipated that at some point in the race she'd miss a cut-off. Ethel shared the same view, and kept a close eye on the live online race tracker as we waited at the first checkpoint.

'Mum is still moving,' she said, as runners flowed by, including Dimi and her husband, who confirmed she was doing just fine.

As well as food and drink, we brought with us the canvas camping seat. Over time, it had become known as The Hundred Chair. With cup holders on each arm, and a deep, inviting backrest, I had grown to love flopping into it. Opinion is always divided among distance runners about sitting at crew points and aid stations in case you never get up again. Many see it as the mark of an amateur, but I was hardly going to upset my sponsors by resting my feet for a moment. When Emma appeared, however – working hard to keep to her set pace – she paused to refill her flasks, grabbed a sandwich from me and shook her head when I showed her the chair.

Throughout the day, as we drove from one checkpoint to the next, Emma gradually began to build a buffer against the cut-offs. It had been tight for a while, but she seemed to draw strength from finding herself with thirty minutes in hand, and then steadily extended that to just over an hour. Both Ethel and I agreed that it was a really impressive performance as well as quite a relief. With six miles to go, looking like every footstep was a conscious effort, Emma didn't even stop at the final crew point.

'You don't need us!' I joked, and crunched on the cheese straw she had declined.

'I do,' she called back over her shoulder.

With time on our hands before driving to the finish line in Eastbourne, and confident that Emma would now make it, Ethel and I decided to visit the coast beside the town. We left the South Downs basking in the afternoon sun, and parked in front of the cafe at Beachy Head. Ethel had never visited this stretch of cliffs before, which formed part of the course I had run on the coastal ultra when the Beast from the East blew in. Now, as we sauntered along a headland softened by wild flowers and grasses, that memory of freezing winds felt like it belonged to a different era. This long, tranquil day had yet to end, but in view of what Emma was set to achieve it felt close to perfect.

And then, in the near distance, a man who had been looking out to sea stepped off the cliff edge.

By the time we arrived outside the athletics track that marked the finish of the South Downs Way 50, Emma was just a mile away. We hadn't planned to cut it so fine, but then the clock felt like it had stopped abruptly one hour earlier. Ethel hadn't seen the man just drop out of sight, which was a small mercy, but I had. So too had the coastal ranger who had been seeking to talk him back from the edge, and also several bystanders who first raised the alarm and then witnessed him go. In the car, all the way into Eastbourne, I kept checking that Ethel was all right. She insisted that she hadn't seen anything, and appeared more concerned about me. I was fine, I told her, though life seemed incredibly precious just then.

Having positioned ourselves on the approach road to the stadium, it felt strange to reclaim some sense of normality by applauding runners ahead of their victory lap. These men and women had reached the end of a challenging journey, and we were here to celebrate. We saw Dimi run in, hand in hand with Andrew, and cheered as they passed through the entrance gates. Covid restrictions meant only the runners could enter, which led to supporters yelling encouragement over the fence in their wake. A few minutes later, as predicted by the tracking app that Ethel had been monitoring, her mother rounded the corner. With long shadows crossing the tarmac in front of her, she set eyes on us and a weight seemed to leave her shoulders. For someone who once doubted she could finish a parkrun, Emma had just discovered that she was capable of so much more than she imagined.

'This has to be one of the best days of my life!' she said on emerging from the stadium with a medal around her neck, and we laughed as she backtracked and added that marriage and childbirth ranked higher. 'It was really hard. At one point I just wanted to give up, but I didn't and that moment passed.'

'You did great,' said Ethel, while I suddenly found myself on the brink of tears.

'There's no way I could have done it without you two,' she continued, unaware that I had dropped back to wipe my eyes. 'In fact, all these guys were amazing.' Emma gestured at exhausted but elated finishers in the care of friends and family across the car park. 'I had no idea there'd be so much love and support out there.'

'Days like this bring out the best in everyone.' I said, thinking in the same breath that it was high time we went home. 'It's why we run.'

A few weeks after Emma finally climbed the stairs again without clinging to the banisters, I made my second attempt at the Thames Path 100. In contrast to her race, it was pouring with rain. With a two-hour window in which all competitors could start, which had become a feature of racing under Covid restrictions, I set out along the riverside path on my own. Raindrops hammered the surface of the water and pooled into puddles in front of me.

The forecast didn't look too positive, and yet I felt alive with every step. Emma's day had been memorable to me for several reasons, and now that became one motivating force. I didn't want to waste moments like this. Life was just too short. I would get out of it what I put into it, and I intended to give it everything I could to collect that one-day buckle at the end.

My approach this time was really very simple: *don't be a dick.* That meant going out steady, keeping on top of my fuel and hydration strategy, and not seeking reasons to mentally withdraw from the race. It could be easily done when fatigue kicked in, but this time I was determined to seize the day. I had trained constructively, and my head was in a good place. My crew were on hand to see me as far as Henley. Twenty miles upriver, I had even talked my trusted pacer into joining me.

My running clubmate, Emma, had taken a little persuading. I could've asked someone else, as she suggested. Given that she had all but hung up her pacing shoes the last time, I felt pretty bad about seeking to bring her on board one more time. I just felt she had come to understand me in a phase of the race when I wasn't at my best. She was good company, happy to run without talking too much, possessed a competitive streak and knew when to push when it mattered most. While I felt like I now had the experience to attempt 100 miles in twenty-four hours or less, I really needed her help.

Emma had listened to my pitch at her front door. Having promised her I wouldn't burn up by going out too urgently, she agreed on one condition. It amounted to one blunt but insightful phrase, and came to underpin my race outlook from the moment I set off.

I had a time in mind as the early morning downpour turned to blustery showers, but an awareness that I also had a very long way to run. So I just aimed to enjoy it, and when the clouds finally broke and the sun shone down, that felt like a bonus. I made friends along the way, minimised my time in The Hundred Chair but relished a moment off my feet, and pressed into the second half of the race as night fell with continued respect for the distance ahead.

'I'm not being a dick,' I promised my pacer when she called me in the early hours. 'I should be with you shortly.'

I had been flagging when my phone's ringtone cut into the silence. A low mist had settled across the fields under moonlight, which had become a playground for my imagination. While I was wondering whether my head torch was trained on another runner in front of me or a cyborg wearing groovy flares, I remained focused on the task in hand.

'You're doing really well,' Emma told me, though it sounded like a tone she might use on one of her children who had half finished their homework, 'but if you want this sub-twenty-four then now is the time for you to *run faster!*'

It was the alarm call I needed. Even though it had just gone two in the morning, I told myself that I had worked hard to get this far. Yes, I'd slipped into tired complacency for a short while, but it hadn't cost me too much time. And so at seventy miles I ran like it was a race, and it hurt, and that continued even after Emma collected me for the remaining quarter. If anything, she pushed me harder. I walked when I had to, and in the closing stages I had very little else left, but my pacer made sure those moments didn't control me. As soon as I said I needed to stop running, I'd have to negotiate when I'd start again based on some landmark up ahead. And so, as we agreed to resume at the next sign, hedge, gate or even a cow on one occasion, each break lasted no more than seconds.

As the sun came up and briefly transformed the river into a ribbon of fire, Emma stopped to take photos on the understanding that I continued running and she would catch me up. In short, she did exactly what I needed her to do while keeping a close eye on the time.

'It's going to be really tight,' she told me almost twenty-two hours in, 'but if we don't stop at the final aid station, we can make it.'

'I've had it,' I complained behind her. 'I'm not sure.'

'Yes, you are,' she said to correct me. 'Stay positive.'

A moment later, having checked her watch once more, Emma slowed to a walk.

'I've got my sums wrong,' she said. 'Matt, we're not going to make it. I'm really sorry.'

'That's fine,' I said, trying hard not to sound too relieved. 'It was worth a go.'

Emma said nothing. She just went back to her watch once more while I gave silent thanks that this ordeal was now over. We were well within the cut-off to just walk the rest of the way, I thought to myself. And maybe run for the photographer at the finish line.

'Wait!' she said, stopping in her tracks. 'I'm *not* wrong!'

'What?'

I sensed my heart sink.

'We can still do this! Come on! *Let's go!*'

Those closing kilometres were the most challenging I had ever run. Emma switched from imploring me to keep moving to simply feeding me the time we had left to complete the distance. Even though my head had gone, and my legs threatened to do likewise, I could still work out that we stood a chance of earning that one-day buckle.

Uploading a race of this length to Strava takes a little longer than normal. There's just a lot of data to process, including a seemingly endless list of segments. I wasn't in a big hurry to see the breakdown, having flopped over the finish line. The result on Centurion's official race clock was all that mattered to me, which confirmed that I had completed my first 100-mile ultramarathon seventeen minutes inside my dream time. Without a pacer to keep me focused, and on the limit towards the end, I would have fallen short. Eventually, when I scrolled through the Strava segments, I found that between two short points on the last leg of the Thames Path I had managed one of the fastest times of the day. It was a meaningless metric, of course, but a measure of how much I wanted to run 100 miles in under twenty-four hours. Even if it proved to be a once-in-a-lifetime achievement, that was fine by me.

'Thank you,' I said to Emma as we nursed cups of tea by the finish line. 'I think we're done now.'

'You're on your own,' she agreed. 'Even if they allowed pacers at the Dragon's Back, you can count me out.'

'Pacers aren't permitted,' I confirmed. 'And now I've got three months of hill training ahead of me. I don't suppose anyone from the club will be rushing to keep me company.'

We paused to watch a finisher come in with his poles aloft. I made a note of his shoes, as I had with almost every runner throughout the race, for that quest was far from over.

'I believe you can do this,' Emma said after a moment. 'But only if you stick to the strategy.'

17

THE HILLS HAVE EYES

As a runner, I always considered it unfortunate that we live at the highest point in the village. It means every single time I take off from home I have to finish with a hill climb. Whether I head out for a short burst on roads or a long trail session, there is only one way home. The lane leading up to our house doesn't exactly take me above the clouds. It's only about fifty metres of elevation across just over half a kilometre. Still, it's stupidly steep in sections and enough to get the legs and heart pumping. As I write, in fact, a cyclist has just pulled up outside to catch his breath. So many runners and riders stop at this spot that I sometimes think I should set up a refreshment stand to compensate for the endless sound of people dying outside my window.

Entering the second phase of my training for the Dragon's Back Race, my long-standing resentment of the hill softened considerably. In this neck of the woods, there are no brooding crags and snow-capped peaks on the horizon line. At best, the landscape could be described as 'rolling', and so I made the most of the climb on my doorstep.

On the upside, I could literally start my new regime of hill repeats outside the gate to my house. On the downside, I felt like I was going nowhere in more ways than one.

'It's good base training,' I said to Emma and Ethel on finishing one morning, 'I just can't help feeling that it's not enough.'

The concept of tyre-pulling as a means of training for ascent struck me as a blatant act of self-masochism. The additional weight and drag it provided also struck me as an effective means of loading the muscles required to power up hills. So I set out to make one. Having equipped myself with two eye bolts from the DIY store, a length of rope and a gym belt I could wear as a harness, I visited the local garage for the final piece of the puzzle.

'Do you have any old tyres?' I asked the mechanic, which was a formality given the pile in the corner.

'Take your pick,' he said breezily. 'What size did you have in mind?'

This was something I hadn't considered. I also wasn't busting to tell him why I wanted one.

'Nothing like a tractor tyre,' I said. 'And definitely not from a lorry.'

'How many inches?' he asked as if that would be more helpful.

It wasn't.

'Six?' I said, guessing wildly, and then doubled it when he laughed.

'How does fourteen sound?' he asked on picking his way through the assorted rubber behind him.

'Perfect,' I lied, resigned to anything he rolled out for me.

Having strung all the components together, and undertaken a very short test run across the patio, my homemade tyre-pull felt good. As it turned out, the mechanic had made a decent choice. It required some effort to haul behind me, but not enough for my eyeballs to pop from my sockets.

The biggest challenge it presented, I discovered, came from going public.

'That looks ridiculous,' observed Ethel as I prepared for my debut on the lane.

'I am aware,' I said, locking off the belt. 'Do you want to try it out?'

'Absolutely not,' she said, but followed me out anyway so she could capture the moment on her phone camera.

When it came to passing cars, I just kept my head down. It wasn't difficult given the effort that the climb demanded. What I couldn't ignore were the villagers out walking their dogs. In the same way, given the spectacle and the awful rasp of rubber on tarmac, they couldn't ignore me.

'Morning!' I said brightly, seeking to own the moment, but it did nothing to stop the comments.

A week passed before I stopped feeling like some massive try-hard. For one thing, I could appreciate the benefit. The muscles in my legs burned after the first few sessions, but slowly it felt like a decent pay-off. Within a month, I gave up feeling self-conscious, pretended to laugh at the same old jokes about looking worn, and just sought to style it out.

'People are talking,' said Emma.

'Not for much longer,' I told her, and shared my intention to graduate from the lane and escalate my hill training to the South Downs.

Every weekend, accompanied by Sprint instead of a tyre, I drove to the foot of the steepest, most technical chalk path I could find. It was a good couple of kilometres to the top, followed by a long roll down a flint-strewn farm track. While the ascents burned my quads, I found the descents to be equally intense. Mostly this was down to the demands on my vision in placing my feet as I barrelled downhill. Essentially, all the rapid eye movement just made me feel unsteady. When I did finally stack it, gouging all the skin off my palms, I tried to tell myself it was progress.

'I won't do that again,' I told Sprint, who had just made impatient noises as I washed the blood from my hands in a puddle.

The tumble was a setback. Not to my hill training but my ongoing search for the ultimate shoes. I had brought an old pair out of retirement, with a view to replacing them with the latest model. I liked them because they were lightweight, but the lack of lug had let me down. At least that's what I told myself as I struck them from the shortlist. In truth, I needed to practise my descents over difficult ground within the limitations that the wonky gyroscope in my head could handle.

Throughout the summer, I anticipated that I would feel increasingly nervous. Pre-race jitters are natural, I think. As a runner, it's a sign that you're taking things seriously. On a Friday night before parkrun, I had been known to lie in the bath with my eyes closed while I visualised the course. Some might say that's taking things too far, and indeed my entire family mocked me for it, but it just helped me to feel ready and then relax.

This time, I had far more than five kilometres to consider. It wasn't just the distance or the terrain but the logistics involved in preparing for a six-day race. Arriving at camp at the end of each day, competitors would be given medical attention if required and then allocated a space in a tent for eight. A field canteen offered supper and breakfast, providing we brought our own plate and utensils and washed up after ourselves. Beyond that we were on our own. Everything a runner needed for the duration had to fit in a regulation-issue dry bag. As this would magically reappear at the next camp, thanks to the army of behind-the-scenes volunteers, it had to come in under fifteen kilograms for the sake of practical transportation. With no aid stations throughout the race, we were also each permitted a small re-supply bag that would be waiting for us at the halfway checkpoint. Restricted to 2.5 kilograms, we could fill it with provisions from our main bag, drop it off at the start and then dream of diving into it all morning. For those who survived the whole day, the bag would be returned to us at the finish line, where we would duly repeat the whole process.

Combined with all the stuff we had to run with, it was a lot to take in. I certainly didn't want to mess up in the mountains, and after my recce weekend in Wales I came home with a to-do list that had doubled in length. Much of this was down to *admin*. As a trail term, I had picked it up from Joe, Kate and the RAW Adventures crew. It had nothing to do with filing on the move, but seemed to cover all aspects of a competitor's race apart from the actual running. From checking my bearings on a regular basis to making sure I zipped into my sleeping bag nice and dry at night having prepared to move out efficiently at first light, I needed to be on top of everything at all times.

Increasingly, I had to make a conscious effort to believe in my own preparations. As the weeks ticked by, my fear of tackling Crib Goch all over again became overshadowed by the risk of minor oversights in my packing that could lead to major problems for me at any point between the two castles. With so much ground to cover, I realised a lot could go wrong. Unlike a 10K, it wasn't just a question of popping a gel in the back pocket of my shorts and hoping for the best. I very much doubted anyone could just rock up at a race like the Dragon's Back and expect to wing it. This wasn't about running fast, though no doubt it helped at the sharp end. It was about being organised.

I decided this should begin at home, and designated a sofa bed upstairs to assemble everything I required for the week. Much of it was mandatory, which was straightforward because I couldn't question whether I needed it. My worries, I discovered, came from reading the Facebook community page to see what everyone else was packing. In a rising state of anxiety, I didn't want to dismiss anything and then discover it to be vital.

'What is that?' asked Wilf as I unboxed what was perhaps my most questionable panic-buy.

'Sniper tape,' I told him with a poker face. 'As a precaution.'

My son shot me a look.

'What are you doing in Wales again?'

While the tape was intended for bolstering the grip on gunstocks, a runner in the group had sworn it was invaluable for strapping rips and tears in shoes and rucksacks. Further research told me it could also protect hammered toes in an emergency, and on that basis I figured I couldn't be without it. I already had a roll of elastic tape, but what if that didn't stretch to saving my race? Now I had the sniper tape in my hands. Apart from the camouflage print, which made me cringe, it didn't look much different from the civilian counterpart. Unless I planned on arming myself for this race, it suddenly seemed less than essential.

As I resisted the urge to swap out cereal bars for some supercharged snack that appeared to be the choice of everyone else but me, I was at least decisive with one aspect of my kit. Granted, it had taken me the best part of six months, but after reading every blog and watching all the video reviews, I selected my running shoes for the race. Inov-8 are a British outfit with a fell-running pedigree. I'd worn their shoes in the past and crucially they had never given me blisters. I knew there were no guarantees when it came to running for a week in Wales, but my chosen pair from the X-Talon range were grippy on wet rock and along muddy trails when I tested them out. They also drained fast enough to head off a meltdown on my part when it came to wet feet.

My masterstroke, or so I thought, was to create space for a secondary pair of shoes that were more suited for the longer tarmac section as the race evolved. This would be my first pair of Altras. I chose a model that boasted more cushioning than a nightclub VIP section. The clincher for me was

Altra's foot-shaped toe box. Even though it looked a little bit like I was rocking hooves, they felt incredibly comfortable. Through packing, weighing, ruthless jettisoning and then repacking, I had mined enough space in my big bag to bring them along for the ride. Then I discovered online that almost half the field had pursued the same two-pair strategy. It left me feeling less like a running genius, but at least helped me to believe I was beginning to make decent judgements.

When it came to everyday conversation at home, however, it seemed the blinkers had come down.

'Can we please talk about something else?' asked Emma one day when I showed her a function on my watch that I had previously overlooked. 'There is more to life than the Dragon's Back.'

'You're right,' I said, but by then it felt like everything else was on hold. 'So, do you think socks with a liner might cut the chances of blisters?'

While I still had some time to continue panic buying, Ethel turned eighteen. In celebrating her milestone year, she entered that year's edition of Race to the King.

'I'm just going to run a half and see how I feel,' she said, before crossing the start line alone and then sailing past her first target, as her parents had foreseen.

'Are you sure you want to continue?' I asked her at the marathon mark. It was a fifty-two-mile race in total, and I wasn't sure she fully appreciated how much further she had to run. 'Do you feel OK?'

'I feel fine,' she said, and somewhat sickeningly looked that way as well.

Later that afternoon, five miles out from the finish, Ethel encountered her only wobble in the race. She didn't get emotional. I did. I was just so proud of her. She'd set herself this challenge on her own terms, and seen it through with remarkable poise and determination. I was a little unnerved by the fact that the support point happened to be at the same place where I had passed my team on the 100-mile relay before disappearing into club infamy. Ethel encountered no such navigational issues, and cruised home to collect her first ultramarathon medal at an age when I was busy dropping shots into pints of cider.

In the run up to the race, Ethel had kept her plans to herself. She knew I'd worry that it was a long way to run at her age, and then feel like somehow I had drawn her into it. A fiercely independent young woman, Ethel had trained responsibly and prepared without drama.

'You should follow in your daughter's footsteps,' said Emma after the event.

'I'm not sure I could keep up,' I said, but I took her point on board.

Things became progressively easier once I placed a tick beside the last line on my checklist. With my two bags packed and weighed, in the week before the race, I felt like I could put the practicalities behind me. I didn't stop feeling keyed up, of course, but having worked through a preparation plan on paper I could afford to relax.

In reality, I knew that the chance of me adopting a Zen-like calm ahead of the Dragon's Back Race was about as likely to happen as finding myself at the top of the timesheets throughout the following week. Nevertheless, this was my opportunity to taper. I had been dropping my distance and running intensity over the final three weeks until I was left with nothing but dog walks for seven days. I recognised the importance of allowing my body to rest and recharge. The older I became, the more I appreciated what a difference it could make.

Physically, the taper can only help to deliver a runner to the start line in the best condition. The inbuilt flaw in this universally recognised strategy is the fact that it completely does your head in at a time when you need to feel relaxed. We all know the benefits of running for our mental health, and yet just as we're facing a stress-inducing challenge we go and wind it down. Having gone cold turkey from the trails in the previous week, I was left practically climbing the walls with anxiety.

'You don't need to repack,' Ethel suggested from the doorway. 'Not again.'

'It makes me feel better,' I said thinly.

'Why don't you take Sprint for a walk?'

'I've only just come back from the last one,' I said, pausing to count the electrolyte sachets in my race vest to cover me for the first morning. The number hadn't changed since the last time I checked the night before. 'I'll give him half an hour.'

'Dad,' she said, sitting on the edge of the bed now, 'you'll be fine. You've done the work. You just need to remind yourself of that. Then go out to enjoy it. Whatever happens, you can say you did your best. Nothing else matters.'

I zipped up the pocket and took a step back. For such a young woman, Ethel had a wise runner's head on her shoulders. While I kept rushing to repack, she had spent the week quietly gathering her things to begin her first year at university. By the time my race was over, she would be gone.

'That walk,' I said, mindful that Emma and Wilf might also want to stretch their legs. 'I'm sure Sprint will be delighted if we all take him out.'

'He's as twitchy as you right now,' agreed Ethel.

'Dogs are strange like that. It's as if they have a sixth sense.'

'No they don't!' Ethel laughed. 'It's just he hasn't been for a run all week.'

PART

4

18

NO SLEEP 'TIL SNOWDONIA

In terms of organisation alone, the Dragon's Back Race is a beast. I had been so caught up in my preparations that I didn't stop to consider how much behind-the-scenes work it would take to stage a six-day mountain ultra-marathon for close to 400 runners along the spine of an entire country. Only when I arrived outside the registration marquee, which was grand enough to stage a circus, did I come to appreciate the sheer scale of the undertaking.

'I've got that first-day-at-big-school feeling,' I told Emma, who had driven down with me to watch the beginning of the race. 'And not just because I'm wearing a cap and shorts.'

The marquee was located under the great walls of Conwy Castle. Inside, an army of event staff and volunteers at a production line of tables were busily processing race entrants. I watched as they bussed each hopeful from one station to the next; handing out numbers and course maps in turn, strapping GPS locators to race vests, attaching electronic checkpoint check-in tags – or dibbers – around wrists and inspecting items of mandatory kit. Finally, each competitor filed past a photographer for a mugshot that would be used for the live race tracker. Some runners grinned. Others stood like they were facing execution.

'Are you ready?' asked Emma.

I picked up my bag. Packed, weighed, lightened, repacked and finally locked down, this top-loaded cylinder of heavy-duty fabric looked and felt like it should be strung from the rafters of a boxing gym.

'Ready as I'll ever be,' I said while attempting to anchor my smaller resupply bag under one arm.

'You can relax once you're done here,' she said. 'How's the toe?'

On Friday evening, I had completed the final task on my to-do list. My plan had been to get everything signed off so that I could just enjoy my last day with the family. All I had to do was slip my compass into the pocket of my race vest, which was hanging from the back of my office chair. All afternoon, I had been preparing the vest with everything I would need to hand, and this was the final piece of the puzzle. I had crossed the floor in bare feet, distracted in part by what a good job I had done, only to smash my middle toe into the chair leg.

The pain was intense, not just physically but in terms of the immediate anguish I felt in terms of the possible consequences. That night, unable to put weight on that foot without drawing the air between my teeth, I had gone to bed hating myself.

'I don't think it's broken,' my eldest daughter and newly qualified doctor had advised me during a face-to-toe videoconference with her the next morning. The digit in question was angry and swollen, but the joint seemed intact, as did my decision not to worry her about my impending week in the mountains. 'Just be brave, Dad, and make sure you rest.'

I didn't feel that courageous as I filed through registration. With my glasses fogging thanks to my face mask as I dragged my bags from one desk to the next, I just felt harassed and out of sorts. I attempted a smile for the camera like I'd just been coached in how to do it for the first time in my life, and then moved on to the bag weigh-in. This was the moment that had been playing on my mind throughout the journey from West Sussex to Wales. The main bag was limited to fifteen kilograms. Anything over that would have to go. Having spent way too much time reducing the content to within a few grams of the limit, I handed it over to the lady with the scales and waited nervously for the numbers to settle.

'Thirteen point two kilograms,' she said, upon which the breath I'd been holding spilled forth with a declaration of complete surprise. 'You're travelling light.'

'That can't be right,' I said, like this was a competition or something.

I had sacrificed vital food supplies in my bid to comply. I had also purchased the cheapest hand-held travel scales I could find online, though it didn't stop me from asking if she might just weigh it again.

'You can take them away to fill up,' she suggested instead, having complied with my request only to reach the same results, and then determined that my drop bag was also on the lighter side.

For a moment, I considered rushing around Conwy to see what I could find. It was getting late in the afternoon, however, and my troublesome toe had already furnished my day with enough stress.

'It's fine,' I said, thanking her anyway. 'I'll survive.'

That evening, following a mass race briefing in the tent that did little to settle my nerves, I sat on the harbour wall beside Emma and ate what felt like my last supper.

'Apparently we're all at high risk of picking up ticks,' I told her, reflecting on the points that had stuck in my mind as I toyed with my fish and chips. 'We're encouraged to help each other remove them. Only last time some guy got one on his todger.'

With her plastic fork in hand, Emma turned to face me.

'You don't have to do this, Matt.'

'I know,' I said, and then paused for a moment. 'Let's just hope tick season is over.'

'I mean this whole race,' said Emma. 'You're all out of your minds, but I can see it takes courage just to get here.'

I picked at my chips. My appetite had left me at lunchtime.

'It's been twelve months in the making,' I said. 'This doesn't feel like the start of a long race. If anything, it's the end.'

As soon as we had sat down, we expected to be descended upon by seagulls. Instead, a couple of fledglings looked on from a distance but chose to leave us in peace. I offered them a chip and binned what I had left. I just couldn't face a big meal. All I wanted to do was head for the hotel with Emma, close the door on the world and try to clear my thoughts.

That night, staring at the ceiling, I resigned myself to the fact that I wasn't going to get much sleep. While Emma's breathing had told me she was out just minutes after the light, I lay awake with the enormity of what lay ahead squatting on my chest. My race vest hung from the rail beside the kettle. All night, a green light on the GPS locator had been flashing sedately as if in some kind of sleep mode. Just as I was drifting off, it began to flicker madly. As well as the tick story, we had been warned at the briefing that accidently pressing the emergency button on this box of tricks would summon all manner of rescue services, and should only be used in extreme cases.

Naturally, I worried that somehow it had pressed itself.

At any moment, I thought in a stew, I would hear beating rotor blades as a rescue helicopter descended out of the night sky and into the hotel car park. Had I somehow fallen asleep and sleepwalked my way into mischief? It was enough to leave me wide awake with worry. Even though I told myself that all the boxes were probably in the process of being primed remotely, ready for the race, I couldn't help thinking that the seemingly random blinks made up a Morse code to alert the organisers to an imposter.

It was just one of those nights where it seemed like sleep would never arrive. Like so many runners ahead of a race, I probably got a few hours without realising, only to awake shortly before my clock was scheduled to go off in a natural state of alarm. By the time Emma opened her eyes, I was showered, standing in front of the mirror in my shorts, carefully applying strips of zinc tape to my nipples.

'Morning,' I said, concentrating hard. 'For the chafing. Not that I get it, but y'know … '

Emma groaned, which may or may not have been related to this breaking early-morning news.

'How are you feeling?'

I pulled my shirt on and turned to face her. There was no need for me to answer.

Conwy Castle is an imposing medieval fortress built on a rock promontory. Huge curtain walls and towers loom large over the harbour and the town's narrow streets. As well as being a big tourist attraction, the ruins within have offered a dramatic start to a legendary mountain ultramarathon since its inaugural edition in 1992. Having struggled to find the main entrance, which didn't bode well with regard to my navigation skills, I followed a clutch of runners up a flight of steps to be ushered onwards by yet more cheery and highly efficient volunteers and members of the team. After several twists and turns along stone passages, I joined a steadily growing throng inside the castle courtyard.

Despite the presence of several hundred runners, it was as quiet as the prelude to a church service.

Family and friends lined the battlements above. As the space continued to fill, I looked up in the hope of seeing Emma. She had thrown me out of the car on a road with waiting restrictions, which appeared to apply to the whole of the town. Such a hasty goodbye wasn't quite what I'd had in mind ahead of such a massive undertaking. I really wanted to see her again before I set off.

'Are you looking for the emergency exit?'

I turned to find a runner with a banana in one hand and a clear need to lighten the moment.

'I think it's too late for that,' I said, for by now we were all facing in the same direction behind the starting gantry.

There was only one way out.

I glanced at my watch. With minutes to go before the race commenced on the hour, I closed my eyes and just sought to relax. Reaching this point had taken me more than a year, I realised now. In some ways it had begun when I first joined my dad to the end of the pavement. Back then, there was no way in the world I could have imagined my running journey would bring me to this moment. It had been difficult to conceive when I first entered this event. Throughout my training, I had questioned what I was doing. Even now, I knew full well that I was about to set out on a race that was very possibly beyond my abilities. I didn't have to ask anyone around me to find out if they shared the same outlook. Apart from a handful of athletes on the front row, everyone here was lined up on the edge of the metaphorical pool facing bottomless and shark-infested waters.

Despite feeling completely out of my depth, I had ticked every box on my training schedule. I had learnt from setbacks and mistakes. I had grown stronger from the experience of pushing how far I could go as a runner. Not just in terms of distance but elevation, self-navigation and even mountain survival. It had brought me the confidence to move out of my comfort zone, and though I was hardly cool, calm and collected, I was quite clear in my mind that I had prepared for this moment to the best of my abilities.

'Welcome, everybody, to the Dragon's Back Race ... '

From the battlements in front of the start line, the race director prepared to send the runners into the wild. Shane Ohly might look like he'd prepare you a fine double shot, cold-foam frappuccino, but beneath the man bun and indecently youthful exterior is a vastly experienced mountain runner and adventurer with an unsurpassable reputation as an ultramarathon impresario. I had no doubt we were in capable hands. At the same time, this was a race that demanded complete self-sufficiency across remote and wild terrain. It wasn't just a question of running without the comfort of signage or food laid out at aid stations. From the start to the finish of each day, every assist had been stripped away.

As Shane began the countdown, and was quickly accompanied by every runner and supporter in the castle grounds, I had never felt more alone.

I took a step forward, along with everyone else, looking up at the eastern battlement before the momentum took me under the start gantry. Against a clear and brightening sky, a line of spectators waved us off. Many were swinging huge flags to represent every nationality in the field. I cupped my hand to my brow, scanning what was just a parade of silhouettes as the early morning sun strengthened over the wall.

In the weeks leading to this moment, I had been studying the forecast. Conditions had spun from wet to fair and windy, like some meteorological fruit machine, before slowly settling on warm conditions. It wasn't ideal, but I had always banked on the weather in Wales working in my favour. Even if we couldn't expect fog and drizzle, I told myself before spotting a familiar figure waving at me, a clement day would at least bring out the best in the landscape. I raised my hand at Emma to register that I had seen her. It was heartening to catch sight of my wife as I crossed the line, even if it was just a glimpse in view of the menacing glare from behind her.

19

INTO THE FIRE

No matter what the distance, my race nerves always take a while to settle. Whether it's the first few minutes of a Saturday morning around the park or the opening miles of a marathon, it can feel like I've forgotten how to run. Every footfall feels like a conscious effort, while my heart rate and breathing send strong messages to my brain that this is not what they would consider to be a state of flow. It all calms down in due course, as it did on that Monday morning as a caravan of runners climbed the foothills out of Conwy into the Carneddau mountain range.

'You don't see this from the office window,' said a guy just ahead of me. He gestured across at the band of haze where the land met the ocean.

I glanced across, but frankly the terrain was my central focus. We were following a narrow path across a steep slope, deep set in heather and gorse. In such a close succession of runners, and with an unpredictable camber, I was finding that my eyes had to work hard to keep my balance. On several occasions I had to spread my arms to keep myself from tipping too far, which simply served to remind me that I couldn't allow myself to be distracted.

The ground took priority in terms of my attention. At the same time, I made sure I glanced regularly at the map on my watch. I had prepared myself to check the route but frankly it was evident from the number of runners stretching towards the next summit in the range. The climbs weren't steep here, but each one felt like a slog. We were free to pick our own lines from one checkpoint to the next, and sure enough a handful of runners were fanning out here and there, hoping to save time wherever they could. This early in the race, I didn't have the confidence to leave the recommended route, and yet I continued to pay close attention to the only other data field that accompanied the map on my watch. I wasn't interested in distance. I knew that I faced forty-nine kilometres and also 3,800 metres of elevation. As long as I stayed on course, I just had to take on whatever lay in front of me.

What concerned me was the elapsed time.

As I registered at one checkpoint after another, slotting the dibber around my wristband into a box of tricks, I had noticed that I wasn't pulling away from the cut-offs as much as I had liked. To begin with, I put this down to course congestion. Early on, we'd had to queue on a summit to take our turn clocking in, and yet even as the pack began to spread I found myself building only a very small advantage. We had fifteen hours available to complete the first day. This had been reduced by an hour from previous editions, which meant the two mandatory cut-offs en route – at the midway support point and before the Snowdon Horseshoe – were tightened accordingly. It didn't seem like much on paper, but I felt it on the ground. It just meant I had to keep moving as efficiently as I could, from ascending and descending without faffing to running at every opportunity.

As a result, as the sun continued to strengthen, I found myself becoming uncomfortably hot and bothered.

I was carrying two litres of water in four soft flasks, which needed to last me to the midway point where I could refill. At the briefing, we had been encouraged to use mountain streams wisely. I was just aware from reading accounts by race veterans that on this first day such water sources were practically non-existent, so I had worked out a routine in my head. While I hadn't anticipated that heat would be a burning issue, I knew how important it was to keep sipping from my flasks and eating from the range of food packed in the pockets of my race vest.

I might have been dressed like a mountain runner, but in my head I felt more like an airline pilot in the cockpit. Mentally, I had panels of levers, buttons and dials in front of me, but so long as I stayed on top of it all the plane would effectively fly itself.

As the morning progressed, so the landscape became increasingly challenging. The climbs turned steeper and the drops on the other side sharp enough to be race-ending with one misplaced step. The paths also became less defined, eventually giving way to an elevated landscape of shattered rock. Here, I switched from running to hopping, skipping and jumping. While I made sure that I took every step with a purpose, the humidity and temperature continued to rise.

'This isn't Wales,' said a woman I had been running alongside for a short while. 'It would be great if I could book this for my holiday, but not for a run.'

'It can't get much warmer,' I said, keen to sound positive.

By now, I had almost worked through the two bottles in the chest pockets of my race vest. Aware that I also needed to fuel this undertaking, I pulled out a bag of banana chips. I placed one in my mouth, only to spit it out a minute later as I pressed on.

It had only been a momentary feeling, but I was all too familiar with what it meant. My appetite just wasn't there. While compensating for my balance issues could still leave me feeling a little sick on long runs, this was different.

Seeking to keep calm, I told myself that it was basically a sign that I hadn't quite been drinking enough in conditions that were shaping up to be one step ahead of me. I'd followed my plan. I just hadn't modified it for the rising temperature. Having been defeated by heat on my second attempt at the North Downs Way 100, I knew it wasn't something I could ignore. So, I finished what little water was left in the first two flasks, and then used the opportunity to swap them with the full ones I was carrying. As I swung the vest from my shoulders, however, I realised that my back was slick with sweat.

In the cockpit of my plane, several dials in front of me showed unusual readings. It was nothing to panic about, I told myself, and promptly began to do just that.

Problem-solving on the move is one aspect of ultrarunning that I find quite challenging. I'm quick to register an issue. It's just when I'm against the clock I tend to stew over my options and prioritise progress rather than act decisively. In this case, while trying to focus on my footing across technical terrain, I realised I needed to add a sachet of electrolyte powder to the water in one of the replacement flasks. I just worried that stopping would cost me time I couldn't afford to lose.

Another ten minutes passed before I decided to address the issue on the move. Having fumbled around for a powder sachet, I unscrewed the lid of the soft flask in my chest pocket and instantly came to regret it. With much of my precious water slopped down my front, I poured in the electrolyte and hoped it might still be drinkable.

It wasn't.

One sip of the rich, concentrated fluid told me that if I tried any more in my current condition I'd probably bring it straight back up again. All I could do was take a slug of water from the other flask and then attempt an in-mouth dilution process. I was just over twenty kilometres into a 240-kilometre race, and in trouble. The sun continued to intensify as we plugged on, raising the temperature beyond anything I had anticipated. By the time we approached midday, I clearly wasn't alone in finding the heat to be a serious challenge.

'I'd been looking forward to my lunch,' grumbled a guy just ahead of me. We had just left behind the mountain plateau to begin a long descent to the checkpoint where our drop bags awaited us. 'Not any more.'

In the valley below, as we picked our way around and over rocky out-crops, drop steps and tussocks, I could see the layby car park that served as our midway destination. That the checkpoint gazebos were shimmering in a heat haze didn't bode well. From up high, and several kilometres away, the reservoir in front of it looked more inviting. I was sweltering and on the edge of feeling sick. Despite knowing that I needed to cool off, I couldn't see how that was possible. The reservoir was clearly out of bounds for that sort of thing. Just then, the vast expanse of water felt like it was taunting us all.

A moment later, as I ran through my mental checklist, it occurred to me that I hadn't taken a salt capsule since switching over my bottles. I had been so caught up with the mess I'd made trying to add a powder that I'd just completely overlooked the one measure I'd come to rely on to keep me ticking over in these conditions. I had planned on taking one capsule every hour, and though it was an inexact science I was certainly paying a price for the oversight.

As my inner pilot finally registered that a red light was blinking, I scrambled to react. Even so, I found it a struggle to swallow just one capsule. Before braving another, fearing it might come back up, I focused on trying to get into some kind of rhythm as I descended this endless, technical mountain flank. Flustered and annoyed at myself, the basic pillars behind my hydration strategy just fell apart. I glanced at my watch, and then decided to just forget the timings and proceed on instinct. If I couldn't rely on my brain with everything going on around me, I simply needed to listen to my body and do what I could to stop it from suffering any further in these conditions.

'Just don't be a dick,' I reminded myself out loud. 'From now on.'

While the checkpoint was at hand, where I could at least stop for a few minutes and regroup, I felt no sense of relief. The gazebos offered some shade, but space was at a premium. With so many runners squeezed under the canopy, most looking utterly baked, I just had to join the overflow and stay out in the sun. By now, the heat was proving both relentless and inescapable. What seriously troubled me, however, was the sight of those pressing on with the next stage of the race. For the car park wasn't just located off a road that skirted a long reservoir but at the base of a gigantic mountain. The foothills rose up into three formidable fins that looked unscalable at a glance. Then I set eyes on a path up this colossus, exposed to the full force of the sun, and noted what looked like a caravan of ants picking their way towards the summit.

'How is it going?' asked a volunteer marshal as I dropped into a blade of thin shade cast by one of the feather flags.

'Great,' I lied before resting my head in my hands. 'I just need a moment.'

Inside my drop bag, I had prepared everything I needed to fuel me to the finish line of this first day: a calorie-packed, vacuum-sealed pack of vegetarian chilli and a pot of pineapple chunks in coconut water. I didn't even dare think about the chilli, while I forced down the fruit one miserable chunk after another. I told myself I could not leave until I'd finished a whole flask of water, which I did in a hurry because one of the crew was helpfully calling out the time to cut-off. I had about twenty minutes in hand, but it didn't seem like much given the climb I faced. So, feeling even more sick than when I arrived, I gathered my stuff and pressed on.

Tryfan, as the mountain is called, is Welsh for 'absolute bastard'. It isn't really, but that felt appropriate as I joined the convoy of overcooked competitors. To the sound of retching from above and below, and in suffocating heat, I marched onwards and upwards in what felt like slow motion. At just over 900 metres high, it took an age to get within eyeshot of the summit. Along the way, I had joined the club in losing my lunch, and flopped off the path a couple of times just to seek out some shade and squeeze down a few drops from my bottle. When the ordeal finally ended, my race strategy had boiled down to not dying of heatstroke while hoping I could achieve just one objective. I had until five o'clock to reach the all-important checkpoint before the final assault of the day around the Snowdon Horseshoe. I just had no idea how far I had to go to reach it.

With such a long and miserable ascent behind me, something that should have taken at least half the time in cooler conditions, I was determined to put in some running where possible. Even though it came in fits and bursts, along with yet more throwing up, scrambling and clambering over giant rises, I knew that I had to keep moving. The terrain was tough, but no surprise. It was the heat that simply drained me. I felt about as poached as I had the last time the sun came out to play with me during an ultramarathon. The only difference was that all the climbs on this race had been cranked up to close to vertical. Despite it all, I just could not entertain the idea of crashing out within hours of getting underway. I had been preparing for just so long. It had occupied my thoughts, alone and with my family, and I had committed to a training regime throughout that time in order to turn this undertaking from a terrifying prospect to a realistic challenge.

If I could just get through this freakishly slow-roasted day, I told myself, I would have a chance to reset overnight and go again.

The bus stop, youth hostel, cafe and car park at Pen y Pass represent an unassuming gateway to the mighty geological formation beyond. The Snowdon Horseshoe comprises rugged peaks and ridges, including the indecently airy ridge of Crib Goch, the summit of the highest mountain in Wales and a formidable monolith called Y Lliwedd. By the time I arrived at the roadside checkpoint ahead of this final, mighty section of the day, I was in no doubt that I had to cool down, hydrate and eat at any cost. I had touched nothing but tinned fruit since lunchtime, and even that was left on the mountainside. If I simply punched in with the electronic key around my wrist and then clambered to the foot of the great knife-edged band of rock that I had been dreading for so long, I knew I'd never make it. I was hot, weak, nauseous, short of breath and dizzy. In that moment, as a marshal hurried me into the checkpoint from a long and challenging descent, along with a straggle of sun-dried runners, I felt like my brain and body were running separate races. I was committed to reaching the finish line to the south of the Horseshoe. On a day when the heat had left me for dead, however, I didn't have the energy to carry me up there.

'You have ten minutes until cut-off,' the marshal announced to the new arrivals, and then kindly offered to refill my flasks. I accepted, despite doubting that I could keep a sip down. 'You're not alone,' he said on turning the tap. 'Just over 100 runners have dropped out already.'

'What?' The number took me by complete surprise. It was far higher than I had imagined, and also hardened my resolve not to add to the toll. 'How long have I got left?' I asked, aware that he could've interpreted that to mean my time on earth rather than what remained of my fifteen hours to reach the finish line at the end of day one.

The marshal swung his attention towards the looming edifice of rock beyond the foothills on the other side of the road. In the fierce afternoon light, Crib Goch and the mountain peak behind it possessed an air of absolute supremacy over the landscape.

'It's nearly five o'clock,' he said. 'Course closes at ten.'

'How far away is the finish line?'

'Just over 10K.'

It didn't sound like much, but then I was hardly facing a straightforward sprint from here.

'Do I have enough time?'

The marshal handed me my flasks in turn.

'Only one way to find out,' he said, and then appeared to remind himself of something. 'The bar inside sells ice creams,' he told me. 'If you're quick.'

Despite his grizzled beard, and my dry, cracked lips, I could've kissed him. The water in my flasks did not appeal to me, but just then I would've remortgaged my house for the prospect of a lolly on a stick.

Very shortly afterwards, carrying not just a Solero but also a bottle of ginger beer from the fridge behind the bar, I flopped into a meagre band of shade under the wall on the other side of the road. There, I embarked on a last-ditch effort to salvage my race. To the sound of the runner beside me retching convulsively on to the hot tarmac, I savoured that ice cream and drained the bottle dry. The effect was miraculous. I gave myself thirty seconds to be sure my stomach wasn't going to mount an insurrection. Then I clambered to my feet and left the checkpoint with renewed determination. I refused to be timed out on this day. Even if it killed me.

20

UNDER THE STARS

At the beginning of the race, as we climbed away from the castle, it had been hard to find much space on the trail. Now, that file of runners had thinned considerably. I could still see competitors ahead, and when I glanced over my shoulder I spotted several others following some way behind. It just served to remind me of the attrition rate. In this heat, even before the most challenging final section of the day, almost one third of the field had gone. Frankly, it sounded like carnage. With my hopes recharged by a lolly and a cold soft drink, I swore to myself that I would make every effort not to add to that statistic.

Approaching the giant rock stack at the head of Crib Goch, I was relieved to find myself in shade. We were heading towards six o'clock in the evening. It was still unbearably hot, and yet the shadows were beginning to lengthen at last. In my mind, I told myself this was my opportunity to stop feeling sorry for myself and push.

'Come on, Matt,' I muttered as the ascent demanded that I use my hands as well as my feet. 'Just get this done.'

During tough times on the trail, I never normally had an open word with myself. All the swearing and self-loathing I conducted in my head. This time, conditions had been so challenging and cut-offs so fiendishly tight that I also hadn't spoken much to anyone. Beyond the odd shared comment or curse about the heat, most runners had simply strapped into their own thoughts and got on with the fight on their own terms. Now, I felt like I needed to hear from someone so I didn't feel so alone.

Having scaled this infamous wall once before, I knew exactly what was in store at the top. On my first visit to Crib Goch, I had crossed in a slow-moving state of terror. With time running out, however, I couldn't afford to let nerves get the better of me. With this in mind, my inner coach took over the conversation. There was no play in my voice. I wasn't fooling around. Every time I reached for a handhold and then hauled myself upwards, a voice ruled out any thought of quitting. I didn't look down on my clamber towards the 900-metre mark. Nor did I pause to catch my breath. With the sugar hit subsiding from my brief stop at the checkpoint, it would not be long before I returned to a state of waking death.

Since setting off from the last checkpoint, I had tentatively sipped at my flasks as if fearing they might poison me. Having managed to hold down the ginger beer, thanks to a rest stop I couldn't afford to repeat, I was scared that gulping down the volume of fluid I really needed risked undoing that good work. As I began to feel the heat sickness returning, it seemed like the only effective cure lay just beyond the finish line for that day.

At the eastern summit of Crib Goch, as the ridge came into view, I climbed back up into sunlight now shining horizontally from the opposite horizon. The sky was infinitely clear, while the world stretched out in every direction under an early evening haze. There was not a breath of wind in the air. For a moment, it felt like I had just ascended into a higher plain of existence. The checkpoint box was the next thing to seize my attention. I punched in with one minute to spare, confirming my arrival on the ridge. Then, feeling strikingly calm after calling on my last reserves to get here, I spread my arms and stood tall.

A razor's edge of rock, some 200 metres in length, stretched out in front of my feet. It dipped towards the middle before curving and rising towards the pinnacle I knew that I would have to face again. On my first visit here, I had inched towards it using the ridge as a handrail. Fear had gripped me by the throat on that day, and threatened to squeeze every time I dared to look down.

This time, as I paused to steel myself, I just felt completely focused on the task at hand. I had a race to complete, and once I committed to this crossing there could be no time to hesitate. On that basis, I let go of having to consciously think about my balance and began to walk as if crossing a tightrope.

I wasn't frightened at all, and that felt like a sweet release. My heart rate held steady as I placed one foot after another, before I finally dropped down to use my hands where the ridge became more technical. Ahead, I saw another competitor make her way around the dreaded rock stack that stood in my way. It was an option, but one that would cost me in time. Clambering down into the pocket in front of the third pinnacle, I knew exactly which line I needed to take.

'I was terrified the first time I did this,' I said on finding that the race organisers had stationed a climbing guide midway up. 'I just don't care now.'

'That's the spirit,' he laughed, and then seemed to reconsider what I'd just said as I picked my way upwards. 'I think.'

I felt no sense of achievement as I lowered myself back on to the ridge from the other side of the pinnacle. Instead, the calm I had found on clambering on to Crib Goch accompanied me as I continued over and around the broader knuckles and scales of rock that would eventually lead to Snowdon. I was conscious that in my exhausted state I had lost all fear. I also didn't want to overthink it in case I somehow broke that spell and froze.

It was then, as if to test me, that a silhouette crossed behind two huge molars of rock. With the setting sun directly in front of me, and in my ragged state of mind, my first thought was that the devil had just made an appearance poorly disguised as a sheep. Picking up on my presence by squaring its head and huge horns to face me, the mountain goat simply stared like I needed its permission to be here. Which, to be fair, I probably did.

'I know I'm in your house,' I said, and searched for a way to negotiate the rock in my way, 'but I'm just passing through, OK?'

At any other time, I would've backed off until it left me alone. I just refused to entertain a situation where anything but the rules of the race could stop me now. Even if the goat started addressing me in tongues, I still would have brushed by with the same respectful nod.

Quite simply, my uncharacteristic fearlessness came from being utterly frazzled. I had reached a point where I was beyond caring if I died trying to do my best here. It also felt like a superpower that might get me over the line in time. A small part of me was also furious that I had got my strategy all wrong for the conditions. I thought I had cracked it after being caught out by the heat once before. Instead, my inner pilot had taken his eye off the dials before realising he was flying too close to the sun. Now, it was too late to make minor adjustments. An emergency landing was our best outcome. As I left, the mountain goat watching me, it was just a case of hanging in with both engines compromised and hoping the aircraft didn't ditch before the runway.

The ridge widens out considerably just before it joins Snowdon. It's only a short stretch, but with no perilous edges it proved to be runnable ground. I only paused briefly at the next checkpoint, dibbing in to confirm I had earned my big boy shorts by crossing Crib Goch. As I set off again, aware that time was really quite pressing, I squinted into the light to see the silhouette of a fellow competitor. The guy was facing the setting sun, sitting with his back to a signpost. His race vest lay in a heap beside him, as if it had been abandoned.

'Everything OK?' I asked, slowing to a walk as I approached. 'Do you need help?'

The guy raised his hand to acknowledge me, but didn't turn around.

'I'm good,' he said and then gestured at the molten orb on the horizon. 'Will you look at that?'

The view was indeed spectacular. As the sun settled under blankets of fiery colours, the earth before it had transformed to a spread of darkening contours. It was entrancing, but the time field on my watch was more important to me.

'You can still make it,' I said, feeling like I was addressing a sailor at the brow of his ship as sirens called to him.

The guy dragged his attention from the horizon line.

'I'm done,' he said, facing up to me now. 'But it was worth it just for this.'

The next checkpoint was just minutes away. At the summit of Snowdon, where I punched in with the cut-off hot on my heels, I mentioned to the marshal that he might want to check on the competitor I had just passed.

'We'll pick him up,' he said, like he wasn't the first or the last, and then urged me to press on if I stood a chance of reaching the finish.

By now, the heat was finally slinking away from the day. It took the edge off the nausea that had been holding me back since late morning, but left me with no taste for the remaining water in my flask or food in the pockets of my race vest. Still, in cooling temperatures as twilight settled, I found some pace returning to me. Coming off the summit, I caught up with two runners who were also determined to beat the clock. In terms of distance, we had five or maybe six kilometres left. As for the course, another mountain stood between us and our camp beds. I was too far gone to lift my head and look at my new fellow survivors as we talked on the move. They were just as beat. Names were no longer important at this point. All we shared was a desire for the same outcome and a kind of survivors' solidarity. That was enough to bring us together, and puncture the silence every now and then as we checked in on each other. At the same time, I did learn from one of them as we scaled Y Lliwedd that Sir Edmund Hillary and his expedition team had trained here ahead of their conquest of Everest in 1953.

'That makes me feel a bit better,' I said as this final climb began to bite. 'But not much.'

By the time we reached the highest point and commenced the long, steep descent from the nose of the mountain, darkness had settled and tucked in at the four corners. We paused very briefly to fish our head torches from our packs, and then continued with three light beams sweeping over the rockscape. Overhead, shoals of stars emerged with breathtaking intensity. I sensed the same pull as the runner who had found himself entranced by the sunset, but now was not the time to stop in awe. Soon after the final checkpoint, as the warm glow of lights from a grid of tents far below came into view, I knew the end was within reach. With a vast drop to our right, however, and a mandatory section to follow, all we could do was follow the path off the mountain as it delivered us to ground level.

'How long have we got left to reach camp?' asked the runner in front of me.

I checked my watch. We had a little over sixty minutes available. On this terrain, however, it was impossible for me to judge how long it would take from here.

'We just need to keep moving,' said the other guy, who had also consulted his watch and seemed more confident than me in assessing our chances. Having made it this far, I refused to entertain the possibility that I might miss the final cut-off. My brain was too fried to make an informed assessment of our chances. I just knew it would be tight. I also had no doubt my view was held in equally strong terms by my partners in hope against adversity.

By now, we were moving with an increased sense of urgency. As the rocks underfoot turned to grass and gorse, we ran at every opportunity, and then slid, slipped and stumbled where the slope steepened so sharply it was hard to control our descent. Finally, we plunged through a forest of ferns, finding a path that crossed a stream several times and then spat us out at a farm gate on to a lane. I stepped on to the tarmac with the kind of quiet euphoria reserved for Apollo astronauts, and then turned to see what I had just conquered.

There in the darkness, reaching back for miles, a trail of lights defined the mountain's spine. For a moment, with only a short run to camp, I watched with a sense of sadness, knowing that so many of those competitors behind me would fail to make the finish line in time. Minutes later, I would cross the line in 240th place. Just nine more runners succeeded in completing that opening day of the Dragon's Back Race. Behind them, another 118 competitors, including those represented by a dot of light on the mountain, either retired or failed to make a checkpoint in time.

'All that way,' I said, feeling like we had come off a battlefield.

'It's still a massive achievement,' one of my new, nameless friends replied.

'Today has been off the scale for all sorts of reasons,' the other guy added as we turned to run the final stretch into camp. 'And tomorrow is forecast to be even hotter.'

Up until this point, my experience of finishing an ultramarathon usually involved flopping around in plastic chairs with a cup of sweet tea while trading stories about the race. On this, my first multi-day experience, I arrived in camp to be greeted by a whole new challenge. This was mostly down to the fact that many runners who finished ahead of me had gone to bed. They had done their admin, which was shorthand for preparing what they needed in order to get up and seize the second day of the race. They had also eaten, no doubt, and generally decompressed from everything they'd been through to get this far.

'Sorry,' I whispered in the darkness as I picked through the contents of my main bag. I was kneeling in the communal area of the eight-berth tent I'd been allocated. It was dark. It was late. I was shattered. Several of my tentmates were asleep, which was no surprise given the demands of the day. Another was dry-heaving inside a pod intended for two, which was sufficient for me to rule out asking if we could share.

Despite arriving at camp far later than anticipated, I had come prepared for this moment. Back home, I had filled five small bags with all the provisions I required to refill my race vest and drop bag in readiness for the second day onwards. It was simple, so I had thought. I had even labelled each bag with a number from one to five. All I had to do was open up the mothership holdall, find the number, restock and relax.

A number of reality checks hindered what I had hoped would be an act of efficient admin. Firstly, I hadn't anticipated having to do it in the dark. I had a head torch. I just didn't want to be that guy who crashes into the shared tent late and then keeps everyone awake. Secondly, I had been working on the basis that I'd arrive at camp each day with the pockets of my race vests empty, having stuck to my food and hydration plan. I had weighed and measured everything I needed to keep me in good shape throughout that first day. Thanks to the sun going supernova, however, I'd hardly touched a thing. It meant I had to fumble around checking what I needed to replace, only to make a wild guess and see what fitted.

I faced one final hurdle in getting myself race-ready before bed: after nearly sixteen hours in the mountains, battling suffocating heat and intense nausea, I was completely wiped out. I had no blisters to report, no strains, pulls or pains. I was just so exhausted that I struggled with what needed to be done before I went to sleep. I also had no appetite, but knew I needed to get food inside me if I stood a second chance in this race.

So, with my race vest packed somewhat randomly, I headed to the camp canteen to eat. Thirty minutes later, I returned to my tent, having stared at a bowl of soup but at least drained a bottle of water with a strong electrolyte mix. With my air mattress and sleeping bag laid out beside some poor unfortunate who at least didn't look like he was going to vomit on me, my final task was to set the alarm on my watch to vibrate. If I wanted to get on top of this race, I had to be ready when the gate opened at six in the morning. In order to leave camp at that time, I decided that I needed ninety minutes beforehand to pack up my stuff and straighten myself out. It wouldn't give me much sleep, given that it was approaching midnight, but that seemed secondary to the hope that I'd be able to get a decent breakfast down me.

That night, I didn't exactly fall asleep. I spent a brief moment holding a very low opinion of my performance under the sun, and then effectively lost consciousness. I went down so deep that it felt like I was asleep for seconds before I stirred in the grey light to register that outside our tent half the camp were up and about. Peering at my watch, it took me a moment to realise that as we were close to five in the morning, my alarm had failed to go off.

'Amazing,' I muttered under my breath, aware that even though I'd over-slept by half an hour I was still the first to rise in our tent. As runners had been given departure times based on their position completing the previous day, with the fastest going last, I didn't want to disturb what I presumed were a bunch of elites as I scrambled to be ready.

21

THE UPS AND DOWNS OF THE LONG-DISTANCE MOUNTAIN RUNNER

It wasn't pretty, but somehow I managed to leave the camp on time. Finally, as I punched in for the day, it seemed that I could leave behind the wreckage of the plane that I had managed to land the night before in a shower of sparks and debris.

I had also been quite keen to get away before my tentmates emerged from their pods. This was down to the fact that I had returned from breakfast to find my watch alarm bleating repeatedly. I'd left it in the communal area to charge it while I forced down eggs and beans in the camp canteen. Not only had I accidentally set it for an hour later than planned, it was quite clear that my attempt to also restrict it to vibrate mode had come to nothing. Mortified at the constant trilling, and yet another screw-up on this race to add to my list, I had scooped up all my stuff from the tent and finished packing on the grass beside the kit check table.

Now, as I set off in the cool morning air – and for the first time since the heat from the previous day had conspired to scupper my race – I felt quite positive. Granted, I was deep in a valley and sheltered from the early sun. While it looked set to be another very hot day, I did at least have a chance to prepare myself for the worst. I was carrying four flasks of water, and though I started early on the salt capsules, I was still concerned. This was down to the simple fact that I had awoken with a raging thirst. It was no surprise, given what I'd been through, but there had only been so much that I could drink the night before and with my breakfast. Water was available on the course, but only at a checkpoint that I couldn't expect to reach until lunchtime. As my flasks wouldn't get me that far, I would just have to be on the lookout for streams.

In that first hour, as I left the valley behind and followed a gentle rise through forest paths, I wondered whether perhaps the worst was over. While the first day was the shortest of the race, it packed the most elevation. The mountains had been as exposed and relentless as the heat, but I did at least feel that all the tyre-pulling and hill repeats had served me well. Nevertheless, such barren, rocky, technical and often uncomfortable terrain wasn't second nature to me. Sometimes I had felt like I didn't deserve a race bib but a learner plate, and yet this early phase of the second day was completely different. Running on soft trails under canopies of conifer, I began to feel quite at home. With so many dropouts from day one, the field was considerably more spaced. I always had sight of someone in the distance, and as the second hour ticked by, the race leaders who had left camp later began to catch up and overtake. That was fine by me. It was nice to use my voice briefly to exchange a few words of support, and then quietly wish that I possessed the same speed and efficiency. When the leading woman in the race slipped by, thanking me cheerily as I stepped aside on a narrow stretch to let her go, I even attempted to keep the same pace. For a few minutes I tried to mimic the ease with which she ran, only to fall back to a plod on realising that it was already quite humid.

'Drink,' I said out loud, as if adding a voice to my thoughts might finally teach me to do it automatically. I would've followed it up with a reminder to eat. Having managed a full breakfast, however, I just didn't feel I had much room.

So, pausing to walk and check nobody was about to bust me for the heinous ultrarunning crime that followed, I opted for a gel.

I had thought that a quick hit like this would keep me ticking over until a proper hunger kicked in. Instead, I found myself struggling to get it down without wanting to gag, and that felt like an ominous sign.

'How is it going?'

The question came out of nowhere. With a start, I turned to see another runner had drawn alongside me. Instinctively, I closed my fist around the empty gel sleeve.

'Fine,' I said, forcing myself to swallow, and then picked up the pace alongside him. 'Actually, not great. I'm still burnt out from yesterday.'

'It's the heat again,' he said, glancing at his watch. 'Somehow we've got to stay cool.'

'Well, that would mean slowing things down,' I said. By now we had reached another country lane. It was lined by tall, wild hedgerow on one side. We ran in file in the shade it afforded. 'The trouble is if I drop the pace I'll be chasing cut-offs.'

'There's no scope at all for hanging around,' he said, only to gesture towards a steep hillside in the middle distance. 'But it's going to be slow going from there.'

My new friend wasn't wrong. Within minutes of turning off the lane and following a steep and rutted hill path, I was reduced to a trudge. By now, the field had compressed somewhat, and I fell into what felt like a sub-dued procession. I continued to sip at my flasks as I climbed, aware of the growing humidity. On the upside, I was within sight of the hill brow, and imagined those competitors who had made it that far were enjoying a breeze on their faces.

It wasn't until I arrived at that point a few minutes later that I paused for a second just to process how wrong I had been.

There was no breeze at the top. Instead, I found myself in the full glare of the morning sun and the realisation that the plodding ascent I had just completed was little more than a warm-up to the main event.

'Oh, you're joking!' declared another runner as he drew level with me on what was an annoyingly false summit.

Cnicht is a 689-metre rock goliath with what felt like a nursery slope in the foothills compared to the climb that would take us to the pyramidical peak. It's known as the Welsh Matterhorn, and a gateway to the Moelwynion mountain range. That morning, thanks to the increasingly oppressive conditions, it just felt like the day's boss level had come early. We were at oven temperature, so it seemed to me, and nothing in my flasks could match the sweat I was in from the undertaking. The ascent itself was deeply demanding, but I had been preparing for terrain like this. I just hadn't considered that Wales might be in the grip of a record-breaking heatwave in September. Rather than facing a challenge I could get stuck into, I began to feel more like I was on a conveyor belt of suffering. By the time I followed the train of competitors to the summit checkpoint, I had drained all four flasks dry. While I'd been measured with the salt capsules, mindful that my water was limited, my appetite had died on the climb. Once again, having started from the disadvantage of being dehydrated at dawn, I found myself approaching the dreaded death march.

To be fair, there wasn't much running to be had off the south side of the mountain. A minority just let go and hoped to stay on their feet. Others picked their way down gingerly. Then I saw one innovative individual employ a method of descent that looked deeply appealing to me for the simple reason that he seemed to be sitting down. Considering it to be a chance to rest on the move, I dropped back on the seat of my shorts, lifted my heels off the long grass and loose scree that covered the slope and let gravity do the hard work. I must have reclaimed several places in the process, which only encouraged yet more competitors to unleash their inner child and follow suit. The slide lasted no more than thirty seconds, but the smile on my face as I picked myself up felt like a small act of defiance against the furnace of the day.

Later, I would learn that the temperature across that wilderness touched thirty degrees. As the mercury climbed and I soldiered on with a sense that time could now be moving against me, I knew that I was in trouble once again. With cut-offs in mind, I didn't feel like there was much that I could do to minimise the symptoms. I couldn't go much slower in a bid to cool off and stop feeling so wretched. Any faster, it felt like I might faint.

I faced an expanse of undulating moorland carved up by the ruins of old drystone walls, with the prospect of another monumental ascent about a kilometre away. At any other time, with a checkpoint at the summit, I would have considered this stretch to be runnable. One or two competitors plugged on at pace, but most had dropped to a disconsolate plod. The will was there, but the heat now weighed heavily on my back. I had no water left, and was rapidly beginning to feel like I wouldn't be able to keep a drink down if I tried.

It was then, for the first time since I had started this epic ultramarathon, that I wondered if I might not complete it.

Ever since I signed up, I had been well aware that the Dragon's Back Race would be the greatest running challenge I ever faced. I was under no illusion about the scale of the challenge, which is why I had committed to the training. I didn't want to blow it because I wasn't fit enough or unprepared for the sheer scale of the mountains. I felt ready to face the distance, elevation and terrain. I'd even braced myself to share a sleeping compartment under canvas with a stranger. I had done everything in my power that I believed I needed to do in order to become a Dragon slayer. In storm-force winds and horizontal rain, I would have been in my element. That was the brand of bad weather I'd been preparing to face.

I just hadn't banked on the ferocity of the sun.

It had taken me down once before, of course, ending my dreams of a Double Grand Slam in the first race of the Centurion series, and though I had made every effort to learn from the experience it threatened me again. If heat exhaustion was my Achilles heel, it had the capacity to stop me in my tracks. At the same time, I had no intention of just giving up. Even if I was just too far gone to run, I was still marching with purpose. The race might come back to me, I told myself. It wasn't a question of digging deep or putting more effort into it. As much as I had responded positively to the constant needling of a pacer in the past, my elevated core temperature dictated my rate of progress here. Unless my clubmate, Emma, materialised with a pitcher of ice-cold ginger beer on a tray, even she would be powerless to improve my situation.

I was following a stone track across undulating fields of reed clumps and grazing sheep. A scattering of competitors marked the route, both in front and behind me. Nobody looked like they were skipping over the course. The ruinous temperature kept every runner at bay. Returning my attention to the way ahead, I noted some figures peeling off from the track and dropping down a steep bank. It caught my attention because they seemed to have come alive for some reason. I broke into something vaguely resembling a jog, and then picked it up considerably on registering the stream that had drawn them all.

'Is it safe?' a young guy asked those at the bank as I stopped to shrug off my race vest.

The water was good enough to bottle. At least that was my reading of the scene as I watched runners filling their flasks and sinking their caps into what was really a bubbling brook. I was mindful of the advice I had learnt on my recce, but this felt like an emergency. Unless I spotted chemical drums when I glanced upstream, it passed my quality threshold. At least it would once I utilised a tool I had packed that would minimise the chance of me self-administering tapeworm.

I hadn't just packed chlorine tablets, which required thirty minutes to take effect in the bottles I refilled. I also had a filter straw that would allow me to drink directly from the source. While it was packed with all kinds of mesh and gauze, and claimed to make any water safe for consumption, it still looked like something you'd stick through the lid of a milkshake. Lying on my belly, I leant over the bank and drew through the device as if someone had just bet that I couldn't drain the stream dry.

'It tastes amazing,' I said, breaking off for air after a moment.

Beside me, the young guy who had approached the stream with caution didn't hear me the first time. I went back to drinking enthusiastically through my straw, and then offered it to him once he'd lifted his head and shoulders out of the water.

Even as I climbed away from the stream, I knew it wasn't enough. The water was so refreshing, and while I had also splashed myself down I still needed more time to cool off. Within minutes of moving off once more, running gently in a bid to make up lost ground, the creeping listlessness and nausea returned. In many ways, it felt like the onset of flu. Every movement required more effort than usual, but with limited return. I felt sluggish, short of breath, prone to retching on a regular basis and with a looming sense that unless I stopped I might just collapse. All I wanted to do was seek out shade and simply lie there. Across this terrain, however, with the sun welded into the sky overhead, there was no escape.

The next mountain to stand in my way looked like some angry god had pinched the earth and then pulled to see how far it would go before tearing away. It was effectively just one giant grass slope that did nothing to soften the severity of the climb. I could make out competitors making their way along a ridge to the summit, but they were little more than specks against the skyline. I had barely started to work my way up the path before I was using my hands, and I wasn't alone. It was also quite clear that others were suffering just as acutely under this relentless sun. For a steady half an hour, I crawled past those who had peeled away to catch their breath or vomit. None of them looked unfit for the climb. The heat was simply intolerable. As much as I wanted to pause, I knew that time was running out on me. I had to keep moving, and yet with every step forward it felt like this accursed mountain was rising up and over me like some breaking wave. I reached the point where I was just so crushed by the conditions that I could no longer scramble. Instead, I found myself crawling on my hands and knees, cursing at the same time but willing myself not to stop.

My progress was pitiful. I was moving like a baby who hadn't quite grasped walking, and could not ignore the fact that I had almost sixty kilometres to cover. Despite it all, I kept telling myself that I would punch in at that summit checkpoint. By the time I reached the ridge, where I could at least death-march on by foot, I wondered how many of my lives I had left below me. Looking down at the bodies on each side of the path, knowing exactly what those poor souls were going through, I just hoped we all had enough to get through this.

'Well, that's not good.' Ahead of me, as I approached the trig point and the magic box below it, a runner had just consulted his watch. 'We're half an hour behind the advisory time.'

'I couldn't have gone any quicker,' I said, resting a hand on my knee to dib in. 'We'll just have to make up time from here.'

We set off on the descent together. It was just as steep as the other side, but technical and generally nastier. Without word, I followed him on a course that twisted around rocks and drops, and forced us at times to use our hands as anchors. It was too demanding for me to do anything but glance across the valley and register the next climb rippling in the heat haze, and clearly more than enough for one of us.

'I'm done,' the guy said breathlessly, and pulled away for me to pass. 'We're never going to make the midday cut-off.'

'Yes, we can,' I said, but even though I continued to barrel towards the foothills, a looming sense of resignation followed me down.

I had already registered the possibility of failure. Once it had entered my head, it never left. While I had the means to remove ticks from my body, which was a mandatory item in my medical kit, there was little I could do to extract the thought that I might not make it. I had ignored it until the last checkpoint, where the cut-off that had passed by thirty minutes forced me to confront the facts. Yes, I could refuse to give in. I could fight against all odds to catch up on lost time. I always had hope, but in the same way that I liked to dream of winning a race, it counted for nothing. When I consulted the map, registering the contours ahead of me, there wasn't even a chance that I would reach the lunchtime checkpoint successfully. That was where those who came in after the cut-off would be pulled from the race. Ultimately, my inability to move quickly in heat combined with the uncompromising time demands of the race placed me in an inevitable checkmate.

Naturally, I spent the next hour in denial underpinned by a hint of panic and dismay. I had devoted just so much time and effort into preparing for this challenge. For so long, I had lived and breathed as a Dragon in Training, only to be derailed by temperatures that had sucked the life out of my chances. The only way that I could possibly stay in the game, I calculated to myself, was if I miraculously shrugged off the fire blanket of exhaustion that still weighed me down and sprinted for the next six miles. As the terrain ruled that out as much as my physical abilities, I prepared myself for the inevitable. I called upon all the motivational quotes I could remember. None of them could overcome reality.

That so many others in the field were reaching the same conclusion came as little consolation to me. Over the next few miles, as I caught up with others or they caught up with me, I sensed a desolate mood of resignation set in among my fellow competitors. The heat made running impossible, even as we came off the mountains, and that was hard to handle.

Defeat was now staring me in the face, and yet I couldn't quite bring myself to call it. I had assumed that task would fall to the poor marshal at the mandatory cut-off point. It was only when I fell in with two guys who had made peace with their decision that I realised I could at least take responsibility for my own retirement.

'We're not going as far as the checkpoint,' one told me when I asked him how far we had left. 'It's at least an hour away.'

'We'll be timed out,' his companion said without looking up from his feet. 'No question.'

'Then we'll have to wait for the minibus of shame to take us to the finish line,' the first guy added, only to glance across with a glimmer in his eye. 'Or we could stop at the pub.'

Now he had my full attention. Even as a teetotaller, my parched mind absorbed the vision of a table at a beer garden under a giant umbrella. All of a sudden, the prospect of an ice-cold soft drink seemed like heaven.

'Really?'

'It's a couple of kilometres before the checkpoint. We go straight past it at a road crossing. We can chill out there and then catch the bus to the finish line in our own time.'

'How do you know this?' I asked.

'Recces,' he said simply, and that was enough for me. While I had learnt about the dangers of drinking unfiltered water from streams on my exploratory visit to Wales, this man had clearly done his research in other ways that sounded like it could also save my life at that moment.

My race was over, but for a moment I pondered how comfortable I would feel knowing I had voluntarily retired. Then I considered the hard fact that slogging on to the checkpoint would lead to the same inevitable outcome. The only difference was that I would be offloading the awful responsibility for being pulled off the course on someone else. I was in a mess under a pulverising sun. In this view, was it worth putting my pride before my health?

'I'm in,' I said before introducing myself.

'Then we should contact race control and let them know we're done.'

I checked my phone for a signal, and volunteered to ring in. I relayed our race numbers, confirmed that we were retiring but otherwise OK, and would take responsibility for ourselves from here on out. The race controller sounded like he'd been taking calls like this for hours. The other two watched me in silence as I finished up. All of a sudden, as I pocketed my phone, it felt somewhat final. In the silence, the guy who had suggested a way out extended his hand.

'We gave it everything,' he said as we all exchanged handshakes. I drew breath to agree, but was stopped by a catch in my throat. 'Nobody can ask for more than that.'

To be frank, I was far too dehydrated to shed a tear. I was also in no fit state to remember any names, but struck by the fact that my other new friend looked completely destroyed. He barely looked up from the path as we trudged towards the fabled road crossing.

'Everything will be all right, mate,' his buddy said at one point, and patted him reassuringly on the back. 'Don't beat yourself up about it.'

I looked across at the pair.

'We can go home with our heads held high,' I said, hoping to help.

'I don't know about that,' said the downcast guy, and showed me his left hand as if in surrender. 'I lost my wedding ring in the mountains yesterday.'

'Oh.' I was all out of words for a moment, though now I understood why he looked beyond help. Failing to finish a race with a marital band on your finger was a double blow that would clearly take some work to overcome. 'Maybe she won't notice?' I offered brightly, concluding in the awkward silence that followed that a premature end to this phase of the race was both devastating and couldn't come soon enough.

22

THE RIVER OF LOST DREAMS

Mr Fuck was on his second pint of lemonade when we asked if we could join him at the picnic table. There was only one in the shadow of the stone-walled pub that marked the place where our GPS trackers came to a halt.

'Fuck,' he said again as we lowered ourselves painfully on to the benches with our soft drinks, and this was pretty much all he seemed to repeat. '*Fuck!*'

I couldn't blame him. As a fellow competitor, I understood his bitter disappointment. Like us, he too had found his hopes and dreams of reaching Cardiff Castle go up in smoke. As enough time ticked by for me to drink four pints of Coke and still feel thirsty, the courtyard filled with yet more heat-stricken retirees who had bowed to the inevitable. Everyone seemed to process their defeat in different ways. Some cracked jokes at their own expense just to lighten the mood. Several runners had completed the previous edition of the race and were in shock that it had come to this. One even took himself to the car park and wept, while most of us just sat and stared into the middle distance with a glass in our hands and broken hearts.

When I entered this race, stopped freaking out and then faced up to the challenge, I was in no doubt that it might be a humbling experience. At the same time, I had not anticipated being defeated so early on. I knew exactly why I had now joined the ever-growing list of DNFs. I just needed a little time to come to terms with the fact that a heatwave across a region known for cool, windy or wet conditions had cooked my race. I had been defeated by the temperature once before, but this was off the scale. Even if I just sucked at running under the sun, I had to make peace with what had happened to my hopes and dreams here.

It was a process that would begin later that afternoon, following a public bus ride to the next camp in which most of the seats were occupied by runners who had retired on the course or missed a cut-off. It had been a quiet, subdued journey in stifling temperatures. By then, word had spread through the field that the attrition rate was even greater than the first day. I thought about those who were still in the race, and wondered what it would have taken for me to be among them. Whether it was down to strategy, some natural propensity to move efficiently in very hot conditions, or a combination of both, I began to recognise why this edition of the Dragon's Back Race had beaten me.

At the finish line, after about twenty of us had trudged in from the bus stop, I opted to have my plastic dibber cut from my wrist. There was an option to continue as a non-competitive runner, taking on half days through the week at will, but I'd lost the drive. I had learnt that the heatwave was set to continue for at least another day, and had no desire to repeat the same experience as I had that morning in the mountains. I needed to rest, rehydrate and find a way to live with an abrupt end to a race that had been the focal point of my life for such a long time.

Back at my tent, I found I wasn't alone. By the end of that day, in fact, all eight runners under canvas with me had either retired from the race or timed out.

'It's a sad camp,' said the guy I had heard dry-heaving the night before, who I found packing to leave, and he wasn't wrong. 'I just want to be with my dogs.'

Despite the lengthening shadows, it was still roasting hot. When things had got really challenging under the sun, I fantasised about climbing into the river that ran alongside this second camp. I had seen it on finishing a recce of this second day with RAW Adventures. Even though I'd dropped out of the race before the Rhinogydds, I knew exactly where to find the waterway. Leaving my campmate to complete his packing, and agreeing that dogs made everything better, I trudged across the field towards the treeline. After everything I had been through, just glimpsing a broad, sparkling band behind the trunks and low-hanging branches was enough to lift my spirits. My plan had been to strip naked, lie in the shallows and just wait for my core temperature to come back to me. Dipping under the branches on to a bank of smooth stones, I realised that probably wasn't going to be appropriate.

It was a scene I had not expected. The sun glittered brightly on the surface of the river, sufficiently shallow to reveal a bed of smooth, polished stones, and with a current just strong enough to cause ripples and eddies. This was what I had come to enjoy, just to escape the heat once and for all and dwell on how I'd arrived here. Only it seemed I wasn't alone in being drawn by the same idea. For this stretch of the river was filled with dozens of race casualties who simply sat in the shallows in quiet reflection.

Like me, these competitors had suffered a cruel end to their race. Nobody spoke. This was not the time for conversation. I removed my shoes and socks, ruefully noting that I hadn't really gone deep enough into the week to run the risk of blisters. Then, wearing only my shorts, I ventured into the river with my phone in hand. The water rushed around my ankles, which I relished for a moment before parking myself at a respectful space from anyone else. Nobody seemed to register my arrival. Everyone was lost in thought. At any other time, I might have found the cold shock a bit much, but just then it felt cleansing. It wasn't just the fact that this was my first chance to wash in two days. In the gentle but persistent current, it felt like the sense of melancholy that had accompanied me into camp just swept away.

I looked up and around at this scene of strange, communal ritual, and knew that for all my disappointment everything would be all right.

I felt no need to conjure up excuses for retiring so early in the race. Despite all the support I had received from friends and family, I wasn't too proud to hold myself accountable for falling far short of the finish line. Yes, it was impossibly hot, and at the end of that week the figures spoke for themselves. At the start of the race, 367 runners had set off with high hopes and dreams. Six days later, just 90 survived to cross the finish line and I remain in awe of their achievements. While they had found a way to overcome the heat, it could not have been easy. When I stood among so many excited hopefuls inside Conwy Castle, I did not imagine that for just over three quarters of us the race would end like this. Despite such impossible temperatures, however, I felt no temptation to claim that I might have succeeded otherwise. The heat was a variable beyond my control and possibly just one of many that could have derailed me. I might have twisted an ankle, woken up with a head cold or chosen to drink from a malevolent stream. Quite simply, as I told anyone who asked, I wasn't good enough to complete that year's edition of the race.

Looking at it in this light, I had arrived at the start line with no margins to overcome adversity. I like to think I was trained and capable of completing six days in ideal conditions, but in all my years of running there has always been something that doesn't go to plan. The key to succeeding, I think, is setting out with the capacity to adapt and get through the worst thing that could happen. For there's no such thing as the perfect race. What matters is your ability to conquer the problems along the way. Not only the ones in your path, or up in the sky, but also those of your own making. In the opening hours of the first day, before the sun turned up the dial, I had simply forgotten to get started on my salt capsules. I have no doubt that contributed to my downfall. In a race of this scale, it just kick-started an escalating chain of events that would see me literally crawling on my hands and knees the next day. We all make mistakes as runners because no two races are ever the same. What matters is how we solve problems, not just of our own creation but those sent to test us all, and that can make the difference between disappointment and success.

Sitting in that river, processing my thoughts, I felt no sense of regret. I was sorry that my race was over, but proud of the fact that I had signed up to something so clearly in the outer region of my abilities. I had spent twelve months raising my game, getting to grips with the skills and fitness that I needed to take on the world's toughest mountain race. Dropping out at this point couldn't take that experience away from me. Nor could it undermine the courage I'd had to find to toe the start line. In the build-up, I had been quite freaked out by the enormity of what I faced, and overcoming that could only serve me well as I moved on.

Just then, and when entries opened the following week for the next edition of the race, I felt no urge to sign up again. I have every respect for those who get back on their feet to give these things another shot at the first opportunity. Personally, if I really had discovered my limit in running, I didn't want to constantly bang up against it. First I needed time to work out if I had any room left for improvement. It wasn't just a question of staring at the sun until one of us stood down. The last two days had demonstrated that I was only fit for purpose on a race of this magnitude so long as *everything* unfolded in my favour. If I could still raise my game, and so long as age allowed it, then perhaps I would remind myself what a boxing legend once showed me with a simple magic trick and return for a future edition. All was not lost for now, however. My journey on the Dragon's Back had ended in failure, but also opened new pathways I wanted to explore on my own terms.

The mountains had taken me far from my comfort zone. It had been a huge challenge to climb high and then cross them at pace, and an experience that was hard to beat. I'd had to build my confidence and overcome wobbles, including those that once stopped me from running in a straight line on flat ground.

I'd been just as daunted by the prospect of self-navigation, only to feel empowered by the map in my hand. It felt liberating, in some ways, to run a race free from the breadcrumb trail of tape. There had been a moment, in fact, shortly after I recognised that the cut-offs had outrun me, when I took a quicker line off the foot of a mountain than the advisory one on the map. It was something we were all free to do on non-mandatory sections of the course, and when several runners had followed me on a kilometre of my own making I felt like Sherpa Tenzing. While I would have needed to uncover a wormhole in order to stay in the race, pursuing that small, single time-saving strategy had been a precious consolation prize.

Most importantly, there had been highlights across both days when I wished I'd had a chance to just pause and absorb it all. From the vastness of the landscape to the sense of freedom that comes with running across the roof of the world, I didn't need to take on a six-day ultramarathon to experience these things again. I could get away in my own time, alone or with those who might share my newfound love of being in the wilderness.

'Hi,' I said when Emma picked up. 'It's me.'

'We've all been watching the race tracker online,' she said in a way that told me she knew the big picture. 'I'm sorry.'

'It's fine,' I said, and then paused for a moment. 'Well, it *will* be fine.'

'Where are you now?' she asked.

'In a river.'

'Right,' she said. 'I'll come and get you.'

'That's kind, but don't worry,' I said. 'I can work my way back by bus and train. It might take forever, but let's face it, I'm equipped for survival.'

'I'll leave first thing in the morning,' insisted Emma.

'You only dropped me off two days ago. There's no need.'

'You've been away for a year now,' she said to me. 'It'll be good to have you back home.'

ACKNOWLEDGEMENTS

Endurance running might seem like a solo pursuit. In reality, it means being out on the trails for long periods, and that absence is felt at home. First and foremost, I should like to thank my wife, Emma, for her understanding, support and encouragement, as well as our four children (and Sprint) for cheering me on along the way. You make a great crew. I'd also like to include my father here. He hung up his running shoes long ago, but follows my race weekends via the wonders of live online tracking. He's also learnt not to fear that I've fallen off a cliff when my dot-on-the-map freezes unaccountably. I'm all right, Dad! It's just a glitch.

Running long has introduced me to people I wouldn't otherwise have had the pleasure of meeting in everyday life. Ultramarathons are about highs and lows, and sharing that experience forges friendships – not just with other runners but the volunteers and race organisers who share the passion and make it happen. In particular, among what can feel like a second family, I'd like to thank Jay McCardle, James Elson and Shane Ohly for getting things off the ground, as well as Dimi and Andrew Booth, Karen Harvey, Matthew Simpson and Dave Douglas for their good cheer and gallows humour in the face of adversity. To Kate Worthington and the team at RAW Adventures, and, of course, Joe Faulkner, my thanks for showing me just how far I had to go.

Closer to home, I'd like to give a wave to my HJ running club friends, Geri, Alan M. & Alan P., Richard, Kath, Neil, Mark, Paul, Matt, Phil, Keith,

Paul Burgess and Speedy Pete, and to Emma Walters for being the pacer who never gave up hope. Thanks also go to Nick Walters for the salted potatoes.

To Ben Clark and Philippa Milnes-Smith at The Soho Agency, my thanks for running with me from the start. At Vertebrate Publishing, I'm indebted to Jon Barton and Stephen Ross, John Coefield and Emma Lockley for such care and attention to the words on the page. Thanks also to Jane Beagley, Laurie (The Line) King, Cameron Bonser, Shona Henderson, Lorna Brogan, Moira Hunter and Phill Rodham. Finally, I would like to make a special mention to Kirsty Reade not just for commissioning this book but also the wisdom and advice she provided me with as an accomplished ultrarunner and actual finisher of an earlier edition of the Dragon's Back Race. It's one thing tackling it on paper ...